# A Crash Course in Composition with Readings

## Fourth Edition

Elizabeth McMahan
*Illinois State University*

## McGraw-Hill Book Company

New York  St. Louis  San Francisco  Auckland  Bogotá  Caracas
Colorado Springs  Hamburg  Lisbon  London  Madrid  Mexico  Milan
Montreal  New Delhi  Oklahoma City  Panama  Paris  San Juan
São Paulo  Singapore  Sydney  Tokyo  Toronto

**A CRASH COURSE IN COMPOSITION WITH READINGS**

1 2 3 4 5 6 7 8 9 0 FGR FGR 8 9 3 2 1 0 9 8

ISBN 0-07-045479-5

This book was set in Times Roman by Automated Composition Service, Inc.
The editors were Susan Hurtt, Judith R. Cornwell, and James R. Belser;
the production supervisor was Salvador Gonzales.
The cover was designed by John Hite.
Arcata Graphics/Fairfield was printer and binder.

Acknowledgments appear on pages 271–272; 449–450 (for readings); and on this page by reference.

**Library of Congress Cataloging-in-Publication Data**

McMahan, Elizabeth.
 A crash course in composition, with readings.
 Includes index.
 1. English language—Rhetoric. 2. College readers.
I. Title.
PE1408.M3947 1989  808′.0427  88-13284
ISBN 0-07-045479-5

# About the Author

Elizabeth McMahan grew up in College Station, home of the "Fightin' Texas Aggies," where her father taught physics at Texas A & M University. Her BA and MA degrees in English are from the University of Houston; her PhD (in American literature) is from the University of Oregon, where she enjoyed the benefits of a National Defense Education Act Fellowship. She is presently Professor of English and Director of Writing Programs at Illinois State University.

While still in graduate school, McMahan completed the first edition of *A Crash Course in Composition*. Since then, she has embraced the joys of collaborative writing with Susan Day. These two have composed *The Writer's Rhetoric and Handbook*, *The Writer's Handbook*, and *The Writer's Resource: Essays for Composition*, all published by McGraw-Hill. With another firm and with a third collaborator, Robert Funk, they have produced *Literature and the Writing Process*, *Keeping in Touch: Writing Clearly* (a basic writing text), and *The Elements of Writing about Literature and Film*.

McMahan considers herself most fortunate in having a husband who is a feminist; four cats (one crazy); two fat, white geese; one beige, rotund corgi; and a house on Lake Bloomington where she composes on an IBM PC.

*To my dear Aunt Helen,
with love and admiration.*

# Contents

# 2

# FURTHER ADVICE FOR THOSE WHO NEED IT

# 3
# READINGS TO INSPIRE YOUR WRITING

# Preface

*A Crash Course in Composition with Readings* provides exactly what the title promises—all the materials necessary for a complete course in composition. In addition to concise writing instruction that is pleasant to read and easy to understand, this expanded edition of *Crash Course* also includes appealing essays to serve as models of various rhetorical strategies and to spark the invention of ideas. Nobody writes well who has nothing to say. These thematically arranged essays are carefully chosen to produce interesting topics for students to write about.

*Crash Course* is a text for people who want help in learning how to organize ideas, develop paragraphs, craft sentences, and insert punctuation; who want to know what is acceptable and what is not in standard English—and who want to acquire all this information as quickly and painlessly as possible. Part One, "How to Put a Paper Together," explains just that, including advice for writing a paper drawing on library sources. Part Two, "Further Advice for Those Who Need It," offers in easy-to-find alphabetical entries all the information needed to revise a paper—brief, clear explanations of problems related to punctuation, grammar, and usage. Part Three, "Readings to Inspire Your Writing," opens with a few words of advice on improving reading and responding to it. The next eight chapters present twenty-six essays on themes of interest to everyone. Each selection is followed by "Questions for Discussion" to nourish ideas; each chapter concludes with "Suggestions for Writing" to focus these ideas on a purpose, an audience, and a thesis for the actual writing. Indeed, this single text does provide all the instruction necessary for a complete course in composition. Any teacher who prefers to organize the course according to rhetorical modes will find a list of the essays arranged by mode at the end of the Instructor's Manual.

My sincere thanks to the people who have assisted me with this new edition: my astute reviewers—John Gensler, Onondaga Community College; Mary Gilliand, Cornell University; Ray Pedrizetti, St. John's University, and Joel Zienty, Lake Michigan College; my literate helpmate—Dan LeSeure; my friends—Michele and Russell Finley; my invaluable editors—Judith Cornwell, Emily Barrosse, Sue Hurtt, and James Belser as well as their efficient assistants—Kathleen Francisco, Christina Cenker, and Pat Pfaus. I am especially grateful to my colleagues Susie Day and Janet Youga, who have taught me much about the teaching of composition.

*Elizabeth McMahan*

Part One

# How to Put a Paper Together

# Chapter 1

# Ponder Your Approach

Writing well involves hard work. There's no sense in pretending otherwise. But as my colleague Charlie Harris says, "I hate to write, but I love to have written." That's it, exactly. Writing is challenging but rewarding—if you do a good job. And if you're not going to do a good job, you might as well not do it at all.

## WHY BOTHER?

The rewards are more than psychological. Writing skillfully is one of the most useful crafts you can develop—essential even—and valuable to prospective employers. You will greatly improve your chances of landing a good job if you can write clear, correct expository prose. That's the kind of writing dealt with in this book: not poetry or drama or fiction, but informative writing. If you'd like to consider a more immediate need, there's no honest way to get through college without being able to write. You simply can't hope to get into law or medical school without a thorough knowledge of *standard English*—the language spoken and written by educated people in this country. Whether you're planning to enter engineering, teaching, social work, or any business or professional career, you'll have to write: memos, letters, reports, instructions, lesson plans, summaries, case files.

Let's face it. You need to be able to write. This book can help you learn to write well. I've tried to make the process as painless as possible, but writing is seldom easy. It requires precision. It requires thinking. I struggle and sigh and squint and swear; I chew my nails, twiddle my thumbs, furrow my brow, gnash my teeth—but eventually I write. And you can, too, if you're willing to work at it.

## CLARITY IS THE KEYNOTE

The important thing to get straight in the beginning is this: You want your readers to *understand what you write*. No need for suspense. No call for ambiguity. Let your readers know at the outset what you're going to discuss and then discuss it. Graceful phrasing and a rich vocabulary are welcome stylistic adornments, but compared with the necessity for *total clarity*, they are secondary. Such refinements can wait until the polishing process—the revising that every good writer feels compelled to do after completing a first draft.

## THINK BEFORE YOU WRITE

As you begin to plan your paper, you need to consider three things:

1　Your purpose: Why am I writing?
2　Your audience: Who am I writing for?
3　Your thesis: What am I going to write about?

These questions are equally important, and your answer to one will often affect your response to the others. For purposes of discussion, let's consider them one by one.

## DECIDING YOUR PURPOSE

Before you start writing, you need to ask yourself what your purpose is. Why are you exerting all this energy and straining your brain to do this piece of writing? It may be an honest answer to say because your teacher or your boss told you to, but it's not a useful answer. Think beyond that immediate response to the reason that makes writing worthwhile. What do you hope to accomplish? Are you writing *to inform* your readers? Do you hope *to persuade* your readers to change their minds about some issue? Perhaps you simply want to *entertain* them. Or you may be keeping a journal or a diary just for your own uses, with no need to consider any other readers than yourself.

Your purpose affects your whole approach to writing: how you begin, whether you state or imply your thesis, what specific details you choose, how you organize the material, how you conclude, as well as what words you select for each sentence. You should give thought to your purpose before you start even the preliminary planning stage.

## CONSIDERING YOUR AUDIENCE

You can't successfully determine why you're writing without also considering this question: Who is going to read what you write? Your audience may be a single person—your boss, perhaps, your history professor, your senator. Or you may sometimes wish to reach a larger audience—your city council, your composition class, the readership of some publication like your campus or city newspaper, *Time* magazine, or *Rolling Stone*.

If your purpose, for instance, is to inform, you need to think about how to present your information to your specific audience most effectively. You can see at once that the larger your audience, the more touchy the problem. If you're writing a letter to the editor of your local newspaper explaining the appeal of reggae music, you'll be addressing people of all ages with assorted dispositions and prejudices. You need to choose your words carefully and present your information calmly—or you may end up with next to no readers at all.

If, however, you're writing a letter to the editor of *Rolling Stone*, your verbal tactics would need to be different. Since your audience here would be primarily people who know a lot about popular music, you should omit background information explaining how reggae originated. You would write in a more conversational manner, using current slang and even music jargon, since your audience could be expected to understand the jargon and not be put off by the slang.

## Audience Analysis Checklist

In order to increase your abilities in evaluating your audience, ask yourself the following questions during the process of planning your paper.

1  How much will my readers already know about my topic?
2  Will they respond emotionally to my topic? Will I need to be especially careful not to offend them? If so, how?
3  Will they be interested in my topic? Perhaps bored by it? If they may be bored, how can I get them interested?
4  Will they be in agreement with me? Opposed? Neutral?
5  How well educated in general are my readers?
6  Do they fall into any particular age group?
7  Is it important to consider their race, sex, marital status, possible parenthood, or religion?
8  Do they identify with any political groups (like Republicans, Democrats, libertarians, socialists)?
9  Are they members of any public interest group (Moral Majority, Common Cause, National Organization for Women, American Civil Liberties Union, Sierra Club, etc.)?
10  How do they make their living? Are they rich, poor, middle-class?

## Temper Your Tone

Although on occasion you may want to make your audience angry about something—injustice, poverty, bigotry—you always want to avoid making them angry at you. Your purpose in writing is to persuade them to agree with you. Therefore, try to adopt a tone that won't antagonize your readers.

*Tone* means the attitude of the writer toward what is being written. Tone can be gentle, sad, strident, angry, serious, sympathetic, supercilious, humorous, playful, poignant, admiring, earnest, curt, sarcastic, ironic, sardonic, or neutral. Since tone always depends to some extent upon how the words are received by the readers, be careful if you decide to adopt an ironic or sarcastic tone. You could easily be misunderstood. Remember that the tone of your voice does not carry over to the written word. A neutral tone may be the best tone for most writing. Before you write, consider your purpose and choose a tone that seems appropriate.

You may sometimes *want* to write abusively when you feel

abused, but try to resist the temptation. You'll only turn your readers off. Mark Twain never published a line or even mailed a letter until his gentle wife Olivia had cleared his prose. You can begin to see why if you'll read his famous letter to the gas company.

Hartford, February 12, 1891

Dear Sirs:

Some day you will move me almost to the verge of irritation by your chuckle-headed (expletive deleted) fashion of shutting your (expletive deleted) gas off without giving any notice to your (expletive deleted) parishioners. Several times you have come within an ace of smothering half of this household in their beds and blowing up the other half by this idiotic, not to say criminal, custom of yours. And it has happened again to-day. Haven't you a telephone?

Ys

S L Clemens

Needless to say, Livy didn't let that one pass. Twain revised his correspondence daily as his rage subsided, until he produced a temperate version that wouldn't invite a libel suit. Try to do the same with your own writing. Adopt a tone that will allow you to be convincing but not offensive.

## ANALYZING THE EFFECTS OF AUDIENCE AND PURPOSE

Think carefully about both purpose and audience as you plan your paper. Continue to keep them in mind as you write. Consider them again as you revise. These overlapping concepts are crucial, for they affect your tone and your tactics.

Notice, for instance, the extensive changes that occur in the following three short passages as I write every one on the same topic (the lack of vegetarian fare in the Snack Shop) but change the purpose each time. The audience here is the Director of Food Services in the Student Union.

### 1. Purpose: To Inform

Although the food served in the Snack Shop of the Union is appetizing and economical, the menu offers only a single entree suitable for a vegetarian—a grilled cheese sandwich. An expanded menu would better serve the needs of all students.

### 2. Purpose: To Entertain

Even a toasty, golden-brown grilled cheese sandwich becomes a loathsome thing if the hungry person is trying to choke one down for the twenty-seventh day in a row. Our friends munch contentedly on a whole array of sandwiches—hamburgers, reubens, ham and turkey combinations, hot pastrami—while we vegetarians chew sullenly on our same old grilled cheese.

### 3. Purpose: To Persuade

While the food served in the Snack Shop of our Union is appetizing and economical, the menu offers little variety for vegetarians. Besides your tasty grilled cheese sandwich, could you perhaps also offer egg salad or fried egg sandwiches? We would especially appreciate your adding a salad bar, which should prove popular with many of your patrons and thus profitable for you as well.

Note what happens in the next three examples when the topic remains the same but the *audience* changes. This time I will address my fellow vegetarians in a letter in the student newspaper.

### 4. Purpose: To Inform

Every day we eat lunch in the Snack Shop of the Union because it's the closest and the cheapest place. And every day we end up ordering the same thing—a grilled cheese sandwich—because that's the only vegetarian item on the menu. We're astonished that at a university the size of ours the food service takes no account of vegetarians' preferences.

### 5. Purpose: To Entertain

When we trudge over to the Snack Shop for lunch—exhausted from our morning classes, perishing for some wholesome food—

we're confronted by a menu offering nothing but a disgusting array of dead animals: dead cow on a bun, dead pig on rye, dead fowl on a roll. We starving vegetarians must make do with a barely edible slice of imitation cheese grilled between two pale pieces of greasy balloon bread. We could get a more nutritious and tasty meal by munching grass out on the quad.

## 6. Purpose: To Persuade

Vegetarians, unite! Our reasonable requests have so far produced no changes in the meat-laden menu at the Union Snack Shop. In order to convince the food service people that a substantial number of vegetarians are potential customers, we need to state our appeal collectively. Stop by the Food Services office next time you're in the Union and tell the manager that we need a salad bar.

---

**Discussion Exercise**                                     **1-1**

1  In the first group of examples, addressed to the Director of Food Services, what details change when the purpose becomes to entertain rather than to inform? Can you tell why? What differences do you notice in word choice? Do you find them appropriate? Why?

2  What different details do you find in the third passage? Why are they introduced? Why do you think the terms *appetizing*, *economical*, and *tasty* appear?

3  In the second group of passages, addressed to fellow vegetarians, the words chosen to describe the meat sandwiches in example 5 are quite different from those used in example 2. Can you explain why?

4  Consider the descriptions of the grilled cheese sandwich in examples 2 and 5. Can you account for the differences? Would a nonvegetarian find example 5 amusing, do you think? If not, why?

5  If you examine all six passages, you will notice that the most pronounced changes occur when the purpose becomes to entertain. What significant difference can you observe when you compare the passages aimed to inform (1 and 4) with those designed to persuade (3 and 6)?

---

**Writing Exercise** 1-2

Choose either of the following topics.

1 Write a letter to the School Board of your former high school suggesting that too much (or too little) emphasis is being given to the Latin Club, to the vocational program, to the cheerleading squad, to the baseball team, or to counseling students.

Then rewrite the letter to address the President of the Student Council. Try to convince that person to rouse the student body to action on your issue.

Your purpose in both letters will be to persuade, but remember that a humorous approach can sometimes be the most persuasive—depending upon the topic and the audience.

If you don't know the correct form for writing a business letter, follow the format used in the sample job application letter in Appendix B.

2 Write a brief account of Moses parting the Red Sea and marching his people across. First write a version to present at the Wednesday Night Bible Study Group. Then write a version to appear as a news story in *Time* magazine. Your purpose in both is to inform. If you don't remember the biblical story, choose some historical event, like the assassination of President Lincoln, and write a version first for the grade school publication *The Weekly Reader*; then write another account for *Time* magazine.

---

## FINDING A THESIS

One of the early decisions in the process of writing involves choosing (or being assigned) a subject of some sort to write about. In composition class you may be allowed to choose your topic. In history class you are more likely to be told the topic. On the job you will probably be required to report in writing on an assigned subject. After you have chosen or been assigned a topic, you need to find an approach that allows you to cover the subject within your word limit. Eventually, you should be able to write out this main idea in a single sentence— your *thesis statement*.

Once you have worked it out, your thesis should clearly state the point you want to make about your subject. If, for instance, your topic is conservation, you need to narrow it considerably for a three-page paper. You might decide to write just about protecting wildlife. But even that is too broad an idea to cover in a brief essay. You could then limit yourself to seals. But now, ask yourself, what *about* seals? What is the point you want to make? You could assert that seals should be protected from industry by international treaty. Or you could argue that people should not buy any product made of sealskin in order to keep industry from finding the slaughter profitable.

**REMEMBER:**   **Your thesis should contain a verb to say something about your subject.**

| | |
|---|---|
| Topic: | Drugs |
| Topic: | Drug abuse |
| Workable thesis: | Drug abuse can occur with perfectly legal prescription drugs. |
| Workable thesis: | Excessive use of alcohol constitutes the number 1 drug abuse problem in the United States. |

A good thesis should make your readers want to read further in order to find out what you have to say about this interesting idea. Be sure the idea is indeed interesting, not a trite or simple-minded idea like "Sports build character" or "Motherhood is a joyful experience that no woman should miss." The writer of that last sentence hadn't thought about the idea. Is motherhood joyful for a poor woman with no husband and nine children? Are women's personalities so similar that such a generalization could be true? We all find ourselves writing down unexamined ideas once in a while. A thoughtful rereading of whatever you write can help you avoid making this weakness public.

<hr>

**Discussion Exercise**                                                    **1-3**

Some of the sentences below are workable thesis statements for an essay of about 500 words, but some need to be made more specific. Pick out the successful ones, and indicate what's wrong with the others.

See if you can make every one into a reasonably good thesis. But first, here are five workable thesis statements to inspire you.

**A**  Many Americans spend so much time in front of the TV set that they never really experience their own lives. (In the introduction of your paper, this thesis might appear in a livelier form, like "Turn off the TV and turn on to life!")

**B**  I think that college students and teachers would be happier with education if people didn't enroll in college before the age of 25.

**C**  On a sunny summer morning last year, I realized that I was ultimately alone.

**D**  The perfect omelet is fluffy, light, delicately browned, and even attainable if the cook follows five practical guidelines.

**E**  In Shakespeare's *Hamlet*, Ophelia's insanity and suicide represent what would have happened to Hamlet had he been female.

Now try to whip these into shape:

**1**  Television commercials are an outrage.

**2**  Freedom and independence carry with them responsibilities and consequences.

**3**  I'm going to describe the dying flowers and yellowing leaves outside my window.

**4**  My dog and my boyfriend are much alike.

**5**  I learned not to worry when I was 16.

**6**  Thousands of Americans go through the vicious cycle of eating until they are overweight and then dieting until they reduce.

**7**  People's views on capital punishment are very controversial.

**8**  The purpose of of this paper is to compare and contrast the Catholic schools and the public schools.

**9**  Do you feel cheated because you can't grow a beard?

**10**  Making a lemon pie is easy.

## MUDDLING MAY BE PART OF THE PROCESS

As you are working on your thesis and thinking about audience and purpose, you will probably also be dredging up ideas to use in the paper, a task I have not yet touched on. The writing process is too involved, too recursive, to be described as a neat and orderly progression. But since my writing in this textbook must be neat and orderly to be easily understood, you can see the problem. I can scarcely avoid explaining the process one part at a time. So, let me make clear that these parts can often overlap, can occur simultaneously, or can even sometimes be done in reverse order (as, for example, when you write your introduction after finishing your paper).

If you are a dedicated writer, you will likely spend a lot of time mucking about—scratching out words, tossing out paragraphs, squeezing sentences between the lines, scribbling new ideas on your outline, drawing arrows to insertions, gazing into space as you search for the right word or the perfect example, and sometimes throwing it all in the wastebasket and starting over.

## A FEW WORDS ABOUT WORD PROCESSORS

Since writing well is such a messy process, a writer's best friend is not diamonds or a dog but a word processor. If you can lay hands on one, by all means do so. It won't by itself make a better writer of you, but it will enable you to become a better writer with greater ease. Here are some of its advantages.

1   You don't have to worry about any kind of errors as you compose because they can be corrected with no muss, no fuss, no bother.
2   You can erase with the touch of a key.
3   You can insert words or move them around wherever you want them (even whole paragraphs) with astonishing ease.
4   You can use a spelling checker to tell you which words you have spelled too creatively. It will catch your typos, too—except when you have typed the wrong word (like *their* for *there*, *car* for *cat*); so you must still proofread.
5   You can turn out perfect copy, even though (like me) you're a hopelessly incompetent typist.

Programs are available that will even help you with revision by analyzing your writing and then telling you if you're using the passive voice too much, if you've made an error in grammar, or if you're using too many multisyllable words. But whether you have access to one of these magical programs or not, you should start processing your words if possible. You'll find it's easier than putting pen to paper. It's more efficient. And it's more fun.

# Chapter 2

# Produce a Plausible Plan

In my opinion, the most efficient method of writing involves thinking about what to say and how to say it before beginning to compose. What major points will you present? In what order? What specific details will you include? To structure all this information, you need a plan of some sort.

You don't necessarily need a tidy, formal outline, complete with roman numerals and A, B, C headings like the ones in this chapter. But you should at least get down on paper the main ideas you intend to present and figure out the order in which you will take them up. You can, if you're eager to get started, think up your supporting evidence as you go. Or you can supply missing examples and illustrations as you revise your first draft. Your scratch outline is a flexible guide. You can rearrange points, add ideas, or leave out portions if you discover a better arrangement as you write.

## START BY BRAINSTORMING

As you're working out a thesis, jot down every idea that comes to mind pertaining to your subject. After you've come up with a workable thesis, continue searching your mind (and maybe a few magazine articles or books) for more information. Consult your friends, also, to see whether they have any ideas or further knowledge on the matter. Write down every notion, whether it seems exactly to the point or not. You can easily scratch out things you don't need, and you may end up altering your thesis slightly to suit the available facts.

Let's assume that in horticulture class you have been assigned a 500-word paper on home gardening. Since you're not interested in growing flowers, you narrow the topic at once to home vegetable gardening. That's still a subject more suited to a book than a short essay. How about organic vegetable gardening? Better, but 500 words isn't much—only three or four well-developed paragraphs, plus a brief introduction and conclusion. You need to narrow the topic some more. How about fighting bugs organically? That sounds promising.

Now, what *about* fighting bugs organically? "Fighting bugs organically allows home gardeners to avoid the dangers of pesticides." There you have a good preliminary thesis. What supporting evidence can you think of that might prove useful in such an essay? If you think awhile, you may end up with a jumbled list something like this:

Some insects eat garden pests.
Soapy water kills some insects but not hardy plants.
Strong garlic water discourages some pests.
Slugs like beer—and will drown themselves in it, given the chance.
Useful insects can be purchased by mail order.
Praying mantises like to eat caterpillars and mites.
Ladybugs zap aphids.
Milky spore disease kills Japanese beetles.
Cabbage worms are zonked by *Bacillus thuringiensis*.
Pick off insects by hand (drown or suffocate them in a jar).
Birds eat insects.
Laying aluminum foil on the ground will drive aphids to suicide.
Green lacewings eat mealybugs like crazy.

## BRINGING ORDER OUT OF CHAOS

You now need three or four main ideas—in this case, methods of controlling insect pests—to serve as the major points in your outline. Keep looking over your list to see if you can discover patterns. Try to determine which are major ideas, which are supporting details.

Note that "Some insects eat garden pests" is a major idea. You have several examples to support it. Perhaps you'll want to rephrase the idea for greater clarity: "Bring in natural enemies to kill pests." As supporting evidence, you can mention praying mantises, ladybugs, and green lacewings (plus the specific insects they control) and note that these useful insects can be purchased by mail. That's plenty for one paragraph.

You may detect several supporting details that are similar and only need to have a major heading added. Notice in your list that these items all share a common trait:

Putting out beer for slugs
Laying down aluminum foil to entrap aphids
Squirting soapy water or garlic water on plants

These methods all use products found usually in the kitchen. You could group these three under the heading, "Try safe and easy household remedies."

Two other items on the list clearly belong together: milky spore disease and *Bacillus thuringiensis*. (You discover such unusual remedies through research—in this case, by reading Lawrence Sheehan's "Garden Club Notes: Fighting Bugs Organically," in *Harper's*, April 1979, which served as a model for this sample outline.) Since these techniques work by introducing diseases fatal to insects but harmless to plants and people, you could head this section, "Introduce insect diseases to destroy pests."

Only two items in the brainstorming list remain unused: picking insects off by hand and encouraging birds to come to your garden. Probably picking bugs off by hand is too tiresome to be a practical suggestion. And enticing birds may hurt more than help. Birds eat bugs indiscriminately—the ladybugs along with the aphids—and are exceptionally fond of many succulent garden vegetables as well. You'd better let those leftover ideas go, unless you decide to mention in your conclusion that if all else fails, the dedicated gardener can always pick off the beastly bugs one by one.

## ARRANGING YOUR POINTS

After you've chosen the main ideas and supporting details, the last step involves deciding in what order to present your ideas. Since there's no chronology (time order) involved in this particular plan, begin with a fairly strong and interesting point to get your readers' attention. End with your strongest point to leave the readers feeling that you've said something worthwhile. With this pest-control outline, you could almost flip a coin. But since the household remedies are the cheapest and most entertaining to describe, you might well begin there. Save the section on importing natural enemies for the end, since it sounds like a dramatic and effective solution.

## SAMPLE OUTLINE

Your outline, then, will look something like this, if you take time to make it look neat:

**THESIS:**   **Fighting bugs organically allows home gardeners to avoid the dangers of pesticides.**

Introduction
  I  Try safe and easy household remedies.
     **A**  Set out trays of beer to attract slugs, which drown in it.
     **B**  Spray soapy water (not detergent) or garlic water on plants.
     **C**  Spread aluminum foil under plants to disorient aphids, thus luring them to their doom.
 II  Introduce insect diseases to destroy pests.
     **A**  Milky spore disease kills larvae of Japanese beetles.
     **B**  *Bacillus thuringiensis* sprayed on soil is deadly to cabbage worms.
     **C**  Both remedies are available at garden stores.

**III**  Bring in natural enemies to fight pests.
    **A**  Praying mantises devour caterpillars and mites.
    **B**  Ladybugs consume quantities of aphids.
    **C**  Green lacewings feed on mealybugs.
    **D**  These useful insects can be ordered by mail.
Conclusion

In the essay from which this outline was adapted, Lawrence Sheehan uses these more imaginative (but less informative) headings for his main points:

| | | |
|---|---|---|
| **I** | Hand-to-hand combat | (for "Household remedies") |
| **II** | Biological warfare | (for "Insect diseases") |
| **III** | Hired-guns approach | (for "Natural enemies") |

In writing your paper, you may want to employ such colorful language, but in the planning stage, clarity is more important. In the outline set your ideas down in a clear and orderly fashion. Then, when you revise your first draft of the paper, you can make the phrasing witty and entertaining. Remember, though: *Clarity is the keynote.*

---

**Exercise**                                                                        **2-1**

The following outline illustrates a number of weaknesses: supporting points that don't really support, minor points that pose as major points, major points that lack supporting evidence, etc. Study this sorry example until you have located all its shortcomings; then revise the whole by adding, omitting, and rearranging as necessary to produce a tidy outline.

**THESIS:**    **Studying in a dorm is impossible for anyone who lacks unswerving discipline.**

  **I**  Phones ringing and stereos playing keep me from concentrating.
 **II**  Friends drop in and keep me from studying.
    **A**  Card playing and bull sessions interrupt me.
    **B**  Watching TV is more fun than studying.

**III** Neighbors are forever partying.
    **A** Loud music, talking, and laughing disturb me.
**IV** Studying is really hard for me.
    **A** I fall asleep.
    **B** Chemistry 101 is beyond me.

## CHECK YOUR PLAN FOR UNITY

Unity is something we never require of casual conversation: it's fine if you wander a little off the track and tell about the Bluebird Saloon in Denver in the middle of a discussion about Humphrey Bogart films.

But in an expository essay, unity is important: you must not go on about the Bluebird in the middle of an *essay* about Bogart films, even though you had a beer there after seeing *The Maltese Falcon* at a nearby theater. Such a departure from the main subject is called a *digression*. A paragraph or essay has unity if it sticks to the main point. It lacks unity if it wanders across the street for a drink.

Since the unity and coherence of your paper depend largely on the way you order your ideas—that is, on your plan or outline—you should take a few minutes to go over it after you finish it. Check these points carefully:

**1** Make sure every major heading or idea relates to your thesis.
**2** Make sure every major heading has adequate supporting details.
**3** Make sure every supporting detail relates to its major heading.
**4** Don't let any major point get buried as a supporting detail or any minor points get elevated as major headings.
**5** Don't allow any careless repetition of ideas anywhere.

If you will take the trouble to unify your outline this way, you can't possibly end up with slipshod organization or an essay that wanders away from the topic.

## PATTERN YOUR DEVELOPMENT

The sample outline about battling bugs was put together by classification—by sorting out the methods of killing garden pests without using insecticides. While classification is a common method of organizing material, experienced writers employ a number of patterns for ordering and developing their ideas—quite often using several different methods in the same piece.

Practicing these various ways of organizing material is a lot like doing finger exercises when learning to play the piano. Through practice you internalize a skill: you make the execution of that skill second nature so that you can use the techniques without having to think about them consciously. Once you become an expert writer, you'll not need to mull over which patterns to use as you develop your ideas. By then you'll have the various methods stored in your brain, and you'll use them to structure your material without giving the techniques themselves a moment's thought.

Your instructor may perhaps wish to have you practice these patterns by writing paragraphs instead of essays in each mode. You are, of course, more likely to employ these patterns in developing individual paragraphs and passages instead of complete essays.

## SPATIAL STRUCTURE

This first method of development, used for description, will seldom form the basis of an entire paper, unless you're writing for practice or for pleasure. But you will probably use description in virtually everything you write—especially if you write interestingly.

### Description

Most authorities on writing suggest that you can organize descriptions spatially—top to bottom, left to right, near to far, etc. This is true. You can describe your cat from nose to tail. But where do you include the texture of the fur, the stripes or spots, the color of the paws? And what about the meow? And the various ways the cat moves? Good description involves working a number of details into some spatial arrangement.

First, consider your purpose. Do you want to arouse an emotional response in your readers? Or are you trying to convey a word picture, without emotion but sharp and clear as a photograph? Your choice of words and details will differ according to the effect you want. Before you begin writing, look—really *look*—at what you plan to describe. Maybe you'll want to smell and taste and touch it as well. Then try to record your sense impressions—the exact shapes, the lights and shades, the textures, the tastes, the sounds, the smells. Don't include everything, of course, or you may overwhelm your readers. Carefully select the details that suit your purpose in order to give your audience a sharp impression of what you're describing. Then search for the precise words to convey that picture.

In this choice descriptive paragraph. Mark Twain takes his readers with him through the woods and into a meadow:

Beyond the road where the snakes sunned themselves was a dense young thicket, and through it a dim-lighted path led a quarter of a mile; then out of the dimness one emerged abruptly upon a level great prairie which was covered with wild strawberry plants, vividly starred with prairie pinks, and walled in on all sides by forests. The strawberries were fragrant and fine and in the season we were generally there in the crisp freshness of the early morning, while the dew-beads still sparkled upon the grass and the woods were ringing with the first song of the birds.

—Mark Twain's *Autobiography* (1924)

A contemporary master of description is Annie Dillard, who allows us both to see and hear the ocean through her selection of details and choice of words in this brief passage from her article "Innocence in the Galápagos," in *Harper's* magazine (May 1975):

The white beach was a havoc of lava boulders black as clinkers, sleek with spray, and lambent as brass in the sinking sun. To our left a dozen sea lions were body-surfing in the long green combers that rose, translucent, half a mile offshore. When the combers broke, the shoreline boulders rolled. I could feel the roar in the rough rock on which I sat; I could hear the grate inside each long backsweeping sea, the rumble of a rolled million rocks muffled in splashes and the seethe before the next wave's heave.

Out of thousands of possible details, Dillard chooses a few that are powerful and appeal to our senses. Remember that good descriptive details will enliven almost any kind of writing. Be sure to observe carefully, select telling details, and search for the exact words.

## Topics for Descriptive Writing

1 Describe as thoroughly as possible in one sentence how a cat's fur feels, how modeling clay feels, how soft rain feels, how hard rain feels, how a hangover feels. Or describe in a sentence how a snake moves, how a cat walks, how a dog greets you; or how a vampire looks, or a werewolf, or a visitor from outer space.

2 Describe a food you hate or love with as much sensory detail as possible.

3 Choose one brief experience that has sensuous association for you— something like this: A person walks by wearing the same perfume you wore in the eleventh grade, or you pet a dog that looks just exactly like old Spot, your devoted companion all through grade school, or you hear a special "golden oldie" on the radio. Write a descriptive paragraph in which you develop that brief experience.

4 Describe a place (like a classroom, the cafeteria, the coffee shop, the dorm lounge, the Dean's office) and try to convey your attitude toward it through your use of specific details. Avoid making a statement about your feelings.

5 Describe the place in which you feel most at peace—or most ill at ease. Choose details that appeal to the senses.

## CHRONOLOGICAL STRUCTURE

Most of the time, writers organize material in two ways: according to chronological sequence or according to logical sequence. Let's take up chronological development first because it's easier.

### Narrative Writing

Brief narratives are frequently used in introductions to gain the readers' interest. Narratives are also useful as supporting evidence—to prove a point through an account of a personal experience. Although narratives are seldom appropriate in academic essays or business writing, you will find that telling an entertaining story proves a good way to enliven various other kinds of writing. And sometimes a narrative may prove to be the perfect form for an entire essay, article, or speech.

Since a narrative recounts an event or an experience, you can simply arrange the details in the order in which they happened. Of critical importance, though, is choosing the right details and focusing on the most significant happenings. While narrative is perhaps the easiest kind of writing to do, it is surely one of the hardest to do well. You may find it necessary to fictionalize the details of your experience somewhat in order to keep your readers interested. And you must be especially careful to maintain a consistent point of view.

But take note: In a piece of pure narrative writing, do not state your thesis in your introduction. Put your thesis or purpose on your scratch outline; then leave the main idea implied in the paper itself. You don't want to take the edge off.

You need in all good writing to make a point of some sort, but you want to avoid just tacking on a moral as the conclusion of your narrative. Say you're asked to write a narrative account of some experience you remember from your childhood. Anything you can recall vividly probably has some significance. Be sure to have in mind before you write what that significance is and how you're going to bring it out. If you remember, for instance, one awful day in sixth grade when your gym teacher made you—a 97-pound weakling—wrestle a 150-pound tarzan, you'll want to include the bloodthirsty cries of your classmates and the sadistic chuckles of your gym teacher in order to emphasize the inhumanity of the incident. You don't have to tell your readers the point: if you write it well, they'll see it for themselves.

## Topics for Narrative Writing

1   I learned _____ the hard way.
2   Write an account of your initiation into some element of the adult world of which you were unaware as a child: violence, hypocrisy, prejudice, sexuality, etc.
3   Tell about the first time you remember being punished at school (or at home).
4   Tell the story of a tough ethical decision you once had to make and of what happened afterward.
5   Write a narrative to support or deny some familiar proverb, like "Honesty is the best policy," "Nice guys finish last," or "Home is where the heart is."

## Process Papers

One of the most practical kinds of writing explains a process, i.e., tells readers how to do something or how something works. Often explaining a process provides the material for a complete essay or set of instructions, but you may, on occasion, want to explain a process as a section in a longer piece. An essay focusing on the advantages of organic gardening, for instance, might well include a paragraph explaining how to make compost.

Chronological structure, point by point, is the usual way to organize process writing. Remember to start at the beginning. If you're going to explain how to bathe a large, reluctant dog, you'll want first to suggest putting on old clothes or a bathing suit and proceed from there. Your outline might look something like this:

**THESIS:**     **How to wash a dog without losing your temper or frightening the washee.**

  **I**   What to wear.
     **A**   In summer—old clothes or bathing suit.
     **B**   In winter—next to nothing in the shower.
 **II**   Gathering the implements.
     **A**   Mild soap or dog shampoo.
     **B**   Lots of old towels.
     **C**   Hand-held hairdryer—if winter.
**III**   Where to do it.
     **A**   In summer—on driveway or patio to avoid killing grass with soap.
     **B**   In winter—in bathtub with shower curtain drawn.
     **C**   If no shower curtain, wait till summer.
 **IV**   Reassuring the animal.
     **A**   Dog thinks you plot a drowning.
     **B**   Talk continually in comforting tones.
  **V**   The actual washing.
     **A**   Wet entire dog, apply soap or shampoo, work up lather.
     **B**   Keep soap out of eyes and ears.
     **C**   Don't forget the underside and tail.
     **D**   Rinse very thoroughly.

**VI**  Drying the dog.
   **A**  Dog will shake—like it or not.
   **B**  Rub damp-dry with towels.
   **C**  If winter, finish with hand-held hairdryer.

You might conclude that having a shiny, fragrant, flealess dog makes all this tribulation worthwhile. Or you might instead conclude that dog owners in their right minds who can afford the fee should pack the beast off to the veterinary clinic and let the experts do it.

A process paper, although easy to organize, is difficult to make interesting. Include as many descriptive words and lively verbs as you can without making the whole thing sound grotesque. You may assume if you're describing a technical process, such as how to clean a carburetor or how to replace a light switch, that probably your readers will follow out of a desire for enlightenment, so there's no obligation to entertain. But instead you must be doubly sure to identify all parts and to explain each and every step.

Identify your audience before you plan. Who are your readers? How much do they already know about the process? How much more do they need to know about it? Instructions for tuning a TV, for instance, will be written entirely differently for the person who owns the set than for the person who repairs it.

Here are some tips for good process writing: (1) Define any unfamiliar terms; (2) be as specific as possible; (3) include reasons for each step; and (4) provide warnings about typical mistakes or hazards.

Some processes do not lend themselves to an easy chronological organization—subjects like "How to choose a suitable marriage partner" or "How to care for a praying mantis." For such topics you must fall back on logical organization, which is covered in the next section.

---

### Topics for Process Writing

1  How to train an animal (dog, parrot, turtle, cat, etc.).
2  How to get rid of a bad habit. Choose only one habit to discuss: nail biting, smoking, interrupting others, or the like.
3  How to build a successful campfire.

4  Find out and describe how some simple, familiar thing works (for example: soap, can opener, hand eggbeater, wart remover, ballpoint pen).
5  How to come about on a windsurfer, or how to impress someone by doing a stunt on a skateboard.

## LOGICAL STRUCTURE

Most of the writing you'll be called upon to do will probably require organizing according to some sort of logic. For instance, if you're writing a paper which suggests no special kind of structure, your most logical approach is probably to arrange your ideas from the least impressive to the most compelling point. Since your final point remains foremost in the minds of your readers as they appraise the quality of your paper, you might as well make it your best idea. Or you might decide to arrange your concepts from the least complicated to the most complex. Or you could work from the smallest to the largest, like this:

1  Tolerable bores
2  Agonizing bores
3  Stupefying bores

But finding an organization for more complex material requires thought and ingenuity. Following are some suggestions that you may find helpful in various writing situations.

### Classification and Analysis

When you *classify*, you take many items and sort them out into a few groups. When you *analyze*, you take one item and divide it into its component parts. Say your subject is squashes. If you outline ''Three Types of Edible Squash,'' you're classifying; if you outline ''Three Parts of a Squash Blossom,'' you're analyzing. Both processes are based on logical division, and both require the same kind of organizational pattern.

We classify and analyze things all the time with no struggle at all. We classify political candidates into Republican, Democrat, Populist, or Socialist; we classify doughnuts into plain, glazed, chocolate-covered, and jelly-filled. We analyze whenever we reveal and explain the parts of something. Solving a problem, explaining a process, arguing a point, speculating on cause and effect, interpreting literature—all involve analysis.

To organize a classification or an analysis essay, you need to find a basis for division which does not shift. The divisions should also have the same rank. That sounds tricky, so let me show you what I mean. Here's a sketchy outline that shifts its basis for division:

**Types of Aardvarks**
Introduction
1  The fuzzy aardvark
2  The hairless aardvark
3  The friendly aardvark
Conclusion

The first two types are divided according to physical characteristics, while the last type is defined by its personality. You see the worry this causes: Can a hairless aardvark be friendly? Are fuzzy aardvarks ill-tempered? How much hair does a friendly aardvark have?

This next skimpy outline demonstrates a shift in rank:

**Types of Recorded Music**
Introduction
1  Classical
2  Easy listening
3  The Rolling Stones
Conclusion

Although the Rolling Stones represent a type of music distinct from classical and easy listening, the category is not parallel (or equal) to the others; it's too small. It should be rock and roll or hard rock or acid rock, with the Stones used as an example.

### Topics for Classification and Analysis Writing

1  Classify the cartoons in the Sunday funnies.
2  What types of TV shows are the most popular this season? Analyze the appeal of each type.

3 Contemplate a magazine advertisement or a television commercial. What emotions and thoughts is this advertising designed to appeal to?

4 Choose a hero you've had in your lifetime and analyze what qualities made this person your idol.

5 If you've ever been a salesperson, waitress, or waiter, how would you classify your customers?

6 Divide into types and analyze any one of these subjects: neighborhoods, marriages, laughter, dreams, teachers, students, tennis players, drinkers, pet owners.

7 Explain what qualities would make up the ideal roommate, dinner date, novel, Saturday afternoon, parent, child, spouse.

## Definition

You will always need to define any abstract or controversial terms that figure importantly in your writing. Sometimes this requires only a sentence or two. But sometimes definition can become the structural basis for an entire paper, as when you're isolating, analyzing, and defining a social group such as bores, hippies, or hockey fans. Florence King in the April 1974 issue of *Harper's* presents an extended definition of ''The Good Ole Boy,'' which she organizes using description, narration, and analysis:

**THESIS:**     **The Good Ole Boy is a Southern WASP type, easy to recognize but difficult to define.**

1 Description of general physical characteristics
   A   Middle-aged, jowlish
   B   Drinks beer, wears white socks, etc.
2 Good Ole Boys I have known
   A   Pearl—the playful masher
   B   Calhoun—the kindly fascist
3 Analysis of Good Ole Boy behavior
   A   The Little Dinky syndrome
   B   The search for an oversexed Melanie
   C   An excursion to Johnny's Cash 'n' Carry tavern

Another method of developing a definition involves exclusion, i.e., explaining what something is *not*. If you're going to argue, for instance, that society needs protection from lethal bores, you might begin by presenting examples of several kinds of bores who are bearable, making clear that these are *not* the ones from whom we need protection. Then you zero in on what constitutes a really paralyzing bore, identifying several types and offering more examples. Finally, if possible, mention suggestions for coping with the problem, ideally something more humane than the electric chair.

---

## Topics for Writing Definitions

1  Think of a word or phrase that you use a lot, and then define what you mean by it in different situations.
2  Define a slang term and discuss its possible origins and significance.
3  Define a certain type of person. Examples: the perfectionist, the male chauvinist, the intellectual, the slob, the egomaniac, the life-of-the-party.
4  Write about a term you feel is used in more than one way. Examples: love, friend, materialism, hippie, ugly.
5  Write the definition of an abstract concept. Examples: alienation, eccentricity, power, happiness, progressive, loving.

---

## Comparison and Contrast

One of the most common methods of organization involves focusing on similarities and differences—or more likely on one or the other—in order to make a point. Sometimes we use this technique to clarify: an effective way, for instance, to explain impressionism in literature is to compare it with impressionism in painting, which is visual and hence easier to grasp. Sometimes we use a comparison to persuade, as Naomie Weisstein does in her article, ''Woman as Nigger,'' in the October 1969 issue of *Psychology Today*. Weisstein sets up this analogy in an attempt to jolt readers into seeing that women are conditioned with the slave mentality and exploited for the economic benefit of society just like black people.

When we focus on differences, we often seek to show that one category is somehow better than the other. You could establish a useful comparison between two products, focusing on their differences, in order to recommend one as a better buy than the other. Or you could humorously contrast the differences between toads and snakes in order to contend that toads make more companionable pets than snakes.

Whether focusing on differences or similarities, you have two ways of organizing a comparison or contrast paper. If, for instance, you decide to contrast the relative merits of toads and snakes, you can simply list and illustrate all the ingratiating characteristics of toads first. Then, using a single transition (something like "Snakes, on the other hand, seldom inspire affection"), you repeat the criteria for snakes, emphasizing their lack of congeniality. Your conclusion needs only to prod your reader to observe that, indeed, as you have shown, toads do make more lovable pets than snakes and don't bite in the bargain.

That's the easy way. A more elaborate way involves establishing the comparison point by point, as shown in this outline:

**THESIS:**     **Toads make more desirable pets than snakes.**

I   Personality traits
   A   Snakes
      1   Messy, lose their skins
      2   Introverted, noncommunicative
      3   Speak only in a menacing hiss
   B   Toads
      1   Clean, tidy
      2   Placid, undeceptive
      3   Speak in a warm, friendly croak
II   Physical characteristics
   A   Snakes
      1   Fixed, glassy stare
      2   No ears or legs, loathsome forked tongue
      3   Difficult to cuddle
   B   Toads
      1   Large, languid eyes
      2   Quaintly bowlegged
      3   Plump, soft, snuggly

If you're an inexperienced writer, you might do well to try the easy method first and work up to the sustained, point-by-point contrast.

You'll find another point-by-point comparison outline (this one on a serious topic) on pages 34–35.

---

**Topics for Comparison and Contrast Writing**

1 Discuss one or more illusions that are presented as reality on television and compare the illusion with the reality as you know it.
2 Compare and contrast: two lifestyles you have experienced, two artists, two films, a film and the book it was based on, two people (e.g., two of your friends, two television characters, a friend and an enemy).
3 Compare how you perceived some person, place, or situation as a child with how you perceive the same thing today.
4 Write about a situation in which you expected one thing and got another— in other words, the expectation and the reality were different. Many times these situations are "firsts": your first day of school, your first roommate, your first wedding, your first health food restaurant.
5 Find a typical magazine for men and one for women. Discuss three or four major differences that distinguish these publications.

---

**Cause and Effect**

When you develop a topic by analyzing *causes*, you are explaining to your readers why something happened. If you go on to explore the consequences of that happening, you are organizing your analysis of the *effects*. Probably you'll want to content yourself with doing only one or the other in a single piece of writing, but you might attempt both if you should get turned loose without a word limit.

You may be able to fall back on chronological arrangement if you can trace the causes from earliest to most recent. If you're explaining "Why my honeymoon was a disaster," you might trace the cause back to the moment you decided to get married and then pinpoint several unfortunate decisions that followed, like this:

1 My first small mistake: I got engaged (cite details).
2 My next big blunder: I decided to have an elaborate wedding (cite details).
3 My final egregious error: I got smashed at the reception (cite details).

More likely, though, your organization will fall into some simple, logical pattern that has more to do with the importance of the causes or effects than simply with chronology—as from the least significant to the most important. Or from the fairly obvious to the exceedingly subtle. Or from local causes to nationwide causes. The possibilities are endless. Simply present your ideas in the order you consider most clear and emphatic.

If you're seriously analyzing causes or effects, you must be wary of logical fallacies—especially oversimplification and the old post hoc pitfall. Do not write a syllable until you've consulted Chapter 6, especially pages 97 to 101.

## Topics for Cause and Effect Writing

1  A group of extraterrestrial beings visits Earth. On their planet people are neither male nor female: each person is both. Using one of these beings as a first-person narrator, explain how their society is different from ours.
2  Explain what causes some natural phenomenon (for example: rain, dew, blue sky, twinkling stars, sweat, hiccups, the phases of the moon).
3  Describe a failure you once had, and tell its causes or effects (or both).
4  Explain the causes (or effects) of any drastic change of opinion, attitude, or behavior you've undergone in your life.
5  Investigate and discuss the possible causes for any opinion, prejudice, interest, or unreasonble fear that you feel strongly.

## Persuasion and Argumentation

*Persuasion* refers to provocative appeals to emotion; *argumentation* refers to logical appeals to reason. In everyday language, the terms are used almost interchangeably; they are used that way here, also, to simplify matters. Most of what we write is intended to be persuasive to some degree. At least it should have a point. Sometimes, though, we write for purely persuasive reasons: We hope to get our readers to agree with our point of view on a debatable subject. That's the kind of writing this section deals with.

Any or all of the organizational patterns covered so far can be used to persuade your readers or to argue a point. Usually you will combine many patterns of development when you write a persuasive paper. You will also need to give extra consideration to your purpose and your audience. Be charming. Be persuasive.

If you're writing on any sort of controversial topic, you'll do well to familiarize yourself with both sides. Not only will you understand the issue better this way, but you'll be able to deal more effectively with the opposing viewpoints—some of which may be lodged firmly in your readers' minds. Your best bet for convincing the nonbelievers is to adopt a rational tone and trot out plenty of telling evidence for your side. But you may first want to present briefly the case for the opposition in order to demolish it with your own irrefutable evidence, clinching your argument with a compelling restatement of your thesis. Or, if you're up to it, use the contrast pattern (page 30) for your outline; present point by point the opposing argument followed point by point with your own, making clear the failings of the opposition while emphasizing the validity of your own.

### Topics for Persuasive Writing

1  Partners in a marriage should (should not) write their own detailed marriage contracts.
2  Marriage is (is not) an outmoded custom.
3  Think of one of our popular maxims—like ''Absence makes the heart grow fonder'' or ''Love is never having to say you're sorry.'' Write about whether you consider the message truth or propaganda, and why.
4  Argue for the alteration or abolition of one of our culture's rituals. Examples: traditional wedding ceremonies, funerals, high school graduation ceremonies, Christmas gift giving, proms, baby showers, presidential elections, dating, beauty contests, and so on.
5  Argue for public ownership of now privately owned services, such as electric companies, phone companies, oil companies, railroads, airlines, and hospitals. Or argue for private ownership of now publicly owned services, like the U.S. Postal Service.

## ORGANIZING ESSAY EXAMINATIONS

While you are in college, you may be called upon to use your composition skills as often in writing essay examinations as in composing actual papers. The technique is exactly the same: You still need a thesis statement, and you still need to plan your main points quickly—either in your head or on scratch paper. Finding a thesis presents no problem since you are usually supplied with one. Simply turn the question or topic into a statement, and there you have it. You may want to sharpen the focus if time permits, but always begin by restating the question as a thesis.

You might employ any of the patterns of organization just discussed in ordering your response. Suppose you are asked, "What were the major political events leading up to the Spanish Civil War?" You'll probably write a chronologically arranged answer quite automatically. Often essay exam questions request comparisons or contrasts. Suppose you have to deal with a topic like this one: "Discuss the major differences between Puritanism and Transcendentalism in America." If you're writing in class and are pressed for time, you'll do well to organize your answer the easy way: Set down all the important elements of Puritanism; then, using a single transition, present *in the same order* the main elements of Transcendentalism.

But if you should be given a take-home exam, you can at your leisure think of three or four major points on which to set up the contrast; then trot out examples for each movement alternately under these generalizations, something like this:

**THESIS:**  **The major differences between American Puritanism and Transcendentalism involve several basically opposing attitudes.**

  **I**  Attitude toward human nature.
     **A**  Puritanism considers human nature corrupt.
        **1**  "In Adam's Fall we sinned all."
        **2**  Doctrine of Original Sin.
     **B**  Transcendentalism views human nature as essentially good.
        **1**  Rejects idea of the fall of humanity.
        **2**  Declares human nature perfectible.
 **II**  Attitude toward God and salvation.
     **A**  Puritanism sees God above as sovereign ruler.
        **1**  Chief end of humanity is to glorify God.
        **2**  Bible is sole authority on religion and morality.
        **3**  No one is saved by good works—only by divine election.

    **B**   Transcendentalism finds God everywhere.
       **1**   God is in Nature and within each person.
       **2**   One comes to know God through "intuition" and the study of Nature.
**III**   Attitude toward society.
    **A**   Puritanism enforces conformity.
       **1**   Little tolerance for beliefs and customs of others.
       **2**   Each person responsible for overseeing behavior of neighbors.
    **B**   Transcendentalism encourages self-reliance.
       **1**   Rejects traditional authority.
       **2**   Advises individuals to follow decrees of their own consciences.

This outline should certainly produce a complete and well-organized response to an essay examination topic. It should, in fact, produce a good paper in its own right. There really is no difference in the writing process.

Naturally you can't hope to dash off an outline as complete as the one above when you must write in class, but remember that spending a short time thinking through what you're going to say—that is, planning your main points—can greatly improve your response, and thus your grade, on essay exams.

# Chapter 3

# Compose Pleasing Paragraphs

Your paper will be made up of paragraphs: first, a brief, fascinating introduction; then several interesting, unified, well-developed body paragraphs; and finally, a splendid, emphatic conclusion. Since the opening and closing paragraphs require special attention, let's begin with them.

## ADVICE ABOUT INTRODUCTIONS

A friend once told Robert Benchley, the humorist, that introductions were easy if you knew how to start. All you had to do was type "the" at the top of the page, and the rest would come by itself. Next morning Benchley tried it. Tap, tap, tap, t-h-e. Nothing came. He thought, he fidgeted, he fretted, he chewed his nails and popped his knuckles. Finally, in exasperation, he typed "hell with it" and abandoned the project.

Unlike Benchley, you cannot afford the luxury of abandonment. But postponing the introduction until you've gathered momentum and are writing at the height of your powers is probably a good idea. You already know the main idea of your paper (otherwise you couldn't begin writing it), so scrawl your thesis statement across the top of that blank page and get going on the first section of your outline. Think about the introduction in spare moments. Solicit divine inspiration, if possible. Should your introduction still be unfinished when the paper itself is done, you will find that a deadline looming ahead serves wonderfully to focus the mind.

## State Your Main Idea

While engaging your readers' attention is an important element of introductory paragraphs, their primary function is to let your readers know what that piece of writing is about. You won't always need a bold statement of your thesis, but the more formal the writing, the more likely you'll need a straightforward statement. In the following introduction, the writer comes directly to the point:

> Today in the United States there is one profession in which conflict of interest is not merely ignored but loudly defended as a necessary concomitant of the free enterprise system. That is in medicine, particularly in surgery.
>
> —(George Crile, Jr., "The Surgeon's
> Dilemma," *Harper's* (May 1975)

This whole introductory paragraph consists of only his thesis statement since the second sentence just concludes the idea begun in the first. It's really point-blank as introductions go.

Normally, you'll take several sentences to introduce your controlling idea. You can give a little background information or begin with some fairly broad remarks about your subject, then narrow the focus down to the specific idea covered by your thesis. You can see this method illustrated in the following example. (Thesis statements are italicized throughout this section.)

> To her, tight jeans and no bra mean she's in style. To him, they mean she wants to have sex. So it goes among adolescents in Los Angeles, according to a survey by four researchers at U.C.L.A. Despite unisex haircuts, the women's movement, and other signs of equality between the sexes, *boys still read more sexual come-ons into girls' behavior than the girls intend.*
>
> —*Psychology Today* (October 1980)

The article then presents other examples of dress and behavior that are often misinterpreted, just as the introduction promises. Be sure to give your readers at least the main idea of what your essay is going to be about somewhere near the beginning.

## Get Your Readers' Attention

If you're going to write skillfully, you need an introduction that makes your prospective readers eager to peruse your essay. You need to capture their interest at the outset.

**Use Fascinating Facts**  You can catch your readers' attention with facts and statistics—if you can find some real eye-openers like the ones in this introduction to an essay on the need for gun-control laws:

Every two-and-a-half minutes someone in the United States is robbed at gunpoint, and every forty minutes someone else is murdered with a gun. The weapons find their way into the hands of the criminals in a manner that almost nobody understands. Made in factories owned and operated by the most secretive industry in the country, the guns move through various markets and delivery systems, all of them obscure. Each year police seize about 250,000 handguns and long guns (rifles and shotguns) from the people they arrest. *Given the number of guns that the manufacturers produce each year (2.5 million long guns and 4 million handguns) the supply-and-demand equation works against the hope of an orderly society.*

—Steven Brill, ''The Traffic (Legal and Illegal) in Guns,'' *Harper's* (September 1977)

**Pose an Interesting Question**  Another way to arrest your readers' attention is by asking a tantalizing question—or maybe a whole series of them, as does the writer of this introduction for a *Newsweek* article:

Do Whitey Ford and Mickey Mantle *really* favor Miller's new Lite beer over all the others and hoist it off-camera as well as on? And how about Morris, the finicky cat? Does he dart for that other bowl of cat food once the floodlights fade? *Starting in mid-July, Whitey, Mickey, Morris and other celebrity hucksters better be prepared to back up their television-commercial claims by*

*actually drinking, eating, or using the products they advertise—or answer to*
*the Federal Trade Commission.*

—"Say It's Really So, Joe!" *Newsweek*, June 2, 1975

Notice how handy those rhetorical questions are for sneaking in the main idea. You pose a question, then answer it yourself, and you're off. But be reasonable. Don't use something simpleminded (like "What is sorority life?" or "Were you ever so mad you could scream?") just because it's an easy way to get started.

### Imply Your Thesis Occasionally

In narrative and descriptive essays your thesis idea is often so easy to grasp that you don't want to state it directly. Here's an example of an implied thesis from *Harper's* "Wraparound" section (April 1975). The author, who is not a professional writer, by the way, is simply leading up to the details of his disillusionment with his new car:

> Watching the auto ads on TV is pretty much like visiting a zoo or a game preserve. After observing leopards and other ferocious felines perform seductive antics for some time, I succumbed and went to a Chevrolet salesroom to get one of these creatures. Unfortunately, the station wagon I purchased did not belong to the cat family. It was a dog.

The double meaning in the slang use of *dog* is a touch that any reader will likely appreciate, probably sympathize with.

And my sympathy to you, as you're sweating out your introduction. Herbert Gold once complained about a similar difficulty—trying to make literature interesting to students. "Moses," he sighed, "only had to bring the Law down the mountain to the children of Israel; I had to bring it pleasingly." If you should manage to come up with something pleasing, you'll be rewarded with a feeling of satisfaction. You can count on that. Probably the only joy involved in writing comes from doing it well.

## ADVICE ABOUT CONCLUSIONS

Like introductions, conclusions ought to be forceful and to the point. Work especially hard on your last paragraph. Its effectiveness will influence the way your readers react to the whole paper. If you trail off tiredly at the end, they will sigh and feel let down. Avoid any sort of apology or hedging at this point. Don't end with a whimper. You want something impressive, but don't overdo it.

## Conclude Concisely

In fact, if you're writing a short paper and have saved your strongest point for the end, you may not need a whole new paragraph in conclusion. Instead, a sentence or two at the end of the final paragraph providing a sense of closure will do nicely. Here, for example, is the conclusion of Joan Didion's essay analyzing her experiences with migraine headaches. The first part of the paragraph continues describing her suffering, but then shifts ("For when the pain recedes . . .") to convey her final point—her acceptance of "the usefulness of migraine."

> And once it comes, now that I am wise in its ways, I no longer fight it. I lie down and let it happen. At first every small apprehension is magnified, every anxiety a pounding terror. Then the pain comes, and I concentrate only on that. Right there is the usefulness of migraine, there in that imposed yoga, the concentration on the pain. For when the pain recedes, ten or twelve hours later, everything goes with it, all the hidden resentments, all the vain anxieties. The migraine has acted as a circuit breaker, and the fuses have emerged intact. There is a pleasant convalescent euphoria. I open the windows and feel the air, eat gratefully, sleep well. I notice the particular nature of a flower in a glass on the stair landing. I count my blessings.
>
> —"In Bed," from *The White Album* (1979)

## Restate Your Thesis Only When Necessary

If you've written something long and informative, like a term paper of ten to twenty typed pages, you'll do well to summarize and restate your main idea. What you want, of course, is a tidy ending that reinforces the point you set out to make in the beginning. The writer of *Psychology Today's* article on misinterpreting sexual signals (the introduction is on page 37) closes with a reinforcement of the thesis:

> The young people's ethnic backgrounds, ages, and previous dating and sexual experiences had almost no effect on their reactions. The girls' "relatively

less-sexualized view of social relationships,'' the psychologists suggest, ''may reflect some discomfort . . . with the demands of the dating scene''; women do, after all, have more to lose from sexual activity, facing risks of pregnancy and/or a bad reputation. The girls in the study were much more likely than the boys to agree with the statement, ''Sometimes I wish that guys and girls could just be friends without worrying about sexual relationships.''

The quotation at the end reflects the thesis idea (''. . . boys still read more sexual come-ons into girls' behavior than the girls intend''), but does so in quite different terms and in a touching way.

### Try an Echo

If you can bring it off, the technique of echoing some element from your introduction is an especially good one. It gives your essay unity. The *Newsweek* article about a new policy requiring people or pets who push products to actually use them concludes with a reference to the same celebrities mentioned in the introduction (on page 38):

> Most advertisers do not feel that the proposed regulations will cramp their style. In any event, it is unlikely to have much effect on Mantle and Ford, who are known to like their beer, and Morris seems honestly to savor 9-Lives cat food. But the rule could have posed a problem for Joe Namath, the nonpareil quarterback. Until recently, he did commercials for Beauty Mist pantyhose.

### Offer Encouragement

Often you can fittingly close with a few words of encouragement for your readers. Tell them how delicious they will find the cheesecake if they follow your instructions to the letter. Or how rewarding they will find growing their own tomatoes, as Mark Kane does in this conclusion:

> When you shop for tomato seeds or plants this season, consider trying at least one new variety. There are hundreds to choose from and if you keep looking, one of them may find a home in your garden. Even if you find nothing to match your favorite, you'll have fun, and the pleasure of gardening is not just in the eating.

—''The Tomato: Still Champion,'' *Organic Gardening* (March 1982)

## Suggest Solutions

If you're writing analysis or argument, a useful closing device involves offering suggestions—possible solutions for problems discussed in the essay. This technique is valid only if you can come up with sound ideas for solving problems. Steven Brill ends his article about the proliferation of guns in the United States (the introduction is on page 38) with some practical suggestions:

> All these small steps toward sanity are possible if we force the people who profit from America's free-wheeling gun traffic to be open, accountable, and fully responsible to law-enforcement needs. If we're going to continue to allow the RGs or the Smith and Wessons to make guns at all for civilian use, we ought to at least demand that they become partners in the effort to curb the carnage their weapons cause. When we think of people murdered or robbed at gunpoint, we have to start thinking of brand names.

Just be sure, though, that your suggestions are truly sound ideas, not facile advice borrowed from a TV commercial or a Hallmark card.

## Provide a Warning

At some time you may desire to inform your fellow citizens about a grave danger which they are comfortably ignoring—AIDS, acid rain, nuclear waste, chemical dumps, or the arms race. Then your conclusion can appropriately be a warning, something similar to the following paragraph, the final one in an article written by Dr. Richard Champlin, a specialist in bone marrow transplants. Although Dr. Champlin's article describes the plight of dying radiation victims following the Chernobyl nuclear power plant disaster in 1986, notice that he takes the opportunity in his conclusion to broaden the context of his warning:

> The disaster at Chernobyl demonstrated the devastating effects of radiation exposure. It illustrates the fact that adequate medical care would be impossible in a larger nuclear catastrophe. As a cancer doctor, I'm accustomed to dealing with patients who die. This was different; I was *overwhelmed* by the human suffering. But the fact is that the damage and human misery that would be wrought by nuclear weapons would be immeasurably worse. Chernobyl would pale by comparison.

—"With the Chernobyl Victims,"
*Los Angeles Times Magazine* (July 6, 1986)

Conclusions aren't really all that difficult. Often they turn out weak because we write them last, when our powers are under a cloud. Treat your conclusion like your introduction: think about it off and on while you're writing the paper—during coffee breaks or whenever you pause to let your mind rest. Jot down anything promising that comes to you. Concentrate on the conclusion, just as you will on the introduction, when you revise.

## ADVICE ABOUT BODY PARAGRAPHS

If you are doing academic, business, or technical writing, the paragraphs that constitute the body of your paper should each have a topic sentence supported by plenty of concrete details. A friend of mine says that all through college she got her papers back with "Underdeveloped ¶" scrawled in the margins. To correct this problem, she would carefully restate the topic four or five different ways in each paragraph, and she'd still get "Underdeveloped ¶" marked in her margins.

My friend finally realized, too late, what *underdevelopment* meant. She wonders why her teachers never wrote in her margins, "Add an example or illustration here," or "Give some specific details," or "Describe your reasoning step by step." She would have understood *that*.

When you find one of your skimpy paragraphs marked *undernourished* or *¶ devel*, you'll know what it means: Add examples, provide specific details, describe your reasoning, or do all three.

### Use Topic Sentences in Informative Writing

Put the topic sentence first whenever you write to inform—that is, in doing summaries, reports, academic papers, and examinations. When you're composing narratives or descriptions, you may often imply your topic sentence, just as you imply your thesis statement in those modes of writing. Like the thesis sentence for an essay, a topic sentence states the controlling idea for the paragraph. The details within that paragraph will support, illustrate, expand, explain, or justify that idea. If you follow your unified outline, you will automatically write unified paragraphs. But if you need to dredge up more details while in the process of writing the paper, be sure those additions are to the point—i.e., that they pertain to the idea stated in the topic sentence.

If, for instance, you are planning a paragraph about the undeserved reputation of dogs, you might use this topic sentence: "Far from being one's best friends, dogs tend to be slow-witted, servile, slobbering beasts seldom deserving of their board and keep." Next you need to trot out examples of slavish spaniels and doltish Great Danes you have known in order to convince your readers that dogs make wretched companions. But if you then observe, "Cats are pretty contemptible also," you need a new paragraph. Or else you need to toss that bit of evidence out as being beside the point, the *point* being whatever idea you committed yourself to in the topic sentence. You can, of course, broaden the topic sentence if you decide cats are essential to your argument. You can expand the topic sentence to read something like this: "Both dogs and cats are exceedingly disagreeable creatures to have around the house." Now the way is clear to discuss all the skittish cats of your acquaintance as well as those loutish dogs in a comparison and contrast paragraph.

### Furnish the Facts and Figures

Supply enough examples to convince your readers that what you assert is true. If you say that members of Congress have too many special privileges, then *prove* it. Mention that Congress members enjoy free medical care at taxpayers' expense. Mention that Senate restaurants in 1975 were subsidized by the taxpayers to the tune of $240,000. Mention that plants and flowers to beautify congressional offices set the taxpayers back $1.2 million each year.[1] Convince your readers that these expenditures and many more are unnecessary to the orderly function of government. Insist that members of Congress should pay their own way, just like the rest of us. Don't expect your readers to take your word about anything without evidence, though. They won't—unless they just happened to agree with you in the first place.

Notice how the plentiful details in the following paragraph allow us to see clearly how the McDonald's chain pioneered in delivering fast food:

The new McDonald's system was predicated on careful attention to detail. The McDonald brothers shortened the spindles on their Multi-Mixers so that

[1]These facts and figures, by the way, come from Robert Shrum's "The Imperial Congress," *New Times*, March 18, 1977, pp. 20–34.

shakes and malts could be made directly in paper cups; there would be no metal mixing containers to wash, no wasted ingredients, no wasted motion, no wasted time. They developed dispensers that put the same amount of catsup or mustard on every bun. They installed a bank of infrared lamps to keep French fries hot. They used disposable paper goods instead of glassware and china. They installed a microphone to amplify the customer's voice and reduce misunderstandings about what was being ordered. By 1952 the McDonald brothers' employees, all men dressed neatly in white, were said to be capable of serving the customer a hamburger, a beverage, French fries, and ice cream in twenty seconds. Word of their proficiency began to spread through the restaurant industry.

—Philip Langdon, "Burgers! Shakes!"
*Atlantic Monthly* (December 1985)

## Include Concrete Details

Whenever possible, use examples that your readers can *visualize*. If you say that motorcycle riding can be dangerous, mention the crushed noses, the dislocated limbs, the splintered teeth, the crushed skulls. Be as concrete and specific as possible. You can't avoid abstractions entirely, of course, but try to follow abstract words—like *dangerous*—with concrete illustrations—like *broken bones*.

You must be especially wary of abstract terms like *democracy*, *truth*, *justice*, *liberty*, and such familiar-sounding words. They mean different things to different people. And sometimes they convey little meaning at all. Consider the following paragraph which purports to explain what a "democratic" education can do for a child:

A democratic plan of education includes more than the mere transmission of the social heritage and an attempt to reproduce existing institutions in a static form. The purpose of democratic education is the development of well-integrated individuals who can live successfully in an ever-changing dynamic culture. The democratic school is also required to indoctrinate individuals with the democratic tradition which, in turn, is based on the agitative liberties of the individual and the needs of society.

No reader can be expected to make sense out of that string of abstract ideas. If you can divine meaning there, it is a vague, shadowy sort of understanding that can't be pinned down precisely because of the numerous abstract words: *democratic*, *social heritage*, *well-integrated*, *dynamic culture*. And what *agitative liberties* are, only the writer knows. He didn't provide us with even a hint. The entire passage contains not a single concrete example to help us grasp the ideas that he was trying to express. You need to train yourself to write in concrete terms as much as possible and to provide definitions and examples when you have to deal with abstractions.

Particularly in writing research papers, you must guard against the tendency to omit examples. Since you are reading widely and condensing material, you'll naturally be leaving out a lot for the sake of compression. What you'll probably be leaving out most often will be the examples. Remember that in order for your own writing to be as convincing as that in your sources, you must get some of those examples back in—either those from the original or some new ones of your own.

## KEEP YOUR READERS WITH YOU: COHERENCE

As you are writing along on your paper following your outline (having either mastered the introduction or postponed it for later), you may encounter another minor difficulty in tying your major points together. Again, remember to keep your readers in mind. You want them to understand what you're writing and understand it easily on the first reading. So, don't let your readers get lost when you move from one idea to the next or when you change the direction of your ideas. The things you do to make your paper hang together, to make it *coherent*, are relatively simple; yet they can often mean the difference between a first-rate paper and a merely passable one.

## DON'T LOSE US ON THE TURNS: TRANSITIONS

The abiding principle of good coherence lies in presenting your ideas in an orderly fashion and then providing transitions when you go from one idea to the next. All this means is that you put up verbal signs showing your readers that you're moving to another point, which usually means to the next section of your outline. The indention for a new paragraph does this to a certain extent. But indenting could also mean that you're going to amplify the same idea. And often your thought changes direction in the middle of a paragraph when you're organizing through contrast or when you add examples or note an exception.

These signals can be as pointed as "Next let us consider the problem of . . ." or "As I have shown in this paper. . . ." That's pretty obvious and creaky transition. You can do better. Figure 3-1 provides a slew of transitional words neatly classified according to meaning. Take note of the different types of transitions illustrated; then tuck in a bookmark in case you get stuck and need a transition to help you over a rough spot.

Be careful, though, not to overuse these transitional terms or your prose will be plodding. Here are some other ploys for slipping smoothly from one paragraph to the next.

### Try a Rhetorical Question

If you're stuck for a logical way to lead from one point to the next, you can occasionally pose a question and then answer it, like this:

> How do we stop people from breeding? First, by not constantly brain-washing the average girl into thinking that motherhood must be her supreme experience. Very few women are capable of being good mothers; and very few men of being good fathers. Parenthood is a gift, as most parents find out too late and most children find out right away. So a change in attitude will help; and that seems to be happening.
>
> Gore Vidal, "The State of the Union,"
> *Esquire* (May 1975)

Or as a last resort, you can fall back on "The question now arises . . . ," which allows you to inject your new idea. Say you're discussing dope addiction among the young. You've just proved satisfactorily that this is a problem. You slide into your next point by writing, "The question now is, what can society do to discourage drug use among teenagers?" Then you trot out one by one the preventive measures that you think might be effective. This device, useful though it is, will seldom work more than one time per paper. You must have others in stock.

### The Short-Sentence Transition

Like the rhetorical question, the short-sentence transition must not be used often but comes in handy when you need it. You simply state

**Figure 3-1**   Useful transitional terms.

---

**To move to the next major point:**   *too, moreover, in the first place, next, second, third, again, besides, in addition, further, likewise, finally, beyond this, admittedly, like*

Examples:      We can see *also* that the quality of most television programs is abysmal.
               *Furthermore*, the commercials constantly assault our taste and insult our intelligence.


**To add an example:**   *for example, such as, that is, in the following manner, namely, in this case, as an illustration, at the same time, in addition*

Examples:      The daytime game shows, *for instance*, openly appeal to human greed.
               Soap operas, *in the same manner*, pander to many of our baser instincts.


**To emphasize a point:**   *especially, without doubt, primarily, chiefly, actually, otherwise, after all, as a matter of fact, more importantly*

Examples:      The constant violence depicted on television, *in fact*, poses a danger to society.
               Even more offensive are deodorant commercials, *without question* the most tasteless on TV.


**To contrast a point:**   *but, still, on the other hand, on the contrary, nevertheless, contrary to, however, nonetheless, conversely, in contrast, neither*

Examples:      We abhor the violence, yet we don't like censorship.
               Although commercials may enrage or sicken us, they do, *after all*, pay the bills.
               *Granted that* advertising picks up the tab, the deceptiveness of commercials remains indefensible.

**To conclude a point:**   *consequently, so, accordingly, then, hence, as a result, in sum, in conclusion, in other words, finally, at last, after all*

Examples:      Soap operas *thus* contribute to the subtle erosion of moral values.
               Commercials, *therefore*, are not worth the sacrifice of our integrity.
               Television, *in short*, costs more than society should be willing to pay.

---

briefly and graciously in advance what you intend to discuss next, like this:

> Europeans think more highly of Americans now than they ever did. Let me try to explain why.

> > —Anthony Burgess, "Is America Falling Apart?"
> > *New York Times Magazine* (November 7, 1971)

John Kenneth Galbraith uses a slightly more formal version:

> Economics, foreign policy, the split in the party as it relates to racial equality, and some resulting questions of political style all require a special word. To these matters I now turn.

> > —"Who Needs the Democrats?" *Harper's* (July 1970)

## Something Subtle for the Skillful: Echo Transitions

Often you won't need such obvious transitions. The smoothest and the most effective method involves touching on the idea from your previous paragraph as you pick up and introduce the idea for your next one. Sounds tricky, I know, but it's worth working on if you want to write readable prose. Pay close attention to these examples. The first one gives you the final sentence from a paragraph by Frederick Lewis Allen about the big Red scare in the twenties, and it is followed by the opening sentence of his next paragraph which explains the reasons for the scare. The transitional words are italicized. Notice how "this national panic" refers back to "a reign of terror," while at the same time leading into the new idea of justification for the scare:

> It was an era of lawless and disorderly defense of law and order, of unconstitutional defense of the Constitution, of suspicion and civil conflict—in a very literal sense, *a reign of terror*.

> For *this national panic* there was a degree of justification.

> > —*Only Yesterday* (1931, p. 39)

The next example is taken from Stewart Alsop's analysis of the drug problem in New York City. You have the last two sentences of his paragraph citing the monetary cost of heroin addiction, followed by the opening sentence of the next paragraph. Note that Alsop repeats the same key phrase:

... addicts must steal more than $1.5 billion from the people of New York every year. But that sum is a tiny fraction of *the real cost*.

*The real cost* is the death of New York as a city in which people who have any choice at all will be willing to live.

—"The Smell of Death," *Newsweek* (February 1, 1971, p. 76)

Here is an example from James Baldwin. Notice that the transitional phrase "this perpetual dealing with people" in the opening sentence of the new paragraph refers back to the whole idea stated in the last sentence of the previous paragraph. At the same time, the phrase leads smoothly into his next point—how this wide acquaintance with people helped to get rid of his preconceived ideas:

I love to talk to people, all kinds of people, and almost everyone, as I hope we still know, loves a man who loves to listen.
*This perpetual dealing with people* very different from myself caused a shattering in me of preconceptions I scarcely knew I held.

—*Nobody Knows My Name* (Dial Press, 1959)

In the final example, Katherine Anne Porter combines an echo with a regular transitional sentence to gain emphasis. She's writing about the peaceful protests preceding the execution of Sacco and Vanzetti in 1927. The paragraph just concluding here describes the frightening tactics of the mounted police:

I do not believe the police meant for the hoofs to strike and crush heads— it was just a very showy technique for intimidating and controlling a *mob*.

This was not a *mob*, however. It was a silent, intent assembly of citizens. . . .

—Katherine Anne Porter, "The Never-Ending Wrong,"
*Atlantic Monthly* (June 1977)

## Echoes within Paragraphs

You don't have to work as hard on transitions *within* paragraphs, since
most of these echoes occur automatically. But it's well to understand
the process in case you have to patch up a paragraph sometime. Mainly
transition within paragraphs occur through words deliberately repeated
and the echo of pronouns as they refer back to their antecedents. You
may, also, use any of the standard techniques for achieving transition
between paragraphs. In the following example, I've italicized the
typical transitional devices and have used capital letters to show the
repetition of the key term ADDICT and the unfortunately sexist
pronouns that refer to it:

> *What to do about drug addiction?* I give you two statistics. England with
> a population of over fifty-five million has eighteen hundred ADDICTS. The
> United States with over two hundred million has nearly five hundred thousand
> ADDICTS. *What are the English doing right that we are doing wrong?* They
> have turned the problem over to the doctors. An ADDICT is required to register
> with a physician who gives HIM at controlled intervals a prescription so that
> HE can buy HIS drug. The ADDICT is content. *Best of all*, society is safe.
> The Mafia is out of the game. The police are unbribed, and the ADDICT will
> not mug an old lady in order to get the money for HIS next fix.
>
> —Gore Vidal, "The State of the Union,"
> *Esquire* (May 1975)

Notice that sentences 3 and 4 (both citing statistics) are approximately
parallel in structure; i.e., the second echoes the structure of the
preceding sentence, which helps give coherence. And besides the
repetition of the word ADDICT, we get echoes from *England/English/
they;* from *United States/we/society;* and from *doctors/physicians/who.*
Even more subtle are the echoes from *content* and *safe*, words with a
similar comforting meaning. It's a nicely coherent paragraph, and you
can do as well if you'll put your mind to it.

Remember this, though: Your best chance of getting coherence in
your paragraphs over the long haul involves keeping a clear continuity
of ideas. You need transitions only to direct the flow.

# Chapter 4

# Style Your Sentences

The previous chapter explained how to put ideas together into well-developed paragraphs. Those ideas should, of course, be expressed in clear, concise, shapely sentences. Such sentences do not simply flow from a good writer's pen—nor do they appear perfectly formed following the touch of a keyboard. Effective sentences are constructed. They are written and rewritten, moved around, added to, and sometimes scratched out. As you know, this tinkering with words and the ideas they convey is called *revising*, and it is a crucial step in the writing process.

Whether you do this rewriting as you struggle to get through a first draft or whether you postpone it until a second or third draft makes little difference. Do it the way that feels most natural for you—but don't fail to do it.

## WRITE NATURALLY, AS YOU SPEAK

Lewis Lapham, editor of *Harper's* magazine, complains: "I have found that few writers learn to speak in the human voice, that most of them make use of alien codes (academic, political, literary, bureaucratic, technical."[1] Strive for a human voice when you write—preferably your own. Many people produce on paper a kind of artificial language that writing specialist Ken Macrorie calls *Engfish*—a language much different from the kind people speak or the kind most professional writers write. Engfish is invariably stuffy and abuses the third-person approach to writing. (Writing in the *third person* means adopting an impersonal approach by using *one*, *he*, *she*, *it*, or *they*, instead of the more personal *I*, *we*, or *you*.) Engfish sounds like this:

> One can observe that athletics can be beneficial to the health of one who participates as well as entertaining for one who watches.

Put that sentence into English and you get:

> Athletics can be healthful for the players and entertaining for the fans.

Eventually you must master the third-person approach without lapsing into Engfish. But unless the occasion requires the formality of third person, I suggest that you use the first-person *I* or *we* (as I just did in this sentence). Most professional writers use *I* and *we* when expressing their own opinions, and many of them address their readers directly as *you*. If you do the same, you'll find Engfish easier to avoid.

### Avoid the *Indefinite You*

But take caution: The word *you* should always refer to the readers, unless you intend to be funny. You may get an unexpected laugh if you're explaining how to prune a tree and write, "Grasp your diseased limb firmly and saw it off immediately above the joint." Reserve this *indefinite you* for humorous writing in which no one will mind if you write, "The behavior of your average alligator tends to be torpid."

---

[1] "The Pleasures of Reading," *Harper's*, May 1975, p. 50.

---

**Exercise**                                                                    **4-1**

Translate these sentences from Engfish into clear, straightforward English. You may have to guess at the meaning sometimes, but do your best. I'll rewrite the first one to get you started.

  1  The causal factors of her poverty become obvious when one considers the number of offspring she possesses.

     *Translation:*    Her poverty is increased because she has so many children.

  2  This writer's report enjoyed a not unfavorable reception by the committee.
  3  The fire department is requesting additional funds for effective confinement and extinguishment of unwanted and destructive fires.
  4  The level of radiation in the immediate vicinity of the nuclear power plant was evaluated and found to be within acceptable danger parameters.
  5  Consumer elements are continuing to stress the fundamental necessity of a stabilization of the price structure at a lower level than exists at the present time.
  6  The unacceptability of one's lifestyle can result in the termination of one's employment in some firms.
  7  Police involvement in the conflict was considered to be an inhibiting factor to the peaceful progress of the protest.
  8  It was with no little enthusiasm that one's peers inflicted various contusions and lacerations on members of the opposing affinity group.
  9  These new economic statistics have validated the essentiality of the President's policies effected to mitigate the inflation rate.
  10  It is the feeling of the committee that the established priorities in management-employee relations are in need of realignment.

---

## USE THE ACTIVE VOICE

If your writing is generally lifeless, turgid, and wordy, the *passive voice* may be the culprit. The passive construction (in which the subject is acted upon instead of doing the acting) is less economical than active voice in conveying the same information:

> *Passive:*    Because patriotism was lacking in their hearts, the battle was lost by the mercenaries.
> (14 words)

> *Active:*    Because they lacked heartfelt patriotism, the mercenaries lost the battle.
> (10 words)

That's not many extra words, I'll grant, but if you add only a couple of unnecessary words to each sentence in a paper, you will seriously pollute your prose.

Even when not wordy, the passive construction leaves out information—sometimes essential information. Take this typical concise passive construction:

> The prisoner was fed.

That's not an objectionable sentence. Nobody is perishing to know who fed the prisoner. But consider the same sentence with only one word changed:

> The prisoner was beaten.

At once we want to know *by whom*? By the sheriff? By one of the deputies? By a guard? By a fellow prisoner? There is no way to tell from the passive construction. In his article "Watergate Lingo," Richard Gambino observes, "The effect of the habitual use of the passive is to create a . . . world where events have lives, wills, motives, and actions of their own without any human being responsible for them."

Notice: It's the *habitual use of the passive* that is treacherous. I do not mean that you should never use the passive voice. Sometimes it can be the best way to convey information. You would likely choose the passive "The President was elected by a comfortable majority" rather than the active "A comfortable majority elected the President." No reader will be troubled by not being told who elected the President because everyone knows that the voters do the electing. The passive is also appropriate when you want to stress that an action is *happening to* or being *inflicted upon* the subject:

The city hall was damaged by an earthquake.

My bicycle was demolished by a truck.

The candidate's credibility has been questioned by the media.

---

**Exercise**                                                        **4-2**

Rewrite the following passive sentences in the active voice and eliminate any wordiness. I'll get you started by doing the first one.

1  An empty disposable lighter is used by folksinger Utah Phillips to store kitchen matches in.

   *Revised:*     Folksinger Utah Phillips stores kitchen matches in an empty disposable lighter.

2  Several disposable lighters were lost by Seymour last week.
3  It is probable that matches should be used by people who often lose things.
4  Matchbooks have been found to be more versatile than disposable lighters by some people.
5  No mail-order opportunities to become electricians, locksmiths, and engineers are offered by disposable lighters.
6  How many matches are left in a book can be easily seen by the match user.
7  Let our daily bread be given to us this day.
8  It was stated by the author in the introduction that several approaches to grammar would be discussed.
9  Several secondary sources were studied in order to gain additional information for this paper.
10  The demand for shirts bearing alligators was artificially stimulated by advertising.

---

## Practice the Passive

Despite all my warnings against habitual use of the passive, I'm aware that writers in a number of jobs and in some academic disciplines are expected—even required—to use the passive voice. If you are taking courses in education, corrections, or any of the hard sciences (chemistry, biology, physics, and the like), you must learn to write gracefully in the passive voice. It can be done. But you will need to practice diligently.

Proceeding from the pen of an accomplished writer, the passive voice is not in the least objectionable. Jessica Mitford, for one, employs the passive so skillfully that you never notice its presence:

Today, family members who might wish to be in attendance would certainly be dissuaded by the funeral director.

That sentence will not be noticeably improved by making it active voice:

Today the funeral director would certainly dissuade family members who might wish to be in attendance.

In order to help you perfect your use of the passive, we have collected some useful and fairly simple sentences as models. If you must become a practitioner of the passive, you'll do well to work this exercise twice, thinking of different material to use the second time.

**Writing Exercise** 4-3

Copy each sentence carefully. Then, choosing subject matter from your academic major, write five sentences imitating the passive structure of each of the originals. Work on them a few at a time. Do two or three, take a break, then come back and do some more. I'll do the first one to give you the idea.

Certain things were not mentioned.     (Jane O'Reilly)

1 *Imitations:*     Synthetic fertilizers were not unknown.
                    Pesticides were not advised.
                    Crop rotation was not used.
                    Early harvesting was not recommended.
                    Organic methods were not tried.

2 The entire body of a tarantula, especially its legs, is thickly clothed with hair.     (Alexander Petrunkevitch)

**3** All others, except apprentices, are excluded by law from the preparation room.    (Jessica Mitford)

**4** The poor are slated to take the brunt of the federal budget cuts.    (Barbara Ehrenreich)

**5** The SKIP option can be used in input and output statements.    (J. S. Roper)

**6** The emphasis is generally put on the right to speak.    (Walter Lippmann)

**7** This could be done either by the accumulation of observed evidence or by mathematics.    (Sir Kenneth Clark)

**8** But—poor little thing—the boundary ought in its turn to be protected.    (E. M. Forster)

**9** Negotiations over a strike of factory workers were conducted among trade union leaders, the minister of labor, and the commander of an infantry brigade.    (Lucy Komisar)

## SENTENCE COMBINING

You can enhance a sentence (or a series of sentences) by *subordinating* some of the elements—that is, by tucking less important ideas into dependent clauses and small details into phrases. Thus major ideas are elevated in independent or main clauses, where they receive the proper emphasis.

### A Word about Clauses and Phrases

If you're hazy about the meaning of some of those terms I just used, let me explain that an *independent clause* can stand as a sentence all by itself. A *dependent clause*, which begins with a subordinating word (see list, page 203), must be attached to an independent clause (or else it is a *fragment*). In case you're also hazy about the difference between clauses and phrases, remember that a clause has both a subject and a verb; a phrase does not.

|            |                    |                 |
|------------|--------------------|-----------------|
| *Phrases:* | having lost my head |                 |
|            | to lose my head     |                 |
|            | after losing my head |                |
| *Clauses:* | after I lost my head | *(dependent)*   |
|            | I lost my head       | *(independent)* |
|            | that I lost my head  | *(dependent)*   |

## Subordinating Ideas

Although simple and compound sentences may be the easiest ones to write, they don't always get across the relationships between your ideas in the clearest way possible. And if you use simple sentences too often, you'll have a third-grade writing style. Here are a couple of plain, simple sentences:

Lucy forgot how to spell *exaggerated*. She used the word *magnified* instead.

The idea in the first of those sentences could be subordinated in these ways:

**a** By using subordinating conjunctions and adverbs (Examples: *after*, *when*, *because*, *if*, *while*, *until*, *unless*):

*Since Lucy forgot how to spell exaggerated*, she used the word *magnified* instead.

**b** By using an adjective clause:

Lucy, *who forgot how to spell exaggerated*, used the word *magnified* instead.

**c** By using a participial phrase or an adjective:

*Having forgotten how to spell exaggerated*, Lucy used the word *magnified* instead.

## Combining Sentences to Avoid Repetition

You should consider sentence combining if you find yourself writing too many simple, monotonous sentences or if you see that you are repeating the same word without meaning to, like this:

The pontoon boat had stalled in the middle of the lake.

The boat stalled because it ran out of gas.

You'll notice when you start to revise that you've got too many *stalled*s and too many *boat*s there. Using subordination, you can combine those sentences and the problem is solved:

> The pontoon boat, which ran out of gas, had stalled in the middle of the lake.

Or, if you want to emphasize the reason the boat was stranded, you can combine the sentences this way:

> The pontoon boat, stalled in the middle of the lake, had run out of gas.

## A Word of Warning

Although skillful sentence combining serves to focus your ideas and add sophistication to your style, don't get carried away. *Remember: Clarity is the keynote.* Don't get so enthusiastic in your use of subordination that you try to compress too much into a single sentence and thus obscure your meaning.

**Writing Exercise**                                                4-4

The following sentences were written by students. Combine each pair into a single clear, concise sentence.

1  The second type of day is a blah day. Most days, especially in the middle of the semester, fall into this category.
2  While the goals of music therapy are nonmusical, the activities prescribed to reach these goals are musical. Musical activities include singing, listening, playing instruments, writing songs, dancing, and moving.
3  Kate Chopin wrote a short story called "The Storm." As the title suggests, the story is about a savage storm and shows how the characters respond to the downpour.
4  There are three major aspects to consider in examining this character. These aspects include what the author tells us about this character, what she herself says and does, and what other people say to her and about her.
5  Most of the incidents that inspire Walter Mitty's fantasies have humorous associations. These incidents can be broken down into basically two groups, with the first one being his desire to be in charge.

## CONSTRUCTING IMPRESSIVE SENTENCES
## FOR SPECIAL OCCASIONS

Another good way to make your prose effective involves writing an occasional forceful sentence. If every sentence built to a climax, your readers might well be bowled over, so don't work at it too hard. But in a key position—such as at the beginning or end of a paragraph, or to emphasize a point anytime—a carefully controlled sentence is worth the time it takes to compose it.

### Save the Clincher for the End—Periodic Structure

Most of the time we don't deliberate about our sentence structure. We attach ideas together, automatically subordinating the less important ones, until we come to the end of the thought, where we put a period and start in on another one. These everyday sentences—like the one I just wrote—are called "cumulative" and constitute the bulk of our writing. If, however, you need a Sunday-best sentence, you either consciously plan it or later rearrange it: you want to order the details to build to a big finish. You don't disclose your main idea until just before the period, which accounts for the label "periodic." Let me show you the difference with a few examples.

| | |
|---|---|
| *Cumulative:* | Seymour made the honor roll while holding down a part-time job and playing the lead in *Hamlet*. |
| *Periodic:* | While holding down a part-time job and playing the lead in *Hamlet*, Seymour made the honor roll. |
| *Cumulative:* | Our first consideration is the preservation of our environment, even though preventing pollution costs money. |
| *Periodic:* | Even though preventing pollution costs money, our first consideration is the preservation of our environment. |

If you have a feel for prose, you probably already write periodic sentences when you need them without being aware that you're doing it. If, on the other hand, you're not long on style, you can develop some by cinching up a few of your sentences. Here are a few more pointers.

## Try a Short One for Emphasis

The really brief sentence is easier to handle than the periodic sentence and is remarkably effective—as long as you don't overdo it. Often short-short sentences appear at the beginning or at the end of a paragraph, since these are the most emphatic positions. You can lob one in, though, anytime you feel brave enough as long as you have a point to make. Notice the emphasis achieved in the following examples by the short sentence following one of normal length:

> Cavett's purpose was to ensure that I would suffer all the shocks, surprises, pitfalls and confusions that afflict the host five shows a week. He succeeded.
>
> —Jesse Birnbaum, *Time* (June 7, 1971)

> Webster's dictionaries and the endless multiplication of handbooks and courses in English composition represent a desperate effort to prevent class distinction from revealing itself in language. And, of course, it has failed.
>
> —John H. Fisher, *School and Society* (November 1969)

The short sentence also functions effectively as a transitional device. In the following examples, the short transitional sentences are italicized:

> "No man," wrote John Donne, "doth exalt Nature to the height it would beare." He saw the discrepancy between dream and reality.
> *Great minds have always seen it.* That is why man has survived his journey this long.
>
> —Loren Eiseley, *Horizon* (March 1962)

> Economics, foreign policy, the split in the party as it relates to racial equality, and some resulting questions of political style all require a special word. *To these matters I now turn.*
>
> —John Kenneth Galbraith, *Harper's* (July 1970)

## Experiment with the Dash

Since the end of a sentence is an emphatic position, you can use a dash there to good advantage, as Woodrow Wilson did in this warning: "I have seen their destruction, as will come upon these again—utter destruction and contempt.'' Note the deliberate repetition of the word *destruction*, amplified by *contempt*. The dash can be used to tack on afterthoughts, but you'll find it more effective for reinforcement of a point or for elaboration, like this:

> Hollywood offered the public yet another marvel—talking films.

> This was the year of the big spectaculars—biblical extravaganzas spiced with sex and filmed in glorious Technicolor.

Sometimes you may want to call attention to an idea in midsentence. Again, dashes will do it:

> The President was beginning—though he did not suspect it—his last month in office.

If you prefer *not* to call attention to the thought inserted, use commas instead of dashes:

> The President was altering, though he neglected to tell the press, his firm commitments on foreign aid.

The dash, like the short sentence, can't retain its effect if overused. In fact, a flurry of dashes produces an unfortunate, adolescent style. So experiment with the dash in your first draft. Leave it in only if you're sure it works well.

For more information, look up *Dash* in the ''Revising Index,'' Chapter 8.

### Balanced Sentences

Another way to keep your ideas clear and to make them emphatic is to use *balanced sentences* (or *parallel structure*). Balanced sentences depend upon repetition: sometimes of the same words, always of the same grammatical structures—phrases, clauses, now and then whole sentences. Virginia Woolf repeats the same adverb, changing the verb each time to achieve this impressive sentence:

> One cannot think well, love well, sleep well, if one has not dined well.

Mark Twain balances independent clauses for a comic effect in this line spoken by the narrator of "A Dog's Tale":

> My father was a St. Bernard, my mother was a collie, but I am a Presbyterian.

**For Everyday Writing**  While parallel structure lends itself particularly well to emphatic sentences, the technique is fundamental to all good writing. If you by chance put together a sentence involving two similar elements or a series of them, your readers *expect* these similar parts to be balanced (or parallel). Such a structure may occur whenever you join parts of sentences with any of the coordinating conjunctions (*and*, *but*, *or*, *for*, *nor*, *yet*, *so*).

Consider the problem first in this simple example:

> Clyde likes *to smoke* and *drinking*.

Your readers expect those italicized parts to sound alike, to be balanced in construction, like this:

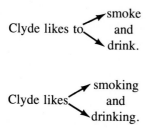

Let's try a more typical example—the kind of sentence you're likely to write in a hurry and should put into parallel structure when you revise:

> Politicians today face the difficult tasks of *solving* urban problems and *how to find* the money without raising taxes.

This one is easy to repair. You need to balance the two grammatical structures connected by *and: solving* urban problems and *how to find* the money. The easiest way is to make *how to find* sound the same as *solving*—that is, use *finding*:

Politicians today face the difficult task of *solving* urban problems and *finding* the money without raising taxes.

**For Sunday-best Sentences** Once you become adept at constructing balanced sentences, you'll find the technique perfect for composing *climactic* sentences—the kind you need to emphasize key points, to conclude paragraphs, and to bring essays to a resounding finish. Martin Luther King, Jr., learned from the Bible how to balance phrases with ringing effect:

With this faith we will be able to work together, to pray together, to struggle together, to go to jail together, to stand up for freedom together, knowing that we will be free one day.

Here's a first-rate concluding sentence written by John Kenneth Galbraith, the noted economist:

To summarize, our present situation is not military need in response to tension and hostility; it is tension and hostility in the service of military need.

—*Harper's* (November 1986)

Parallel structure also provides the most effective way to compress a number of ideas into a single sentence with perfect clarity. In this next example let me show you graphically how *Time*'s drama critic, T. E. Kalem, balances phrases in a sentence about George Bernard Shaw's *Man and Superman*:

Shaw steadily sounds his pet themes:

| | |
|---|---|
| the chicanery | of politics, |
| the corruptive power | of money, |
| the degrading stench | of poverty, |
| the servile dependencies | of marriage and family, |
| the charlatanism | of medicine, |
| the fossilization | of learning, |
| the tyranny | of the state, |
| the stupidity | of the military, and |

the bigoted, sanctimonious zeal of the church.

There's no other way to deliver so many ideas so clearly in so short a sentence.

You can also use parallel structure to good effect in separate sentences by repeating the same grammatical structure in each sentence. This technique involves building to a climax, which means you can't use it often, but the effect is impressive when well done. Here is Maya Angelou repeating balanced clauses (beginning with *because*) to emphasize the reasons she undervalued the virtues of her race:

> Because Southern black people move slowly, I was quick to think they did not move at all. Because many Southern black people speak in black English, I had taken too lightly the wisdom of their words. Because Southern black Americans had employed a gargantuan patience, I had not fully appreciated the splendor of their survival.

Finally, notice how Pastor Martin Niemoeller, a Lutheran minister, achieves eloquence by using simple, precisely balanced sentences to explain how he ended up in a Nazi concentration camp during World War II:

> In Germany, the Nazis first came for the Communists, and I didn't speak up because I wasn't a Communist. Then they came for the Jews, and I didn't speak up because I wasn't a Jew. Then they came for the trade unionists, and I didn't speak up because I wasn't a trade unionist. Then they came for the Catholics, and I didn't speak up because I was a Protestant. Then they came for me, and by that time there was no one left to speak for me.

---

**Exercise**                                                                    **4-5**

The following sentences were written by students whose grasp of parallel structure was less than perfect. I want you to restore the balance. Don't aim for impressive, emphatic sentences in this exercise. Just try to produce good, clear, everyday sentences.

First, read each sentence and decide which parts need to be parallel. Look for elements in series and phrases or clauses connected by coordinating conjunctions (*and, but, or, for, nor, yet, so*). Then, change the part that's irregular so that its grammatical structure matches the structure of the coordinate parts. Often you can find several ways to improve each sentence, each way equally good. I'll do one first to show you the technique.

1  The plan is not workable; it delegates a dangerous amount of power to
   the government, and because it is unconstitutional.

   That sentence consists of three clauses in series. All three should be
   parallel. The first two are both independent clauses (subjects are underlined once, verbs twice):

   > The <u>plan</u> <u>is</u> not workable
   >
   > <u>it</u> <u>delegates</u> a dangerous amount of power to the government

   Fine so far. The clauses don't have to be precisely parallel as long as the
   basic pattern (in this case, subject-verb-complement) is the same. The
   trouble comes with the third clause, which is not independent but dependent (beginning with the subordinating conjunction *because*):

   > because <u>it</u> <u>is</u> unconstitutional.

   Probably the easiest way to revise the sentence is to make all three clauses
   independent by dropping the subordinating word *because*:

   > *Revised:*    The plan is not workable; it delegates a dangerous
   >               amount of power to the government, and it is uncon-
   >               stitutional.

   You could also make both the second and third clauses dependent by
   adding another *because*, like this:

   > *Revised:*    The plan is not workable because it delegates a
   >               dangerous amount of power to the government and
   >               because it is unconstitutional.

2  The first part of the Bus Stop, a disco dance, consists of three steps
   backwards, a touch step, and then stepping forward three times.
3  The dancer should remember to act unruffled, self-composed, and as
   though the steps came naturally.
4  After the dancer repeats the first part, a sideways two-step is executed,
   and the dancer then two-steps back into the starting position.
5  Experienced dancers say that the hops and touches in the third part of the
   Bus Stop are the most exciting and also hard to teach to others.
6  The final step is executing a ninety-degree kick-turn and to start the pattern
   over from the beginning.

7  European trains are frequent, punctual, provide easy connections, and travel at high speeds.

8  In the movies all college men are portrayed as single and having other attributes such as money, good looks, and a great personality.

9  You have never heard so many joyous cries and laughter in your life.

10  Progressive education aims to teach children to be open-minded, logical-thinking, collecting evidence to make wise choices, self-discipline, and self-control.

11  This caused me to return home with a feeling of being a number in his appointment schedule and that there are other numbers just like me every day.

12  I feel quite uneasy when a commercial comes on about feminine hygiene spray or have Jane Russell come out and tell me she can't believe she's got a girdle on.

## STRAIGHTENING OUT SCREWED-UP SENTENCES: MIXED CONSTRUCTIONS

Some sentence errors are impossible to categorize as anything other than messed up. And they are the worst kind because they make no sense. These semantic disasters are sometimes called—for lack of a better term—*mixed constructions*. They apparently result when the writer begins to say something one way, loses track in the middle, and finishes another way. That's a guess anyway. Heaven only knows how they actually happen because the students who write them are more surprised than anybody when confronted with these prodigies. These are the kinds of sentences that make readers do a double take—we shake our heads, rub our eyes, and read them again, hoping for a better connection next time. But we never get it from mix-ups like these:

> When students have no time for study or moral training also breeds a decadent society.

> The first planned crime will tell how well a boy has learned whether or not he is caught to become a juvenile delinquent.

Now those are pretty hopeless cases. They need to be scrapped. You'll lose more time trying to patch up a troublesome sentence than you will by backing off and beginning a different way. Take that last example. It needs a totally different beginning:

> Whether or not he is caught in his first planned crime may determine whether a boy will become a juvenile delinquent.

Occasionally a screwed-up sentence can be easily revised, like this one:

> When frequently opening and closing the oven door, it can cause a soufflé to fall.

All you need to do to correct that one is scratch out the *when*, the *it*, and the comma:

> Frequently opening and closing the oven door can cause a soufflé to fall.

These mixed constructions seem to reflect varying degrees of illiteracy, but I imagine they usually result from nothing but sheer, unpardonable carelessness. For this reason I beg you to proofread. And pay attention while you do it so that these linguistic misfortunes won't slip by you.

---

**Exercise** 4-6

Try to straighten out the following mixed constructions. Some of them cannot be easily patched up: you need to back off and begin in a different way. I will revise the first one.

1 Sherry, hoping to find a job that interests her, and so she doesn't have to type.

*Revised:* Sherry is hoping to find a job that interests her—one that doesn't involve typing.

*Revised:* Sherry is hoping to find an interesting job in which she doesn't have to type.

2 The Rites of Spring festival has been postponed because of too many students are sick with the flu.

3 Marijuana users should stop being made into criminals.

4 Only through constant study will achieve academic excellence.

5 In time of crisis must be handled with cool judgment.

# Chapter 5

# Work on Your Words

In order to produce first-rate writing, you need to revise each sentence—to make it more clear perhaps, more vivid, more concise, more interesting, or more forceful. At the same time, you need to consider how your audience may respond to your word choice. You want to make sure that the terms you have chosen will be pleasing to your readers.

## SELECT AN APPROPRIATE USAGE LEVEL

The nature of your audience and your purpose will determine whether you should use slang or contractions or six-syllable words—that is, your *level of usage*. The three main usage levels—*formal*, *informal*, and *colloquial*—overlap considerably. You need different levels of usage for different writing occasions, just as you sometimes need formal and informal clothes, plus your grubbies for around the house. Good usage is a matter of using language appropriate for the occasion. Figure 5-1 provides an illustration of these usage levels.

**Figure 5-1**   Usage levels for all occasions.

| | |
|---|---|
| Formal: | One should not admit defeat too quickly. |
| | I shall not admit defeat too quickly. |
| Informal: | We should not give up too quickly. |
| | I'll not give up too quickly. |
| Colloquial: | I'm not going to throw in the towel too quick. |
| Nonstandard: | I ain't gonna throw in the towel, nohow. |

| Formal | Informal | Colloquial (slang) |
|---|---|---|
| automobile | car | wheels |
| comprehend | understand | dig |
| depart | leave | split |
| residence | house | pad |
| odious | offensive | gross |
| debilitated | exhausted | wasted |
| dejected | sad | down |
| hyperactive | jittery | wired |
| intoxicated | drunk | sloshed |

**Formal Writing**

Formal writing is a lot less formal than it used to be. Many textbooks (not this one, though) are written in formal English, as are most scholarly articles and books and a few magazines. Most business communication still observes many of the rules of formal usage, but recently the use of *I* and *we* is replacing the strictly formal, third-person approach. Here are the main characteristics of formal usage:

**1**   No contractions
**2**   No slang
**3**   Third-person approach (*one, he, she, it, they*) (Do not address readers directly as *you*.)
**4**   No sentence fragments for emphasis (Look up *fragment* on page 202 if you don't know what one is.)
**5**   A serious or neutral tone

In order to get the feel of writing in the third person, try turning the sentences in the following exercise from first person into the more formal third. The more you practice writing in third person, the more natural—and thus effective—your use of it will become when your purpose requires it.

---

**Exercise**                                                    **5-1**

The following sentences are written using the first person (*I* and *we*) and the informal second person ( *you*). Rewrite each sentence to eliminate every *you*, as well as all slang and contractions. Try to use the formal third person (*one*, *she*, *he*, *it*, or *they*). But if the sentence sounds stilted, go back to *I* or *we*. The use of first person—especially *we*—is acceptable in much formal writing today. I'll show you how with the first one.

1 The point I want to make is quite simple.

    *Revised:*    The point is quite simple.
    *Revised:*    The point one wants to make is quite simple.

2 We hold these truths to be self-evident.
3 We must suppose, then, that the figures cited are OK.
4 You should eat nutritious foods if you want to stay healthy.
5 You can't help expressing yourself, unless you live in a vacuum.
6 If you would hold the attention of your readers, you should cultivate a pleasing style.
7 We shouldn't make editorial decisions solely upon our personal likes and dislikes.
8 The very people who most try your patience are often those who want to please you.
9 If you attain high office, your responsibility to other people increases.
10 We often find ourselves unable to resist temptation.

---

**Informal Writing**

The bulk of the writing you'll be called upon to do will probably be *informal*, which means ordinary, familiar, everyday writing. Here are the guidelines for informal usage:

1 You can use contractions, if you want to.
2 Use slang *only* if appropriate for your audience.

**3** Write in the first person; address your readers as *you*, if you wish.
**4** You may use an occasional sentence fragment—as long as each fragment is stylistically effective.
**5** Adopt any tone appropriate for the audience and the purpose.

### Colloquial Writing

In colloquial writing you have a lot of leeway, since *colloquial* means the language of the everyday speech of educated people. There's not much call for colloquial writing, of course, but it comes in handy for reproducing the flavor of a person's actual speech in an essay that is otherwise informal. Be careful if you decide to use colloquial language because your readers may be annoyed if they feel such extreme informality is not suitable for the subject under discussion. Remember also that usage levels are seldom pure, except perhaps for the formal. This textbook, for instance, is written on an informal level but occasionally has touches of the colloquial. Here are the characteristics of colloquial writing:

**1** Contractions are expected.
**2** Slang is fine.
**3** First person and second person (*I* and *you*) are typical.
**4** Sentence fragments are characteristic.
**5** Tone is light, often humorous.

### Nonstandard Usage

Since *standard usage* means the language used by educated people, *nonstandard usage* means any language (like *he don't*) that fails to conform to the accepted standard. (This textbook, by the way, offers advice on standard usage.) Unfortunately, dialectical expressions are considered nonstandard. Some dictionaries even label nonstandard constructions *illiterate*, which seems harsh, but you should be advised that many people are unalterably prejudiced against nonstandard English. Avoid it in writing, or use it only with extreme caution for stylistic effect.

---

### Writing Exercise                                              5-2

Compose a brief paragraph in which you try to persuade a group of your peers that they should conserve electricity or gasoline or natural gas. Then rewrite the paragraph twice more, choosing a suitable usage level to address each of the groups below. Be prepared to explain the differences in your three versions.

1  The Lost Souls Motorcycle Club
2  The Presbyterian Ladies' Missionary Society

---

## AVOID SEXIST LANGUAGE

In considering your audience, keep in mind that many of your readers may be displeased by sexist language. The word *sexist* (coined by analogy with the word *racist*) means stereotyping females and males according to traditional sex roles.

Our language reflects a sex bias that is ingrained in our society. Since it's awkward to repeatedly say *he or she*, *his or hers*, or *him or her*, it was long ago decreed by an act of the British Parliament that *he*, *his*, and *him* would refer to both sexes. That probably doesn't even sound unfair, unless you're female—or unless you've encountered William F. Buckley's extension of this principle. Mr. Buckley assures us that "the phrase 'will appeal to adventure-loving boys' is not an exclusionary phrase because the word 'boys' in this case means not only boys but also girls."[1] Now, everyone can at once see the injustice of that assertion because we're not accustomed to having the word *boys* mean *girls*.

Feminists would like for people to get *un*accustomed to accepting male orientation in language. Probably the easiest way to achieve non-sexist pronoun reference is to write whenever possible in the plural. We have perfectly neutral plural pronouns: *they/their/them*. Dr. Spock in his best-selling baby book no longer refers throughout to the *mother/ she*, but to the *parents/they*. He even goes one step further: When he can't avoid using *baby* in the singular, he no longer says the *baby/he* but rather, the *baby/she*. If this reversal seems too daring, go ahead and use an occasional "his or her." The double pronoun has now become standard usage and really isn't cumbersome—as long as you don't overdo it.

---

[1]William F. Buckley, "Give the Lady an Inch," Bloomington *Daily Pantagraph*, July 13, 1974, Sec. 1, p. 4, col. 4.

REMEMBER:        **If you can write what you want to say just as
                 well in the plural, the problem won't even come
                 up.**

For more information on avoiding sexist language, see the entries for *he or she*, *man/person*, and *Ms.* in Chapter 7, "Glossary of Usage."

---

**Exercise**                                                          **5-3**

See if you can eliminate all the sexist language from the following sentences without changing the meaning or causing awkwardness. I'll work out the first one for you.

1  Man must work in order to eat.

    *Revised:*    One must work in order to eat.
                  People must work in order to eat.

2  Anyone with a brain in his head can see the dangers of utilizing atomic reactors.
3  The citizen may pay his water bill by mail or at city hall.
4  The gregarious dog is man's best friend, but the more aloof cat keeps his own counsel.
5  He who laughs last laughs best.
6  "As long as man is on earth, he's likely to cause problems. But the man at General Electric will keep trying to find answers." (advertisement for GE)
7  Clyde was patched up by a lady doctor who stopped her car at the accident scene.
8  Gertie's mother is a computer repairman at IBM.
9  The hippopotamus is happiest when he is half submerged in mud.
10 The American pioneers loaded their wagons and moved their wives and children westward.

---

## BE WARY OF EUPHEMISMS

While considering word choice, you should give a fleeting thought to the sensibilities of your readers. If they have led a sheltered life, you may want to soften your language when saying something unpleasant, unpopular, or sexy. You can employ linguistic smokescreens called *euphemisms*, most of which are quite innocent. Rather than say bluntly, "He died of cancer," you can say, "He passed away after a lingering illness." It takes the shudder out and cloaks the whole grim business of dying in a soothing phrase. Undertakers (or "funeral directors," as they prefer to be called) sometimes carry euphemism to grotesque extremes, like calling the room where the body lies the "slumber chamber." And my dear little Victorian mother quaintly used to refer to the "white meat" of the chicken (instead of the "breast") and to the "second joint" (instead of the "thigh").

Such delicacy is amusing and does no harm, but some people also use a sinister kind of euphemism, called *doublespeak*, to mask realities that ought not be concealed. The CIA, for instance, substitutes the meaningless phrase "to terminate with extreme prejudice" for the blunt word "murder." The Pentagon refers to weapons designed to kill human beings as "antipersonnel implements" and civilian casualties of a nuclear war are designated "collateral damage." Instead of "bombings," the Air Force announces "protective reaction strikes." Such transparent attempts to make human slaughter sound inoffensive are far from innocent.

This deceptive misuse of language is becoming widespread in our society. Police officers are no longer taught to aim to kill. Now they aim "to neutralize the adversary." The nuclear power industry refers to an accident as an "abnormal evolution," speaks of a fire as a "rapid oxidation," and calls an explosion an "energetic disassembly." Such euphemisms are deliberately misleading and border on being immoral.

You need to decide according to the nature of your audience whether innocent euphemisms are appropriate or not. Certainly you should never use deceptive ones. Be honest both in what you say and in the way you say it.

## BE CAUTIOUS ABOUT PROFANITY AND SLANG

There remains the question of whether to use yet another kind of euphemism. Many people consider it euphemistic to substitute more socially acceptable terms for our frank and forceful four-letter words. You should, again, consider your readers. You don't want to put them off; you want to communicate with them. Different people are shocked by different things, but all of us are offended by something. To some people violence is the ultimate obscenity. To some the sight or sound of four-letter words is obscene. We could argue about whose concept of obscenity is valid and whose isn't, but that wouldn't necessarily help you avoid offending your readers. You'll need to size them up for yourself. Before you toss in four-letter words for emphasis, try to decide whether your readers will find them forceful or merely offensive. And when in doubt, leave them out.

A number of readers object also to the use of slang in writing—on any level, even informal. Slang terms like *nerd*, *wimp*, *woozy*, and *slammer* and phrases like *psyched up*, *shagged out*, and *down the tube* can be lively and descriptive, but F. L. Lucas, for instance, considers slang ''a kind of linguistic fungus; as poisonous, and as short-lived as toadstools.'' Your dictionary will tell you if a word is slang; if you don't find it listed, you may assume that it is slang. Remember, you don't want to put your readers off; you want to communicate with them. Slang often is an in-group language known only to those of a certain age or ethnic background. As a matter of courtesy, you should never use slang that your readers won't understand or may find offensive.

## CUT OUT UNNECESSARY WORDS

Try to make your writing clean, clear, and concise. I don't mean to deprive you of effective stylistic flourishes, but *ineffective* stylistic flourishes have got to go. So does just plain lazy wordiness. It's far easier to be verbose than it is to be concise. In *Provincial Letters*, *XVI* (1657), Pascal wrote, ''I have made this letter longer than usual because I lack the time to make it shorter.'' And Hugh Henry Brackenridge in *Modern Chivalry* (1792) observed, ''In order to speak short on any subject, think long.'' Nothing will annoy your readers more than having to waste time plowing through a cluttered paragraph because you neglected to spend your time cleaning it up.

You must be diligent and prune your prose. Sentences like the following cause any reader to contemplate justifiable homicide:

It is believed by a number of persons in this country that the young people of today do not assume as much responsibility toward society as it might be hoped that they would.   (33 words)

You can say the same thing better with fewer words:

Today many people believe that our young people assume too little responsibility toward society.   (14 words)

Notice, for instance, that *at this point in time* means exactly the same thing as *at this point*. *During this period of time* means the same as *during this time*. Spare your readers the unnecessary words.

---

**Exercise**                                                                      **5-4**

Sharpen your editing skills by tidying the following littered sentences. Try to keep the same meaning but eliminate all unnecessary wordiness. I will show you how with the first one.

1   It has been in the most recent past that many different groups of citizens have joined together in completely unanimous protest against the concept of nuclear war.

   *Revised:*   Recently many groups have joined in unanimous protest against nuclear war.

2   It is my desire to be called Ishmael.
3   There is a general consensus that the paper which is judged to be the most original should be awarded the prize.
4   By and large a stitch sewed or basted as soon as a rip is discovered may well save nine times the amount of sewing necessary if the job is put off even for a short time.
5   At future meetings, please do not request an exemption from being present at the meeting.
6   We finally selected a desk that was small in size and grey in color.
7   The participants who engage in polo playing seem to be few in number.
8   It is absolutely essential that we do something about the complete absence of members of minority groups among the members of this important committee.
9   The reason that I think we should postpone our decision on this problem is because this problem is a complex matter.

**10**   There was a feeling, at least on my part, based upon a number of true
facts that I had been reading, that the food that we buy at the supermarket
to eat may be poisoned with food additives.

---

### Use Repetition Wisely

Deliberate repetition, such as you observed in those impressive,
balanced sentences in the previous chapter, can be one of your most
effective rhetorical devices. But *careless repetition* may offend your
readers as much as wordiness. Ineffective repetition is often the result
of thoughtlessness, as in this student's sentence:

> Walking up to the door, I came upon the skeleton head of a cow
> placed next to the door.

That's too many *to the door* phrases. Just changing the first phrase
solves the problem:

> Walking up to the house, I came upon the skeleton head of a cow
> placed next to the door.

You need to eliminate any word or phrase that's been carelessly used
twice.

*Effective repetition* is an entirely different matter. You can achieve
both clarity and emphasis by repeating a key term deliberately, as
Katherine Anne Porter does in this sentence describing the execution
of Sacco and Vanzetti (my italics):

> They were put to death in the electric chair at Charlestown Prison at
> *midnight* on the 23rd of August, 1927, a desolate dark *midnight*, a *night* for
> perpetual remembrance and mourning.

Just be sure the word deserves the emphasis before you purposely repeat
yourself.

### BE SPECIFIC AND VIVID AND CLEAR

Paul Roberts once wrote that most subjects—except sex—are basically
boring, so it's up to the writer to make the topic interesting. Since you

can't write about sex *all* the time, you need to incorporate some of the following suggestions aimed at keeping your readers awake.

**Choose Lively Words**

One way to liven up your sentences (and hence your writing) is to use lively, specific words whenever possible. You can't avoid the limp *to be* verb (*am, was, been, is, are, were,* etc.) a great deal of the time, but given a chance, toss in a forceful verb. James Thurber, in his essay "Sex Ex Machina," speaks of a "world made up of gadgets that *whir* and *whine* and *whiz* and *shriek* and sometimes *explode.*" (Italics mine.) The force of the verbs conveys the feeling of anxiety produced by machine-age living. In his essay "A Hanging," George Orwell describes a dog that "came *bounding* among us with a loud volley of barks, and *leapt* round us *wagging* its whole body, wild with glee at finding so many human beings together." (Italics mine.) The verb *leapt*, plus the italicized verbal adjectives, here enable the reader to visualize the energy and excitement of the dog. Thomas Heggen, in the introduction to *Mr. Roberts*, writes, "Surely an artillery shell fired at Hanover *ripples* the air here. Surely a bomb dropped on Okinawa *trembles* these bulkheads." (Italics mine.) These verbs produce precisely the effect he wants in the two sentences: the suggestion of being touched, but only barely touched, by events far away.

There are, of course, other stylistic elements combining to make the above examples effective. But if your writing is colorless and tiresome, you may need to practice using lively verbs and specific details. Instead of writing, "We got into the car," try "All four of us piled into Herman's Honda." You can, of course, overdo the use of forceful verbs and specifics, but most of us err in the other direction and our writing comes out flat.

---

**Exercise**                                                    **5-5**

In order to limber up your imagination, try rewriting the following dull sentences, substituting vivid, precise words for any general or lackluster terms. I'll do the first one to give you an example.

1   Seymour was up late last night trying to finish typing his term paper.

*Revised:*    Seymour sat hunched over his typewriter, pecking away doggedly until three o'clock in the morning, trying to finish his paper on the mating habits of hippopotamuses.

2  My friend, who exercises as a hobby, studies at night in order to have his afternoons free for sports.
3  That cat is behaving in a most peculiar fashion.
4  Some person had removed the very article I needed from the magazine in the library.
5  She came into the room, removed her shoes, and sat down.
6  Hearing someone make even slight noises at a symphony is distracting.
7  The woman left her office, walked hurriedly to the store, and made a purchase.
8  The man (woman) I went out with last night was a real character.
9  Clyde and I have just been out driving around in his new car.
10  Near the window was an attractive plant in an interesting container.

## FIND THE EXACT WORD

Mark Twain once observed that the difference between the right word and almost the right word is the difference between the lightning and the lightning bug. Our language is full of synonyms; but synonyms have different shades of meaning. Although a *feeling* is a *sensation*, the two words are not interchangeable. A pen is not a writing *utensil*; it's a writing *implement* or *instrument*. And *uninterested* does not mean the same thing as *disinterested*.

### Dust off Your Dictionary

Any good desk-size dictionary can enlighten you on these distinctions if you'll take the trouble to look the words up. But in order to get reliable help from your dictionary, you should first learn how to use it. For some reason, myths abound concerning dictionaries. Many people believe that the first meaning listed for a word is the "best" one. Not true. There is no "best" one. The first meaning will often be the oldest meaning; hence, it could be the least common one. The same thing is true of alternative spellings. Unless some qualifier is inserted (like "also" or "variation of"), multiple spelling listings are equally acceptable.

The only way to find out how your dictionary handles these matters is to force yourself to read the "Explanatory Notes" at the beginning. It's not the liveliest reading imaginable, but it can be rewarding. You'll find out, for instance, that in most dictionaries the principal parts of verbs, degrees of adjectives, and plurals of nouns are not listed unless irregular. You'll find, if you persevere, explanations of various usage labels, which warn you about words with limited uses (archaic, slang, substandard, etc.). You may also, if you have an inquiring mind, discover interesting material in the back that you never suspected was there: many dictionaries include lists of abbreviations, proofreader's marks, signs, and symbols; rules for spelling, punctuation, and capitalization; and sometimes a list of all the colleges and universities in the United States and Canada. A good college dictionary is something you will use often if you write well. If the only thing you ever do with your dictionary is use it to prop up other books, that may be part of your problem.

### Trot out Your Thesaurus

A pocket-size thesaurus (dictionary of synonyms) comes in handy for locating just the right word. If you need a synonym for a word, either because you think it's not the precise word or because you've used it three times already, locate that word in your thesaurus just as you would in a dictionary. Instead of a definition, you'll find a handsome selection of words with related meanings. Remember, though, that synonyms aren't always interchangeable. Never choose an unfamiliar word unless you first look it up in the dictionary to make sure it conveys the exact meaning you want.

### Increase Your Vocabulary

The only safe, sure way to increase your vocabulary is to take note of new words as you encounter them in reading, in the classroom, in conversation, in movies—in other words, as they appear in context. If you become conscious of new words, you'll start absorbing them almost by osmosis. I have used in this book a number of words that I wouldn't expect a college freshman to understand in hopes that you might take a fancy to some and look them up. You'll encounter them again and they'll be familiar next time. Before long, you'll be using them in your own writing—and using them correctly.

## SAY WHAT YOU MEAN

Sometimes a sentence comes out as nonsense not because the writer confuses unusual words but because the person somehow fails to pay attention to what common words mean. The following sentences *sound* all right—until you think about them. A police officer recently announced in the local paper:

> We are trying to put some teeth into the law to help enforce narcotics abuse.

We can hope he doesn't really intend to force everyone to abuse narcotics. More likely he meant "to help *curb* narcotics abuse," but he actually *said* he intended to make drug abuse mandatory. A student confidently made this observation in an essay:

> Many important factors are determined by the way one dresses: the person's personality, lifestyle, profession, age, and sex.

She couldn't seriously believe that changing one's manner of dress could also change one's "profession, age, and sex," but that's what she *said*. Another student wrote this puzzler:

> Some wives have to hold jobs to help support the family's low income.

That is a grammatically correct but confusing sentence. The student meant "to help *supplement* the family's low income"—or else simply, "to help support the family."

Some people mix up words that sound alike—which confuses readers who know what the words actually mean. If you write, "Tighten all the lose screws," people may think *you* have a screw loose. Consult Chapter 9, the "Glossary of Usage," if you are in doubt about whether to write *effect* or *affect*, *lie* or *lay*, or any of those other words that are hard to keep straight.

When you write, pay attention to the words you choose. When you revise, study your word choice again. Be sure that each sentence is perfectly clear and means exactly what you want to say. Try also to make sure that you have said it in the best possible words.

**Exercise**                                                    **5-6**

The following sentences—all taken from actual usage—employ words
without regard for meaning. First, point out what's wrong with each
one, and then rephrase it accurately. You may need to revise some
extensively in order to repair them. I'll rewrite the first one, which
appeared on a sign in a parking lot.

1  Illegal Parking Will Be Towed Away At Their Expense.

   *Revised:*     Illegally Parked Cars Will Be Towed at Owners' Expense.

2  Because she was disinterested in the novel, she called it "boring."
3  Despite the enormous number of books in the world, it is possible to
   generalize them into three categories.
4  My brother confides in me not to tell on him.
5  Today's society has been pilfered with a barrage of illegal drugs.
6  These figures deduce that the firm could expect a loss.
7  I have apprised the situation and find it perilous.
8  But I am going irregardless of what you say.
9  There are a variety of media under the classification of painting.
10 Myself and Officer Smith responded to the eighth floor by way of the
   stairwell.

### Avoid Jargon and Clichés

As you search for the right word, be careful about words that may
sound grand but have vague meanings. Avoid elevated language if you
can say the same thing clearly and plainly without it.

*Jargon* usually means pretentious language used by people to make
themselves sound smarter than anybody else. Such language is always
ineffective because it sets up a barrier to communication. Jargon can
also refer to language used within a trade or profession which is understood perfectly well among that specialized group but not among
outsiders. Bridge players mean something entire different by *rubber*,
*dummy*, and *slam* than the rest of us do.

Consider your audience and your purpose. If your readers are all
familiar with the jargon, use it—provided it's the best way to make

your meaning clear. But the kind of jargon you should try to avoid includes those monstrous new words that creep into the language via the federal bureaucracy, the educational establishment, and the social sciences—phrases like "increased propensity to actualize" (meaning "apt to occur"); "facilitate the availability of funds" (meaning "to help get money"); and "sociologically compatible behavioral parameters" (meaning who knows what).

*Clichés* are phrases we pick up because they sound good, but then we use them over and over until they lose their force and become annoying. Some *old chestnuts* are *cool as a cucumber*, *ship of state*, *rugged individualist*, and *frontiers of knowledge*. The simple word *fine* is preferable to the tarnished phrase *worth its weight in gold*. Here is a list of currently popular clichés that you may be tempted to use. Try to resist the temptation.

| | | |
|---|---|---|
| acid test | doomed to failure | interface with |
| at this point | few and far between | in this day and age |
| in time | first and foremost | last but not least |
| ball park figure | for all intents and | paid my dues |
| bottom line | purposes | pretty as a picture |
| burning questions | have a nice day | state of the art |
| crystal clear | history tells us | untimely death |
| crucial test | high and mighty | user-friendly |
| cutting edge | high tech | |

## USE YOUR IMAGINATION

Try to come up with at least a few lively *figures of speech*—analogies, metaphors, similes—to give zest to your writing. If you set your imagination loose, you'll be able to come up with imaginative comparisons that will give your writing greater interest and clarity. Ralph Waldo Emerson once remarked that "New York is a sucked orange." Now that's an observation full of insight, phrased with great economy. Maya Angelou, speaking of the struggle for civil rights, mentions that some changes "have been as violent as electrical storms, while others creep slowly like sorghum syrup." Such comparisons are a form of *analogy*, a useful method of comparing something abstract (like the quality of life in a city) to something concrete (like a sucked orange). Here's a simple but effective analogy from J. F. Kobler: "Like really good tomatoes, performance standards in each department must be home grown."

When Dorothy Parker declares, "His voice was as intimate as the rustle of sheets," she lets us know that the man was speaking seductively. Certainly her *simile*—an imaginative comparison stated with *like* or *as*—is more interesting than just telling us so. Notice how forcefully Barbara Ehrenreich conveys the hazards of smoking when she asserts that the "medical case against smoking is as airtight as a steel casket." Brigid Brophy uses a *metaphor*—an implied or suggested imaginative comparison—to assert her belief that monogamy is a confining relationship: "At present, monogamy is the corset into which we try to fit every married couple—a process which has on so many occasions split the seams that we have had to modify the corset."

The only thing you need to be wary about is the *mixed metaphor*—the comparison that doesn't compare accurately, like this choice one from the *Nashville Tennessean:* "I may be just a little grain of salt crying in the woods, but I deplore this kind of thing." Just try to visualize that image and you'll see why it's a mistake. Better no metaphor at all than one that's confused.

Most importantly: Remember that *figures of speech should clarify your meaning* through comparisons that increase your readers' understanding.

---

**Exercise**                                               **5-7**

If writing analogies doesn't come naturally to you, try practicing by filling in the blanks to finish these comparisons:

1  Kissing my lover is like _____ .
2  Failing an exam is like _____ .
3  Eating in the cafeteria is like _____ .
4  Going to the health service is like _____ .
5  Getting busted is like _____ .
6  Losing a lover is like _____ .
7  My room looks like _____ .
8  Falling in love is like _____ .

**9** Writing a theme for English class is like _____ .
**10** Washing the dog is like _____ .

███████████████████████████████████████████████████████


## REVISING THE WHOLE (IF YOU SKIP THIS STAGE, I CAN'T HELP YOU)

When you've finally completed your rough draft, you'll feel elated, as if the task is finally done. And indeed, you are practically through. But many students at this point rush the manuscript to a typist—either a professional one or a handy, inexpensive one located on the premises. Don't do it. Not without some further revising.

If you haven't yet hit on a good introduction or conclusion, you must now apply yourself to that task—with or without inspiration. You'll need a title, too. For advice, look up *Title Tactics*, Chapter 8, the alphabetized "Revising Index." Now is a good time also to look up word meanings in doubtful cases and to check your thesaurus if necessary.

Also, pay attention as you reread the paper to be sure your paragraphs are fully developed with clear transitions between ideas. Be sure that you haven't strayed from your outline and taken any little side trips with only a passing relationship to your thesis.

Most important of all, be sure that the whole makes sense—that each sentence is clear, not just to you but to anyone who chances to read the paper. Be sure that each sentence *is* a sentence, not a fragment, unless you have used a fragment deliberately for stylistic purposes.


### Cajole a Loved One into Reading It

Finally, try to talk someone else into reading your paper—and not just for spelling, punctuation, and typographical errors. Ask your benefactor to call your attention to any sentences that don't make sense, any points that aren't clear. Then rework those sentences; add illustrations to clarify the weak points. You may have to rewrite a page or two, but do it, and try to be grateful for having caught the problems before instead of after turning in the paper. Most humane teachers will overlook a typo or a minor spelling error, but few will forgive a breach in communication. And rightly so. Work hard to make your content clear. Try also to make it graceful, make it persuasive, make it forceful. But primarily make it communicate, and you will have fulfilled your chief obligation as a writer.

Following is a revising checklist that will help you (as you go over your draft yet one more time) make sure you have given your work the proper polish.

### Revising Checklist

In order to make this piece of writing a paper to be proud of, be sure that your

1 Thesis involves an idea worth developing.
2 Level of usage is appropriate for your audience.
3 Language is not sexist, profane, or unduly slangy.
4 Introduction makes the point of the paper clear and catches the readers' interest.
5 Ideas are logically arranged and easy to follow.
6 Ideas are completely clear throughout.
7 Paragraphs contain plenty of examples.
8 Sentences are well constructed and precisely worded.
9 Conclusion makes or reinforces the point of your thesis.
10 Final sentence is pleasing, maybe even emphatic.

### PROOFREAD THE FINAL DRAFT

Even after you've typed or printed out a clean copy, you must force yourself (or someone completely trustworthy) to read the paper once more to pick up assorted minor mistakes that didn't show up in the rough draft but will glare like neon signs in the final draft. Jessica Mitford rightly says that "failure to proofread is like preparing a magnificent dinner and forgetting to set the table, so that the wretched guests have to scramble for the food as best they can." So, be polite: proofread.

Careless errors can be funny and Freudian, like this one from a student discussing public reaction to the changing morality of the twenties: "Ladies' skirts finally rose so high that the public was shocked." But careless errors can also be witless and annoying—like repeating a word needlessly ("and and") or leaving off an *s* and producing an illiteracy: "The protester were arrested and herded off to jail.'' Such errors do nothing to encourage the readers' admiration for the brilliance of your observations—no matter how keen they are. So watch the little things, too. Don't write ''probable'' for ''probably,'' or ''use to'' for ''used to,'' or ''you'' for ''your,'' or ''then'' for ''than.'' Check possessives to be sure the apostrophes are there—or not there in the case of *its*. You'll momentarily confuse your readers if you get that one wrong. (If you are at all in doubt about the distinction between *its* and *it's*, consult Chapter 9, the ''Glossary of Usage.'')

### Proofreading and Editing Checklist

Reread the paper one more time *paying no attention to content* but checking to be sure that

**1**  No words are left out or carelessly repeated.
**2**  No words are misspelled (or carelessly spelled—*use to* for *used to*).
**3**  No plurals are left off.
**4**  No apostrophes are omitted (for possessives or contractions).
**5**  No periods, dashes, commas, colons, or quotation marks are left out.

Make the necessary corrections. If you're using a word processor, this step will take only a matter of minutes. Remember, a handsomely typed paper has a psychological advantage. It suggests to your readers that time and effort went into the preparation, that it wasn't tossed off at the last minute. If you're typing, make corrections neatly in black ink above the line, and retype any page that looks like it's ready for urban renewal.

Chapter 6

# Smart Reading and Straight Thinking

Just as important as the writing process is the reading process that transmits the ideas into your head. The writing you do in college and thereafter will probably demand that you go beyond relating personal experiences as such. You'll find it necessary to write about issues and events—to deal with ideas, theories, and opinions as well as facts. And you'll be continually reading in order to acquire informed ideas of your own on various subjects. Reading, discussing, synthesizing all this new information constitutes a large part of becoming educated.

## CULTIVATE A QUESTIONING ATTITUDE

But the educational process bogs down unless you keep an open mind. You shouldn't reject a new idea just because it conflicts with an opinion you presently treasure. Because you've heard and accepted a statement all your life doesn't make that statement true. As Mark Twain observed, in his *Notebook*, "One of the proofs of immortality is that myriads have believed it. They also believed that the world was flat.'' You should be willing to consider new ideas, examine them, think about them, and decide on the basis of the available evidence what is and is not valid. You'll be bombarded by facts and opinions from all sides. In self-defense you must try to distinguish the truth from the tripe. It's not easy. Truth may be mighty, but it doesn't always prevail.

## DEFINE YOUR TERMS

Most of our abstract words mean slightly different things to different people. Some of them mean entirely different things, depending on the point of view. ''Individual freedom,'' for instance, means to some people the absence of governmental control in business, i.e., the freedom to pursue profits without restraint. To other people, though, ''individual freedom'' means the liberty to read whatever they wish, to see any movies they find interesting, to make love to any person of either sex in any manner agreeable to all: that is, strictly personal freedom. Virtually all terms dealing with morality and ethics need to be clarified.

If one of those slippery, abstract terms figures importantly in your writing, you should probably define it. Usually a brief, dictionary-type definition is all you need, like the one Gore Vidal provides here:

> Put simply, fascism is the control of the state by a single man or by an oligarchy, supported by the military and the police. That is why I keep emphasizing the dangers of corrupt police forces, of uncontrolled *secret* police, like the F.B.I. and the C.I.A. and Army counterintelligence and the Treasury men—what a lot of sneaky types we have spying on us all!

> —''The State of the Union,''
> *Esquire* (May 1975)

You may consider his charge exaggerated, but his tactic of defining the term *fascism* encourages us at least to examine the possibility that what he says may be true. Notice also the ease with which he inserts his definition: ''Put simply, fascism is. . . .'' That's much more graceful than ''According to the dictionary . . .'' or (shudder) ''Webster says. . . .'' You should, of course, consult the dictionary, but then define the terms in your own words, making your definition parallel in form (i.e., same part of speech or same verb tense as the word defined).

## BE SUSPICIOUS OF SLOGANS

As you form the habit of questioning statements, the first ones to examine are the ones that come in the form of epigrams or slogans. These prepackaged ideas are all neat and tidy, easy to remember, pleasant to the ear. We've been brought up on them and have Ben Franklin to thank for a sizable number, like "A stitch in time saves nine," and "Early to bed and early to rise makes a man healthy, wealthy, and wise." *Epigrams* usually state a simple truth, but often they cleverly disguise opinion as fact. For instance, we've always heard that "home is where the heart is," yet George Bernard Shaw says, "Home is the girl's prison and the woman's workhouse." Clearly, the absolute truth of either statement is debatable. In my opinion, Shaw's version has more of the ring of reality.

A *slogan* is a catchword or motto designed to rally people to vote for a certain party, agree with the opinions of a particular group, or buy a specific product. Bumper stickers reading "America—love it or leave it" or "America—change it or lose it" may inspire you, but don't mistake them for reasoned arguments. Your job as reader is to question such statements: Demand evidence and decide rationally rather than emotionally which opinions are valid, which are propaganda, which are a mixture of both.

## BE CAUTIOUS ABOUT CONNOTATIONS

More difficult to perceive than the bias of slogans is the subtle persuasion of slanted writing. But once you become aware of the emotional quality of many words, you'll not likely be taken in by slanted writing.

Words are symbols with *denotative* meanings (the actual concrete property or abstract quality referred to) and *connotative* meanings (the emotional responses stimulated by associations with the word). The term *mother*, for instance, *denotes* the woman who gives birth to a child, but the term often *connotes* warmth, love, security, comfort. Most of our words have connotations in varying degrees—some so strong that the words should be considered "loaded." Whether you choose to refer to the President as a "statesman" or a "politician" may well reveal your political affiliation. Consider the connotations of these pairs of similar words:

| | |
|---|---|
| smut | pornography |
| mob | gathering |
| cur | pup |
| smog | haze |
| egghead | intellectual |
| prudish | chaste |
| jock | athlete |
| penny-pinching | thrifty |
| foolhardy | courageous |

Your attitude will be fairly transparently revealed by whether you choose from the strongly negative words on the left or the more favorable words on the right.

Consider, for example, Frederick Lewis Allen's description of Woodrow Wilson as a "Puritan Schoolmaster. . . . cool in a time of great emotions, calmly setting the lesson for the day; the moral idealist . . . , the dogmatic prophet of democracy. . . ." The word *Puritan* suggests a moralist devoid of human warmth. Allen could have said "high-minded" and lessened the chill factor. And what does the word *schoolmaster* suggest that the neutral word *teacher* does not? Again, a strict, no-nonsense, unsmiling disciplinarian. The word *cool* reinforces this same feeling, as does *calmly*. The term *moral idealist* should be totally complimentary. But is it? We associate idealists with good intentions, but a tinge of daydreaming impracticality clings to the word. *Dogmatic* denotes closed-mindedness. And *prophet* suggests an aura of fanaticism, since the Biblical prophets were always exhorting the fun-loving Old Testament sinners to repent of their evil ways or face the wrath of Jehovah. Allen has told us perhaps more through connotation in the sentence than he did through denotation. He slants the writing to convey a picture of Wilson that he feels is accurate—the image of a cold, determined, perhaps misguided man with the best of intentions.

Thus you shouldn't get the impression that connotative language is necessarily bad. It isn't. In fact, without the use of emotional words, writing would be virtually lifeless. But you must be *aware* of connotations, both as you read and as you write. The rhetoric in the following passage by Theodore Roosevelt is first-rate. The utterance has impact, conviction, persuasion. See if you can detect how much connotative words lend to the writer's effect:

If we stand idly by, if we seek merely swollen, slothful ease and ignoble peace . . . , then bolder and stronger peoples will pass us by, and will win for themselves the domination of the world.

Note that he says not "stand by" but "stand *idly* by." He fears we may seek "ease"—but not the ease that brings rest after wearying toil; instead, "*swollen, slothful* ease." Certainly the word *peace* alone would not serve: it is "*ignoble* peace." Notice, too, that the peoples who are going to "pass us by" and leave us with no world to dominate are "*bolder* and *stronger* peoples": we're subtly asked to envision not Turks and Visigoths slaughtering innocent hordes, but rather to picture clean-limbed, fearless types pressing onward against obstacles, propelled by what is presented as an admirable vision of world conquest. Surely the piece deserves high marks as effective propaganda. But you as reader must be able to detect that the chinks in his logic are effectively plugged with rhetoric. Your best protection from propaganda is your ability to think—to examine the language and the logic, to sort the soundness from the sound effects.

## CONSIDER THE SOURCE

You could be reasonably sure, even before reading it, that you wouldn't get an unbiased comment from Theodore Roosevelt concerning the Spanish-American War. This doesn't mean, however, that you should ignore Roosevelt's statement if you're writing an appraisal of the reasons the United States entered that war. Neither should you ignore the opinions of William Jennings Bryan or H. L. Mencken if you're analyzing the fairness of the Scopes trial. But you should be constantly aware that the sources you're reading could hardly be considered impartial.

You might expect an unprejudiced analysis of an event from journalists who were present, but here again you must stay alert because not all publications achieve—or even *try* to achieve—objective reporting. You may be certain that the conservative *National Review* will offer an appreciably different appraisal from that of the ultraliberal *Mother Jones*. And the *Congressional Record*, which sounds like an unimpeachable source, is actually one of the least reliable, since any member of Congress can have any nonsense whatsoever read into the

*Record.* You must sample enough authorities so that you are able to weigh the matter and discount the prejudices. This is one reason that research papers require extensive bibliographies. You could probably scare up most of the facts from reading one *unbiased* source, but the problem is discovering which one—if any—that is. You'll have to read opinions on both sides of the middle in order to recognize the center— if and when you find it.

Don't make the mistake of embracing what you consider a reliable source and then placing your trust in it till death do you part. Too many of us do just this: we plight our troth to the Bible, to *The Nation*, to the *Wall Street Journal*, or to *Time* magazine, and assume we never have to think again. You will discover writers and publications whose viewpoint is similar to yours. These will naturally strike you as the most astute, cogent, perceptive, reliable sources to consult. But be careful that you don't fall into the comfortable habit of reading these publications exclusively.

The *date* of a publication often makes some difference in its value or reliability. If you're doing a paper analyzing the relative safety of legal and illegal abortions, you'll find an article written in 1936 of little use. If, on the other hand, you're writing a paper on the *history* of the long struggle to legalize abortion, a 1936 article could be quite important. In general, we place the highest value on recent articles simply because the latest scholar or scientist has the advantage of building on all that has gone before. Dr. Christiaan Barnard might never have been able to perform the first heart transplant had it not been for the pioneering genius of the seventeenth-century surgeon William Harvey, who first theorized the circulation of blood. But if you're writing about the effectiveness of heart transplants, your paper need not mention Harvey. Obviously, your data must be current to be of value in such an investigation.

## Appealing to Authority

You're probably going to want to cite authorities whenever you write on any controversial subject. You can lose arguments, though, if your authority isn't convincing to your readers. Some people feel that once they've clinched a point with "The Bible says . . . ," they've precluded any rebuttal. If your reader happens to be Billy Graham or one of the faithful, you'll be on solid ground. But not everyone would agree with the upright citizen who offers this solution for helping the poor:

The only remedy against poverty is to worship God as God, honor His word and obey His doctrines, call upon Him and humble ourselves. Then He will hear and heal the land.[1]

The more practical-minded your readers, the less likely they will be to accept an argument requiring divine intervention to solve social problems.

You should cite authorities, by all means, but be sure they are recognized authorities on the subject you're considering. You might find some people who would value the opinion of the Pope on pornography, George Wallace on race relations, or Hugh Hefner on women's rights. But try for authorities who would come closer to being considered impartial experts on those subjects by the majority of reflective, educated people.

## A QUICK LOOK AT LOGIC

Whenever you write using sources, your purpose is to convey your thoughts and ideas into the minds of your readers. But in order to be convincing, these thoughts and ideas must be logical. You should be aware of the common pitfalls of slippery logic so that you can avoid them in your own thinking and writing, as well as detect them in the arguments of others.

### Avoid Oversimplifying

Most of us have a tendency to like things reduced to orderly, easily grasped *either/or* answers. The only problem is that things seldom are that simple. Be wary of arguments that offer only *either/or* choices, as if there exists no middle way—the "either we win the war, or we sacrifice our national honor" sort of reasoning. This fallacy is sometimes called the *false dichotomy*.

**Stereotypes** The same people who produce these alternatives will usually come up with *stereotypes* as well. They will be aware of only two types of students, for instance: the loud, rowdy, alcoholic hell-raisers; and the quiet, studious, well-mannered kids. Such stereotypes are based on the combination of a few facts and a lot of prejudice.

[1]Letter to the editor of the *Eugene* (Ore.) *Register-Guard*, September 18, 1969.

They seldom give a truthful picture of anyone in the group and could never be accurate to describe all the members.

**Hasty Generalizations**   You'll do well to question people who present easy solutions to complex problems. This ability to simplify could reflect genius, but more often it will stem from a lack of completely understanding the situation in the first place. Single-minded people, confident that they have all the answers, are always happy to enlighten you with what are called *hasty generalizations*, like this one:

> If the demonstrators had left when the police told them to, there would have been no trouble, and no one would have been killed.

The statement, which on the surface seems entirely plausible, conveys no force to anyone who doesn't share in the hidden premises (the underlying assumptions): that all the laws are just and are fairly administered; that all the actions of the government are honorable and in the best interest of all the citizens. The statement presumes, in short, that the demonstrators had no right or reason to be there and hence were entirely wrong not to leave when told to do so. Such a presumption overlooks the possibility that the demonstrators might legitimately protest the right of the state to silence their protests.

Oversimplification can also be achieved by merely stating opinions as facts. The Kansas lady who wrote the following letter to the editor of the *Wichita Eagle-Beacon* (June 17, 1965) has the technique down nicely:

> Liquor is something that we can get along without to a very good advantage. The problem of jazz music is a very grave one in this city, also, as it produces an attitude of irresponsibility in the listener. . . . The fact that it originates from undesirable heathen rituals should keep us from performing it.
>
> Let's keep Kansas attractive to God-fearing people. This is the type industry is interested in hiring and this is the type needed in government and the armed forces.

The letter is a study in logical fallacies. It's not necessary that you be able to distinguish them from one another. The name of the error isn't important: avoiding the error *is*.

## Sweeping Generalizations

Since you can't avoid making general statements, you should be careful to avoid making them without sufficient evidence to support them. Suppose you write:

> All Siamese cats are extremely nervous creatures, far more jumpy than alley cats. My sister has a Siamese cat that will allow itself to be petted only with great hissing and trembling. But my striped tomcat is so friendly, he jumps up in the laps of complete strangers.

Personal experience is always convincing but you're not likely to prove to anyone's satisfaction that *all* Siamese cats are edgy by describing the behavior of only one. Neither have you proved that alley cats are indeed friendly by trotting out one pushy tomcat. You must either draw on a much larger body of experience, or else you're going to need to qualify your assertion considerably. Statements involving *all*, *none*, *everything*, *nobody*, and *always* are tough to prove. You may so damage your readers' confidence by exaggerating your point that they won't accept even the smaller truth that you can support.

So tone it down. *Qualify* your statement. If you really have seen several high-strung Siamese, and if you know of at least three or four out-going alley cats, you might try saying it like this:

> Siamese cats are often aloof and edgy around strangers, but alley cats will sometimes be as friendly as a beagle pup.

Then you mention your experience with lots of cats, and your readers will be more likely to accept your generalization.

## Jumping to Conclusions

The foregone conclusion fallacy is one of the most common errors in logic because we slip into it so easily and so unobtrusively. Suppose you've just discovered that the early symptoms of mercury poisoning are restlessness, instability, and irritability. Since ecologists have warned that our waters are polluted with mercury in dangerous amounts, and since everybody you know is restless, unstable, and irritable these days, you conclude that the population is succumbing to mercury poisoning. And we may well be, for that matter, but if you expect to convince anyone who wasn't already eager to make the same leap in logic, you'll need to garner more evidence—such as some medical reports showing that human beings (as well as fish and cattle) are actually ingesting dangerous amounts of the poison.

## Dodging the Issue

There are a number of handy fallacies that people press into service in order to sidestep a problem while appearing to pursue the point. One of the most effective and the most underhanded—a favorite device of politicians—involves attacking the opponent, rather than the issue, and usually entails playing on emotional reactions, prejudices, fears, and ignorance instead of directly addressing the problem. You are probably familiar with the discrediting tactic which involves an appeal to popular opinion. If you would believe certain writers, the United Nations is trying to deliver the United States of America into the bloodstained hands of Soviet Russia; President Dwight D. Eisenhower was a willing tool of the Communist Party; the Supreme Court of the United States is dedicated to serving the interests of big business. A variation on the same approach goes like this:

> If we allow sex education to be taught in the public schools, the young will be corrupted, the moral fiber of the nation will be endangered, human beings will become no better than animals, and the Communists will just walk right in and take over.

## Begging the Question

This common fallacy involves a circular argument: you offer as evidence premises which assume as true the very thing you're trying to prove. These premises, of course, are usually hidden or at least disguised; otherwise no one would even try this deception. Ex-Attorney General John Mitchell apparently considered his reasoning sound when he rejected the finding of the President's Commission on Obscenity that pornography is harmless:

> If we want a society of people who devote their time to base and sensuous things, then pornography may be harmless. But if we want a society in which the noble side of man is encouraged and mankind itself is elevated, then I submit that pornography is surely harmful.

Now, we could with hindsight observe that John Mitchell is hardly the person to instruct the citizenry about elevating the noble side of humanity. We could argue that it's better to have sensuous things than conspiracy, perjury, and obstruction of justice. But that would be *name-calling* or *ad hominem*—attacking the person rather than the issue. So let's look at his logic.

The basic issue that Mitchell is concerned with is the value of pornography. He appears to argue that pornography is undesirable by alluding to its baseness and by deploring its lack of elevating qualities. Yet by calling pornography base and ignoble, Mitchell is already *assuming* its undesirability. His argument is invalid since the truth of the conclusion is assumed in the premises. I happen to agree with Mitchell, by the way, that pornography can be harmful. But I still object to his statement on the grounds that he hasn't supplied any valid reasons.

## Sliding Down the "Slippery Slope"

The *slippery-slope* fallacy assumes that one instance will automatically lead to thousands of similar instances, and thence directly to chaos. And that's not necessarily so. The *slippery-slope* argument goes like this: "If we grant this student's request to take the final examination early, then every student in the university will want to take early exams; so we'll have to deny the request."

## KEEP AN OPEN MIND

All these techniques are frighteningly successful with untrained, unanalytical minds. And they get to many of us who are educated also. You should try never to use them, and you must be armed against them. Thinking is your best defense. *Think* while you're reading, and *think* some more before you write. Be prepared to change your mind. Instead of hunting for facts to shore up your present opinions, let the facts you gather lead you to a conclusion. And don't insist on a nice, tidy, clear-cut conclusion. There may not be one. Your conclusion may well be that both sides for various reasons have a point. Simply work to discover what you honestly believe to be the truth of the matter, and set that down as clearly and convincingly as you can.

# Chapter 7

# Writing About Your Reading: The Documented Essay

At some time you may be asked to write a paper that doesn't spring entirely from your own fertile brain. You may be expected to do research—to read fairly widely on a certain subject, to synthesize (to combine a number of different ideas into a new whole) and organize this accumulated information, and then get this new knowledge down on paper in clear and coherent prose.

Traditionally research papers involve *argument*. You may be expected to choose a topic which is somewhat controversial, investigate thoroughly the issues on both sides, and take a stand. Otherwise, the writing process for a research paper is the same as for any other. You'll still need to narrow the subject to a topic you can handle in the number of pages assigned. And you'll have to come up with a thesis statement and an outline before you begin writing. But first you'll locate the material you're going to read; then you'll take notes as you read so that you'll be able to give credit to various sources as you write the paper.

## SCHEDULING YOUR RESEARCH PAPER

Writing a research paper is a time-consuming job. This is one paper that you simply cannot put off until the last minute. If you divide the project into units, you can keep the work under control.

### Set Deadlines for Yourself

If your completed paper is due in, say, six weeks, you could put yourself on a schedule something like this:

*1st week:*   Complete stack of cards listing possible sources.
Try to narrow your topic down to a workable thesis question to investigate.

*2d week:*   Read and take notes.
Settle on a preliminary thesis question.
Try to come up with a preliminary outline.

*3d week:*   Continue reading and taking notes.

*4th week:*   Complete reading and note taking.
Turn your thesis question into a statement.
Wrestle the outline into shape.

*5th week:*   Write the first draft.
Let it cool—rest yourself.
Begin revising and editing.
Get someone reliable to read your second draft and tell you whether every sentence is clear, every quotation properly introduced, and every paragraph nicely coherent.

*6th week:*   Polish the paper.
Type the final draft.
Let it rest at least overnight.
*Proofread* it carefully.

That is a fairly leisurely schedule. You can, of course, do the work in a shorter time if required to. You will just have to be more industrious about the reading. Some instructors deliberately ask students to complete the project within a month in order to allow no chance for procrastination. Whatever your time limit, devise a schedule for yourself and stick to it.


## NARROWING YOUR TOPIC

If you have an area of interest but no ideas about any way to limit that topic, your first step might be to consult a good encyclopedia. Perhaps your father recently underwent abdominal surgery; as a result of spending many hours with him, you have become interested in hospitals. An encyclopedia article on hospitals will briefly discuss their history, some specialized kinds, services provided, intern training, difficulties with sanitation, and cost of care, among other things. Remembering that your dad contracted a staph infection while recovering from his operation, you might decide to investigate the problem of infections in hospitals. Why have they become prevalent? What is being done about them? Or, as you read the article, you might encounter a new term and become interested in *hospices*—specialized hospitals that attempt to provide comfort and dignity for the dying. Are these proving successful? Should we have more of them in this country? Something in an encyclopedia article on your subject is likely to provide the spark needed to fire your curiosity and give you a focus for your research.


## EXPANDING YOUR ASSOCIATIONS

Once you have narrowed your topic, you may need momentarily to expand it again in order to locate all the relevant information in the library. As indexes and other reference tools do not necessarily classify information the way you do in your brain, you need to think of other headings under which your subject might be indexed. Before going to the library, you should make a list of topics related to your research subject. If you are planning to investigate hospices, your list might go like this:

| | |
|---|---|
| Hospice | Geriatrics |
| Dying | Health care |
| Death | Old people |
| Aging | Euthanasia |

For each of the following subjects, list at least three related topics that you could look under in reference books.

1  No-fault divorce
2  High school students' legal rights
3  Fad diets
4  Detective fiction by women
5  Use of the word *ain't*
6  Tax shelters
7  Horror movies

## TOPICS FOR RESEARCHED WRITING

If your mind remains a blank and your instructor will allow you to borrow a topic from this book, here are some ideas that might be interesting to research.

### For Writing an Informative Paper

1  Research the history of a familiar product or object, such as Coca-Cola, Mickey Mouse, the dictionary, the typewriter, the nectarine, black mass, black magic, vampire movies.
2  Research and analyze a fad, craze, or custom: fraternity initiation, pierced ears, "smile" buttons, any fad diet, punk fashions, Cabbage Patch dolls.
3  How can autistic children be helped?
4  How can alcoholics be helped?
5  How can rape victims be helped?
6  Why do people become alcoholics?
7  What is *anorexia nervosa*, and can it be prevented?
8  What is *agoraphobia*, and what can be done about it?
9  How can battered women be helped?
10  Why do women allow themselves to be beaten by their husbands?

### For Writing About Literature

1  How effective is the ending of *Huckleberry Finn*?

**2**  Is the governess sane or insane in James's "The Turn of the Screw"?

**3**  What are the characteristics of the "Hemingway hero"?

**4**  What are the mythological implications of Eudora Welty's "Moon Lake"?

**5**  What was Zola's contribution to literary naturalism?

## For Persuasion or Argumentation

After doing the appropriate research, defend either side of one of the following issues:

**1**  Is nuclear waste disposal safe—or suicidal?

**2**  The use of animals in research should (should not) be allowed.

**3**  Clear-cutting of forests should (should not) be stopped.

**4**  It is (is not) better for children if their incompatible parents get a divorce.

**5**  The children's toys now on the market often encourage (discourage) destructiveness and discourage (encourage) creativity.

**6**  The federal government does (does not) have the right to monitor activities of U.S. citizens whom it regards as possible terrorists.

**7**  The fashion industry does (does not) exploit consumers. Or substitute any area of business that interests you: the cosmetics industry, the funeral business, the car manufacturers, the oil industry, etc.

**8**  Having a working mother does (does not) harm a child's development.

**9**  Automation has (has not) hindered our culture more than it has helped.

**10**  Violence on children's TV shows is (is not) harmful to children.

**11**  Newspaper reporters should (should not) have the right to protect their sources.

**12**  Parents should (should not) have the right to censor the textbooks and literature taught in their children's schools.

**13**  Internment of Japanese-American families after the United States entered World War II was a grave injustice (was necessary for the national security).

**14**  Is sexual harassment in the workplace a serious problem—or a myth?

**15**  The government should provide more (fewer) benefits for single parents on welfare.

## SOME CLUES ON USING THE LIBRARY

Most college libraries offer orientation courses to show students how to find things in that clean, well-lighted place. If the course isn't required, take it anyway. An orientation course is your surest bet for learning your way around a library. If no such course is offered, your library will at least have available a handbook explaining what's where. A few minutes spent studying these instructions may save you many hours of aimless wandering. If after reading the handbook carefully you search and still can't find what you're looking for, ask for help. Librarians are seldom snarly about answering questions and will often take you in tow, lead you to the material you need, and give you valuable advice.

### How to Find What You're Looking for If You Don't Know What It Is

When you begin making out a preliminary list of sources, you're looking for books, articles, and chapters in books on your topic, but you haven't the vaguest notion what these are or where to find them. Do not despair. What sounds like an impossible task is actually quite simple.

### Begin with the Card or Computer Catalog

You will find the books available on your topic by looking it up by subject in the card catalog—or by using the handy computer, which provides the same information at the touch of a keyboard. Remember to look under related subjects if you fail to find enough material on your first try.

Remember also to have notecards handy when you begin this project, since you'll need to record authors, titles, and call numbers of any materials that appear useful. In the same area are the encyclopedias, the *Dictionary of National Biography* (British), and the *Dictionary of American Biography*, *Who's Who*, and various almanacs and dictionaries of famous quotations. These may or may not be of use to you, depending on what kind of research paper you're writing.

**Indexes and Bibliographies**   Things begin to get a bit tricky when you move onto the next step, which involves finding out what articles and essays are available on your topic. You'll find the chief tools you need in the reference room. These are mammoth sets of books which index, year by year, all the articles in a multitude of magazines.

You need to know first which indexes cover what type of magazines (or you could waste a lot of time scanning titles that have no potential usefulness). The *Readers' Guide to Periodical Literature* (familiarly known as the *Readers' Guide*) would be of little value if you're writing a paper on Edgar Allan Poe, for instance, because it indexes popular magazines, not scholarly ones. And how often does *Mechanics Illustrated* come out with a big spread on Poe? But if you're investigating the possibilities for cutting down pollution from automobile exhaust, *Mechanics Illustrated* may have just the article you want. Of if you're writing on some aspect of current events, the *Readers' Guide* will lead you to articles in *Newsweek*, *Time*, *U.S. News and World Report*, as well as to magazines which analyze current events, like *Harper's*, the *Atlantic*, and the *National Review*.

Another useful index for any research involving current events is the *Public Affairs Information Service Bulletin* (PAIS). Here you'll find indexed articles dealing with diverse topics of public interest. PAIS indexes the *Bulletin on Narcotics* published by the United Nations, the *Journal of Gerontology*, the *Journal of Forestry*, the *Journal of African and Asian Studies*, various legal journals, and countless other esoteric magazines and pamphlets.

For that Poe article, you'd be better off consulting the *Humanities Index* (formerly part of the *International Index*) or, if you want the really scholarly articles, the MLA *Bibliography* (which works just like the other indexes)—but you may have to troop off to the humanities area to find it. And if you'd like to find out what Poe's contemporaries thought of his writing, look him up in *Poole's Index to Periodical Literature*, which covers the major nineteenth-century magazines.

There are several other reference works of general interest. One of the most valuable is the *Essay and General Literature Index*. This treasure allows you to locate essays buried in books and to find chapters of books that may pertain to your topic, even though the title might give no clue. Then, there's the *Book Review Digest*, which tells you briefly what various reviewers thought of a book when it came out (if it came out since 1905) and gives you the information necessary to look up the actual review should you want to know more. All you need is the approximate year of publication in order to know which volume to consult. And the *New York Times Index* will furnish you with the date of any noteworthy event since 1851, allowing you to look it up in the files of your local newspaper—or in the *Times* itself, on microfilm. The *Social Sciences Index* (formerly part of the *International Index* and, until very recently, combined with the *Humanities Index*) should prove useful if you're looking for articles related to sociology, psychology, anthropology, political science, or economics. Articles pertaining to history or literature are listed in the *Humanities Index*.

One more tip: Just because some periodical index lists a magazine doesn't mean that your library will necessarily *have* that magazine. Before you tire yourself searching the stacks, spend a minute checking the list of periodical holdings for your library to find out whether the magazine will be there.

Also, just because a magazine or book is supposed to be in the library does not, in fact, guarantee that the item *will* be there. Theft is a major problem in libraries these days. You should report lost (or ripped off or ripped out) materials to someone at the circulation desk so that the missing materials can be noted and eventually replaced.

**Ask About the Others**  If you're planning some really high-powered research, you may need more specialized indexes than the ones discussed here. There are countless more covering every conceivable field. In order to use these, you'll need to go to the section of the library where the books and magazines in this field are located. Find a librarian in that area and ask for help.

## SWEATING THROUGH THE RESEARCH

Once you've located the sources—the books and articles that you'll need to read and assimilate—you can begin the actual research.

### Get It All Down

Every time you consult a new source, copy all the information necessary for indicating your source to the reader. If you fail to record all the pertinent data, you may find yourself tracking down a book or article weeks later in order to look up an essential publication date or volume number that you neglected to record initially. The book may by this time be checked out, lost, or stolen, so get it all down the first time.

You should probably use three- by five-inch notecards to keep track of this information, and they should come out looking something like the examples in Figures 7-1 through 7-4. Note the pertinent data. Always get it *all*.

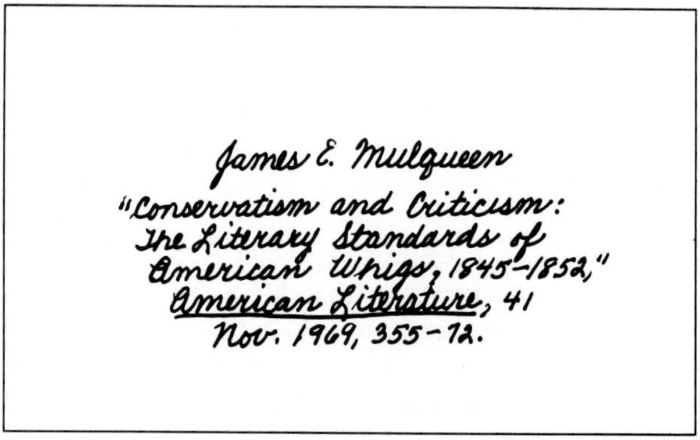

James E. Mulqueen
"Conservation and Criticism:
The Literary Standards of
American Whigs, 1845–1852,"
American Literature, 41
Nov. 1969, 355–72.

**Figure 7-1**    Article from magazine with volume number.

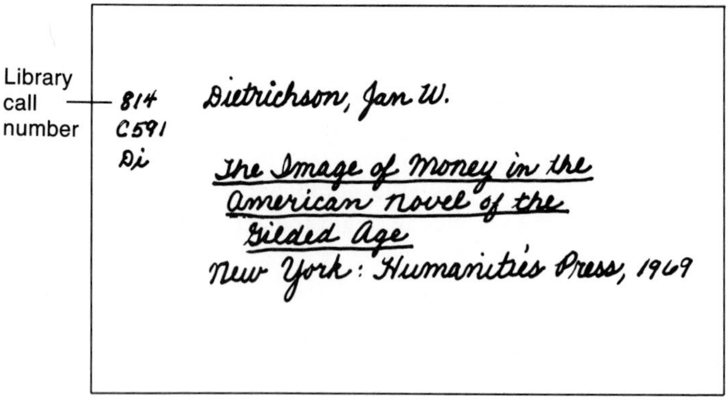

Library
call — 814
number   C591
           Di

Dietrichson, Jan W.

The Image of Money in the
American Novel of the
Gilded Age
New York: Humanities Press, 1969

**Figure 7-2**    Book.

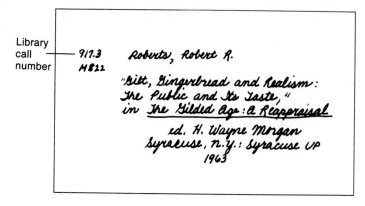

Library
call
number

*917.3*
*M822*

*Roberts, Robert R.*

*"Gilt, Gingerbread and Realism:*
*The Public and Its Taste,"*
*in* *The Gilded Age: A Reappraisal*
*ed. H. Wayne Morgan*
*Syracuse, N.Y.: Syracuse UP*
*1963*

**Figure 7-3**   Essay in a collection.

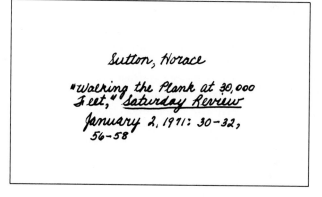

*Sutton, Horace*

*"Walking the Plank at 30,000*
*Feet," Saturday Review*
*January 2, 1971: 30–32,*
*56–58*

**Figure 7-4**   Article from magazine without volume number.

*For Books:*

**1**  Author or editor
**2**  Title (underlined)
**3**  Place of publication
**4**  Publisher
**5**  Date of publication (plus date of edition, if the book has more than one)
**6**  Call number at your library

*For Articles:*

**1** Author (or "Anonymous")
**2** Title (in quotation marks)
**3** Name of magazine or newspaper (underlined)
**4** Volume number (if the journal uses them)
**5** Date of the issue
**6** Pages the article covers

## On to the Reading

Keeping your thesis in mind, you can get started on the reading. Have your notecards handy. At the same time you're doing your research, you'll be working out your outline. These notecards, each containing information related to a single idea, can be shuffled around later and slipped into appropriate sections of your outline. Taking notes consecutively on regular sheets of paper makes this handy sorting of ideas impossible.

As you take notes, put subject headings in the upper righthand corner of your notecards indicating in a word or two what each note is about. Eventually these subject headings will probably correspond to sections of your outline. Chances are that your outline won't really take shape until you're fairly well along with your research—possibly not until you've finished it. As you collect more and more cards, leaf through them occasionally to see if they can be arranged into three or four main categories to form the major headings of an outline. The sooner you can get one worked out, the more efficient becomes your research. You can see exactly what you're looking for and avoid taking notes that would eventually prove off the point and have to be discarded.

But if an idea sounds potentially useful, copy it down whether it fits exactly or not. If the idea recurs in your reading and gathers significance, you may decide to add a section to your outline or to expand one of the present sections. Then later, at the organizing stage, if you have cards with ideas that just don't seem to fit in anywhere, let them go. Let them go cheerfully. Don't ruin the focus and unity of your paper by trying to wedge in every single note you've taken. Unless you're an uncommonly cautious notetaker, you'll have a number of cards that you can't use.

Your notecards may look something like the one shown in Figure 7-5.

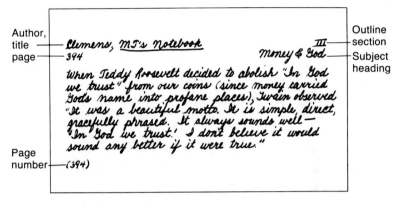

Author, title page ──

Page number ──

Outline section ── Subject heading

**Figure 7-5**    Sample notecard.

Again, don't forget to record *on each card*:

1  Author's last name
2  Abbreviated title
3  Page number

If you'll get in the habit of writing down these essentials before you take the note, there's less chance of forgetting an item—or all the items, for that matter.

## TIPS ON AVOIDING PLAGIARISM

Plagiarism, as you know, means using somebody else's writing without giving proper credit. You can avoid this dishonesty by using a moderate amount of care in taking notes. Put quotation marks around any material—however brief—that you copy verbatim. As you're leafing through the cards trying to sort them into categories, circle these quotation marks with a red pencil so you can't miss them. There remains the problem of avoiding the author's phrasing if you decide not to quote directly but to paraphrase. This dilemma is not so easily solved.

You naturally tend to write the idea down using the same phrasing, changing or omitting a few words. This close paraphrasing is, in the minds of many, still plagiarism. To escape it, you must not even look at your source as you take notes that aren't direct quotations. I suggest that you use both methods—verbatim notes and summarizing notes—and let the summaries be just that, condensing several pages of reading on a single card. You'll scarcely be able to fall into the author's phrasing that way. Or if your writer uses an eyecatching phrase—something like Veblen's "code of pecuniary honor"—get that down in quotation marks in the middle of your summary. A summarizing notecard will look something like the card shown in Figure 7-6.

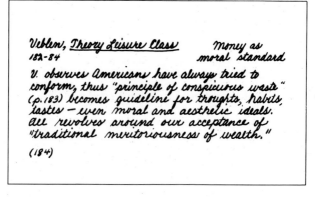

**Figure 7-6**   Summary notecard.

### Paraphrase Carefully

Sometimes, of course, you must do fairly close paraphrasing of important ideas. Since plagiarism is often accidental, let me give you a couple of examples to show you exactly what plagiarism is. Here is a passage from Marvin Harris's *Cows, Pigs, Wars, and Witches: The Riddles of Culture* (1978), which, let's assume, you need to use in making a point in your paper:

> No one understood better than Gandhi that cow love had different implications for rich and poor. For him the cow was the central focus of the struggle to rouse India to authentic nationhood.

If you incorporate that material into your paper in the following words, you have plagiarized, even though you've cited Harris as your source:

> Gandhi understood the different implications of cow love for rich and poor. He saw the struggle to rouse India to authentic nationhood focused on the cow (Harris 21).

The fact that the source is cited suggests that this plagiarism might have resulted from ignorance rather than deception, but it is plagiarism nonetheless. Changing a few words or rearranging the phrases is not enough. Here is another version, somewhat less blatant but still plagiarism:

> Gandhi well knew that rich and poor were affected differently by cow love, which he saw as a means of inspiring his people to authentic nationhood (Harris 21).

There are still two phrases there that are distinctly Harris's: *cow love* and *authentic nationhood*. It is quite all right to use those phrases but *only if you put them in quotation marks.* You should also acknowledge your source in the text of your paper—as well as in your citation—whenever possible, like this:

> According to Harris, Gandhi well knew that rich and poor were affected differently by ''cow love,'' which he saw as a means of inspiring his people ''to authentic nationhood'' (21).

Notice, by the way, that the phrase *rich and poor* in the original does not appear in quotation marks in this acceptable version. The phrase is so simple, so commonly used—and so nearly impossible to replace without using many more words—that quotation marks are unnecessary. Here is another acceptable version in which none of the original phrasing is used:

> Harris suggests that Gandhi well knew that rich and poor were affected differently by reverence for the sacred cow but saw this symbol as a means of uniting his people (21).

**REMEMBER:**    **If you are paraphrasing, put the passage into your own words; if you are quoting directly, put the passage in quotation marks.**

## FINISHING THE PAPER

After you've read all the material you feel is necessary to cover your topic thoroughly, gather up your notecards and shuffle them to fit the sections of your outline. If your outline is still hanging fire, now is the time to wrestle it into shape. The actual writing of the paper is the same as writing any other paper, except that you'll incorporate the material from the notecards into your text (either in your own words or through direct quotes) and give credit to the original authors for ideas borrowed and actual passages quoted. The following sections will give you advice on how to handle quotations and documentation (crediting the quotations).

### To Quote or Not to Quote

Never quote directly unless (1) the material is authoritative and convincing evidence in support of your thesis, or (2) the statement is happily phrased, or (3) the idea is controversial and you need to assure your readers that you aren't slanting or misinterpreting the source. You would want, for instance, to quote directly an observation as well-put as this one:

> Bernard Rosenberg defines "pragmatism" as "a distinctly American philosophy whose only failing is that it does not work."

There is no need, however, for the direct quotation in the following sentence:

> The ICC, in an effort to aid the rail industry, has asked for a "federal study of the need and means for preserving a national passenger service."

You could phrase that just as well yourself. But remember, even after you put the statement into your own words, you'll still need to indicate where you got the information.

### Quoting Quotations

Sometimes in your reading you will come across a quotation that says exactly what you have been hoping to find. If the quotation is complete enough to serve your purpose, and if you honestly don't think you would benefit from tracking down the original, then don't bother. Instead, include that quotation in the usual way. But notice that your citation will include "qtd. in" before the source and page number:

> George Cukor once told Scott Fitzgerald, "I've only known two people who eat faster than you and I, and they are both dead now" (qtd. in Latham 39).

> Mark Twain relates that he once knew a Miss Sexton, who pronounced her name "Saxton to make it finer, the nice, kindhearted, smirky, smily dear Christian creature" (qtd. in Wecter 103).

### Working Quotations in Smoothly

If you want your research paper to read smoothly, you must take care in incorporating quotations into your own writing. You must have ready a supply of introductory phrases with which to slide them in gracefully—phrases like "As Quagmire discovered," "Professor Clyde Crashcup notes," and "According to Dr. Dimwit." If you run through the examples in this section on quoting, you will find a generous assortment of these phrases. Borrow them with my blessing.

Notice, please, that the more famous the person, the less likely we are to use Mr., Miss, Mrs., or Ms. in front of the name. "Mr. Milton" sounds quite droll. If the person has a title, you can use it or not, as you think appropriate: Dr. Pasteur or Pasteur, Sir Winston Churchill or Churchill, President Lincoln or Lincoln.

**Introduce Your Quotations**    Most of the time you will introduce a quotation before beginning it, like this:

> As Mark Twain observed, "Heaven for climate, hell for society."*

But you may want to break one up in the middle every so often for variety, this way:

*I have omitted many citations in this book to save space. But remember, you do not have this option in a documented paper. Whenever you quote directly, you *must* cite the source.

"But if thought corrupts language," cautions George Orwell, "language can also corrupt thought."

Or you can make most of the sentence yours and quote only the telling phrases or key ideas of your authority, like this:

Lily B. Campbell considers King Henry's inability to fight "a saintly weakness."

Or this:

The play's effectiveness lies, as E. M. W. Tillyard points out, in "the utter artlessness of the language."

But do introduce your quotations, please. The MLA (Modern Language Association) documentation style suggests identifying the source within the citation immediately following the quotation. But I think that identifying the source before presenting the borrowed material allows your readers a clearer understanding of which ideas are yours and which come from sources.

If you have difficulty introducing your authorities gracefully in the text of your paper, perhaps you are using too many direct quotations.

**Make the Grammar Match**   When you integrate a quotation into your own sentence, you are responsible for making sure that the entire sentence makes sense. You must adjust the way your sentence is worded so that the grammar comes out right. Read your quotations over carefully to be sure they don't end up like this one:

When children are born, their first reactions are "those stimuli which constitute their environment."

"Reactions" are not "stimuli." The sentence should read this way:

When children are born, their first reactions are to "those stimuli which constitute their environment."

What a difference a word makes—the difference here between sense and nonsense. Take particular care when you are adding someone else's words to your own; you get the blame if the words in the quotation do not make sense, because they *did* make sense before you lifted them out of context.

**Use Special Punctuation**   When you write a documented paper, you probably will need to use some rather specialized marks of punctuation: *ellipsis dots* (to show that you have omitted something from a quotation) and *brackets* (to make an editorial comment within a quotation). You will find both of these useful devices discussed fully in the alphabetized "Revising Index," Chapter 8.

## To Cite or Not to Cite

The main purpose of documentation—of citing sources used in a research paper—is to give credit for ideas, information, and actual phrasing that you borrow from other writers. You cite sources in order to be honest and to lend authority to your own writing. You also include citations to enable your readers to find more extensive information than your paper furnishes, in case they become engrossed in your subject and want to read some of your sources in full.

We are all troubled occasionally about when a citation is necessary. I can say with authority that you must include a citation for:

1  All direct quotations
2  All indirect quotations
3  All major ideas that are not your own
4  All essential facts, information, and statistics that are not general knowledge—especially anything controversial

The last category is the one that causes confusion. In general, the sort of information available in an encyclopedia does not need a citation. But statements interpreting, analyzing, or speculating on such information should be documented. If you say that President Warren G. Harding died in office, you do not need a citation because that is a widely known and undisputed fact. If you say that Harding's administration was one of the most corrupt in our history, most people would not feel the need for a citation because authorities agree that the Harding scandals were flagrant and enormous. But if you say that Harding was sexually intimate with a young woman in the White House cloakroom while President of the United States, I strongly suggest that you cite your source. Because such information is not widely known and is also debatable, you need to identify your source so that your readers can judge the reliability of your evidence. Then, too, they might want further enlightenment on the matter, and your citation will lead them to a more complete discussion. Probably it's better to bother your readers with too many citations than to have them question your integrity by having too few.

### Accuracy Is the Aim

After years of being told to be original, to be creative, to think for yourself, you are now going to be told—on this one matter, at least— to fall into line and slavishly follow the authorities. What you might consider a blessed bit of variety will not be appreciated in the slightest. If you put a period after the first citation, put a period after every one. Get the form correct every time, right down to the last comma, colon, and parenthesis.

The information (date, publisher, place of publication) necessary for completing a citation is located on the title page and on the back of the title page of each book. For magazines you usually can find it all on the cover.

### When in Doubt, Use Common Sense

Keep in mind that the purpose of documentation is dual:

**1** To give credit to your sources
**2** To allow your readers to find your sources in case they want further information on the subject

If you are ever in doubt about documentation form (if you are citing something so unusual that you cannot find a similar entry in the samples here), use your common sense and give credit the way you think it logically should be done. Be as consistent as possible with other citations.

## REVISING THE PAPER

Since a research paper requires the incorporation of other people's ideas and the acknowledgment of these sources, you need to take special care in revising.

### Check the Usual Things

1  Be sure the introduction states your thesis.
2  Be sure each paragraph is unified, coherent, and directly related to your thesis.
3  Be sure the transitions between paragraphs are smooth.
4  Be sure your conclusion evaluates the results of your research; if the paper is argumentative, be sure the last sentence is emphatic.

### Check the Special Things

1  Be sure that you have introduced direct quotations gracefully, using the name and, if possible, the occupation of the person quoted.
2  Be sure each citation is accurate.
3  Be sure that paraphrases are in your own words and that the sources are clearly acknowledged.
4  Be sure to underline the titles of books and magazines; put quotation marks around the titles of articles and chapters in books.
5  Be sure that you have written most of the paper yourself; you need to examine, analyze, or explain the material, not just splice together a bunch of quotations and paraphrases.
6  Be sure always to separate quotations with some comment of your own.
7  Be sure to use ellipsis dots if you omit any words from a quotation that your readers would not otherwise know were missing; never leave out anything that alters the meaning of a sentence.
8  Be sure to use square brackets, not parentheses, if you add words or change verb tenses in a quotation.
9  Be sure that you have not relied too heavily on a single source.
10  Be sure to indent long quotations ten spaces—without quotation marks.

Before you work on your final draft, give your entire attention to the following instructions on form.

## Preparing the Final Draft

**1** Provide margins of at least one inch at the top, bottom, and sides.

**2** Double-space throughout.

**3** Do not put the title of your paper in quotation marks.

**4** Insert corrections neatly in ink *above the line* (if allowed by your instructor).

**5** Put page numbers in the upper-right-hand corner. But do not number the title page or the first page of the paper. After the title page and the outline, count all pages in the total as you number. Note correct page numbering on the sample student paper, which follows.

**6** Proofread. You may well be close to exhaustion by the time you finish copying your paper, and the last thing you will feel like doing is rereading the blasted thing. But force yourself. Or force somebody else. But do not skip the proofreading. It would be a shame to allow careless errors to mar an otherwise excellent paper.

## SAMPLE STUDENT RESEARCH PAPER

The following documented essay was written by Kathy M. Donaldson, a student at Illinois State University. Kathy chose to follow the new MLA (Modern Language Association) style commonly used in the humanities. Complete instruction for employing this documentation style follows Kathy's paper.

If you once learned the old MLA style and would feel more comfortable using it, you will find instruction for its use on pages 155–161.

Getting Down to Business with the Liberal Arts


Kathy M. Donaldson


English 145

Professor Susan Day

Getting Down to Business with the Liberal Arts

Prospective graduates in liberal arts fields listen to an accusation that is akin to the sound of nails on a chalkboard from the time they enter the field to the time they receive the sheepskin: "You'll never get a decent job with a liberal arts degree." This liberal arts major is tired of the misbegotten preconceptions of many individuals who view the liberal arts as a luxury that has no value outside the classroom. The business world is currently reporting that a specialized business degree is often not the answer to their administrative employment needs. A number of surveys and articles, produced for and by businesses, report that an overwhelming quantity of technically trained people do not possess the skills needed to guide them to careers in middle and upper management. Experience is still the best teacher, and experience is shining the spotlight on the liberal arts graduates who "are getting offers that rival the stuff of M.B.A.s' dreams" (Byrne 112).

According to William Benton, the outpouring of technically trained graduates is a direct result "of the age of the pat answer" (v). Many students are not choosing their majors on the basis of their interests or their natural abilities. Instead, says Lynne Cheney, business writer for Newsweek, ". . . they are channeling themselves into fields that promise to be profitable: business, engineering, computer science, allied health programs" (7). These fields of study do provide pat answers for their students. However, most of life is not easily reduced to textbook answers, and therein lies the problem. When the answer is not available, the specialized graduates are often trapped because they have not been taught the skills necessary to creatively formulate a solution.

Despite this fact, the trend today is for students to flock to the specialized fields that are currently offering the greatest salary potential. What happens to the specialized graduates when their chosen fields are no longer "hot" and the jobs dwindle? It is difficult, at best, to predict which skills will be demanded years down the road. Therefore, Cheney counsels that ". . . a student's best career preparation is one that emphasizes general understanding and intellectual curiosity: a knowledge of how to learn and the desire to do it. Literature, history, philosophy and the social sciences . . . are the ones traditionally believed to develop such habits of mind" (7).

The surfacing realization that the liberal arts

offer the kind of quality education favorable to business is being reiterated by several top executives who are now voicing their preferences. Arthur F. Oppenheimer, president of Oppenheimer Companies, Inc., asserts that today's management needs the skills of creative and independent thinking, the ability "to make decisions when all the data required to solve the problem are not available; . . . not to rely on quantitative and analytical data, . . . to avoid the obvious and solely subjective. . . . These are all abilities fostered by the liberal arts" (qtd. in Sturman 57–58). In agreement with Mr. Oppenheimer is the president of Chemical Bank, Robert Callander, who claims that ". . . a liberally educated person is still the type of individual needed at the highest levels of corporate life. . . . The technical skills are built upon this base'' (qtd. in Bennett 62–63). General Motors chair, Roger E. Smith, is also in concurrence when he explains in Management Review the valuable role creativity plays in the corporate world. Creativity, he claims, is necessary

> to see relations between things that may seem utterly different, and . . . to connect the seemingly unconnected. The power is quite familiar to people trained to recognize the recurring elements and the common themes in art, literature and history. (36)

Certainly, the importance of creativity in business should not be ignored. However, the top contender among skills necessary to succeed in business is indisputable—effective communication. In a nationwide survey, chief executives ranked verbal communication skills at the top of the list for success in middle and top business positions; these same executives ranked writing skills first by a large

margin in a list of deficiencies reported by business

(Warren 12). A working knowledge of communica-

tion skills is quite often lacking in the specialized

graduate.

> But students of drama, language, litera-
> ture, speech and rhetoric do understand
> what [good communication entails]. They
> learn to arrange their thoughts in logical
> order, and to write and speak clearly,
> economically, and unpretentiously.
> They learn to communicate with a real
> feeling for the flexibility and power of
> language, and with a sensitivity to their
> own purposes and to the needs of their
> audience. (Smith 38)

These corporate leaders exhibit a growing

preference for liberal arts graduates that is filtering

down from the executives to those responsible for

hiring quality people. First Boston Bank, for

example, recently hired graduates for 42 financial

analyst positions. The final tally disclosed that 90 percent were liberal arts graduates (Byrne 114). Liberal arts graduates experience upward mobility after the initial hiring, too. Thirty-eight percent of today's chief executive officers are liberal arts graduates, and the New York Times disclosed that nine of IBM's top thirteen executives are liberal arts majors (Cheney 7).

AT&T has also released some interesting facts about their graduates of the liberal arts in a recently completed study. Their data reveals that:

—Liberal arts graduates enjoyed more mobility than any other group.

—More than twice as many liberal arts graduates made it to senior management than did those with engineering degrees.

## 8

—Liberal arts graduates beat business degree holders in having the best overall records for managerial performance and progress (Byrne 114).

Success stories of liberal arts graduates are often unknown by the general public. Following are the names of well-known figures shown with positions they currently hold or have held in the past. All were educated in liberal arts fields (Cheney 7):

| Name | Position | Degree |
|------|----------|--------|
| Thomas Wayman | Chair, Columbia Broadcasting System | English |
| Cathleen Black | Publisher, USA Today | English |
| William Raspberry | Columnist, Washington Post | History |

| Name | Position | Degree |
|------|----------|--------|
| Tom Brokaw | Anchorman, NBC | Political Science |
| George Schultz | Secretary of State | Economics |
| John Herrington | Secretary of Energy | Economics |
| Donald Hodel | Interior Secretary | Government |
| Elizabeth Dole | Transportation Secretary | Political Science |
| James Baker | Secretary of Treasury | History |
| Ronald Reagan | President | Economics and Sociology |
| William Bennett | Secretary of Education | Philosophy |
| Pat Buchanan | Communications Director | English and Philosophy |
| Donald Regan | Chief of Staff (former head of Merrill Lynch) | English |
| Malcolm Baldrige | Secretary of Commerce | English |

The list could go on and serves to demonstrate that students with a degree in liberal arts are not crippled by their chosen course of study. A liberal arts degree can unlock doors in virtually any facet of life. The Chief Executive Officer of Time, Inc., Dick Munro, states his employment preference with no qualms: "I would personally opt for a liberal arts graduate every time. Almost all the CEOs I know are liberal arts graduates. We still think that liberal arts institutions are putting out the best product" (qtd. in Sturman 58). Thanks to Mr. Munro and other progressive business leaders, liberal arts graduates are indeed being given the opportunity to exercise their diverse skills in the business world and are proving wrong those who said they would never make it.

Works Cited

Bennett, William J. "The Humanities Pay Off."

    Across the Board Apr. 1985: 61–63.

Benton, William. Introduction. Great Ideas from the

    Great Books. By Mortimer J. Adler. New

    York: Washington Square P, 1961. v.

Byrne, John A. "Let's Hear It for Liberal Arts."

    Forbes 1 Jly. 1985: 112+.

Cheney, Lynne V. "Students of Success." Newsweek

    1 Sept. 1986: 7.

Smith, Roger B. "Humanities & Business: The Twain

    Shall Meet—But How?" Management Review

    Apr. 1985: 36–39.

Sturman, Emanuel. "Do Corporations Really Want

Liberal Arts Grads?'' Management Review Sept.

1986: 657–59.

Warren, Russell G.  New Links Between General

Education and Business Careers.  Washington,

DC: Association of American Colleges, 1983. 12.

## THE MLA DOCUMENTATION STYLE

The simplified new MLA documentation style resembles those used in other academic disciplines. It works like this:

**A**   Mention your source (author's last name and page number) within the text of your paper in parentheses, like this:

> One of the great all-time best-sellers, <u>Uncle Tom's Cabin</u>,
>
> sold over 300,000 copies in America and more than 2
>
> million copies worldwide (Wilson 3).

**B**   Your readers can identify this source by consulting your "Works Cited" list at the end of your paper (see items I through N). The entry for the information above would appear like this:

> Wilson, Edmund. <u>Patriotic Gore: Studies in the Literature</u>
>
>     <u>of the American Civil War</u>. New York: Oxford UP,
>
>     1966.

**C**   If you are quoting directly or if you want to stress the authority of the source you are paraphrasing, you may mention the name of the source in your sentence. Then include just the page number (or numbers) at the end in parentheses, like this:

> <u>In Patriotic Gore</u>, Edmund Wilson tells us that Mrs. Stowe
>
> felt "the book had been written by God" (5).

**D**   If you must quote indirectly—something quoted from another source not available to you—indicate this in your parenthetical reference by using "qtd. in" (for "quoted in"). The following example comes from a book written by Donald Johanson and Maitland Edey:

> Richard Leakey's wife, Maeve, told the paleoanthropologist

> David Johanson, "We heard all about your bones on the
>
> radio last night" (qtd. in Johanson and Edey 162).

**E**    If you are using a source written or edited by more than three people, use only the name of the first person listed, followed by "et al." (meaning "and others"):

> Blair et al. observe that the fine arts were almost ignored
>
> by colonial writers (21).

**F**    If you refer to more than one work by the same author, include a shortened title in the citation in your text:

> (Huxley, <u>Brave</u> 138).

**G**    If the author's name is not given, then use a shortened title instead. In your abbreviation, be sure to use at least the first word of the full title to send the reader to the proper alphabetized entry on your "Works Cited" page. The following is a reference to a newspaper article entitled "Ramifications of Baboon Use Expected to Become an Issue":

> The doctor observed that some people objected to the trans-
>
> plant on grounds that were emotional rather than rational
>
> ("Ramifications" A23).

**H**    If you are quoting more than *four* typed lines, you should indent the quotation ten spaces and omit the quotation marks. Cite the page number in parentheses two spaces after the period:

> About Nora in Ibsen's <u>A Doll's House</u>, Liv Ullman writes,
>
>> She says goodbye to everything that is familiar
>>
>> and secure. She does not walk through the door
>>
>> to find somebody else to live with and for; she is

leaving the house more insecure than she ever

realized she could be. But she hopes to find out

who she is and why she is.   (263)

**I**   On your last page, a separate page, alphabetize your "Works Cited" list of all sources mentioned in your paper. Use *hanging indention*: that is, after the first line of each entry, indent the other lines five spaces.
**J**   In your "Works Cited" list, in citing two or more works by the same author, give the name in the first entry only. Thereafter, in place of the name, type three hyphens and a period, skip two spaces, then follow with the usual information. Alphabetize the entries by title:

Lewis, C. S.  The Dark Tower and Other Stories.  Ed. Walter

Hooper.  New York: Harcourt, 1977.

———.  The Screwtape Letters.  New York: Macmillan,

1976.

**K**   Omit any mention of *page* or *pages* or *line* or *lines*: do not even include abbreviations for these terms. Use numbers alone.
**L**   Abbreviate publishers' names. See the list of abbreviations suggested by the MLA on pages 147 through 149.
**M**   Use regular (not roman) numerals throughout. Exception: James I, Elizabeth II. Use *lowercase* roman numerals for citing page numbers from a preface, introduction, or table of contents. You may use roman numerals to indicate act and scene in plays: "In *Hamlet* III.ii, the action shifts. . . ."
**N**   Use raised note numbers for *informational notes* only (i.e., notes containing material pertinent to your discussion but not precisely to the point). Include these content notes at the end of your paper on a separate page just before your "Works Cited" list, and entitle them "Notes."
**O**   If you are writing about literature, you should cite the edition of the novel, play, short story, or poetry collection you are using in an informational note. Thereafter, include the page numbers in parentheses in the text of the paper. The note should read like this:

[1]Joyce Carol Oates, "Accomplished Desires," in

Wheel of Love and Other Stories. Greenwich: Fawcett,

1970: 127. All further references to this work appear in

parentheses in the text.

Your subsequent acknowledgments in the text will be done this way:

Dorie was not consoled, although Mark "slid his big beefy

arms around her and breathed his liquory love into her

face, calling her his darling, his beauty" (129).

Note the placement of the quotation marks—before the parentheses, which are followed by the period. *But* if the quotation is a long one that you need to indent without quotation marks, the period comes *before* the parentheses as shown in item H above.

### Sample Entries for a "Works Cited" List

The following models will help you write "Works Cited" entries for most of but not all the sources you will use. If you use a source not treated in these samples, consult the more extensive list of sample entries found in the new *MLA Handbook* or ask your instructor.

### *Books*

**1**  Book by one author:

Abernathy, Charles F. Civil Rights: Cases and

Materials. St. Paul: West, 1980.

**2**  Two or more books by the same author:

Gould, Stephen Jay. The Mismeasure of Man. New York:

Norton, 1981.

———. The Panda's Thumb: More Reflections in Natural

   History. New York: Norton, 1980.

**3**  Book by two or three authors:

Brusaw, Charles, Gerald J. Alfred, and Walter E. Oliu. The

   Business Writer's Handbook. New York: St.

   Martin's, 1976.

Ciardi, John, and M. Williams. How Does a Poem Mean?

   Rev. ed. Boston: Houghton, 1975.

**4**  Book by more than three authors:

Sheridan, Marion C., et al. The Motion Picture and the

   Teaching of English. New York: Appleton, 1965.

[The phrase "et al." is an abbreviation for "et alii," meaning "and
others."]

**5**  Book by an anonymous author:

Beowulf. Trans. Kevin Crossley-Holland. New York:

   Farrar, 1968.

**6**  Book with an editor:

Zaranka, William, ed. The Brand-X Anthology of Poetry.

   Cambridge: Apple-Wood, 1981.

[For a book with two or more editors, use "eds."]

**7**  Book with an editor and an author:

Shakespeare, William. Shakespeare: Major Plays and the

<u>Sonnets</u>. Ed. G. B. Harrison. New York: Harcourt,

1948.

**8**  Work in a collection or anthology:

Firebaugh, Joseph J. "The Pragmatism of Henry James."

<u>Henry James's Major Novels: Essays in Criticism</u>.

Ed. Lyall Powers. East Lansing: Michigan State P,

1973. 187-201.


Pirandello, Luigi. <u>Six Characters in Search of an Author</u>.

<u>The Norton Anthology of World Masterpieces</u>. Ed.

Maynard Mack et al. 5 ed. 2 vols. New York:

Norton, 1985. 2:1387-1432.

**9**  Work reprinted in a collection or anthology:

Sage, George H. "Sport in American Society: Its Pervasive-

ness and Its Study." <u>Sport and American</u>

<u>Society</u>. 3rd ed. Reading: Addison-Wesley, 1980.

4-15. Rpt. in <u>Physical Activity and the Social</u>

<u>Sciences</u>. Ed. W. Neil Widmeyer. 5th ed. Ithaca:

Movement, 1983. 42-52.

[First give complete data for the earlier publication; then give the reprinted source.]

**10**  Multivolume work:

Blom, Eric, ed. <u>Grove's Dictionary of Music and Musicians</u>.

5th ed. 10 vols. New York: St. Martin's, 1961.

**11**  Reprinted (republished) book:

> Malamud, Bernard. The Natural. 1952. New York: Avon,
>
>    1980.

**12**  Later edition:

> Gibaldi, Joseph, and Walter S. Achtert. MLA Handbook for
>
>    Writers of Research Papers. 2nd ed. New York:
>
>    MLA, 1984.

**13**  Book in translation:

> de Beauvoir, Simone. The Second Sex. Trans. H. M.
>
>    Parshley. New York: Knopf, 1971.

[Alphabetize this entry under *B*.]


*Newspapers*

**14**  Signed newspaper article:

> Krebs, Emilie. "Sewer Backups Called No Problem."
>
>    Pantagraph [Bloomington, IL] 20 Nov. 1985: A3.

[If the city of publication is not apparent from the name of the newspaper give the city and state in brackets after the newspaper's name as shown above.]

> Weiner, Jon. "Vendetta: The Government's Secret War
>
>    Against John Lennon." Chicago Tribune 5 Aug.
>
>    1984, Sec. 3:1.

[Note the difference between "A3" in the first example and "sec. 3:1" in the second. Both refer to section and page, but in the first the pagination appears as "A3" in the newspaper, whereas in the second the section designation is not part of the pagination.]

**15**  Unsigned newspaper article:

> "Minister Found Guilty of Soliciting Murder." New York
>
>    Times 2 Aug. 1984: A12.

**16**  Letter to the editor:

> Kessler, Ralph. "Orwell Defended." Letter. New York
>
>    Times Book Review 15 Dec. 1985: 26.

**17**  Editorial:

> "From Good News to Bad." Editorial. Washington
>
>    Post 16 July 1984: 10.

### *Magazines and Journals*

**18**  Article from a monthly or bimonthly magazine:

> Foulkes, David. "Dreams of Innocence." Psychology
>
>    Today Dec. 1978: 78-88.

> Lawren, Bill. "1990's Designer Beasts." Omni Nov. 1985:
>
>    56-61.

**19**  Article from a weekly or biweekly magazine (signed and unsigned):

> Adler, Jerry. "A Voyager's Close-Up of
>
>    Saturn." Newsweek 7 Sept. 1981: 57-58.

> "Warning: 'Love' for Sale." Newsweek Nov. 1985: 39.

**20**  Article from a magazine with continuous pagination:

> Potvin, Raymond, and Che-Fu Lee. "Multistage Path
>
>    Models of Adolescent Alcohol and Drug Use."
>
>    Journal of Studies on Alcohol 41 (1980): 531-542.

**21**  Article from a magazine that paginates each issue separately or that uses only issue numbers:

> Terkel, Studs. "The Good War: An Oral History of World War
>
>    II." Atlantic 254.1 (July 1984): 45-75.

[That is, volume 254, issue 1.]

### *Other Sources*

**22**  Review (of a book):

> Langer, Elinor. "Life Under Apartheid: The Possible and
>
>    the Real." Rev. of A Revolutionary Woman, by Sheila
>
>    Fugard. Ms. Nov. 1985: 26-27.

**23**  Personal or telephone interview:

> Deau, Jeanne. Personal interview. 12 Mar. 1983.

> Vidal, Gore. Telephone interview. 2 June 1984.

[Treat published interviews like articles, with the person being interviewed as the author.]

**24**  Published letter:

> Tolkien, J. R. R. "To Sam Gamgee." 18 Mar. 1956. Letter
>
>    184 in The Letters of J. R. R. Tolkien. Ed.
>
>    Humphrey Carpenter. Boston: Houghton,
>
>    1981. 244-245.

**25**  Unpublished letter:

> Wharton, Edith.  Letter to William Brownell.  6 Nov. 1907.
>
>> Wharton Archives.  Amherst College, Amherst.
>
> Isherwood, Christopher.  Letter to the author.  24 Apr.
>
>> 1983.

**26**  Anonymous pamphlet:

> How to Help a Friend with a Drinking Problem.  American
>
>> College Health Association, 1984.
>
> Aaron Copland: A Catalogue of His Works.  New York:
>
>> Boosey, n.d.

[The abbreviation "n.d." means "no date given."]

**27**  Article from a specialized dictionary:

> Van Doren, Carl.  "Samuel Langhorne Clemens."  DAB.
>
>> 1958 ed.

[Some commonly used resources, such as the *Dictionary of American Biography*, have accepted abbreviations.]

**28**  Encyclopedia article (signed and unsigned):

> Martin, William R.  "Drug Abuse."  World Book Encyclo-
>
>> pedia.  1983 ed.
>
> "Scapegoat."  Encyclopaedia Britannica: Micropaedia.
>
>> 1979 ed.

[The micropaedia is volumes 1–10 of the *Britannica*.]

**29** Bible:

The Holy Bible. Revised Standard Version. Cleveland:

World, 1962.

The Jerusalem Bible. Trans. Alexander Jones et al.

Garden City: Doubleday, 1966.

[Do not list the Bible unless you use a version other than the King James. Cite chapter and verse in parentheses in the text of your paper this way: (Rom. 12.4–8). Underline only the titles of Bibles other than the King James version.]

**30** Film:

Wyler, William, dir. Wuthering Heights. With Merle

Oberon and Laurence Olivier. Samuel Goldwyn,

1939.

[If you are citing the work of an actor or screenwriter, put that person's name first.]

**31** Lecture:

Albee, Edward. 'A Dream or a Nightmare?'' Illinois State

University Fine Arts Lecture. Normal, 18 Mar. 1979.

*Note:* For any other sources (such as television shows, recordings, works of art), you should remember to include enough information to permit an interested reader to locate your original source. Be sure to arrange this information in a logical fashion, duplicating so far as possible the order and punctuation of the entries above. To be on safe ground, consult your instructor for suggestions about documenting unusual material.

## Standard Abbreviations of Publishers' Names

| | |
|---|---|
| Allyn | Allyn and Bacon, Inc. |
| Appleton | Appleton-Century-Crofts |
| Ballantine | Ballantine Books, Inc. |
| Bantam | Bantam Books, Inc. |
| Basic | Basic Books |
| Bobbs | Bobbs-Merrill Co., Inc. |
| Bowker | R. R. Bowker Co. |
| Cambridge UP | Cambridge University Press |
| Clarendon | Clarendon Press |
| Columbia UP | Columbia University Press |
| Cornell UP | Cornell University Press |
| Crown | Crown Publishers, Inc. |
| Dell | Dell Publishing Co., Inc. |
| Dial | Dial Press, Inc. |
| Dodd | Dodd, Mead, and Co. |
| Doubleday | Doubleday and Co., Inc. |
| Dover | Dover Publications, Inc. |
| Dutton | E. P. Dutton |
| Farrar | Farrar, Straus, and Giroux, Inc. |
| Feminist | Feminist Press |
| Free | Free Press |
| GPO | Government Printing Office |
| Grove | Grove Press, Inc. |
| Harcourt | Harcourt Brace Jovanovich, Inc. |
| Harper | Harper & Row Publishers, Inc. |
| Harvard UP | Harvard University Press |
| Heath | D. C. Heath and Company |
| Holt | Holt, Rinehart and Winston, Inc. |
| Houghton | Houghton Mifflin Company |
| Indiana UP | Indiana University Press |
| Information Please | Information Please Publishing, Inc. |
| Johns Hopkins UP | Johns Hopkins University Press |
| Knopf | Alfred A. Knopf, Inc. |
| Larousse | Librairie Larousse |
| Lippincott | J. B. Lippincott Co. |
| Little | Little, Brown and Company |
| Macmillan | Macmillan Publishing Co., Inc. |
| McGraw | McGraw-Hill, Inc. |

| | |
|---|---|
| MIT P | Massachusetts Institute of Technology Press |
| MLA | Modern Language Association of America |
| Morrow | William Morrow and Company, Inc. |
| NAL | New American Library, Inc. |
| National Geographic Soc. | National Geographic Society |
| NCTE | National Council of Teachers of English |
| NEA | National Education Association |
| New Directions | New Directions Publishing Corporation |
| Norton | W. W. Norton and Co., Inc. |
| Oxford UP | Oxford University Press |
| Penguin | Penguin Books, Inc. |
| Pocket | Pocket Books |
| Prentice | Prentice-Hall, Inc. |
| Princeton UP | Princeton University Press |
| Putnam's | G. P. Putnam's Sons |
| Rand | Rand McNally and Co. |
| Random | Random House, Inc. |
| Ronald | Ronald Press |
| St. Martin's | St. Martin's Press, Inc. |
| Scott | Scott, Foresman and Co. |
| Scribner's | Charles Scribner's Sons |
| Sierra | Sierra Club Books |
| Simon | Simon & Schuster, Inc. |
| State U of New York P | State University of New York Press |
| Straight Arrow | Straight Arrow Publishers, Inc. |
| Swallow | Swallow Press |
| UMI | University Microfilms International |
| U of Chicago P | University of Chicago Press |
| U of Illinois P | University of Illinois Press |
| U of Nebraska P | University of Nebraska Press |
| U of New Mexico P | University of New Mexico Press |
| UP of Florida | University Presses of Florida |
| Viking | Viking Press, Inc. |

| | |
|---|---|
| Warner | Warner Books, Inc. |
| Yale UP | Yale University Press |

**Exercise**                                                                    **7-2**

In order to practice composing entries for a "Works Cited" list, complete an entry for each of the works described below. You need to supply underlining or quotation marks around titles. I'll write the first one for you to show you how.

**1** The author of the book is Charles K. Smith.
The title of the book is Styles and Structures: Alternative Approaches to Student Writing.
It was published in 1974 by W. W. Norton and Co., Inc.

> Smith, Charles K. <u>Styles and Structures: Alternative</u>
>
>   <u>Approaches to Student Writing</u>. New York: Norton,
>
>     1974.

**2** Author: Robin Lakoff
Title of the book: Language and Woman's Place
Published by Harper & Row in New York in 1975

**3** Author: Max Spalter
Title of the article: Five Examples of How to Write a Brechtian Play That Is Not Really Brechtian
Periodical: Educational Theatre
Published in the 2nd issue of 1975 on pages 220 to 235
*Note*: This periodical has continuous page numbering.

**4** Author: Daniel S. Greenberg
Title of the article: Ridding American Politics of Polls
Newspaper: Washington Post
Published on September 16, 1980, in section A, on page 17

**5** Authors: Clyde E. Blocker, Robert H. Plummer, and Richard C. Richardson
Title of the book: The Two-Year College: A Social Synthesis
Published in Englewood Cliffs, New Jersey, by Prentice-Hall in 1965

**6** How would your textbook, *A Crash Course in Composition*, appear in a "Works Cited" list? Include the exact data.

**7** In which order would the publications from 1 to 6 above appear in your list? Write the correct answer.

(a) 5 4 2 6 1 3    (b) 1 2 3 4 5 6    (c) 4 3 6 1 5 2    (d) 6 4 3 5 1 2

## THE APA DOCUMENTATION STYLE FOR THE SOCIAL SCIENCES

You use the APA style this way:

**A** Always mention your source and its date within the text of your paper in parentheses, like this:

> The study reveals that children pass through identifiable
>
> cognitive stages (Piaget, 1954).

**B** Your readers can identify this source by consulting your References list at the end of your paper. The entry for the information above would appear like this:

> Piaget, J. (1954). The construction of reality in the child. New York: Basic Books.

[Note the use of sentence capitalization for titles in the references section.]

**C** If you are quoting directly or if you want to stress the authority of the source you are paraphrasing, you may mention the name of the source in your sentence. Then include just the date in parentheses, like this:

> In Words and Women, Miller and Swift (1976) remind us
>
> that using the plural is a good way to avoid "the built-in
>
> male-as-norm quality English has acquired . . ." (p. 163).

**D**   If you are using a source written or edited by more than two people and fewer than six, cite all authors the first time you refer to the source. For all following references, cite only the surname of the first person listed, followed by "et al." (meaning "and others"):

> Blair et al. (1980) observe that the fine arts were almost
>
> ignored by colonial writers.

When there are only two authors, join their names with an "and" in the text. In parenthetical materials, tables, and reference lists, join the names by an ampersand (&).

> Hale and Sponjer (1972) originated the Do-Look-Learn
>
> theory.

> The Do-Look-Learn theory (Hale & Sponjer, 1972) was
>
> taken seriously by educators.

**E**   If the author's name is not given, then use a shortened title instead. In your abbreviation, be sure to use at least the first word of the full title to send the reader to the proper alphabetized entry in your "References" section. The following is a reference to a newspaper article entitled "Ramifications of Baboon Use Expected to Become an Issue":

> The doctor observed that some people objected to the trans-
>
> plant on grounds that were emotional rather than rational
>
> ("Ramifications," 1979).

**F**   If you are quoting more than *forty* words, begin the quotation on a new line and indent the entire quotation five spaces, but run each line to the usual right margin. Omit the quotation marks. Do not single-space the quotation.

In <u>Language and Woman's Place</u> (1975) Lakoff observes that

> men tend to relegate to women things that are not of concern to them, or do not involve their egos. . . . We might rephrase this point by saying that since women are not expected to make decisions on important matters, such as what kind of job to hold, they are relegated the noncrucial decisions as a sop (p. 9).

**G**　On your last page, a separate page, alphabetize your "References" list of all sources mentioned in your paper. Use *hanging indention:* that is, after the first line of each entry, indent the other lines five spaces.

**H**　In your "References" section, in citing two or more works by the same author, put the earliest work first. When more than one work has been published by the same author during the same year, list them alphabetically, according to name of the book or article and identify them with an a, b, c, etc., following the date:

> Graves, D. (1975). An examination of the writing processes of seven-year-old children. <u>Research in the Teaching of English</u> 9, 227-241.

> Graves, D. (1981a). Writing research for the eighties: What is needed. <u>Language Arts</u>, 58, 197-206.

> Graves, D. (1981b). <u>Writers: Teachers and children at work</u>. Exeter, NH: Heinemann Educational Books.

**I**　Use the following abbreviations: Vol., No., chap., trans., ed., Ed., rev. ed., 2nd ed., p., pp. (meaning Volume, Number, chapter, translated by, edition, Editor, revised edition, second edition, page, and pages). Use official U.S. Postal Service abbreviations for states: IL, NY, TX, etc.

**Sample Entries for a List of "References"**

The following models will help you write entries for your "References" list for most of the sources you will use. If you use a source not treated in these samples, consult the more extensive list of sample entries found in the *Publication Manual of the American Psychological Association* or ask your instructor.

Alphabetize your list by the author's last name. If there is no author given, alphabetize the entry by the title. Use hanging indention; that is, after the first line of each entry indent the other lines five spaces.

### *Books and Journals*

**1**  Book by one author:

Abernathy, C. F. (1980). Civil rights: Cases and materials.

St. Paul: West.

**2**  Two or more books by the same author (list in chronological order):

Gould, S. J. (1980). The mismeasure of man. New York:

Norton.

Gould, S. J. (1981). The panda's thumb: More reflections

on natural history. New York: Norton.

**3**  Book by two or more authors:

Brusaw, C., Alfred, G. & Oliu, W. (1976). The business

writer's handbook. New York: St. Martin's.

Cook, M. & McHenry, R. (1978). Sexual attraction. New

York: Pergamon.

[Note that in your list of references you use the ampersand sign instead of writing "and."]

**4**  Book by a corporate author:

White House Conference on Children and Youth. (1970).

The becoming of education. Washington, D.C.: U.S.

Government Printing Office.

**5**  Book with an editor:

Zaranka, W., Ed. (1981). The brand-X anthology of

poetry. Cambridge: Apple-Wood.

[For a book with two or more editors, use "Eds."]

**6**  Article in a collection or anthology:

Emig, J. (1978). Hand, eye, brain: Some basics in the

writing process. In C. Cooper & L. Odell (Eds.).

Research in composing: Points of departure (pp. 59-

72). Urbana, IL: National Council of Teachers of

English.

**7**  Multivolume work:

Asimov, I. (1960). The intelligent man's guide to science.

(Vols. 1-2). New York: Basic Books.

**8**  Later edition:

Gibaldi, J. & Achtert, W. (1984). MLA handbook for

writers of research papers (2nd ed.). New York:

MLA.

**9** Article from a journal:

> Emig, J. (1977). Writing as a mode of learning. College
>
> Composition and Communication, 28, 122-128.

### Other Sources

**10** Personal or telephone interview, letter, lecture, etc. Not cited in Reference list, only in text citation.

**11** Article from a specialized dictionary or encyclopedia. Treat as an article in a collection (number 6 above).

## THE OLD MLA DOCUMENTATION STYLE

To credit borrowed material using this system, you insert consecutive note numbers (raised a half space above the line) in order to credit a source. That source is then identified with a corresponding number on a page entitled "Notes" or "Endnotes" at the end of the paper. This system would be fairly simple if we never used the same source twice. But, of course, we often do refer to a good source several times in different parts of a paper. Sometimes we quote a couple of ideas in a row from the same author. In order to avoid writing out the complete information each time, the system gives you abbreviated forms which you are expected to use. It works as shown in the following examples.

*First reference to a work:*

> [1]Seymour Savant, Knowledge Is Power (Philadelphia:
>
> Brotherly Love Press, 1960), p. 69.

*Another reference to the same work:* If you have only one author by this name in your bibliography, you simply write the last name, plus the page number, whether other notes have intervened or not:

> [4]Savant, p. 68.

If you've acquired more than one Savant, or if you're using a couple

of books by this particular Savant, you need only distinguish them by
giving a brief title after the last name for repeat entries:

[5]Savant, <u>Knowledge</u>, p. 68.

If you're quoting an unsigned article or pamphlet, you'll have no
author's name for repeat entries. Instead, abbreviate the title and cite
the page number, as shown in footnote 2 below:

[1]"New Places to Look for Presidents," <u>Time</u>, Dec. 15,

1975, p. 19.

[2]"New Places . . . ," p. 20.

**A Minor Complication**  If you're quoting from an introduction,
preface, foreword, or afterword written by someone other than the
author of the main text, cite this writer's name first in the note (but not
in the bibliography). Omit quotation marks around Introd., Pref.,
Foreword, or Afterword, like this:

[1]Hershel Parker, Foreword,  <u>The Confidence Man</u> by

Herman Melville (New York: Norton, 1971), p. ix.

Remember also that brevity in documentation is a virtue. You are
expected to use abbreviated forms and to shorten dates and publisher's
names.

That's about all there is to it, except that different kinds of
materials (books, essays in books, encyclopedias) require different
kinds of citations. The sample entries below should cover all but the
most esoteric sources.

### Sample Notes

**1**  A book with one author:

[1]Seymour Savant, <u>Knowledge Is Power</u> (Philadelphia:

Brotherly Love Press, 1960), p. 69.

If the author's full name is given in the text, you may use only the last name in the note. Repeat the title even if you mentioned it in the text.

**2**   A paperback reprint of an earlier publication:

[2]Frederick Lewis Allen, Only Yesterday (1931, rpt.

New York: Perennial-Harper, 1964), p. 28.

The abbreviation ''rpt'' stands for ''reprinted.''

**3**   A book with two or more authors or editors:

[3]K. L. Knickerbocker and H. Willard Reninger, eds.,

Interpreting Literature, 3rd ed. (New York: Holt, 1965), pp.

78-79.

The abbreviation ''pp.'' stands for ''pages.''

**4**   A work in several volumes:

[4]Albert Bigelow Paine, Mark Twain: A Biography (New

York: Harper, 1912), II, 673.

Note that the abbreviation for page (or pages) is omitted when you use a volume number. This holds true for periodical entries with volume numbers also.

**5**   An essay in a collection, casebook, or critical edition:

[5]William York Tindall, ''The Form of Billy Budd,'' rpt.

in Melville's ''Billy Budd'' and the Critics, ed. William T.

Stafford (Belmont, Calif.: Wadsworth, 1961), p. 126.

**6**   A work in translation:

[6]Eugene Ionesco, Rhinoceros and Other Plays, trans.

Derek Prouse (New York: Grove, 1960), p. 107.

**7**  An anonymous article (magazine):

> [7]"A Beatle Roundup," <u>Newsweek</u>, Sept. 7, 1970, p. 85.

**8**  An anonymous article (newspaper):

> [8]"Smog Group to Consider Tougher Rules," <u>Eugene</u>
>
> (Ore.) <u>Register-Guard</u>, Sept. 13, 1970, Sec. 1, p. 2, col. 3.

**9**  A signed article in a periodical not requiring a volume number (i.e., in a *popular*, rather than a *scholarly*, magazine):

> [9]Tom Wicker, "Nixon's the One--But What?" <u>Playboy</u>,
>
> Oct. 1970, p. 105.

Notice, no comma after the question mark ending the title. Don't stack up punctuation.

**10**  An article in a scholarly periodical requiring a volume number:

> [10]Marcus Smith, "The Wall of Blackness: A Psycholog-
>
> ical Approach to <u>1984</u>," <u>Modern Fiction Studies</u>, 14 (Winter
>
> 1968-69), 425.

**11**  An unsigned encyclopedia article:

> [11]"Abolitionists," <u>Encyclopedia Americana</u>, 1974 ed.

**12**  A signed encyclopedia article:

> [12]T[homas] P[ar]k, "Ecology," <u>Encyclopaedia Britan-</u>
>
> <u>nica</u>, 1968 ed.

**13**  An article from the *Dictionary of American Biography*:

> [13]A[llan] N[evins], "Warren Gamaliel Harding," <u>DAB</u>
>
> (1932).

The entry for an article from the *DNB*, the British *Dictionary of National Biography*, would be done the same way.

**14** An anonymous pamphlet:

> [14]Preparing Your Dissertation for Microfilming (Ann
>
> Arbor, Mich.: University Microfilms, n.d.), p. 3.

The abbreviation "n.d." means there's no date given. Be sure to include this notation; otherwise your readers may think you carelessly omitted the date. If there are no page numbers in your pamphlet, just put a period after the parenthesis.

**15** A reference to the Bible:

> [15]Amos II, 6-7.   or   [15]Amos 2:6-7.

Notice you identify only the book (Amos), the chapter (2), and the verses (6-7). Your readers are expected to recognize the source as the Bible.

**16** A reference to a letter:

In a published collection:

> [16]Twain to James Redpath, Mark Twain's Letters, ed.
>
> A. B. Paine (New York: Harper, 1917), I, 190-91.

An unpublished letter:

> [16]Letter from Wharton to William Brownell, 6 Nov.
>
> 1907, Wharton Archives, Amherst College, Mass.

A personal letter:

> [16]Letter received from Gore Vidal, 2 June 1976.

**17** A personal or telephone interview:

> [17]Personal interview with Ken Kesey, 28 May 1977.
>
> [17]Telephone interview with Joan Didion, 10 April 1977.

**18**   A review, signed or unsigned:

> [18]John Updike, "Who Wants to Know?" rev. of The Dragons of Eden, by Carl Sagan, The New Yorker, 22 Aug. 1977, p. 87.

> [18]Rev. of Ring by Jonathan Yardley, The New Yorker, 12 Sept. 1977, p. 159.

**19**   A lecture:

> [19]Rise Axelrod, "Who Did What with Whom," MLA Convention, Chicago, 30 Dec. 1977.

**20**   A document from ERIC:

> [20]Joseph Lucas, Background for Builders, Curriculum Lab (New Brunswick, N.J.: Rutgers, The State Univ., 1975), p. 6 (ERIC ED 127 459).

## The "Sources Consulted" Section

English instructors now agree that there is no need to include a bibliography with a documented paper since all the information necessary for locating your sources is cited in the notes. But if you have read a number of works that you did not refer to in your paper, you might want to include a "Sources Consulted" page following your "Notes" section. Do not number the entries but *do* alphabetize them. Although the information is basically the same as in your "Notes" entries, the form is quite different, as you can see in this example:

> Kaufman, Sue. Diary of a Mad Housewife. New York: Random House, 1967.

**1** The item is indented backwards: "hanging" instead of regular indention.

**2** The last name is listed first for ease in alphabetizing.

**3** The author's name is followed by a period instead of a comma.

**4** The title is followed by a period instead of a parenthesis or a comma.

**5** No parentheses are used, except to enclose dates for articles in periodicals using volume numbers.

**6** No page numbers are listed for books.

**7** Page numbers for an article or for an essay in a book indicate the length of the selection, i.e., the page on which the piece begins, followed by the page on which it ends: pp. 376–84. [With popular magazines in which articles begin at the front and are continued in the back, the only realistic solution is to give the beginning page numbers and use a plus sign (+) to indicate that there's more at the back.

**8** If you should use two or more books by the same author, don't repeat the author's name. Instead, use a line, followed by a period. Then give the title and the rest of the information as usual:

Savant, Seymour. Knowledge Is Power. Philadelphia:

Brotherly Love Press, 1960.


———. Love and Its Lapses. Philadelphia: Brotherly Love

Press, 1963.

Part Two

# Further Advice for Those Who Need It

# Chapter 8

# Revising Index

Nobody expects you to sit down and read this chapter straight through. You are expected to look up here the entries that cover whatever errors your instructor finds in your writing and correct your paper accordingly. The advice given here applies to current *standard English*, the language used by educated people in our society. While standard English is not necessarily any *better* than the language you may hear at the grocery store or in your local tavern (it may, in fact, be less vigorous and colorful), standard English is the language required of college students and in the business world. I've also included exercises so that you can get some practice on especially knotty problems.

*Abbreviation*   See also *Numbers*.

**1**  If you're writing on a formal level, you'd best not abbreviate any terms, other than the following, which are customary:

  **a**  *Personal titles:* Mr., Ms., Mrs., Dr. Abbreviate doctor only

before the person's name: Dr. Dustbin—*but never* "The dr. removed my appendix."
St. Joan *but:* "My mother has the patience of a saint."

**b**  *Academic degrees:* PhD., M.D., D.V.M., R.N.; or without periods: PhD, MD, DVM, RN

**c**  *Dates or times:* 1000 B.C. or AD 150 (periods are optional here too); 10:00 a.m., 3 p.m., or 10 A.M., 3:00 P.M., *but not* "Sylvester succumbed to intoxication in the early a.m."

**d**  *Places:* Washington, D.C. or DC, the U.S. economy, Boston, MA, *but not* "Ringo flew to the U.S. on a jumbo jet."

**e**  *Organizations:* IRS, FBI, ITT, UNICEF, YWCA. Many organizations are commonly known by their abbreviations (usually written in capital letters without periods). If you're not certain whether your readers will recognize the abbreviation, write the name out the first time you use it, put the initials in parentheses following it, and thereafter use the initials only.

**f**  *Latin expressions:* e.g., (for example); i.e., (that is); etc. (and so forth)—but do not use *etc.* just to avoid thinking of other examples.

**g**  *Citations:* Most documentation styles require abbreviations; consult pages 136 to 149 for information concerning the style of the Modern Language Association.

**2**  Avoid using symbols (%, #, &) except in scientific papers, in which you are expected to use both numerals and symbols.

***Active Voice***   See pages 54–56.

***Adverb/Adjective Confusions***

**1**  Most of the time you can spot an adverb by its customary *-ly* ending which is added to an adjective:

| Adjective | Adverb |
|-----------|--------|
| beautiful | beautifully |
| rapid | rapidly |
| mangy | mangily |

Naturally there are exceptions—adjectives that end in *-ly* such as *sickly*, *earthly*, *homely*, *ghostly*, *holy*, *lively*, *friendly*, *manly*—but these seldom cause difficulty. Also, there are adverbs that don't end in *-ly—now, then, later, there, near, far, very, perhaps*—but hardly anybody messes these up either.

**2**   The trouble stems from choosing the wrong form as a modifier. Remember that in standard usage *adverbs* modify *verbs, adjectives,* and other *adverbs.*

*Standard:*   The car was vibrating badly.

*Faulty:*   The car was vibrating bad.

*Standard:*   The car was moving really rapidly.

*Faulty:*   The car was moving real rapidly.

*Standard:*   The car was badly damaged.

*Faulty:*   The car was damaged bad.

**3**   *Adjectives* modify *nouns* or *pronouns:*

Fido is a frisky pup.

She looks frisky.

**4**   *Adjectives* also follow *linking verbs* (*to be, to feel, to seem, to look, to become, to smell, to sound, to taste*) and refer back to the noun or pronoun subject:

Fido feels bad.

Fido smells bad.

Notice that a verb *expressing action* requires an *adverb* in what appears to be the same construction, but the adverb here modifies the verb:

*subj.*   *vb.*⤺⁀*adv.*

Fido eats messily.

*subj.*     *vb.*⤺⁀*adv.*

Fido scratches frequently.

**5**   Some short adverbs can now be used with or without the *-ly* ending in informal writing:

Drive slowly!     Drive slow!
Yell loudly.      Yell loud.

---

**Exercise**                                                      **8-1**

In the following sentences choose the correct form to use in writing standard English.

1   The candidate talked too (loud, loudly).
2   Onion soup tastes (delicious, deliciously).
3   Sodium nitrite reacts (dangerous, dangerously) in your stomach.
4   Drive (careful, carefully)!
5   Rhinoceroses seldom move very (quick, quickly).

---

### *Agreement (Pronoun and Antecedent)*

**1**   Pronouns should agree in number with their antecedents. Most of the time we have no problem:

Charlene shucked *her* sweater.

Charlene and Susie shucked *their* sweaters.

Neither Charlene nor Susie shucked *her* sweater!

There are some indefinite pronouns that seldom cause difficulty because they can be singular or plural, depending on the construction:

All of my money is gone.

All of my pennies are spent.

Some of this toast is burned.

Some of these peas are tasteless.

**2**  There are a beastly lot of *indefinite* pronouns, many of which *sound* plural but have been decreed grammatically singular:

| | |
|---|---|
| anybody | someone |
| anyone | everyone |
| none | neither |
| no one | either |

Consider, for instance, the logic of these grammatically correct sentences:

Since everyone at the rally spoke Spanish, I addressed him in that language.

Everyone applauded, and I was glad he did.

After everybody folded his paper, the instructor passed among him and collected it.

Robert C. Pooley points out in *The Teaching of English Usage* that grammarians since the eighteenth century have been trying to coerce writers into observing this arbitrary, often illogical, distinction.[1]

Writers—often extremely good writers—have frequently ignored the rule (italics mine):

*Nobody* knows what it is to lose a friend, till *they* have lost him.

—Henry Fielding

I do not mean that I think *anyone* to blame for taking due care of *their* health.

—Joseph Addison

[1](Urbana, Ill.: National Council of Teachers of English, 1946, 1974), pp. 83–87.

If a *person* is born of a gloomy temper, . . . *they* cannot help it.

—Lord Chesterfield

It's enough to drive *anyone* out of *their* senses.

—George Bernard Shaw

*Nobody* likes a mind quicker than *their* own.

—F. Scott Fitzgerald

*Everybody* must develop *their* own standards of morality.

—Dr. Mary Calderone

I firmly believe that the *person* who goes for food stamps does it because *they* are poor.

Sen. Philip Hart

The time has come to use the indefinite pronouns sensibly again, as Fielding and Addison did. Professor Pooley, in summarizing his findings on current usage, reports:

It may be concluded, then, that the indefinite pronouns *everyone, everybody, either, neither,* and so forth, when singular in meaning are referred to by a singular pronoun and when plural in meaning are referred to by a plural pronoun. When the gender is mixed [includes both females and males] or indeterminate [possibly includes both sexes] the plural forms *they, them, their* are frequently used as common gender singulars.[2]

Thus, we may now write in standard English:

*Everyone* should wear *their* crash helmets.

*Neither* of the puppies has *their* eyes open yet.

*None* of those arrested will admit *they* were drinking.

That takes care of what used to be a really troublesome problem with pronoun agreement. But you should realize that there are still

[2]Pooley, p. 87.

plenty of people around who will look askance at this usage. Many people who learned standard English, say, twenty years ago will declare you wrong if you write *everyone* followed by *their*. If you prefer to avoid ruffling such readers, you can simply observe the old rule and consider these pronouns as always singular: *anybody*, *anyone*, *someone*, *everyone*, *none*, *neither*, *either*. Unless you're discussing a group that's entirely female, you'll write:

> *Everyone* should wear *his* crash helmet.

> *Neither* of the informers escaped with *his* life.

> *None* of those arrested will admit *he* was drinking.

There remains, too, the sticky problem of what pronoun to use if your indefinite pronoun is strictly singular in meaning. This dilemma occurs frequently because we are programmed to write in the singular. Many people would write:

> *Each* student must show *his* permit to register.

Just as effectively, you can write:

> *Students* must show *their* permits to register.

Or, if you're fond of the singular, try this:

> *Each* student must show *a* permit to register.

The meaning remains the same and you've included both sexes. Occasionally you may need to write a sentence in which you emphasize the singular:

> *Each* individual must speak *his or her* own mind.

That usage is now quite acceptable in standard English—as long as you don't use the double pronoun very often. I favor writing that sentence this way:

> *Each one of us* must speak *our* own minds.

Try to break the singular habit and cultivate the plural. You can thus solve countless problems automatically.

---

In the following sentences, select one or more words suitable for filling the blank in a nonsexist way. If you can't think of such a word, revise the sentence.

1 Everyone on the plane should fasten _____ seat belts.
2 All the cows were wearing _____ bells.
3 Anyone living outside of town should leave _____ job early to avoid getting _____ car stuck in a snow drift.
4 None of the cats in our house will allow _____ to be picked up.
5 Someone has left _____ car lights on.

---

## *Agreement (Subject and Verb)*

**1** *Agreement in number:* In standard English, subjects and verbs should agree in *number* (singular or plural):

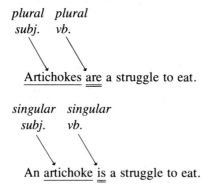

*plural   plural*
*subj.    vb.*

Artichokes are a struggle to eat.

*singular   singular*
*subj.      vb.*

An artichoke is a struggle to eat.

**NOTE:** **The *to be* verb (*am*, *was*, *were*, etc.) agrees with the subject (a noun before the verb), not the predicate nominative (a noun following the *to be* verb).**

         *subj.*    *pr. nom.*

My favorite <u>fruit</u> <u>is</u> peaches.

   *subj.*                   *pr. nom.*

<u>Peaches</u> <u>are</u> my favorite  fruit.

**2**  *Forming plurals:*  There's one bit of confusion about plurals at the outset. With most nouns you add an -*s* to make the plural:

    snips and snails and puppydogs' tails

But with most verbs, the singular form ends in -*s* and you drop it to form the plural.

    One squirrel gnaws; several squirrels gnaw.

**3**  *The intervening modifier menace:*  Sometimes a modifier gets sandwiched in between subject and verb to trip the unwary, like this:

                         *subj.*                  *vb.*

*Wrong:*     The full <u>extent</u> of his crimes <u>have</u> now <u>been</u> <u>discov-ered</u>.

"Crimes have now been discovered" sounds fine, but *crimes* is *not* the subject of that sentence. The actual subject is the singular noun *extent*, with *crimes* serving as object of the preposition *of.* The sentence should read:

                         *subj.*                  *vb.*

*Right:*     The full <u>extent</u> of his crimes <u>has</u>  now <u>been</u> <u>discovered</u>.

Here are more correct examples of sentences with intervening modifiers:

          *subj.*

The <u>boredom</u> of minding children, cleaning floors, washing

                                  *vb.*

dishes, and cooking meals <u>has</u> <u>driven</u> many women to drink.

    *subj.*

<u>Pictures</u> showing nude women and men having sexual contact

*vb.*

<u>are</u> shocking.

*subj.*                          *vb.*

<u>Books</u> full of adventure <u>are</u> what Lucy likes.

**4** *The compound subject syndrome:* We all know that where two singular subjects are connected by *and*, we need a plural verb:

1          +          1          =          *plural*

The <u>pitcher</u> and the <u>catcher</u> <u>are</u> both big drinkers.

But sometimes we complicate matters by connecting singular subjects with *correlative conjunctions* (*not . . . but, not only . . . but also,* neither *. . . nor, either . . . or*) instead of *and.* Then the verb should be singular, although the idea may still come out plural:

Not only the pitcher but the catcher also is sloshed.

Neither the pitcher nor the catcher is sober.

Either the pitcher or the catcher is drunk.

When you use compound *plural* subjects connected by *or*, the verb should be plural:

<u>Fleas</u> or <u>ticks</u> <u>are</u> unwelcome.

If one subject is plural and the other singular, the verb agrees with the subject closest to it:

<u>Leather</u> or <u>hubcaps</u> <u>remind</u> me of you.

<u>Hubcaps</u> or <u>leather</u> <u>reminds</u> me of you.

**WARNING:**     **Some constructions appear compound but really aren't. Singular subjects followed by words like *with, like, along with, as well as, no less than, including, besides* are still singular because these words are prepositions, not coordinating conjunctions. The *idea* in the sentence may be distinctly plural, but the subject and verb remain singular.**

My cat, as well as my parakeet, is lost.

Seymour, together with his St. Bernard, his pet alligator, and his piranha fish, is moving in with us.

Claudia, no less than Clyde, is responsible for this outrage.

**5** *The verb-subject variation:* We don't always follow the usual subject-followed-by-verb sentence pattern. Always be sure of your grammatical subject and make the verb agree:

*vb.*        *subj.*   *vb.*

Where have all the flowers gone?

If the sentence is longer, you may have trouble:

> *Wrong:*     Where has all the hope, gaiety, yearning, and excitement gone?

The adverb *where* can never be the subject of a sentence, so you must look further. The actual subject is compound: "hope, gaiety, yearning, and excitement," which means the verb should be *plural*:

> *Right:*      Where have all the hope, gaiety, yearning, and excitement gone?

We often invert subject and verb for stylistic reasons:

> *Right:*      In poverty, unjustice, and discrimination lies the cause of Juan's bitterness.

> *Right:*      Here are my friend Seymour and his cousin Selma.

Like the adverbs *here* and *where*, the word *there* often poses alluringly at the beginning of a sentence, looking for all the world like the subject. Do not be deceived. *There* can never be the subject; it's either an adverb or an *expletive* (a filler word that allows variety in sentence patterns). So before you automatically slide in a singular verb after *there*, find out what the subject really is:

> *Right:*  There <u>is</u> great <u>hope</u> for peace today.
>
> *Right:*  There <u>are</u> two great <u>hopes</u> for peace today.

The pronoun *it* can also be an expletive, but unlike *there*, it can be the subject of a sentence and always takes a singular verb, even when functioning as an expletive; thus, it causes no problem:

> *Right:*  It <u>is</u> a mile to the nearest phone.
>
> *Right:*  It <u>is</u> miles to the nearest phone.

**6** *The collective noun option:* Some words in the language (like *group, staff, family, committee, company, jury*) are not decreed singular or plural. They can be either, depending upon the context. To suggest that the members are functioning together as a single unit, you can write:

The office <u>staff</u> <u>is</u> <u>working</u> on the problem.

Or to suggest that individual members are functioning separately within the group, you can write:

The office <u>staff</u> <u>are</u> <u>debating</u> that proposal.

---

**Exercise**                 **8-3**

In the following sentences, choose the correct word.

1  There (is/are) Moose and Lenin, scratching furiously.
2  Where (has/have) the toothpaste and the hairbrush gone?
3  Not only Moose but Lenin also (has/have) fleas.
4  Bananas and peanut butter (make/makes) a tasty sandwich.
5  Caffeine or cigarettes, in quantity, (cause/causes) damage to the body.
6  Cigarettes or caffeine, in quantity, (cause/causes) damage to the body.
7  The impact of these statistics (has/have) not yet been fully analyzed.

**8**  Movies packed with violence (is/are) still a favorite with the public.
**9**  In great poetry (lie/lies) many great truths.
**10**  The jury (is/are) in disagreement about the verdict.

---

### Analogy

An *analogy* is a form of comparison, either brief or extended. A brief analogy will be a metaphor or simile. An extended analogy provides a more thorough comparison and can be a means of organizing a paragraph, perhaps even a whole essay. You use something familiar to explain something unfamiliar. Geologists, for instance, often describe the structure of the earth's crust by comparing the strata to the layers of an onion. Sometimes writers use analogy in an attempt to persuade, as advocates of legalizing marijuana do when they argue that the present laws are as ineffective as the prohibition laws were in the twenties.

**Antecedent**  See *Agreement* (*pronoun* and *antecedent*).

### Appositive

An *appositive* is a word or phrase following a noun that renames or describes it. Appositives need commas both before and after:

> Spiny Norman, a huge hedgehog, appears on "Monty Python," a zany television series.

See also pronouns as appositives under *Case of Pronouns*, section 3.

### Apostrophe

**1**  The apostrophe signals possession (except for the possessive pronouns, which don't need one: *ours*, *yours*, *its*, *theirs*):

> Clarence's kittens
>
> the Joneses' junk
>
> Yeats' yearnings

**2**   An apostrophe signals that some letters (or numbers) have been left out in contractions:

> we've (for *we have*)
>
> something's (for *something has* or *something is*)
>
> mustn't (for *must not*)
>
> class of '75 (for *class of 1975*)
>
> o'clock (for *of the clock*)

The chief confusion concerning apostrophes occurs with *its* and *it's*. The context of a sentence usually reveals which one you intended, but you'll mislead your readers if you carelessly choose the wrong one. So pay attention. It's easy really. Use the apostrophe only for the contraction: *It's* = it is or it has. If you use the apostrophe to form the possessive of *it* and write:

> That dumb dog chomped it's own tail.

you've really said:

> That dumb dog chomped it is own tail.

or

> That dumb dog chomped it has own tail.

And your readers may wonder about you as well as the dog. Make a mental note to check every *its* and *it's* when you proofread if you're at all careless about apostrophes.

**REMEMBER:**     **its** = *of it* (possessive:   **The dog chomped its tail.**)

**it's** = *it is* or *it has* (contraction:   **It's not an intelligent dog.**)

**3**  An apostrophe is often optional in forming the plural of numbers, titles, letters, and words used as words:

> Clyde rolled these consecutive 7's [or 7s]. *But:* Clyde rolled three consecutive sevens.

> The 1970's [or 1970s] proved quieter than the 60's [or 60s].

> We hired two new Ph.D.'s [or PhD's].

> Seymour makes straight A's.

> Those two *and's* [or *ands*] are ineffective.

> You're learning the *dos* and *don'ts* of English usage.

**Exercise**                                                       8-4

Choose the correct word in the following sentences.
1  The (Cox's, Coxes) will be gone for two weeks.
2  That donkey is not known for (it's, its) docility.
3  The (begonias', begonias) finished blooming.
4  Some lucky (dogs', dogs) houses are as warm as toast.
5  Mind your (ps and qs, p's and q's).

*Balanced Sentence*  See pages 63 to 66.

*Brackets*

Writers use brackets as a signal for readers in the following ways.

**1**  *To change verb tenses in a quotation:* Usually it's necessary to adjust your phrasing to suit a quotation, but if the quotation is past tense and you're writing in present tense (or vice versa), it's easier to change the verb in the quotation than to rewrite your paper. If you want to make a past-tense quotation about H. L. Mencken fit your present-tense essay, do it as shown in the following example.

*Original in past tense:*

> He defended prostitution, vivisection, Sunday sports, alcohol, and war.[3]

*Changed to present tense:*

> He defend[s] prostitution, vivisection, Sunday sports, alcohol, and war.[3]

**2**  *To clarify any word in a quotation:*

> In those days [the early 1940s] until the postwar repression set in, the [Communist] Party was a strange mixture of openness and secrecy.[4]

**3**  *To enclose* sic*:* When you quote a passage that contains an error, you are expected to copy the error. The word *sic* is Latin and means "thus." It means, "Honest, it really was written that way."

> The correspondent, as he rowed, looked down as [sic] the two men sleeping underfoot.[5]

**4**  *To enclose parenthetical material that is already within parentheses:* Use brackets this way only if you can't avoid it. It's most likely to happen in a scholarly note, like this one:

> (For an informed appraisal of her relationship with the Rev. Mr. Wadsworth, see Richard B. Sewall, *The Life of Emily Dickinson* [New York: Farrar, Straus, and Giroux, 1974], II, 444–462.)

You may not have keys for brackets on your typewriter. Do *not* substitute parentheses. If you use parentheses, your readers will assume that the material appeared in the original quotation and may become either hopelessly confused or endlessly annoyed. All you need to do is

---

[3]William Manchester, *H. L. Mencken, Disturber of the Peace* (New York: Collier, 1962): 79.

[4]Jessica Mitford, *A Fine Old Conflict* (New York: Knopf, 1977): 67.

[5]Stephen Crane, *The Red Badge of Courage* and *Selected Prose and Poetry*, ed. William M. Gibson, 3d ed. (New York: Holt, Rinehart and Winston, 1950): 285.

skip two spaces as you type; then write in the brackets later with a pen. Or you can make brackets with the slash and underscore keys, like this:

$$\sqsubset \quad \sqsupset$$

## Capitalization

**1** Begin each sentence with a capital letter, including sentences you quote:

> Mark Twain observed that "It's a difference of opinion that makes a horse race."

**2** Begin each line of poetry with a capital letter if the poet has used capitals:

> Candy
> Is dandy
> But liquor
> Is quicker.
>
> —Ogden Nash

> God comes in like a landlord
> and flashes on his brassy lamp.
>
> —Anne Sexton

**3** Always capitalize the pronoun *I*.

**4** Use caution in capitalizing words to express emphasis or personification (Truth, Justice, Beauty), unless you're writing poetry.

**5** Capitalize proper nouns—the names of specific persons, places, historical events and periods, organizations, races, languages, teams, and deities.

| Lowercase | Capitalized |
|---|---|
| the town square | Washington Square |
| go to the city | go to Boston |

| Lowercase | Capitalized |
|---|---|
| our club secretary | the Secretary of State |
| traveling east | visiting the Far East |
| a historical document | the Monroe Doctrine |
| reading medieval history | studying the Middle Ages |
| taking Latin, chemistry, and math | Latin 100, Chemistry 60, Math 240 |
| an industrial town | the Industrial Revolution |
| a political organization | Common Cause |
| an ethnic group | the American Indian |
| our favorite team | the Galveston Gophers |
| buttered toast | French toast |
| the Greek gods | Buddha, Allah, Zeus |

**6**  Most people capitalize pronouns referring to the Christian God or Jesus:

Our Father, Who art in heaven, hallowed be Thy name . . . In His name, Amen.

**7**  When in doubt, consult your dictionary. If the word is capitalized in the dictionary entry, you should always capitalize it. If you find a usage label, like "often cap.," or "usually cap.," use your own judgment. Occasionally a word will acquire a different meaning if capitalized:

Abraham Lincoln was a great democrat.

Lyndon Johnson was a lifelong Democrat.

The Pope is Catholic.

Carla's taste is catholic (all-encompassing).

**8**  Capitalize the *first* and *last* words of titles; omit capitals on articles, conjunctions, and prepositions of fewer than five letters:

*Pride and Prejudice*

*Gone with the Wind*

*Shakespeare Without Tears*

*Been Down So Long It Seems like Up to Me*

*One Flew Over the Cuckoo's Nest*

Always capitalize the first word following the colon in a title:

*Problems of Urban Renewal: A Reconsideration*

### Case of Pronouns

**1** Although nouns don't change form to show case when they move from being subjects to objects, pronouns do. We can write:

Martha resembles my sister.

My sister resembles Martha.

But with pronouns, alas, we must use a different form for subjects and objects:

*She* resembles my sister.

My sister resembles *her.*

The case forms are easy:

| Subjective | Objective | Possessive |
|---|---|---|
| I | me | mine |
| he | him | his |
| she | her | hers |
| you | you | yours |
| it | it | its |
| we | us | ours |
| they | them | theirs |
| who | whom | whose |
| whoever | whomever | whosever |

Most of the time the possessives give no trouble at all, except for the confusion of the possessive *its* with the contraction *it's* (see *Apostrophe*, section 2). But problems do come up like the ones in the entries which follow.

**2**   *When the subject or object is compound:*

*Faulty:*         Seymour and *me* went to a lecture.

*Preferred:*      Seymour and *I* went to a lecture.

*Faulty:*       Martha sat with Seymour and *I*.

*Preferred:*      Martha sat with Seymour and *me*.

If you're in doubt about which pronoun to choose, drop the noun momentarily and see how the pronoun sounds alone:

*I* went?    or    *me* went?

Martha sat with *me?*    or    Martha sat with *I?*

Your ear will tell you that "me went" and "sat with I" are not standard constructions.

Remember that although prepositions are usually short words (like *in*, *on*, *at*, *by*, *for*), a few are deceptively long (like *through*, *beside*, *among*, *underneath*, *between*). Long or short, prepositions always take the objective pronoun:

between Clyde and *me*

among Clyde, Martha, and *me*

beside Martha and *me*

**3**  *When pronouns are used as appositives:*

*Faulty:*       *Us* cat lovers are slaves to our pets.

*Preferred:*      *We* cat lovers are slaves to our pets.

*Faulty:*       Spring is a delight for *we* hedonists.

*Preferred:*      Spring is a delight for *us* hedonists.

Once more, if you're in doubt about which pronoun to choose, drop the noun and your ear will guide you: "*We* are slaves to our pets," not "*Us* are slaves to our pets"; "Spring is a delight for *us*," not "Spring is a delight for *we*."

**4** *When pronouns are used in comparisons:*

> *Faulty:* Demon rum is stronger than *me*.
>
> *Preferred:* Demon rum is stronger than *I*.

These comparisons are incomplete (or elliptical). If you finish the statement—at least in your mind—you'll eliminate any problem. You're not likely to write, "Demon rum is stronger than *me* am." Naturally, "stronger than *I* am" is standard English. How about "Henrietta's husband is ten years younger than *her*"? Younger than *her* is? No, younger than *she* is.

**5** *When the choice is between* who *and* whom: Colloquial usage now allows *who* in all oral constructions because when we begin a sentence in conversation, we don't always know how it's going to come out.

But in writing you can always see how your sentence comes out, so you need to know whether to use *who* or *whom*. When the choice occurs in midsentence you can fall back on substitution. Replace the prospective *who* or *whom* with *she* or *her* in the following sentence, and your ear will tell you whether to choose the subjective or objective form:

> Kate Chopin was a superb writer (who/whom) literary critics have neglected until recently.

Ask yourself,

> Critics have neglected *she?*

or

> Critics have neglected *her?*

We'd all choose *her*, naturally. Since *her* is objective, the sentence needs the objective *whom:*

> Kate Chopin was a superb writer *whom* literary critics have neglected until recently.

**6** There's also a sneaky way to avoid the choice. If you're writing an exam and haven't time to think, try using *that:*

> Kate Chopin was a superb writer *that* literary critics have neglected until recently.

Although many people still find this usage distasteful, it is now standard English. But don't ever substitute *which* for *who* or *whom.* Standard usage still does not allow *which* to refer to people.

| | |
|---|---|
| *Preferred:* | the woman *whom* I adore |
| *Acceptable:* | the woman *that* I adore |
| *Faulty:* | the woman *which* I adore |

---

**Exercise**                                              **8-5**

Choose the correct pronoun in each sentence.

**1** You can't win if you run against (she/her) and Clyde.
**2** At the next meeting Sherman and (I/me) are going to present a modern morality play.
**3** For too long (we/us) women have been denied equality.
**4** Monty Python's Flying Circus is the group on (whom/who/which) I base all hope for humor on television.
**5** (Who/Whom) is going to deliver the keynote address?
**6** You'll never persuade the people (who/whom/that) you need the most to go along with your proposal.
**7** The very person (who/whom/that) you're trying to help is the least likely to accept your plan.
**8** If you'll agree to see us tomorrow, Seymour and (I/me) will go home now.
**9** Stanley and (I/me) are planning to become transcendentalists.
**10** The public should be spared commercials (who/whom/that/which) are an insult to our intelligence.

*Clause*   See page 58.

*Cliché*   See page 86.

*Coherence*   See pages 46 to 51.

*Collective Noun*   See *Agreement* (*Subject and Verb*), section 6.

### Colon

**1**   Use a colon to introduce lists of things: items in a series which can be single words, phrases, or subordinate clauses.

> Joe-kitty sometimes catches small animals: birds, snakes, moles, and mice.

> It is by the goodness of God that in our country we have those three unspeakably good things: freedom of speech, freedom of conscience, and the prudence never to practice either of them.

—Mark Twain

**2**   Use a colon to connect two independent clauses when the second enlarges on or explains the first:

> The students had an inspired idea: they would publish an underground newspaper.

> Only later did the truth come out: Clyde had gambled away his inheritance, embezzled the company funds, and skipped town with the loot.

If the second clause poses a question, begin with a capital letter.

> The main question is this: What are we going to do about the shortage of funds?

**3** Formal usage requires a colon following a complete sentence, like this:

> My favorite animals are the following: lions, tigers, aardvarks, and hippopotamuses.

Many writers presently will insert a colon without completing the first independent clause. This usage is widely gaining acceptance.

> *Informal:*     My favorite animals are: lions, tigers, aardvarks, and hippopotamuses.

**4** Use a colon (or a comma) to introduce a direct quotation:

> As Emerson observes: "Travel is a fool's paradise."

**5** Use a colon to separate numerical elements:

> Time: 9:35
>
> Biblical chapter and verses: Revelations 3:7–16 *or*
>                                           Revelations III:7–16
>
> Act and scene: 3:2 *or* III:2
>
> Act, scene, and verse: 4:3:23–27 (*or* IV, iii, 23–27)

**6** Use a colon after the salutation of a business letter:

> Dear Mr. Shuttlecock:
> Dear Service Manager:

**7** Use a colon between the title and subtitle of a book or article:

> *American Humor: A Study in the National Character*
>
> "The Money Motif: Economic Implications in *Huck Finn*"

**NOTE:**     **When typing, usually leave one space after colons, but no space in biblical references, between hours and**

> **minutes, and between volume and page numbers in some endnote styles (5:47–49). Leave two spaces after a colon that separates two complete sentences.**

*Comma*   See also *Comma Splice*.

**1**   Use commas to set off nonessential modifiers. A word, phrase, or clause that interrupts the normal flow of the sentence without changing the meaning is nonessential or nonrestrictive. You need a comma both *before* and *after* the interrupter:

> Clarence, our cat, surprised us with three kittens.
>
> My father, who leads a sheltered life, took a dim view of my being arrested.
>
> My mother, however, saw the injustice involved.

**2**   Do not use commas around essential (or *restrictive*) modifiers:

> *Restrictive:*        All students who can't swim must wear life jackets on the canoe outing.
>
> *Nonrestrictive:*   Melvin, who can't swim, must wear a life jacket on the canoe outing.

Notice that "who can't swim" is essential to the meaning of the first example (it *restricts* the subject) but can easily be left out in the second without changing the basic meaning. Thus in the second sentence the modifier "who can't swim" is nonessential and is set off by commas. But commas around "who can't swim" in the first sentence would mislead readers. Here's another example:

> *Restrictive:*        Reservations which are not accompanied by checks will be ignored.
>
> *Nonrestrictive:*   Reservations, which may be submitted either by mail or by phone, will be promptly acknowledged.

**3**  Do not carelessly allow a *single* comma to separate subject from verb or verb from its complement:

*Wrong:*    Minnie, being unsure of the path stopped suddenly.

*Right:*    Minnie, being unsure of the path, stopped suddenly.

*Wrong:*    I grabbed, without looking the wrong jacket.

*Right:*    I grabbed, without looking, the wrong jacket.

**4**  Use a comma after any longish introductory element (like a dependent clause or a long phrase) to make the sentence easier to read:

Before you complete your plans for vacationing in the Bahamas, you should make plane reservations.

After all the trouble of sneaking into the movie, Seymour didn't like the film.

Even though commas following introductory elements are optional, use a comma if your sentence would be more difficult to read without one.

**5**  A comma precedes a coordinating conjunction (*and, but, or, for, nor, yet, so*) that connects two complete sentences (independent clauses):

Myrtle splashed and swam in the pool, but Marvin only sunned himself and looked bored.

Notice, there are three coordinating conjunctions in that example, but a comma precedes only one of them. The *and*'s connect compound verbs (splashed *and* swam, sunned *and* looked), not whole sentences the way the *but* does. Thus, a comma before a coordinating conjunction signals your readers that another complete sentence is coming up, not just a compound subject or object. Here are two more examples:

Several women's rights groups are active today, yet some housewives oppose them.

Clyde went to the library, so he may well be lost in the stacks.

**6**   Use a comma to separate two independent clauses if they are *short* and *parallel in structure*. Otherwise, you should use a semicolon.

> Heaven for climate, hell for society.
>
> —Mark Twain

> It was the best of times, it was the worst of times. . . .
>
> —Charles Dickens

**7**   Use a comma before a phrase or clause tacked on at the end of a sentence:

> The universal brotherhood of man is our most precious possession, what there is of it.
>
> —Mark Twain

> I just failed another math exam, thanks to Rob's help at the local tavern.

**NOTE:**      **You can use a dash instead of a comma for greater emphasis.**

> I just failed another math exam—thanks to Rob's help at the local tavern.

**8**   Use a comma to separate a direct quotation from your own words introducing it—if you quote a complete sentence:

> F. L. Lucas observes, "Most style is not honest enough."

Omit the comma if you introduce the quotation with *that* or if you quote only a part of a sentence:

> F. L. Lucas observes that "Most style is not honest enough."

> F. L. Lucas observes that in writing we are often "not honest enough."

If your introduction interrupts the quotation (as sometimes it should, for variety), you need to set off your own words with commas as you would any other interrupter:

> "Most style," observes F. L. Lucas, "is not honest enough."

**9**  Use commas to set off nouns of direct address and other purely introductory or transitional expressions:

*Direct address:*

Dr. Strangelove, your proposal boggles the mind.

Your proposal, Dr. Strangelove, boggles the mind.

Your proposal boggles the mind, Dr. Strangelove.

*Introductory and transitional words:*

Well, anywhere you go, there you are.

My, how the child has grown.

In the first place, we must clean up the rivers.

We must, however, consider one thing first.

We must first consider one thing, however.

**10**  Use commas to separate elements in series:

> Gertie ordered tomato juice, bacon and eggs, pancakes, and coffee with cream.

> Some of the old moral values need to be revived: love, pity, compassion, honesty.

For the first sentence above, the comma before *and* is now optional. Here's another option: In the second sentence, try leaving out the commas and replacing them with *and's*. You gain emphasis this way, but don't try it too often.

> Some of the old moral values need to be revived: love and pity and compassion and honesty.

**11**   Use commas to separate numerals and place names and to set off names of people from titles, so they don't clump up in confusion:

> Eudora, who was born November 15, 1950, in Denver, Colorado, moved to Dallas, Texas, before she was old enough to ski.

> You may write to Laverne at 375 Fairview Avenue, Arlington, TX 20036.

> Arthur Schlesinger, Jr., writes intelligently and persuasively. Or: Arthur Schlesinger, Jr. writes intelligently and persuasively.

> The committee chose Lola Lopez, attorney-at-law, to present their case.

> See also *No Punctuation Necessary* for advice about where *not* to use a comma.

**Exercise**                                                    **8-6**

Try your hand at putting commas in the following sentences, if needed.

1   Your new hairstyle is stunning Seymour.
2   Oh I'll finish the job all right but it won't be because you inspired me.
3   My point however must not be misunderstood.
4   In the first place Heathcliff should never have taken the job.
5   Heathcliff should never have taken the job in the first place.
6   Although Irving takes his studies seriously he still flunks math regularly.
7   I said you made a slight miscalculation not a mistake.
8   The tall willowy red-haired girl with the short squinty-eyed bare-footed boyfriend is Jocasta.
9   Anyone who wants the most from a college education must study hard.
10  He intends to help you not hinder you.
11  The principal without a shred of evidence accused Leonard of inciting the riot.
12  If you go out please get me some cheese crackers pickles and a case of cola.
13  ''Whatever you do'' begged Florence ''don't tell Fred.''
14  Clarence had a fearful time talking his way out of that scrape yet two days later he was back in trouble again.

**15**  Barbara's new address is 1802 Country Club Place Los Angeles CA
    90029.

_____

### *Comma Splice*

A comma splice (or *comma fault or comma blunder*) occurs when a
comma is used to join ("splice") two independent clauses together,
instead of the necessary semicolon or colon.

**1**  Use a semicolon or possibly a colon—*not a comma*—to separate
closely related independent clauses. These sentences are correctly
punctuated:

>  Moose-kitty has been listless all day; he appears to have a cold.

>  It's tough to tell when the cat is sick; he just lies around all day
>  anyway.

>  Tonight he skipped dinner; Moose must be sick if he misses a
>  meal.

If you end up with comma splices, you're probably not paying attention to the structure of your sentences. You're writing complete
sentences (independent clauses) without realizing it.

**2**  There's another devilish complication, though, that can produce
comma splices. Conjunctive adverbs—transitional words like *indeed,
therefore, nevertheless, however*—sound for all the world like coordinating conjunctions, but they are not. They cannot connect two
independent clauses with only a comma the way coordinating conjunctions can. The solution to this seemingly baffling difficulty is to
memorize the coordinating conjunctions: *and, but, or, for, nor, yet,
so.* Then all you have to do is remember that all those other words that
sound like pure conjunctions really aren't; hence with the others you
need a semicolon:

>  It's tough to tell when the cat is sick; indeed, he just lies around
>  all day anyway.

**3** One final word of warning: Try not to confuse the conjunctive adverbs (listed on page 224) with subordinating conjunctions (listed on page 203). A subordinating conjunction at the beginning of a clause produces a *dependent*, not an independent, clause. Thus, you don't need a semicolon in the following sentence because there's only one independent clause:

> It's tough to tell when the cat is sick, because he just lies around all day anyway.

If you know you have difficulty with comma splices, slip a bookmark into your textbook to mark the list at page 224, and another at page 203. Get into the habit of checking your punctuation when you revise.

**4** *Remember* that independent clauses (except short, balanced ones) must be separated by something stronger than a comma. You have all these options:

**a**  *Use a semicolon:*

> Moose-kitty feels better today; he's outside chasing the neighbor's dog.

**b**  *Use a period:*

> Moose-kitty feels better today. He's outside chasing the neighbor's dog.

**c**  *Use subordination to eliminate one independent clause:*

> Moose-kitty apparently feels better today, since he's out chasing the neighbor's dog.

**d**  *Use a comma plus a coordinating conjunction:*

> Moose-kitty feels better today, so he's outside chasing the neighbor's dog.

**e**  *Use a semicolon plus a conjunctive adverb:*

> Moose-kitty feels better today; indeed, he's out chasing the neighbor's dog.

**Exercise**                                              **8-7**

Correct any comma splices in the following sentences. Just to increase the challenge, I've included one that is already correct.

1   We just passed Clark Kent, he was changing his clothes in a telephone booth.
2   Doris says she doesn't want to live on a cannibal isle, she'd be bored.
3   Once a week I go out into the country and fill my lungs with clean air, this outing gives me a chance to remember what breathing used to be like.
4   Henrietta spent a grim half-hour shampooing Bowser to get rid of fleas, Bowser probably preferred to keep them.
5   Hunched over her typewriter, Flossie doggedly pecks out her term paper, it isn't even due until Monday.
6   Clyde complains that his history class offers little intellectual challenge, yet he never even reads the textbook.
7   This paper is due at nine o'clock in the morning, thus you'll have to go to the movies without me.
8   You can't control your temper, Throckmorton, you shouldn't be teaching a Carnegie course.
9   Seymour's a polite young man, as far as I know, he never swears.
10  My opinion of Orville is not high, because he has a closed mind, I doubt that he'll be a good teacher.

## Comparisons, Incomplete or Illogical

1   If you're going to draw a comparison, be sure that you mention at least two things being compared:

| | |
|---|---|
| *Incomplete:* | Seymour has the nicest manners. |
| *Improved:* | Seymour has the nicest manners of anyone I know. |
| *Incomplete:* | Eloise has fewer inhibitions. |
| *Improved:* | Eloise has fewer inhibitions now that she's Maybelle's roommate. |
| *Improved:* | Eloise has fewer inhibitions than Maybelle. |

**2** Be sure that the second element of your comparison is not ambiguous or vague. See *Predication, Faulty.*
**3** Do not compare words that denote absolutes, like *unique, omnipotent, infinite, perfect, outstanding.*

> *Illogical:* Russell came up with a very unique design.
>
> *Improved:* Russell came up with a unique design.

**Conciseness** See pages 78 to 79.

**Concrete Examples** See pages 45 to 46.

**Confused Sentence** See pages 68 to 70.

**Conjunctions, Coordinating** See *Comma Splice,* section 2.

**Conjunctions, Correlative** See *Agreement (Subject and Verb),* section 4.

**Conjunctions, Subordinating** See *Comma Splice,* section 2, and *Comma,* section 3. For a list of subordinating conjunctions, see *Fragment,* section 2.

**Conjunctive Adverb** See *Semicolon,* sections 2 to 4, and *Comma Splice,* section 2.

**Connotation and Denotation** See pages 93 to 95.

**Contraction** See *Apostrophe,* section 2.

**Coordinating Conjunction** See *Comma Splice,* section 2.

**Correlative Conjunction** See *Agreement (Subject and Verb),* section 4.

## Dangling Modifier

A modifier is a word, a phrase, or a clause that describes, qualifies, or in some way limits another word in the sentence.

**1**  Be sure every modifier in a sentence actually has a word to modify; otherwise, it will be a *dangling modifier*:

> *Dangling:*  Staring in disbelief, the car jumped the curb and crashed into a telephone booth.
>
> *Improved:*  While I stared in disbelief, the car jumped the curb and crashed into a telephone booth.
>
> *Dangling:*  When only seven years old, her father ran off with another woman.
>
> *Improved:*  When Marcella was only seven years old, her father ran off with another woman.

**2**  Unwise use of the passive voice often causes dangling modifiers. (In the last example below, *you* is understood as the subject of both *pin* and *cut*.)

> *Dangling:*  After carefully pinning on the pattern, the material may then be cut.
>
> *Improved:*  After carefully pinning on the pattern, you may then cut the material.
>
> *Improved:*  First pin on the pattern; then cut the material.

In order to avoid dangling modifiers, you must think carefully about what you're writing. You can eliminate many of your modifier problems by writing consistently in the active voice: "I made a mistake," rather than "A mistake was made."

See also *Misplaced Modifier*.

---

**EXERCISE**                                                    **8-8**

Identify any dangling modifiers in the following sentences, and then revise to eliminate the problem.

1  After subduing the protesters, the meeting resumed.
2  Driving through the lush, pine-scented forest, the air was suddenly fouled by the sulfurous belchings of a paper mill.
3  After bolting down lunch and racing madly to the station, the train left without us.
4  Looking back in history, Americans have often professed individualism while rewarding conformity.
5  To avoid hitting the bumper of the car in front, the pedestrian was struck.

### Dash

The dash—which requires your readers to pause—is more forceful than a comma. You can use dashes to gain emphasis, as long as you use them sparingly.

1  Use a dash to add emphasis to an idea at the end of a sentence:

| | |
|---|---|
| *Emphatic:* | Maybelle had only one chance—and a slim one at that. |
| *Less emphatic:* | Maybelle had only one chance, and a slim one at that. |

2  Use dashes, instead of commas, around an interrupter to emphasize the interrupting material. To take away emphasis from an interrupter, use parentheses:

| | |
|---|---|
| *Emphatic:* | My cousin Clyde—the crazy one from Kankakee—is running for the legislature. |
| *Less emphatic:* | My cousin Clyde, the crazy one from Kankakee, is running for the legislature. |
| *Not emphatic:* | My cousin Clyde (the crazy one from Kankakee) is running for the legislature. |

3  Use dashes around an interrupter if commas appear in the interrupting material:

All the dogs—Spot, Bowser, Fido, and even Old Blue—have gone camping with Clyde.

**4**   Use a dash (or a colon, if you want to be more formal) following a series at the beginning of a sentence:

> Patience, sympathy endurance, selflessness—these are what good mothers are made of.

**NOTE:**     **Do not confuse the dash with the hyphen. On your typewriter, strike *two* hyphens to make a dash. To use a hyphen when you need a dash is a serious mistake; hyphens connect, dashes separate.**

*Diction*   See pages 71 to 87.

### *Ellipsis Dots*

**1**   Use three dots to show your readers that you've omitted words from a direct quotation:

**a**   *Something left out at the beginning:*

> About advice, Lord Chesterfield wrote, ''. . . Those who want it the most always like it the least.''

> —Letter to his son, 1748

**b**   *Something left out in the middle:*

> ''The time has come . . . for us to examine ourselves,'' warns James Baldwin, ''but we can only do this if we are willing to free ourselves from the myth of America and try to find out what is really happening here.''

> —*Nobody Knows My Name*

**c**   *Something left out at the end:*

> Thoreau declared that he received only one or two letters in his life ''that were worth the postage'' and observed summarily that ''to a philosopher all *news*, as it is called, is gossip. . . .''

> —*Walden*, Chapter 2

**NOTE:**     **The extra dot is the period.**

NOTE ALSO:     **An omission which changes the meaning—even
               though you alert your reader with ellipsis dots—
               is misleading and dishonest. You should omit
               from quotations only portions that do not alter
               the meaning.**

**2**   If you're quoting only a snatch of something—and your readers can
*tell* you're doing so—do not use ellipsis dots:

> Occasionally, like Eliot's Prufrock, we long to be "scuttling
> across the floors of silent seas."

**3**   Use either ellipsis dots or a dash to indicate an unfinished statement, especially in recording conversation:

> "But, I don't know whether . . . ," Bernice began.
>
> "How could you—?" Ferdinand faltered.

*Elliptical Construction*   See *Case of Pronouns*, section 4.

*Emphasis*   See pages 61 to 64; 65 to 66; 80.

*Exclamation Point*   See also *Quotation Marks*, section 8.

**1**   Do not use exclamation points merely to give punch to ordinary
sentences. Write a good, emphatic sentence instead:

> *Ineffective:*     LeRoy was in a terrible accident!
>
> *Improved:*       LeRoy, whose motorcycle collided with a semi on
>                   US 51, lies near death from head injuries.

**2**   Use exclamation points following genuine exclamations:

> O kind missionary, O compassionate missionary, leave China! Come
> home and convert these Christians!
>
>                   —Mark Twain, "The United States of Lyncherdom"

> I'm mad as hell, and I'm not going to take it anymore!
>
>                                   —Paddy Chayefsky, *Network*

**NOTE:**     **Never stack up punctuation. Do not put a comma after an exclamation point or after a question mark.**

## *Expletive*

**1**  An *expletive* can be an oath or exclamation, often profane. You'll have no trouble thinking of the four-letter ones, so I'll mention some socially acceptable ones: Thunderation! Tarnation! Oh, drat! Darn! Oh, fudge!

**2**  The words *it* and *there* are also expletives, but of a different sort. These expletives serve as filler words to allow for variety in sentence patterns:

> *It* is raining.

> *There* are two ways to solve the problem.

Remember that you won't achieve variety if you begin more than an occasional sentence this way; instead, you'll get wordiness.

See also *Agreement (Subject and Verb)*, section 5.

## *Figures of Speech*   See pages 86 to 87.

## *Formal Usage*   See pages 72 to 73.

## *Fragment*

**1**  A sentence fragment, as the term suggests, is only part of a sentence but is punctuated as a whole. Many accomplished writers use fragments for emphasis, or simply for convenience, as in the portions italicized in the following examples:

> Man is the only animal that blushes. *Or needs to.*
>
> —Mark Twain

> I did not whisper excitedly about my Boyfriends. *For the best of reasons.* I did not have any.
>
> —Gwendolyn Brooks

No member [of Congress] had ever been challenged or even questioned about taking the exemption. Until my nomination.

—Geraldine Ferraro

If there is to be a new etiquette, it ought to be based on honest, mutual respect and responsiveness to each other's real needs. *Regardless of sex.*

—Lois Gould

She did not suffer any pain, and that is true—if imprisonment is not pain. *While she demanded our love in every way she knew, without sense of shame, as a child will.*

—Alice Munro

**2** Avoid fragments in formal writing (term papers, business reports, scholarly essays):

| | |
|---|---|
| *Fragment:* | Pollution poses a serious problem. *Which we had better solve.* |
| *Complete:* | Pollution poses a serious problem—which we had better solve. |
| *Complete:* | Pollution poses a serious problem, which we had better solve. |

**NOTE:**     **If you write fragments accidentally, remember that a simple sentence beginning with one of the following subordinating words will come out as a fragment:**

| after | since | unless |
|---|---|---|
| although | so as | until |
| as, as if | as far as | when |
| because | so that | whenever |
| before | still | whereas |
| if | through | which |
| only | till | while |

| | |
|---|---|
| *Fragment:* | Although I warned him time after time. |
| *Complete:* | I warned him time after time. |

*Complete:*     Although I warned him time after time, Clyde continued to curse and swear.

**NOTE:**     **Words ending in *-ing* and *-ed* can cause fragments also. Although such words sound like verbs, sometimes they're verbals—actually nouns or adjectives. Every complete sentence requires an honest-to-goodness verb.**

*Fragment:*     Singing and skipping along the beach.

*Complete:*     Juan went singing and skipping along the beach.

*Fragment:*     Abandoned by friends and family alike.

*Complete:*     Alice was abandoned by friends and family alike.

*Complete:*     Abandoned by friends and family alike, Alice at last recognized the evils of alcohol.

**4** Fragments are fine in asking and answering questions, even in formal writing:

When should the reform begin? At once.

How? By throwing the scoundrels out of office.

Fragments are also necessary for reproducing conversation, since people don't always speak in complete sentences. Mark Twain records this conversation he supposedly had with his mother:

"I suppose that during all [my sickly childhood] you were uneasy about me?"
"Yes, the whole time."
"Afraid I wouldn't live?"
After a reflective pause, ostensibly to think out the facts.
"No—afraid you would."

—Mark Twain, *Autobiography*

**5** When you connect two sentences with a semicolon, be sure that both constructions really are sentences:

| *Questionable:* | He looked a lot like Quasimodo; although I couldn't see him too well. |
|---|---|
| *Improved:* | He looked a lot like Quasimodo, although I couldn't see him too well. |
| *Improved:* | He looked a lot like Quasimodo; I couldn't see him too well though. |

**Exercise**                                                                        **8-9**

Some of the following constructions are not complete sentences. Correct the ones that you consider faulty. Defend the ones that you find effective.

1  Marion was late to his own wedding. To his eternal sorrow.
2  Broadcasting moment-by-moment, hour-by-hour, day-by-day reports.
3  Because she is allergic to fleas and scratches her skin raw. Our little dog needs regular bathing.
4  What is the best policy? To do nothing—diplomatically.
5  Rosita passed her exams. By studying twelve hours a day.

*Fused Sentence*   See *Run-On Sentence*

*Hyphen*

Unlike exclamation points, hyphens are much in fashion today as a stylistic device.

**1**  Writers sometimes hyphenate clichés (to revitalize them) or descriptive phrases that are used as a whole to modify a noun:

Emily Dickinson challenges the time-heals-all-wounds adage.

Women today are pressing for equal-pay-for-equal-work laws.

**2** Hyphenate compound adjectives when they come before the noun:

> a feather-light touch
>
> high-speed railroads

But if the descriptive phrase comes after the noun, omit the hyphen:

> a touch light as a feather
>
> railroads running at high speed

**3** Most compound words beginning with *self-* and *ex-* are hyphenated:

> self-employed    ex-wife
>
> self-deluded    ex-slave
>
> self-abuse    ex-President

Never use a hyphen in the following words:

> yourself    himself    itself
>
> themselves    herself    selfless
>
> ourselves    myself    selfish
>
> oneself (or one's self)

**4** Consult your dictionary about other compound words. Some words change function depending on whether they're written as one word or two:

> *Verb:*    Where did I *slip up?*
>
> *Noun:*    I made a *slipup* somewhere.

**5** Use a hyphen to divide words at the end of a line. *Divide only between syllables.* Consult your dictionary if in doubt.

**NOTE:** **In typing, do not leave a space either before or after a hyphen.**

*Incomplete Comparisons*    See *Comparisons, Incomplete and Illogical*

*Indefinite "You"*   See page 53.

*Infinitive*   See *Split Infinitive.*

*Informal Usage*   See page 73 to 74.

*Interjection*   See *Exclamation Point.*

*Irregular verb*   See *Tense*, section 4.

*Italics*   See *Underlining.*

*Levels of Usage*   See pages 71 to 74.

### Linking Verb

Linking verbs do just what the term implies. They connect the subject of the sentence with the complement. The most common linking (or copulative, as they used to be bluntly called) verbs are these: *to be, to feel, to appear, to seem, to look, to smell, to sound, to taste.* See also *Adverb/Adjective Confusion*, section 4.

*Logic*   See pages 97 to 101.

### Misplaced Modifier

Keep modifiers close to what they modify (describe, limit, or qualify).

| | |
|---|---|
| *Faulty:* | Once married, the church considers that a couple has signed up for a lifetime contract. |
| *Improved:* | The church considers that a couple, once married, has signed up for a lifetime contract. |
| *Faulty:* | I had been driving for forty years when I fell asleep at the wheel and had an accident. |

*Improved:*    Although I had driven safely for forty years, last night I fell asleep at the wheel and had an accident.

---

**Exercise**                                                              **8-10**

In the following sentences move any misplaced modifiers so that the statements make better sense.

1  Also soft and cuddly, the main appeal of a kitten is its playfulness.
2  Registration assignments will not be accepted from students until the door attendant has punched them.
3  Although similar in detail, my purpose is to show how these two pussycats differ.
4  I was sure the old fellow even before I hit him would never make it across the street.
5  Clyde was robbed at gunpoint in an elevator where he lives.

---

### Modifiers

The numerous ways of placing modifiers allows almost infinite variety in the English sentence. For a quick run-down of several of these methods, see *Adjective/Adverb*; *Appositives*; *Comma*, sections 1, 3, and 6; *Dash*; and *Sentence Combining*, pages 58 to 60.

For several ways in which modifiers are often misused, see *Dangling Modifier*, *Misplaced Modifier*, and *Squinting Modifier*.

### Mood   See *Subjunctive Mood*.

### Nonrestrictive Clause   See *Comma*, section 1.

### No Paragraph

If your instructor marks "no ¶" on your paper, you have indented needlessly. Journalists tend to indent every two or three sentences for easy readability in narrow news columns, but in an essay or a report, that much indenting produces choppy paragraphing. You should start a new paragraph when you finish developing one idea and move on to the next.

Usually, you can correct choppy paragraphing by simply combining two or more paragraphs, like these written by a student:

> One positive effect of legalization is that marijuana would be safer to use. There would be none of this intervention from the Mafia that introduces poisons into the product before it is sold. ↢
>
> *no ¶*    ⊂ Smokers would be assured of good quality marijuana because competition would arise among the producers. There wouldn't be any additives, such as "angel dust," which can have a bad effect on some people.

Certainly there was no need for the new paragraph, since the first sentence (the topic sentence) is broad enough to include the ideas in both paragraphs.

### No Punctuation Necessary

If you are a comma fancier, you may be in the habit of inserting commas wherever you would pause in speaking. That practice doesn't always work; we pause far too often in speech, and different speakers pause in different places. Here are some situations that seem particularly tempting to comma abusers.

**1** *When main sentence parts are long:* Some writers mistakenly separate the subject from the verb or the verb from the complement, like this:

> *Wrong:*    Tall people with quick reflexes, make particularly good basketball players.
>
> *Wrong:*    By the end of the year we all understood, that using too many commas would make us grow hair on our palms.

Neither of those sentences should have a comma in it. In the second sentence the clause is restrictive (it serves as the direct object of the verb *understood*) and thus should not be set off with a comma.

**2**  *When a restrictive clause occurs in midsentence:* Putting a comma on one end of a clause and no punctuation at all on the other end is never correct. Nonrestrictive clauses always need punctuation on both ends (see *Comma*, section 1), and restrictive ones need no punctuation. Avoid errors like this one:

> *Wrong:*     Ruthie's poem that described the death of her husband,
>                     was the most moving one she read.

No comma is necessary in that sentence.

**3.**  *When the word* and *appears in the sentence:* Some people always put a comma before the word *and*, and they're probably right more than half the time. It's correct to put a comma before *and* when it joins the last word in a series or when it joins independent clauses. But when *and* doesn't do either of those things, a comma before it is inappropriate. This sentence, for instance, should have no comma:

> *Wrong:*     Mark called the telephone company to complain about
>                     his bill, and got put on ''hold'' for an hour.

### Numbers

Spell out the numbers one hundred and under. In general, write numbers over one hundred in figures. Spell out round numbers requiring only a couple of words (two hundred tons, five thousand dollars). If a series of numbers occurs in a passage, and some of them are over one hundred, use figures for all of them. You should also always use figures for addresses (27 White's Place), for times (1:05 P.M.), for dates (October 12, 1950), and for decimals, code and serial numbers, percentages, measurements, and page references.

**EXCEPTION:**     **Never begin a sentence with a numeral; spell it out or rewrite the sentence.**

### Paragraph

The proofreader's mark ¶ means that your instructor thinks you should indent to begin a new paragraph at that point. When all your sentences are closely related, sometimes you forget to give your readers a break by dividing paragraphs.

Remember to indent when you shift topics or shift aspects of a topic. For instance, look at the break between the preceding paragraph and this one. Both of these paragraphs are on the same subject (paragraphing), but the topic shifts from *why* to begin a new paragraph to *when* to begin a new paragraph. Hence, the indentation.

See also *No Paragraph* and *Unity*.

**Parallel Structure**   See pages 63 to 66.

**Parentheses**

**1**   Use parentheses around parts of a sentence or paragraph that you would speak aloud as an aside—a slight digression or some incidental information that you don't particularly want to emphasize:

> John Stuart Mill (1806–1873) promoted the idea of woman's equality with men.

> Russell's lapses of memory (often he forgets what he went to the store to buy) are probably caused by his inability to concentrate.

**2**   Sometimes you'll choose parentheses to separate a part of a sentence that could be enclosed in commas, as in the example above (about Russell's memory lapses). Use commas to separate material that is directly relevant to the main passage, and parentheses to separate material that is indirectly related or less crucial. When you use dashes around a part of a sentence, they strongly stress that part, as neither commas nor parentheses do.

**3**   Use parentheses around numerals when you number a list:

> Her professor did three things that bothered her: (1) He called her "honey," even though he didn't know her; (2) he graded the class on a curve, even though there were only ten students; (3) he complained that male students no longer wore suitcoats and ties to class.

**4** Punctuation goes inside the parentheses if it punctuates just the words inside:

> Consumers can use their power by boycotting a product. (The word *boycott* is from Captain Charles C. Boycott, whose neighbors in Ireland ostracized him in 1880 for refusing to reduce the high rents he charged.)

**5** Punctuation goes outside the parentheses if it punctuates more than just the enclosed material. A numbered list, like that in section 3, is the *only* case in which you would put a comma, semicolon, colon, or dash before an opening parenthesis.

---

**Exercise**                                  **8-11**

Choose the best punctuation (parentheses, dashes, or commas) to put in place of the carats in the following sentences. Remember: Dashes *stress*, parentheses *play down*, and commas *separate* for clarity.

1   The 1960 *World Book Encyclopedia* claims that smoking marijuana ∧*cannabis sativa*∧ causes fits of violence.
2   I tasted his omelette and found∧how disgusting!∧that it was runny inside.
3   Stewart Alsop∧whom my mother claims as a distant relation of ours∧was a well-known conservative journalist.
4   People often mistakenly think that Lenin∧our black and white cat∧was named after John Lennon of the Beatles.
5   Alcohol∧although a dangerous drug∧is considered harmless by many Americans.

---

*Participle*    See *Tense.*

*Passive Voice*    See pages 54 to 57.

*Period*

Use a period at the end of a complete declarative sentence and after most abbreviations (see *Abbreviations*). If a sentence ends with an abbreviation, let its period serve as the final period of the sentence: don't double up.

### Phrase

A phrase is a group of words that does not include a subject and verb combination.

*Point of View*    See *Shifts in Tense and Person.*

*Possessives*    See *Apostrophe* and *Case of Pronouns.*

### Possessives with Gerunds

**1**   A gerund is a verb with an *-ing* on it that acts like a noun in a sentence:

> Squishing mud between your toes is a sensual pleasure.

*Squishing* is the subject of the sentence and thus acts like a noun.

> He got back at the telephone company by folding his computer billing card each month.

*Folding* is the object of the preposition and thus acts like a noun.

**2**   In formal writing, you should use possessive nouns and pronouns before gerunds because gerunds act as nouns. You probably wouldn't forget to use a possessive before a regular noun in a sentence like this:

> I worry about Teddy's impulsiveness.

But people often forget to use the possessive before a gerund.

|              |                                     |
|--------------|-------------------------------------|
| *Colloquial:* | I worry about *Teddy* getting lost. |
| *Formal:*     | I worry about *Teddy's* getting lost. |
| *Colloquial:* | I worry about *him* getting lost. |

*Formal:*   I worry about *his* getting lost.

### Predication, Faulty

**1** This error comes from shifting your thought slightly in midsentence and then not rereading carefully enough to notice the problem. A sentence with faulty predication is one whose predicate doesn't match the subject in meaning:

> *Faulty:*  Your first big city is an event that changes your whole outlook if you grew up in a small town.
>
> *Faulty:*  The importance of graceful hip movement is essential when doing the Bump.
>
> *Faulty:*  Smoothness and precision are among the basic problems encountered by beginning dancers.

In the first sentence, a city is not really an event; in the next, the writer probably didn't want to say something as banal as "importance is essential"; and in the last, smoothness and precision are not problems.

 To correct such errors, you can revise the subject, the predicate, or both to make them match up better. Here are possible revisions of those problem sentences:

> *Improved:*  Your first visit to a big city is an experience that changes your whole outlook if you grew up in a small town.
>
> *Improved:*  Graceful hip movement is essential when doing the Bump.
>
> *Improved:*  Roughness and imprecision are among the weaknesses of beginning dancers.

**2** Your predication can be merely weak instead of utterly illogical. Important words should appear as the subject and predicate:

> *Weak:*  One important point of his speech was the part in which he stressed self-reliance.

In the example above, the key subject and predicate words are *point
. . . was . . . part*, which don't carry much meaning in the sentence.
Here's an improvement:

> *Improved:*     At one important point, his speech emphasized self-
> reliance.

Now the key subject and predicate words are *speech . . . emphasized
. . . self-reliance*, which are more meaningful.

### Preposition Problems

Explaining when to use which preposition or when to leave one out is
next to impossible. But standard English doesn't allow constructions
like these:

> *Colloquial:*     Tyrone did as good of a job as he could.
>
> *Colloquial:*     This is the kind of an example I mean.

If you write sentences like these, you need to find a friend to point out
your surplus words. Those sentences should read like this:

> *Standard:*      Tyrone did as good a job as he could.
>
> *Improved:*      Tyrone did the best job he could.
>
> *Standard:*      This is the kind of example I mean.

### Prepositions, Redundant

Avoid using a preposition at the end of any sentence involving *where*:

> *Colloquial:*     Can you tell me where the action's at?
>
> *Standard:*      Can you tell me where the action is?
>
> *Colloquial:*     Where is our money going to?
>
> *Standard:*      Where is our money going?

### Pronouns

Pronouns, those words that take the place of nouns, have numerous useful functions but can also cause trouble in devilish ways. See *Agreement (Pronoun and Antecedent)*; *Case of Pronouns*; pronouns for coherence, page 51; *Indefinite "You,"* page 53; *Reference of Pronouns (this* and *which* especially); *Shifts in Person*; in the "Glossary of Usage": *he or she/his or her*; *its/it's*; *their/there/they're*; *who/which/ that*; *you (indefinite)*; *your/you're*.

### Proper Noun

A common noun names a class (like *dog, city*); a proper noun names a specific person, place, or thing (like *Rover, Chicago*).

### Qualification    See page 99.

### Quotation Marks

See also *Comma*, section 7 and pages 116 to 118 in the researched writing chapter.

**1** *Quotation marks should appear around words that you copy just as they were written or spoken, whether they are complete or partial sentences:*

> "Gloria, please don't practice your quacky duck imitation while I'm trying to do my income tax," Susie pleaded.

> She said that Gloria's barnyard imitation made her "feel like moving to New York for some peace and quiet."

**2** *A quotation within a quotation should have single quotation marks around it:*

> I remarked, "I've disliked Melvin ever since he said I was 'a typical product of the Midwest.'"

Don't panic if you read a book or article that reverses double and single quotation marks (that is, uses single around quotations and double around quotations within quotations). The British do it the opposite of the American way, so that book or article is probably British.

**3** *If you paraphrase* (i.e., change words from the way they were written or spoken), *you're using indirect quotation and should not use quotation marks:*

Susie observed that Gloria's pig grunt was particularly disgusting.

Her actual words were, "Gloria's pig grunt is the worst of all."

Melvin told me that he despised levity.

He actually said, "I despise levity."

**4** *When you write dialogue* (*conversation between two or more people*), *give each new speaker a new paragraph. But still put related nondialogue sentences in the same paragraph:*

> After our visitor finally left, I was able to ask my question. "What did he mean by calling me 'a typical product of the Midwest'?" I inquired.
> "Maybe he meant you were sweet and innocent," Michele suggested.
> "Fat chance," I replied. "He probably meant I was corny."

**5** *Put quotation marks around titles of works that you think of as* part *of a book or magazine rather than a whole by itself: articles, stories, chapters, essays, short poems. Do not, however, put quotation marks around titles of your own essays.*

"Petrified Man," a short story by Eudora Welty

"We Real Cool," a poem by Gwendolyn Brooks

"My View of History," an essay of Arnold Toynbee

*Underline the titles of works you think of as a* whole: *books, magazines, journals, newspapers, plays, and movies* (Walden, The

<u>New York Times</u>, <u>Casablanca</u>). *Also underline the names of works of visual art* (Dali's painting, <u>Civil War</u>). Italics in print mean the same thing as underlining by hand or on a typewriter.

**6**  *Underline or put quotation marks around words used as words,* but be consistent once you decide which method to use in a paper.

> You used *but* and *and* too often in that sentence.

> He thought ''sophisticated'' only referred to stylishness.

**7**  *In general, don't put quotation marks around words that you suspect are too slangy.* It's tempting to do this:

> *Weak:*     Phys ed was really a ''drag.''

> *Weak:*     On the first day of class, my philosophy instructor showed that he was really ''hot'' on the subject.

But you should take the time to decide whether the informality of the slang suits your audience and purpose. If it does, there's no need to set it off with quotation marks. If it doesn't, you should find a more fitting expression. In the first example, since the writer used the slangy, abbreviated form of physical education, the informal word *drag* is suitable without any quotation marks. In the second example, the writer should probably substitute *enthusiastic about* for ''*hot on.*''

Don't use quotation marks as a written sneer, either. Learn to express your distaste in a more precise and effective way.

**8**  *Periods and commas always go inside quotation marks:*

> ''Never eat at a restaurant named Mom's,'' my brother always said.

> In James Joyce's story ''Eveline,'' the main character is at once frightened and attracted by freedom.

When a quoted sentence is followed by tag words (like *he whined, she said, Gloria grunted*), substitute a comma for the period at the end of the quoted sentence. When the tag words interrupt a quoted sentence, the first part of the quotation needs a comma after it:

"I must admit," Seymour said, "that Gloria sounds more like a rooster than anyone else I know."

**9**  *Colons, semicolons, and dashes always go outside the quotation marks:*

"If at first you don't succeed, try, try again"; "It takes all kinds"; "You can't get something for nothing": these shallow mottos were his entire philosophy of life.

**10**  *Exclamation points and question marks go inside the quotation marks if they are part of the quotation and outside if they are not:*

"That man called me 'Babycakes'!" Sandra screeched.

He said, "Hey there, Babycakes, whatcha doin' tonight?"

Isn't that what my father calls "an ungentlemanly advance"?

**11**  *Do not use quotation marks to indicate sarcasm or a verbal sneer*, like this:

*Wrong:*    The new income tax reform is the "best thing" that Washington has come up with in years.

Instead, make the sarcasm clear without quotation marks, like this:

*Right:*    The new income tax reform is the best thing that Washington has come up with since giving us the Great Depression of the 1930s.

Or else, eliminate the sarcasm, like this:

*Right:*    The new income tax reform is the most disastrous thing Washington has come up with in years.

---

**Exercise**                                                        **8-12**

Add single or double quotation marks to these items.

**1**  Did you see the article Dietmania in *Newsweek*? she asked.

**2**  He called Gloria's performance an embarrassment to man and beast.
**3**  Until I heard Gloria, I though that oink was the basic pig sound.
**4**  At first, Gloria said, I just did easy ones like ducks and lambs.
**5**  In March she mourned, I will never get the emu call right; however, by
May she had learned it perfectly.

---

*Redundant Prepositions*   See *Prepositions, Redundant.*

### Reference of Pronouns

**1**  Pronouns are useful words that stand in for nouns so that we don't
have to be forever repeating the same word. Occasionally pronouns
cause trouble, though, when readers can't tell for sure *what* noun the
pronoun stands for (or refers to). If, for instance, you write:

> Seymour gave Selma her pet parrot.

There's no problem: *her* clearly means Selma. But suppose you write
instead:

> Seymour gave Clyde his pet parrot.

Instant ambiguity: *his* could mean either Seymour's or Clyde's. In order
to avoid baffling your readers in this fashion, you should rephrase such
constructions in a way that makes the pronoun reference clear:

> Seymour gave his pet parrot to Clyde.

or

> Clyde got his pet parrot from Seymour.

If you have difficulty with vague pronoun reference, start checking
pronouns when you proofread. Be sure each pronoun refers clearly to
only *one* noun. And be sure that noun is fairly close, preferably in the
same sentence. You cannot expect your readers to track back two or
three sentences to find the antecedent for a pronoun.

**2**  Use *this* and *which* with care. Whenever you use the word *this*, try to follow it with a noun telling what *this* refers to. We're naturally lazy and take advantage of such a handy word, which can be a pronoun and stand there by all by itself meaning nothing in particular. Naturally, *this* will mean something to *you* when you write it, but you must be sure that the idea also gets onto the page. Too often *this* refers to an abstract idea or to a whole cluster of ideas in a paragraph, and your readers would require divine guidance to figure out exactly what you had in mind. So, if you're going to write:

> The importance of this becomes clear when we understand the alternatives.

at least give your reader a clue: "this *principle*," "this *qualification*," "this *stalemate*" or even "this *problem*," if you can't pinpoint the meaning any better than that. It takes extra time and energy to think of the right word, even though you may know exactly what you mean. But searching for a single word to express the idea will help your readers understand you.

*Which* causes similar problems. Often this handy pronoun refers to the entire clause preceding it. Sometimes the meaning is clear, sometimes not. Suppose you write:

> Jocasta has received only one job offer, which depresses her.

That sentence can be interpreted in two different ways:

> Jocasta is depressed about receiving only one job offer, even though it's a fairly good job.

or

> Jocasta has received only one job offer—a depressing one, at that.

Remember that such ambiguity is undesirable in expository prose. Check every *this* and *which* to be sure your readers will understand these words to mean exactly what you intended.

Look up *Agreement (Pronoun and Antecedent)* for a discussion of more pronoun problems.

**3**  The word *it* can be an *expletive*, a filler word that delays the subject and has no precise meaning:

> Since *it* has rained for ten days straight, *it* looks as if we should start building an ark.

But often *it* is a pronoun and needs a clear antecedent:

> *Unclear:*  The campaign is over and the election starts today. Sometimes *it* is exciting.

Is the campaign sometimes exciting or the election?

> *Clear:*  Now that the dreary campaign is finally over, the election starts today. It sometimes proves exciting.

### Repetition

Eliminate any word that's been thoughtlessly used twice:

> *Careless:*  Marvin considered the opportunity of becoming the troop leader a valuable opportunity.
>
> *Improved*:  Marvin considered becoming the troop leader to be a valuable opportunity.

For advice on using *deliberate repetition*, see page 80.

### Restrictive Clauses   See *Comma*, section 2.

### Run-On Sentence   (Fused Sentence)

Occasionally writers entirely forget to put in a period and run two sentences together, like this:

> Horace has a mangy dog without a brain in his head his name is Bowser.

Such a lapse is guaranteed to drive even the most patient readers to

distraction. When you proofread, make sure that each sentence really
*is* an acceptable sentence.

> Horace has a mangy dog without a brain in his head. His name is
> Bowser.

Those sentences are standard English, but a good writer would revise
further to avoid wordiness:

> Horace has a mangy, brainless dog named Bowser.

---

**Exercise**                                                          **8-13**

Put end punctuation where it belongs in the following items, and revise
to avoid wordiness where necessary.

1  Playing blackjack is an absorbing hobby it might even absorb your bank
   account if you're not careful.
2  Blackjack is the only Las Vegas game in which the house does not have
   an overwhelming advantage in fact the players have an advantage if they
   use a system.
3  The best blackjack system involves remembering every card that has turned
   up the player keeps a running count of what cards are left in the deck and
   makes high or low bets accordingly.
4  The system is based on statistical tables compiled by computer expert Julian
   Braun of the IBM Corporation Braun does not play blackjack himself.
5  System players must be dedicated learning the system well takes 200 hours
   of memorization and practice.

---

## Semicolon

1  The semicolon connects complete sentences that have closely
related content:

> Clarence has three kittens; one of them is uncommonly homely.

> When angry, count four; when very angry, swear.
>
> —Mark Twain

**2** You should be sure to use a semicolon (instead of only a comma) when sentences are joined with a conjunctive adverb rather than with a coordinating conjunction: *and*, *but*, *or*, *for*, *nor*, *yet*, *so*. Here is a list of the most commonly used conjunctive adverbs:

| | | |
|---|---|---|
| accordingly | indeed | nonetheless |
| besides | instead | otherwise |
| consequently | likewise | then |
| furthermore | meanwhile | therefore |
| hence | moreover | thus |
| however | nevertheless | too |

**3** The type of connective you choose need not change the meaning, but it will change the punctuation. The following sentences, for instance, appear to require identical punctuation, but in standard usage the first requires a semicolon, the second only a comma:

> The demonstrators have a valid point; however, I can't condone their violence.

> The demonstrators have a valid point, but I can't condone their violence.

This rule may seem senseless, but there *is* a reason for the distinction. The conjunctive adverb is not a pure connective in the way the coordinating conjunction is. *However* in the first example can be picked up and moved to several other spots in the sentence as it suits your fancy. You could write:

> The demonstrators have a valid point; I can't, however, condone their violence.

or

> I can't condone their violence, however.

or even

> I, however, can't condone their violence.

You'll not be able to take such liberties with the coordinating conjunctions without producing nonsentences like these:

> I can't, but, condone their violence.
>
> I can't condone their violence, but.
>
> I, but, can't condone their violence.

It's easy to tell the difference between the pure conjunctions and the conjunctive adverbs if you've memorized the seven coordinating conjunctions: *and*, *but*, *or*, *for*, *nor*, *yet*, *so*. Other words likely to deceive you into thinking they are coordinating conjunctions are actually conjunctive adverbs.

**4**   Fortunately the problem of whether to use a comma *after* the adverb need no longer trouble you: it's optional now. Use a comma if you want to emphasize the adverb.

> The puppies are only three days old; however, you may pick one out without handling them.
>
> The puppies are only three days old; therefore you must not handle them.

**NOTE:**   **The semicolon also substitutes for the comma in separating items in series when any of the items listed *already contains commas*, as in this sentence.**

> Moose-kitty tangled with an enormous, testy tomcat; triumphed momentarily; lowered his guard; then suffered a torn ear, a scratched eye, and mangled whiskers.

Sometimes the series may follow a colon:

> Clyde made several New Year's resolutions: to eat sensible, well-balanced meals; to study harder, sleep longer, and swear less; and to drink no more rum, tequila, or gin.

**Exercise**                                                    **8-14**

Add semicolons to the following items where appropriate.

1  He believed that spicy foods were good for the heart, therefore, he ate
   jalapeña peppers for breakfast each morning.
2  He was tall, handsome, and rich, everyone loved him.
3  She divided her life into four distinct eras: blissful childhood, 1940–1954,
   carefree student life, 1954–1964, motherhood, 1964–1974, and finally,
   liberation, 1974 to the present.
4  He forgot to add oil, thus finding himself the victim of thrown rods and
   other incomprehensible malfunctions.
5  Seymour asked me to bring wine, preferably a rosé, baby Swiss cheese,
   and rolls, ideally fresh-baked, whole wheat ones, little did he know I'd
   already packed peanut butter sandwiches, strawberry Koolaid, and cheese
   curls.

*Sentence Combining*   See pages 58–60.

*Shifts in Tense and Person*   See also *Tense*, sections 1 to 3.

Sometimes your prose gets rolling along, and you shift into the wrong
gear while you're moving, which results in an unpleasant grinding noise
in your readers' heads. These shifts occur in tense and person.

1  *Don't shift tense without a reason.*

   **a**  You may write in either present or past tense, depending upon
   how you approach your material. This sentence, for instance, is
   written in present tense:

        Bumper *is playing* poker.

   Past tense would be:

        Bumper *was playing* poker.

        Bumper *had been playing* poker for five hours.

There's a good bit of variety within the two tenses, which there's no need to go into. The thing to remember is this: Choose either present or past tense and stay with it unless you have a reason to change. Here's an example of faulty tense switch:

> Bumper *was* intently *examining* his cards, when he *looks* up and *raised* the ante. Susie *yelps* and *gritted* her teeth but finally *throws* in her money.

You can, of course, switch tenses if you want to indicate a change occurring in time:

> Bumper *was raising* every bet for a while, but now he *is* simply *checking*.

Just be sure that you don't shift tenses without meaning to.

**b**   When you're writing about literature, be especially careful to avoid mixing past and present tense in your discussion of what happens in the book. It's traditional to describe literary happenings in the present tense (called the *historical* or *literary present*):

> Kingsley Amis's hero, Lucky Jim, *has* an imaginative humor that constantly *gets* him in trouble.

**2**  *Don't shift person, either.*   Shifting *person* (*I*, *you*, *she*, *they*) in a passage is a similar error. Here's an example of a triple whammy:

> *Faulty:*     As students, we learn the ghastly effects of procrastination. You find out that you just can't appreciate reading ten chapters of geography the night before a test. Most students know the grim thud in the gut that they feel when they stare at an exam and don't even understand the questions.

In that example the writer refers to the students in three different ways: *we* (first-person plural), *you* (second-person), and *they* (third-person plural). To revise the passage, stick to one pronoun:

> *Revised:*     As students, we learn the ghastly effects of procras-

tination. We find out that we just can't appreciate reading ten chapters of geography the night before a test. We become familiar with the grim thud in the gut that we feel when we stare at an exam and don't even understand the questions.

***Spelling***   See *Spelling Appendix*, pages 265 to 266.

If you get certain pairs of words confused, like *accept* and *except* or *affect* and *effect*, the ''Glossary of Usage'' beginning on page 237 will help you.

### Split Infinitive

Current usage finds split infinitives perfectly acceptable:

> He tried *to* secretly *cause* fights between Chris and Ann.
>           *inf.*

*Really* is a common infinitive-splitter that can usually—quite beneficially—be left out of the sentence altogether.

> *Split:*        I began *to* really *appreciate* jug band music.
>                       *inf.*
>
> *Improved:*     I began to appreciate jug band music.

A widely split infinitive can be awkward:

> *Widely split:*   He tried *to* purposely, secretly, and with malicious intent *cause* fights between Ann and Chris.
>
> *Improved:*       Purposely, secretly, and with malicious intent, he tried to *cause* fights between Ann and Chris.

### Squinting Modifier

A *squinting modifier* is one that's ambiguous; it's placed between two words (or phrases) and could conceivably refer to either one of them:

*Squinting:*     Marla thought *secretly* James ate too much.

Move the squinting modifier to a less confusing place in the sentence:

*Clear:*     Marla *secretly* thought James ate too much.

*Clear:*     Marla thought James *secretly* ate too much.

**Subject**   See *Agreement* (*Subject and Verb*).

**Subjunctive Mood**

*Mood* means the manner of expression of a verb. The verb forms you're most familiar with and use most often are in the indicative mood: I *cook*, you *eat*, he *washes* the dishes, they *sweep* the floor. Indicative mood is used for statements of fact. For statements and wishes contrary to fact (or highly unlikely) or for suppositions, many writers use *subjunctive* mood. You'll notice considerable difference in the verb forms for the *to be* verb but not so many for the regular verbs:

| **Indicative** | | **Subjunctive** | |
|---|---|---|---|
| I am | I was | I *be* | I *were* |
| he is | he was | he *be* | he *were* |
| you are | you were | you *be* | you were |
| they are | they were | they *be* | they were |

| **Indicative** | **Subjunctive** |
|---|---|
| I take | I take |
| he takes | he *take* |
| you take | you take |
| they take | they take |

Remember Patrick Henry's "If this *be* treason"? And the phrase "if need be"? Those are examples of subjunctive mood. It used to be commonplace to use the subjunctive mood of all verbs, like, "If he *take* to his bed, he will surely expire." But now the subjunctive mood of the *to be* verb is practically the only one anyone worries about.

Although the subjunctive mood is no longer required in standard English, it's still expected by many people—especially in formal writing. Employing the subjunctive correctly will lend elegance to your writing and mark you as a well-educated user of the language.

**1**   Use subjunctive mood to express something that's contrary to fact, highly unlikely, doubtful, or speculative:

> If I were more refined, subjunctive mood would sound natural to me.

> Suppose he were confronted with an audience of subjunctive mood fanatics: he'd be in trouble if he were to use it incorrectly.

> He acts as though he were the smartest graduate of Podunk High, but he certainly doesn't know subjunctive mood.

**2**   Use subjunctive mood to express a strong necessity or a motion in a meeting:

> I move that all whale hunting be banned.

> It's crucial that you be present at this week's meeting.

***Subordination***   See pages 59 to 60.

***Tense***

Tense indicates time relationships. When you start trying to explain how it all works, you realize how amazing it is that most people do it right. Here are the basic tenses of English:

| | |
|---|---|
| Present: | I walk. |
| Past: | I walked. |
| Future: | I will walk. |
| Present perfect: | I have walked. |
| Past perfect: | I had walked. |
| Future perfect: | I will have walked. |

**1**   When you're writing about an event in present tense, it's natural to use past tense for past events and future for future events:

> I think that Hornsby wanted Clara to quit her job yesterday because he will not need as many clerks after the Christmas rush is over.

When you're writing about an event in past tense, you must use past perfect for events farther back in the past:

> Hornsby regretted that he had hired Clara for a permanent, full-time job.

**2**   The three perfect tenses (present perfect, past perfect, and future perfect) always show completed action:

> I have ridden the bus to campus for the past month.

> I had expected my Subaru to be fixed by last Monday.

> By the time I get my car back, I will have paid $215.39 just to get that windshield wiper fixed.

**3**   Sometimes the tense of a statement gets tricky when the surroundings of the statement are in past or future tense, but the statement itself is presently true or applicable:

> Clara realized last week that Hornsby is a greedy, manipulative phony.

Hornsby is still a greedy, manipulative phony, so the present tense is appropriate even though Clara figured him out a week ago.

> Jacob said that reading fiction is so pleasant it feels sinful.

Jacob said this in the past, but his statement about fiction still applies today, so the present tense is fine.

**4**   Every English verb has three principal parts that you need to know in order to form the tenses. Usually, the principal parts are just the present infinitive plus -*d*, -*ed*, or -*t*):

| Present | Past | Past participle |
|---------|--------|---------------------|
| walk | walked | (have, had) walked |
| dance | danced | (have, had) danced |
| spend | spent | (have, had) spent |

But some verbs are *irregular;* that is, they form their past tense or past participle in odd ways. You just have to memorize the principal parts of these verbs. Here are twenty of the most common irregular verbs:

| Present | Past | Past participle |
|---------|------|-----------------|
| am | was | been |
| begin | began | begun |
| break | broke | broken |
| burst | burst | burst (*not* busted) |
| choose | chose | chosen |
| come | came | come |
| do | did | done |
| drag | dragged | dragged (*not* drug) |
| drink | drank | drunk |
| forget | forgot | forgotten (*or* forgot) |
| go | went | gone |
| get | got | got (*or* gotten) |
| have | had | had |
| lay | laid | laid (meaning "placed") |
| lead | led | led |
| lie | lay | lain (meaning "reclined") |
| ride | rode | ridden |
| rise | rose | risen |
| run | ran | run |
| see | saw | seen |
| swim | swam | swum |
| take | took | taken |
| wake | waked (*or* woke) | waked (*or* woke) |

*Thesis Statement*   See pages 10 to 12.

*Title Tactics*

Your title should tell your readers, as far as possible, what the paper is about.

**1**  Don't use a complete sentence but give more than a hint about your topic:

| *Useless:* | The Teacher and Research |
|------------|--------------------------|
| *Better:* | The Teacher and Research in Education |
| *Good:* | Practical Research Ideas for Secondary Teachers |

**2**  Experiment with a colon. Sometimes a colon can make an uninspired title more impressive:

> Grass Roots Organization:       A Key to Political Success
>
> Legal Liability:                What Everyone Needs to Know About Mercy Killing
>
> Riches of the Heart:            The Characterization of Polly in Cather's "Neighbor Rosicky"

**3**  Titles can be less formal and still be effective:

> Laura's Self-Betrayal in "Flowering Judas"
>
> Aunt Jennifer and Her Tigers

**4**  Do *not* put quotation marks around your own title.

See also *Quotation Marks*, section 5, for advice about punctuating other people's titles.

## Topic Sentence

The topic sentence expresses the central idea of a paragraph. Most of your paragraphs should have one.

*Transitions*   See pages 46 to 51.

*Triteness*   See pages 85 and 86.

*Underdeveloped Paragraphs*   See pages 43; 44–46.

## Underlining

Underlining by hand or by using a typewriter means the same as italics in print. It is used three ways:

**1**  *To indicate titles of long or self-contained works:* See *Quotation*

*Marks* (section 5) for a list of what titles to underline and what titles to enclose in quotation marks.

**2** *To point out words used as words:*

*Manipulative behavior* is my psychology teacher's favorite phrase.

**3** *To indicate foreign words:* In informal writing, you do not need to underline foreign words that are widely used, like etcetera or tortilla. But underline foreign words when they are less familiar or when you're writing formally.

After her marriage, Jocasta seemed to lose her *joie de vivre.*

**Unity**   See page 19.

**Usage**   See "Glossary of Usage," Chapter 8, and *Levels of Usage,* pages 71 to 74.

**Verb**   See *Agreement (Subject and Verb)* and *Tense.*

**Word Choice**   See pages 71 to 87.

**Wordiness**   See pages 78 to 79.

**"You," Indefinite**   See page 53.

**Comprehensive Exercise**                                              **8-15**

Correct or improve each of the following sentences.

1 Care should be taken by new students not to alienate their roommates.
2 Every semester, Sandra makes two resolutions, first, not to spend all her money on tropical fish, and second, not to put off schoolwork, until the last minute.
3 Hubert went to school five days early, and found himself alone on campus.

4   Luckily, he had remembered to actually bring his copy of *Paradise Lost* in case he had leisure reading time.

5   Hubert did feel badly because his roommate was not there to share the fun.

6   Sandra on the other hand did not arrive until a week after registration began.

7   She had only 3 paperback books with her.

8   She surprised her teachers by acting as though she was right on time.

9   Each of the books Sandra brought were special to her.

10  The books were Libra: Your Horoscope, Adventures of Huckleberry Finn, and Webster's New World Dictionary.

11  Although she didn't really believe in astrology Sandra found that reading over the list of Libra's good qualities cheered her up in times of depression.

12  *Huckleberry Finn* also cheered her up, supported her philosophy of life, and she never got bored no matter how many times she read it.

13  These characteristics of the novel were important to Sandra, for it meant that she never lacked a good book to read.

14  She sometimes forgot how to spell long words, therefore the dictionary was essential.

15  The dictionary was frequently used when she wrote papers.

16  It also helped her become drowsy when she'd drank too much coffee.

17  Huberts ability to spell was much better than most peoples.

18  His ability to dance, though, was lower than an elephant.

19  Sandra admired Hubert coming up with the correct spelling of *embarrass* every single time.

20  In her opinion, she had to admit that in the field of dancing, Hubert's Hustle was hopeless.

21  Sandra learned the Hustle at the New Age discotheque.

22  The surprising thing about some of Hubert's dance attempts, that include stumbles, jerks, and sometimes falls, do look quite fashionable sometimes.

23  Spelling, Hubert explained to Sandra, is a problem that can be cured only through memorization.

24  Dancing, Sandra explained to Hubert, becomes easy as pie with practice.

25  Hubert was eager to improve his dancing. Sandra wanted to become a better speller. They agreed to give each other lessons.

26  Hubert suggested, We could create a dance called the disco dictionary.

27  It's already created replied Sandra. I read about it in an article called Discomania in the New York Review of Books.

28  Walking into Sandra's room, Hubert's eye was caught by all the empty bookshelves.

**29** He thought her lack of books was very strange he decided not to mention it, though.

**30** She might still have her books packed up, he thought. Although it was the fifteenth week of the semester.

**31** Sandra wasn't embarrassed by her empty bookshelves, in fact, she thought people often filled their shelves up just to impress others.

**32** After supper on Tuesday, Sandra asked Hubert if he'd like to go to a lecture on how the *Oxford English Dictionary* was compiled in two hours.

**33** She said that if students went to all the lectures that came up, you'd be busy every night of the week.

**34** Hubert believed that people whose interests changed with every passing breeze were building on a foundation of jelly.

**35** Sandra decided to go to the lecture while Hubert practices his Bump in front of the mirror.

# Chapter 9

# Glossary of Usage

This section describes the current usage of terms that are questionable as standard English (like the word *irregardless* and the use of *quotes* as a noun) and provides warnings about expressions that are nonstandard. It also explains the distinction between pairs of words that people often confuse (like *sit* and *set*, *lie* and *lay*, *effect* and *affect*). You will find, too, that quite a few formerly questionable expressions have recently become accepted as standard usage. (In order to refresh your memory about the characteristics of the various usage levels, see pages 71 to 74.) In making decisions on usage, I have been guided by Robert C. Pooley, *The Teaching of English Usage;* Roy H. Copperud, *American Usage: The Consensus;* Theodore Bernstein, *Dos and Don'ts and Maybes of English Usage;* several current collegiate dictionaries; and a stack of popular composition handbooks.

*Usage* simply means the way the language is used. But different people use the language in different ways. And even the same people use the language differently on different occasions. You probably speak more carefully in the classroom or on the job than you do when relaxing at the local pub. Good usage, then, is a matter of using language *appropriate* to the occasion. This chapter will tell you which expressions are appropriate for various occasions.

If you're in doubt about any terms that don't appear in this glossary, consult your trusty collegiate dictionary—but be sure it's of recent vintage. Even the best of dictionaries will be out of date on usage within ten years.

### *a/an*

Use *a* before words beginning with consonant sounds; use *an* before words beginning with vowel sounds (*a, e, i, o, u*).

| | |
|---|---|
| a martini | an Irish coffee |
| a tree toad | an armadillo |
| a hostile motorist | an hour exam (the *h* is silent) |
| a hopeful speech | an honest decision (the *h* is silent) |
| a one-car accident | an only child |
| (*o* sounds like *w*) | an historical event |
| a history text | |

### *accept/except*

*Accept*, a verb, means "to receive or to agree with."

We *accept* your excuse with reluctance.

*Except* as a preposition means "but or excluding."

Everyone's coming *except* Dinsdale.

*Except* as a verb isn't used much but means "to leave out."

The Dean agreed to *except* the foreign language requirement since I have lived in France.

### *advice/advise*

When you *advise* someone, you are giving *advice*.

*vb.*
We *advise* you to stop smoking.

*n.*
Mavis refuses to follow our good *advice*.

### *affect/effect*

The verb *affect* means "to influence." The noun *effect* means "the result of some influence."

*n.*                                    *vb.*
The *effect* on my lungs from smoking should *affect* my decision to quit.

*vb.*
Smoking adversely *affects* our health.

*n.*
LeRoy cultivates a seedy appearance for *effect*.

Just to confuse things further, *effect* can also be a verb meaning "to bring about." And *affect* can be a verb meaning "to cultivate an effect" or a noun meaning "emotional response."

*vb.*
We need to *effect* (bring about) some changes in the system.

*vb.*
Clyde *affects* (cultivates) a seedy appearance.

*n.*
Psychologists say that inappropriate *affect* (emotional response) is a feature of schizophrenia.

These last three meanings are seldom confused with the more widely used words above. Concentrate on getting those first, common meanings straight.

### *ain't*

Still colloquial usage. Don't use it unless you're writing dialogue or trying to get a laugh.

### *all right/alright*

Although *alright* is gaining acceptance in the world of advertising, you should stick with *all right* to be safe. *Alright* is definitely not *all right* with everybody yet.

### *almost/most*

Don't write *most all;* standard usage still requires *almost all.*

> Jocasta ate *almost all* of the chocolate-covered cherries.

> Melvin sloshed down *most* of the eggnog.

### *a lot/alot*

Even though *alike* is one word, *a lot* remains two.

### *already/all ready*

*Already* means "before, previously, or so soon."

> Agnes has *already* downed two cheeseburgers.

*All ready* means prepared.

> Clarence is *all ready* to deliver his anti-junk food lecture.

### *altogether/all together*

*Altogether* means "entirely, thoroughly."

> Clarence's analysis is *altogether* absurd.

*All together* means "as a group."

> Let's sing it *all together* from the top.

### among/between

Use *among* when referring in general terms to more than two.

> Ashley found it difficult to choose from *among* so many delectable goodies.

Use *between* when referring to only two.

> She finally narrowed it down to a choice *between* the raspberry tart and the lemon meringue pie.

You can also use *between* when naming several persons or things individually.

> Seymour vacillates *between* the key lime pie, the Bavarian cream, and the baked Alaska.

### analyzation

Don't use it. The word is *analysis*, and tacking on an extra syllable doesn't make it any grander.

### anyways/anywheres

Nonstandard. Use *anyway* and *anywhere*.

### apprise/appraise

To *apprise* means to "inform or serve notice."

> Marcella said the officer neglected to *apprise* her of her constitutional rights.

To *appraise* means to "evaluate or judge."

> Clarence *appraised* the situation carefully and caught the next plane for Venezuela.

### *as/like*

Hardly anyone takes serious umbrage over the confusion of *as* and *like* anymore, but in formal writing, you should observe the distinction. *As* is a conjunction; hence it introduces clauses:

> This pie tastes good *as* everyone will agree.

> The other pie tastes *as if* he made it with artificial lemon.

> The good pie tastes *as though* he used real lemons.

*Like* is a preposition; thus it introduces phrases:

> The other pie tastes *like* artificial lemon.

### *author*

Some people object to *author* as a verb, but the usage is becoming increasingly common.

> *Colloquial:*     Ann *authors* our monthly newsletter.
>
> *Formal:*          Ann *writes* our monthly newsletter.

### *awhile/a while*

Written as one word, *awhile* is an adverb.

> Moose-cat frolicked *awhile* with Bowser.

*A while* is an article plus a noun.

> After *a while* Moose got bored and chased Bowser home.

*bad/badly*   See *Adjective/Adverb Confusion*, Chapter 8.

### *being as/being that*

Don't use either one. Write *because* or *since*.

### *beside/besides*

Don't use *beside* (at the side of) if you mean *besides* (in addition to).

> He leadeth me *beside* the still waters.

> Brandon has a math exam tomorrow *besides* his physics test.

### *between/among*   See *among/between*.

### *center on/center around*

As a matter of logic, you can't *center around* anything. Instead, you *center on* something.

### *choose/chose*

*Choose* (rhymes with *ooze*) means a decision is being made right now.

> I find it hard to *choose* from a long menu.

*Chose* (rhymes with *toes*) means a choice has already been made.

> I finally *chose* the eggplant surprise.

### *compare/contrast*

These words overlap in meaning. When you *contrast* two things, you are making a comparison. But as most instructors use the terms on examinations or in writing assignments, *compare* generally means to focus on similarities; *contrast* means to focus on differences.

*Compare* the music of the Beatles and the Rolling Stones.

*Contrast* the music of Lawrence Welk and Madonna.

### complement/compliment

A *complement* is something that completes. The verb *to be* usually requires a *complement*.

Sheryl's purple scarf *complemented* her lavender sweater.

A *compliment* is a word of praise.

She got many *compliments* on her purple scarf.

### continual/continuous

Careful writers will make a distinction. *Continual* means "repeatedly."

Bernard was *continually* late to class.

*Continuous* means "without interruption."

We suffered *continuous* freezing weather for almost three months.

### could of/should of/would of

Nonstandard. Use *could have, should have, would have*.

Clyde *should have* (not *should of*) stopped at three beers.

### deduce/infer/imply

*Deduce* and *infer* mean essentially the same thing—to reach a conclusion through reasoning.

Clarence *deduced* (or *inferred*) that Juanita was angry with him when she poured a pitcher of beer over his head.

But do not confuse these words with *imply*, which means "to state indirectly or hint."

> Juanita had *implied* several times earlier in the evening that she was displeased.

### *different from/different than*

To be safe, stick with *different from* in formal writing.

> Gazelles are *different from* zebras in many ways.

You can save words, though, by introducing a clause with *different than;* this usage is now widely accepted.

> | *Wordy:* | Your aardvark looks *different from* the way I remembered. |
> |---|---|
> | *Improved:* | Your aardvark looks *different than* I remembered. |

### *disinterested/uninterested*

Although the distinction between these words is important, many people carelessly confuse them. *Disinterested* means "impartial."

> We need a totally *disinterested* person to judge the debate.

*Uninterested* means "not interested."

> Albert is totally *uninterested* in the moral tension of Renaissance drama.

### *dominant/dominate*

*Dominant* is an adjective or a noun.

> George has a *dominant* personality.
>
> Brown eyes are genetically *dominant*.

*Dominate* is always a verb.

> Cecil's parents *dominate* him.

**effect/affect**    See *affect/effect*.

**enthuse**

Now acceptable in speech, but since the term still offends many people, avoid it in writing. Stick with *enthusiastic:*

> *Colloquial:*     Brandon *enthuses* endlessly about the benefits of jogging.
>
> *Standard:*      Brandon is endlessly *enthusiastic* about the benefits of jogging.

**etc.**

Don't use this abbreviation (meaning "and so on") unless you have a list in which the other examples are obvious (like large cities: Paris, London, Rome, etc.). Don't ever write *and etc.*; it's redundant.

**everyday/every day**

Use *everyday* as an adjective to modify a noun or pronoun.

> Gary is wearing his *everyday* jeans.

Use *every day* to mean "daily."

> It rains in the islands almost *every day.*

**except/accept**    See *accept/except*.

**farther/further**

Either word is acceptable to mean distance.

I can't walk a step *farther*, yet we have two miles *further* to go.

To indicate something additional, use *further*.

The judge would hear no *further* arguments.

### *former/latter*

Unless you are a skillful writer, don't use these terms. Too often readers must look back in order to remember which was the former (the first mentioned) and which the latter (the last mentioned). For greater clarity, repeat the nouns.

### *fun*

Do not use *fun* as an adjective in writing; use it as a noun.

| | |
|---|---|
| *Colloquial:* | We had a *fun time* at the shore. |
| *Standard:* | We had *fun* at the shore. |

### *good/well*

*Good* is an adjective: it can be compared (*good, better, best*). *Well* can be an adverb (as in *Clyde writes well*) or an adjective (as in *Clarissa's kitty is well now*). What you want to avoid, then, is using *good* as an adverb.

| | |
|---|---|
| *Wrong:* | Clyde writes *good*. |
| *Right:* | Clyde writes *well*. |
| *Wrong:* | Clarissa's job pays *good*. |
| *Right:* | Clarissa's job pays *well*. |
| *Right:* | I feel *good*. |

Remember, though, that linking verbs take predicate adjectives, so you're right to say:

Clyde <u>looks</u> good.

Clarissa's attitude <u>is</u> good.

If you're in doubt, find a more precise expression:

>   Clyde looks healthy (or happy or handsome).
>
>   Clarissa's attitude is positive (or cooperative or hopeful).
>
>   I feel frisky (or fine or great).

### got/gotten

Both words are acceptable as past participles of the verb *to get*.

### hanged/hung   See *hung/hanged*.

### he or she/his or her

In order to include women in the language, many socially conscious people deliberately use *he or she* (instead of simply *he*) or *his or her* (instead of simply *his*, as grammarians decreed correct for over a century).[1] Equally as many people, though, still consider the double pronoun awkward, as indeed it can be if used ineptly, like this:

> *Awkward:*     The student must have his or her schedule signed by an adviser before he or she proceeds to pick up his or her class cards.

But that sentence can be easily revised to eliminate the excess pronouns.

> *Improved:*     The student must have his or her schedule signed by an adviser before picking up class cards.

Better yet, that sentence can be recast in the plural to eliminate the problem altogether.

---

[1] For an enlightening historical study explaining how the male bias in our language became so pronounced, see Julia P. Stanley, "Sexist Grammar," *College English*, 39 (March 1978), 800–811. Stanley contends, "The usage of *man, mankind,* and *he* in the early grammars of English was not generic in any sense of that term, however one might wish to construe it" (p. 801), and she supplies the evidence to prove her point.

> *Improved:*      Students must have their schedules signed by an adviser before picking up class cards.

You'll notice that the *idea* in the previous example was plural all along, even though the first two versions were written in the singular. We are taught early on to write singular even when we mean plural. We write sentences like this:

> A child should memorize *his* multiplication tables.

Really we mean *all* children should memorize *their* multiplication tables. We need to kick that singular habit and cultivate the plural, since our language has perfectly good nonsexist pronouns in the plural—*they, their, them.*
     If you can't avoid using the singular—and sometimes you can't—try to eliminate unnecessary pronouns.

> *Avoid:*      The winner should pick up *his* prize in person.
>
> *Better:*      The winner should pick up the prize in person.

If you can't eliminate the pronoun, an occasional *his or her*—or *her or his*—is quite acceptable today.
     See also *man/person.*

### hisself

Nonstandard. Don't use it unless writing dialect. Use *himself.*

### hung/hanged

If you're talking about hanging pictures or hanging out clothes or just letting it all hang out, the verb *hang* has these principle parts: *hang, hung, hung, hanging.* But if you're referring to people hanging by the neck, the verb goes *hang, hanged, hanged, hanging.*

> Everyone felt that Melvin should have been *hanged,* drawn, and quartered for forgetting the hot dogs.

*imply/infer* See *deduce/infer/imply*

*indefinite "you"* See *you (indefinite).*

### in/into/in to

To be precise, use *in* to show location; use *into* to indicate motion.

> I was *in* the back seat when our car crashed *into* the train.

Often we use *in* not as a preposition (as in the previous example) but as an adverb functioning almost as part of a verb; *to go in, to sleep in, to give in*. With these fused verb-adverb constructions, keep *to* as a separate word.

> *adv.*
> Don't give *in* to pressure.
> *prep.*
> Don't play *into* their hands.

### irregardless

Most people still steadfastly refuse to accept *irregardless* as standard English. Don't use it; say *regardless* or *nonetheless*.

### is when/is where

Avoid both phrases, especially in writing definitions and instructions. Use *involves* or *occurs* instead.

> *Avoid:* In tragedy, catharsis is when the audience feels purged of pity and fear.
>
> *Improved:* In tragedy, catharsis involves purging pity and fear from the audience.

### its/it's

*Do not* confuse these two terms. Memorize the two definitions if you have trouble with them, and when you proofread, check to be sure you haven't confused them accidently.

*Its* is a possessive pronoun.

> The dog chomped *its* own tail.

*It's* is a contraction of *it is* or *it has*.

> *It's* not an exceptionally smart dog.
>
> *It's* been impossible to train.

Perhaps it will help you keep these words straight if you remind yourself that none of the possessive pronouns has an apostrophe: *his*, *hers*, *ours*, *yours*, *theirs*, *its*. If you absolutely can't remember which is which, you should quit using the contraction: always write *it is*. Then, all you'll need to remember is *no apostrophe in* its.

### kind of/sort of

Colloquial when used to mean *rather* or *somewhat*.

> *Colloquial:*    Moose is *sort of* snarly today.
>
> *Standard:*    Moose is *somewhat* touchy today.

The phrases can be used in standard English, but not as adverbs.

> *Standard:*    What *kind of* food will Moose-kitty eat?

Be careful, though, to avoid wordiness.

> *Wordy:*    Joe-kitty prefers a less fishy sort of food.
>
> *Improved:*    Joe-kitty prefers a less fishy food.

Never use *kind of a* or *sort of a* in writing.

> *Avoid:*    Moose is kind of a grouch today.
>
> *Improved:*    Moose is grouchy today.

### latter/former    See *former/latter*.

### lay/lie

*To lay* means to put or place; *to lie* means to recline. Be sure you know the principal parts; then decide which verb you need: to place—*lay*, *laid*, *laid*, *laying*; to recline—*lie*, *lay*, *lain*, *lying*. Remember that *lay* requires a direct object: you always *lay* something. But you never *lie* anything: you just *lie down*, or *lie quietly*, or *lie under a tree*, or *lie on a couch*. Notice the difference:

> *No object:* Selma *lies* in the hammock.
>
> *Direct object:* Selma *lays* her weary body in the hammock.

If you absolutely can't keep these verbs straight in your mind, choose another word.

> Selma *lounges* in the hammock.
>
> Selma *plops* her weary body in the hammock.

The verb *lie* meaning "to tell a falsehood" causes no problems since its principal parts are *lie*, *lied*, *lied*, *lying*. Hardly anyone past the age of five would say "Selma *lied* down in the hammock." Similarly, the slang meaning of *lay* never confuses people. Nobody ever asks, "Did you get *lain* last night?"

### lead/led

Pronunciation causes the confusion here. *Lead* (rhymes with *bed*) means a heavy, grayish metal.

> Our airy hopes sank like *lead*.

*Lead* (rhymes with *seed*) is present tense of the verb meaning to guide.

> He *leads* me beside the still waters.

*Led* (rhymes with *bed*) is the past tense of the verb *lead*.

> LeRoy *led* the march last year, but he vows he will not *lead* it again.

### leave/let

Standard usage allows either "*Leave* me alone" (meaning "go away") or "*Let* me alone" (meaning "stop bothering me"). But since *let* really means *to allow*, "*Leave* me give you some advice" is definitely nonstandard. Use "*Let* me give you some advice before you *leave*."

### lie/lay   See *lay/lie*.

### like/as   See *as/like*.

### lose/loose

Another problem in pronunciation and spelling. *Lose* (rhymes with *ooze*) means to fail to keep something.

> *vb.* *vb.*
> If we *lose* our right to protest, we will ultimately *lose* our freedom.

*Loose* (rhymes with *goose*) means not tight.

> *adj.*
> The noose is too *loose* on your lasso.

### man/person

The generic *man* (as the term is called) is supposed to include both sexes—all human beings. But unfortunately the same word, *man*, also means simply a male human being; thus the term is ambiguous. Sometimes it includes both sexes; sometimes it doesn't—and sometimes nobody can tell whether it does or doesn't. Also, *man* is another word, like the generic *he*, that eclipses the female. To avoid this subtle sexism, use *person* or *people* when you mean a person or people, not just males.

> *Sexist:*   We want to hire the best *man* we can get for the job.
>
> *Fair:*   We want to hire the best *person* we can get for the job.

A number of compound words using the word *man* can be avoided with little difficulty.

| Avoid | Prefer |
|-------|--------|
| chairman | chairperson, chair, moderator |
| congressman | representative, senator |
| councilman | council member |
| fireman | fire fighter |
| foreman | supervisor |
| mailman | mail carrier |
| mankind | humanity |
| manpower | work force |
| manmade | artificial, manufactured |
| policeman | police officer |
| salesman | salesperson |

The tough one to replace is *manhole*. But did you ever stop to think that it could just as well be called a *sewer cover*?

See also *he or she/his or her*.

### most/almost    See *almost/most*.

### Ms.

Accepted by most and preferred by many, the term *Ms.* (rhymes with *whiz*) allows us to address women without indicating (or even knowing) their marital status, as the term *Mr.* has always done for men.

### myself

Properly used, *myself* is either an intensive (I am going to fix the faucet *myself*) or a reflexive pronoun (I cut *myself* shaving). Do not use *myself* as a subject or an object in writing.

| *Colloquial:* | Jocasta and *myself* are going to be partners. |
| *Preferred:* | Jocasta and *I* are going to be partners. |

| *Colloquial:* | Will you play tennis with Jocasta and *myself*? |
| *Preferred:* | Will you play tennis with Jocasta and *me*? |

***number/amount***   See *amount/number*.

***ones/one's***

Use the apostrophe only with the possessive.

> To abandon one's friends is despicable.
>
> We were the first ones to report for duty.

***prejudice/prejudiced***

Although we seldom pronounce the *-ed*, do not leave it off in writing.

> *Prejudice* remains engrained in our society.
>
> Our society remains *prejudiced* against minorities.
>
> Almost everyone is *prejudiced* against something.
>
> Almost everyone harbors some sort of *prejudice*.

***principal/principle***

While we have numerous meanings for *principal*, the word *principle* basically means "rule": a person of high moral *principle*, a primary *principle* of physics. You can remember the *-le* spelling by association with the *-le* ending on *rule*. All other uses will end with *-al:* a high school *principal*, the *principal* on a loan, a *principal* cause or effect, the *principal* (main character) in a film or play.

***quite/quiet***

Be careful not to confuse these words. *Quite*, an adverb, means "entirely" or "truly." *Quiet* means the opposite of "loud." Do not confuse the two.

> Stanley was *quite* ready to yell, "*Quiet*, please!"

***quotes***

As a verb, *quotes* is standard English.

Leroy *quotes* Shakespeare even in bed.

But as a shortening of *quotation* or *quotation marks*, the term *quotes* is still considered colloquial by some people. This usage is presently changing, but for now, call them *quotations* in writing.

*Avoid:*     You no longer need to put *quotes* around slang.

### real/really

Don't use *real* as an adverb in writing.

*Colloquial:*     Norman got into a *real* dangerous fight.

*Standard:*     Norman got into a *really* dangerous fight.

But *really* (like *very*) is a limp, overworked word. Either leave it out or find a more emphatic word.

*Improved:*     Norman got into a dangerous fight.

Norman got into an incredibly dangerous fight.

### reason is because

This phrase causes faulty predication. Use instead, "The reason is that . . . ," or rephrase your sentence.

*Avoid:*     The reason we are swamped with trash is because I forgot to put the garbage out.

*Better:*     The reason we are swamped with trash is that I forgot to put the garbage out.

*Better:*     We are swamped with trash because I forgot to put the garbage out.

### rise/raise

You never *rise* anything, but you always *raise* something. Prices *rise*, spirits *rise*, curtains *rise*, but you *raise* cain, or *raise* corn, or *raise* prices.

Taxes are *rising* because Congress has *raised* the social security withholding again.

If you can't keep these verbs straight, avoid them.

Taxes are going up.

Congress keeps increasing taxes.


**she or he**   See *he or she/she or he.*


**should of**   See *could of/should of/would of.*


**sit/set**

You don't *sit* anything and you always *set* something (with these exceptions, which are seldom confused: the sun *sets*, jello and concrete *set*, hens *set*). We *sit* down or we *sit* a spell; we *set* a glass down or we *set* a time or we *set* the table. But for some inexplicable reason, we say in standard English, "The principal *sat* Herman down and gave him a stern lecture." If anyone can figure that one out, please let me know.


**sort of/kind of**   See *kind of/sort of.*


**split infinitives**

Go right ahead and split your infinitives if you feel like it, but don't rend them asunder. A single adverb between *to* and the verb is now acceptable (*to* hastily *plan* a party), but several intervening words are usually considered awkward.


**supposed to/used to**

Since we never hear the *-d* sound in these phrases when we talk, the *-d* is easy to forget in writing. Whenever you write either term, be sure to add the *-d*.

***than/then***   See *then/than*.

***their/there/they're***

Do not confuse these words. *Their* is a possessive adjective or pronoun.

> *Their* dog is friendly. That dog is *theirs*.

*There* is an adverb or an expletive.

> *There* she goes. *There* is no problem.

*They're* is a contraction of *they are*.

> *They're* gone.

If you have trouble spelling *their*, remember that all three—*the*ir, *the*re, and *the*y're—start with *the*-.

***theirselves***

Don't use it unless writing dialect. The accepted term is *themselves*.

***then/than***

These words have quite different meanings. *Then* usually suggests a time.

> First we'll pick up the ice; *then* we'll get the pop.

*Than* usually suggests a comparison.

> No one drinks cola faster *than* Seymour.

***thusly***

Don't use it except for humor; write simply *thus*.

*to/too/two*

*To* is usually a preposition, sometimes an adverb, and also introduces an infinitive.

> *to* the depths, push the door *to*, *to* swing

*Too* is an adverb.

> *Too* much noise.
>
> Selma is going *too*.

*Two* is the number.

> *two* hedgehogs, *two* bricks

*try and/try to*

Although we frequently say, ''I'm going to *try and* get this job done,'' the usage is still informal. In formal writing, stick with *try to*.

*uninterested/disinterested*   See *disinterested/uninterested*.

*used to/supposed to*   See *supposed to/used to*.

*very*

Avoid this colorless, exhausted word. Find one more exact and expressive (extremely, considerably, fully, entirely, completely, utterly) or just leave it out. See also *real/really*.

*weather/whether*

Do not confuse these words. *Weather* is what goes on outside. *Whether* introduces an alternative.

> I can't decide *whether* the *weather* will be suitable for a picnic.

### who/which/that

Use *who* to refer to people (or animals you're personifying).

> The person *who* lost three keys . . .
>
> Lenin, *who* is Susie's cat, . . .

Use *which* to refer to animals or nonliving things.

> The earth *which* blooms in spring . . .
>
> The cat *which* lives at Susie's . . .

Use *that* to refer either to people or things.

> The person *that* lost these keys . . .
>
> The earth *that* blooms in spring . . .
>
> The cat *that* lives at Susie's . . .

If you're in doubt about whether to use *who* or *whom*, see *Case of Pronouns*, section 5, in Chapter 8.

### whose/who's

*Whose* is the possessive pronoun or adjective.

> *Whose* alligator is that? Find out *whose* alligator that is.

*Who's* is the contraction of *who is*.

> *Who's* going to dispose of that alligator?

**would of**   See *could of/should of/would of*.

### you (indefinite)

In informal writing, you may always address your readers as *you* (as I have done in this sentence). Somewhat questionable, though, is the use of *you* to mean just anyone (the *indefinite you*).

In France if *you* buy a loaf of bread, *you* get it without a wrapper.

If you're writing on a formal level, you should use the third-person singular *one*.

In France if *one* buys a loaf of bread, *one* gets it without a wrapper.

### your/you're

*Your* is a possessive adjective or pronoun.

The porpoise is *your* problem; the porpoise is *yours*.

*You're* is a contraction of *you are*.

Let me know when *you're* leaving.

o

**Exercise on Words Frequently Confused**                                9-1

The following sentences contain words that sound alike but mean different things, like *quite/quiet*, *its/it's*, and *sit/set*. In each sentence, choose the appropriate term from the words in parentheses.

1  I have been (lead/led) astray again.
2  Lenin is even plumper (then/than) Spiny Norman.
3  (Its/It's) not the money; (its/it's) the (principal/principle) of the thing.
4  Those most in need of (advice/advise) seldom welcome it.
5  Clyde can't study if his room is (to/too) (quiet/quite).
6  The automobile is a (principal/principle) offender in contributing to air pollution.
7  Our spirits (rose/raised) with the sun.
8  They had a frisky time when (there/their) goose got (lose/loose).
9  Let's (lie/lay) down and talk this over.
10  That (continual/continuous) drip from the faucet is driving me to drink.
11  You ought to (appraise/apprise) the situation carefully before you decide (weather/whether) to file a complaint.
12  (You're/Your) decision could (affect/effect) your career.
13  If you (choose/chose) to file, you should not habor the illusion that all (you're/your) problems will be solved.
14  Why don't we (sit/set) this one out?

15  (Your/You're) going to be sent to Outer Mongolia if you (accept/except) this job.
16  Clyde tends to (dominant/dominate) the conversation with his (continual/ continuous) complaints about the IRS.
17  I could (infer/imply) from his complaints that he owes back taxes.
18  If the (weather/whether) improves, (then/than) we will plant the garden.
19  Any news program will usually (appraise/apprise) you of a late frost.
20  Snow peas will not be (affected/effected) by a light frost.
21  I (advice/advise) you to pick them young.
22  The administration has (lain/laid) down firm (principles/principals) concerning campus dissent.
23  I (chose/choose) strawberry last time, and it was all right, (accept/except) there weren't any strawberries in it.
24  Clyde was (quiet/quite) outraged.
25  How did that dog (lose/loose) (its/it's) tail?
26  Many men mistakenly think (their/they're) supposed to be the (dominant/ dominate) sex.

### Exercise on Assorted Matters of Usage                    9-2

Most of the sentences below contain examples of questionable usage. Revise those sentences that need changing in order to be acceptable as standard English. Some contain multiple mistakes.

1  Stanley and myself moved in a new apartment.
2  We need to quickly, thoroughly, and painstakingly perform the analyzation of that substance again.
3  Did Clyde author that report all by hisself?
4  Having been raised on a farm, Henrietta is disinterested in urban entertainments.
5  Seymour baked alot of cookies.
6  You could of busted the lawnmower on that huge rock.
7  For once, try and do what you're supposed to.
8  Hopefully, we are already to go now.
9  I'm going to put quotes around this slang, irregardless of what the book says.
10  Most everyone which is liable to come has all ready got here.
11  A banquet is where you eat alot of food and can't help but be bored by the speeches.
12  If we go altogether, we should be alright.
13  A person may buy his or her ticket from his or her union representative.

14  You would of had less problems if you would of centered around the main issue better.
15  The real reason I'm not coming is because I'm not interested anyways.
16  My ideas are all together different than those of the speaker.
17  If you live in Rome, you should do like the Romans do.
18  Clyde and Claudia got theirselves involved in a accident all ready on their new motorcycle.
19  Clyde use to enthuse about the virtues of being safety conscious.
20  Now his safety record ain't any different from anybody else's.
21  If you turn the key, thusly, the engine will start.
22  Where is the monkey wrench at?
23  If I'd known you were coming, I would of left.
24  Seymour used to scrub the bathtub every day.
25  Being as you promised, you must come, irregardless of the inconvenience.
26  Clarence is headed for the hospital, as he hurt hisself hunting.

# Appendix A

# Spelling Suggestions

For a time people were considerably more relaxed about correct spelling than we are today. William Shakespeare, demonstrating his boundless creativity, spelled his own last name at least three different ways. John Donne wrote ''sun,'' ''sonne,'' or ''sunne,'' just as it struck his fancy. But along about the eighteenth century, Dr. Samuel Johnson decided things were out of hand. He took it upon himself to establish a standard for the less learned and brought out his famous dictionary. The language has refused to hold still, even for the stern-minded Dr. Johnson, but some folks have been trying to tame it ever since.

Today educated people are expected to be able to spell according to the accepted standard. Nobody encourages a lot of creativity in this area. So if you didn't learn to spell somewhere back in grade school, you've got a problem. At any bookstore you'll find an abundance of pamphlets that promise to place you among the ranks of superlative spellers. But these are seldom helpful. Anybody who memorizes well enough to remember all those rules plus all those exceptions probably knows how to spell already.

## TRY LISTING

My advice is to keep a list of all the words you *know* you misspell. Start now. Add to it whenever you discover you've misspelled a word. If you keep adding the same word—especially an easy, often-used word, like "writing" or "coming"—make a point of *remembering* that you can't spell it so that you can look it up. And keep your dictionary handy when you write.

## TRY DODGING

Sometimes you can switch to another word when you realize you don't know how to spell the one you had in mind. It's tough with little everyday words, but use your ingenuity if you can't use your dictionary. Suppose you want to say, "I have trouble with writing," and you can't remember whether "writing" has one or two *t*'s. Rather than risk a serious spelling error (and the more common the word, the more serious the error), scratch that out and say, "I don't write as well as I'd like to."

## TRY PROOFREADING

Spelling is intimately tied up with proofreading. A quick read-through won't catch careless spelling errors, and it won't make you stop and look up words that just don't look right the way you wrote them. It will do you no good to shrug and say, "Oh, I'm a terrible speller," as though it were the same as "Oh, I'm a hemophiliac." If you know you're a sorry speller, don't worry about it on the rough draft: that could cramp your style. But do look up all words you're uncertain about before you type the final copy, and correct misspellings that you discover when you proofread.

Should you be so fortunate as to have a friend or relative who can spell, you are among the blessed. Beg or bribe this gifted person to check your papers for misspelled words. And don't forget to add these words to your list after you correct them.

# Writing Job Application Letters and Résumés

Whether you go into business as a career or not, you'll eventually need to write at least one extremely important business letter: a job application, accompanied by a résumé listing your qualifications. You will find here a sample of each to use as models.

## TIPS FOR WRITING

When you do your letter, adopt a polite tone and be brief. Your résumé will include most of the pertinent information. Organize before you write. If possible, try to focus your remarks on what you can do for the person you're writing to, rather than the reverse. Be sure to make a rough draft and revise it until it sounds perfect. Get your friends and loved ones to rally round and offer suggestions for improvement. Check your spelling and punctuation carefully.

## TIPS FOR TYPING

In typing the final copy, follow the format of the model closely. Originality is not appreciated in business correspondence. Use the best paper you can afford, and be sure the final version looks handsome—evenly spaced on the page with no more than a couple of inconspicuous corrections.

Your résumé may be duplicated commercially after you've typed it once, but each letter must be retyped individually. Don't forget to proofread—at least twice.

---

### Exercise

Go through the help wanted ads of your local newspaper and choose a job that sounds like one you might like. Write a letter of application and a résumé. Don't mail them unless you want the job, but don't throw them away either. You can use the letter as a guide when you write the real thing. And you'll only need to update the résumé.

500 West Main Street
Normal, IL 61761
March 15, 1988

Ms. Marna Winters
Personnel Manager
Great Western Publishing Corp.
7777 State Street, Room 456
Chicago, IL 60606

Effective opening →

Dear Ms. Winters:

Do you need a good, experienced proofreader or copy editor?

Presenting qualifications {

For two summers I worked as a proofreader at The Daily Deluge in Colfax, Illinois, and for three years as a part-time advertising copywriter for radio station WXYZ in Normal. As the enclosed résumé indicates, I majored in English and minored in journalism at Illinois State University.

Summarizing experience {

My experience with various writing and proofreading assignments should prove useful to your firm. I know a position with your nationally known organization would be satisfying to me, as it would further my professional goal of becoming an editor.

Setting up interview →

May I come in for an interview at your convenience? Thank you for your consideration.

Sincerely,

Sue LeSeure

Enclosure: Résumé

**Figure B-1:**  Sample Job Application Letter

Sue LeSeure
500 W. Main St.
Normal, IL 61761
Telephone: 309/452-9999

### Experience

Oct. 1986 to present
(during school term)

Station WXYZ, Normal, IL
Part-time, 20 hours per week. Wrote advertising copy
and solicited ads.

June-August 1987
June-August 1986

The Daily Deluge, Colfax, IL
Full-time proofreader (substituted for head proofreader, 1987).

June-August 1985

Gilbey's Variety Store, Colfax, IL
Sales clerk (with stocking and pricing duties).
Also made deliveries and called in supply orders.

### Education

Sept. 1985-June 1988

Illinois State University
Will receive B.A. in English, June 1988.

Sept. 1984-June 1985
Sept. 1980-June 1984

Baskerville Community College
Octavia High School

Scholastic honors:

Earned a 3.46 grade point average (on a 4.0 scale).
George Canning Scholarship in English Literature, 1987-88.
Illinois State Scholarship, 1984-1988.

Technical training:

Attended a two-week seminar on "Advertising in Today's
Marketplace," sponsored by College of Business and McLean
County Association of Commerce and Industry.

### Personal Data

| | | |
|---|---|---|
| Age: | 24 | Married, no children |
| Health: | Excellent | Willing to relocate |
| Memberships: | Student Association for Women; Journalism Club (President, 1986-87) | |
| Hobbies: | Photography, swimming | |

### References

Ms. Mary Gilbey, Manager
Gilbey's Variety Store
555 S. Fifth Street
Colfax, IL 61763
Phone: 309/723-9999

Dr. Charles Harris
Prof. of English
Illinois State University
Normal, IL 61761
Phone: 309/436-9999

Mr. Waldo Withersnorp
Advertising Manager
Radio Station WXYZ
112 Beaufort Avenue
Normal, IL 61761

**Figure B-2:** Sample Résumé

# Acknowledgments

Maya Angelou, excerpt from *I Know Why the Caged Bird Sings*, 1969. Reprinted by permission of the publisher, Random House, Inc.

James Baldwin, excerpt from *Nobody Knows My Name*, 1959. Reprinted by permission of Doubleday, a division of Bantam, Doubleday, Dell Publishing Group, Inc.

Stephen Brill, excerpt from "The Traffic (Legal and Illegal) in Guns," *Harper's*, September 1979. Copyright © 1977 by Stephen Brill. Reprinted by permission of Sterling Lord Literistic, Inc.

Richard Champlin, M.D., excerpt from "With the Chernobyl Victims," *Los Angeles Times*, July 6, 1986. © Richard Champlin. Reprinted by permission.

Joan Didion, excerpt from "In Bed," *The White Album*, Washington Square Press, 1979. Copyright © 1979 by Joan Didion. Reprinted by permission of Simon and Schuster, Inc.

Annie Dillard, excerpt from "Innocence in the Galapagos," *Harper's*, May 1975. © by *Harper's* magazine. Reprinted by special permission.

Richard Flint, excerpt from "Corn of a Different Color," *Rodale's Organic Gardening*, November 1982. Copyright 1982 Rodale Press, Inc., USA. All rights reserved. Reprinted by permission.

# Part Three

# Readings to Inspire Your Writing

# Chapter 10

# Responding to Your Reading

The essays in this section are here to provide you with models of various rhetorical strategies and techniques as well as to give you interesting ideas to write about. They will also serve to entertain you and to make you a more intelligent person, but those advantages are fringe benefits. These selections are included primarily to help you become a better writer.

Following each selection you will find discussion questions designed to aid you in understanding the writer's methods. You will be asked to examine strategies used in addressing audience, in crafting introductions and conclusions, and in providing effective organization. You will be asked to comment on narrative and descriptive techniques, on examples of outstanding word choice and sentence construction, on the use of dialogue, and on methods of paragraph development. You will sometimes find questions about the meaning and purpose of each piece. Besides making you more knowledgeable about the way good writers work, these questions should spark lively exchanges in class discussion.

At the end of each chapter appear a number of suggestions for writing essays, letters, or articles in response to the readings in that section. Every idea for writing includes a suggested audience and purpose for your paper, but feel free to change these if you come up with better ones.

## READING FOR MEANING

Just as the key to good writing is rewriting, the key to good reading is rereading. I'm not talking about reading just for pleasure. You can read for pleasure any way you please. I'm talking about reading for meaning, reading for understanding, reading to learn. Here are some suggestions to help you gain more from your reading and retain that knowledge longer.

Read through the essay once as rapidly as you wish—for pleasure and to get a general grasp on what the writer is doing. You should at the end of a first reading be able to tell in general terms what the point is and what the main ideas are. You'll probably be able to identify the tone, if the essay has one worth discussing. You may want to underline slang terms or imaginative phrases that catch your attention. And you may want to circle any words whose meaning is unfamiliar. Perhaps you may want to jot a few responses in the margin as you go—reactions like "Right!" or "Great descrip!" or "What an outrage!"

But the time to get serious about jotting responses in the margin is during the second reading.* Before you begin, look over the discussion questions so you'll have in the back of your mind some ideas about what to look for as you read the essay again. As you go, underline any passages that you find significant, and note in the margin what impressed you—"Well put!" or "Thesis statement?" or "Balanced sentence" or "Great phrase!" or "What does *this* mean?" Make comments about the organization if you find it effective. Note paragraphs that you consider especially well developed, and try to figure out how they got that way. Is the writer using descriptive details

---

*If you're studying a physics or a philosophy text—something truly difficult to understand—you'll want to concentrate solely on meaning during this second reading. You may even want to outline the chapter or at least copy the main points in your notebook because writing something down helps you remember it. These notes will also prove handy for reviewing at test time.

or examples of personal experience? Or presenting facts or offering statistics? Or what? Are any paragraphs especially short? If so, what might be the reason? Don't neglect to drag out your dictionary and look up any unfamiliar words—or familiar words that don't quite make sense in the context, since words often have multiple meanings. Improving your vocabulary will help make you a better writer, and, believe me, learning new words in context is the only safe way.

## RESPONDING WITH RELISH

After reading an essay, you can respond in writing in a number of different ways. The least difficult response involves writing about some way in which the piece touches your life. After reading Russell Baker's account of his experiences selling the *Saturday Evening Post*, you might write about your experiences delivering the *Dallas Morning News*. But a word of warning: Personal experience writing, although fairly easy to do, is fairly hard to do well. You need either an extraordinary experience to recount or a talent for writing entertainingly—preferably both. And besides that, you should somehow manage to make your retelling of the experience convey a point.

Another way of responding to an essay involves taking exception to the ideas expressed by the writer. If, for instance, you have just read Noel Perrin's "The Androgynous Man" (Chapter 14) in which he criticizes society's way of stereotyping human behavior according to gender, you might choose to disagree. You could write an essay in which you argue that such sex role stereotyping is necessary to preserve society as we know it today. Your evidence might be drawn from your personal experiences and observations, but those experiences would probably not serve as the focus of your essay. And such an essay will almost always be more successful if your opinions have been informed through reading on the subject.

You might want to respond to an author's ideas by taking another approach to the same subject. Perhaps you will be so moved by the plight of Michelle Clark in "A Teenager's Tragedy: Birth and Death in a Florida Town" (Chapter 13) that you'll get fired up to write about the need for sex education in the schools. Or maybe you'll work up enough enthusiasm to do some research and then write about the national crisis of teenage pregnancy—perhaps even devising useful suggestions for coping with this disaster. Sometimes personal experiences, your own or someone else's, can be totally convincing in such a paper, as you will discover when you read George Orwell's "A Hanging" (Chapter 13) and John McMurtry's "Kill 'Em! Crush 'Em! Eat 'Em Raw!" (Chapter 16).

Another way to respond in writing to an essay involves conducting a survey on the author's subject and reporting your findings. After reading Ellen Goodman's "Women Divided: Family or Career?" (Chapter 14), you might interview a number of women who work outside the home and an equal number who work at home. If your questions are well chosen, your discussion of their attitudes about women and work should produce a most interesting paper, one providing fresh information and making a valid point.

Finally, you might decide to perform a rhetorical analysis of an essay that lends itself to such an approach. H. L. Mencken's "The Death Penalty" (Chapter 13) would be a good choice. After discussing the appeal of his straightforward approach, the unexpected humorous touches, his subtle antireligious bias, his use of rhetorical questions, his use of slang in an otherwise fairly formal essay, the effectiveness of his organization, and the strength or weakness of his examples, you would then draw a conclusion concerning the overall success of the work. Naturally, you need to know quite a bit about rhetorical strategies in order to do a good job on such a paper, but by the time you have studied a few chapters of readings, you may find yourself relishing the task.

# Chapter 11

# Considering Times Past

## Salvation

Langston Hughes

I was saved from sin when I was going on thirteen. But not really [1] saved. It happened like this. There was a big revival at my Auntie Reed's church. Every night for weeks there had been much preaching, singing, praying, and shouting, and some very hardened sinners had been brought to Christ, and the membership of the church had grown by leaps and bounds. Then just before the revival ended, they held a special meeting for children, "to bring the young lambs to the fold." My aunt spoke of it for days ahead. That night I was escorted to the front row and placed on the mourners' bench with all the other young sinners, who had not yet been brought to Jesus.

My aunt told me that when you were saved you saw a light, and [2] something happened to you inside! And Jesus came into your life! And

God was with you from then on! She said you could see and hear and feel Jesus in your soul. I believed her. I have heard a great many old people say the same thing and it seemed to me they ought to know. So I sat there calmly in the hot, crowded church, waiting for Jesus to come to me.

[3]     The preacher preached a wonderful rhythmical sermon, all moans and shouts and lonely cries and dire pictures of hell, and then he sang a song about the ninety and nine safe in the fold, but one little lamb was left out in the cold. Then he said: "Won't you come? Won't you come to Jesus? Young lambs, won't you come?" And he held out his arms to all us young sinners there on the mourners' bench. And the little girls cried. And some of them jumped up and went to Jesus right away. But most of us just sat there.

[4]     A great many old people came and knelt around us and prayed, old women with jet-black faces and braided hair, old men with work-gnarled hands. And the church sang a song about the lower lights are burning, some poor sinners to be saved. And the whole building rocked with prayer and song.

[5]     Still I kept waiting to *see* Jesus.

[6]     Finally all the young people had gone to the altar and were saved, but one boy and me. He was a rounder's son named Westley. Westley and I were surrounded by sisters and deacons praying. It was very hot in the church, and getting late now. Finally Westley said to me in a whisper: "God damn! I'm tired o' sitting here. Let's get up and be saved." So he got up and was saved.

[7]     Then I was left all alone on the mourners' bench. My aunt came and knelt at my knees and cried, while prayers and songs swirled all around me in the little church. The whole congregation prayed for me alone, in a mighty wail of moans and voices. And I kept waiting serenely for Jesus, waiting, waiting—but he didn't come. I wanted to see him, but nothing happened to me. Nothing! I wanted something to happen to me, but nothing happened.

[8]     I heard the songs and the minister saying: "Why don't you come? My dear child, why don't you come to Jesus? Jesus is waiting for you. He wants you. Why don't you come? Sister Reed, what is this child's name?"

[9]     "Langston," my aunt sobbed.

[10]     "Langston, why don't you come? Why don't you come and be saved? Oh, Lamb of God! Why don't you come?"

Now it was really getting late. I began to be ashamed of myself, [11] holding everything up so long. I began to wonder what God thought about Westley, who certainly hadn't seen Jesus either, but who was now sitting proudly on the platform, swinging his knickerbockered legs and grinning down at me, surrounded by deacons and old women on their knees praying. God had not struck Westley dead for taking his name in vain or for lying in the temple. So I decided that maybe to save further trouble, I'd better lie, too, and say that Jesus had come, and get up and be saved.

So I got up. [12]

Suddenly the whole room broke into a sea of shouting, as they [13] saw me rise. Waves of rejoicing swept the place. Women leaped in the air. My aunt threw her arms around me. The minister took me by the hand and led me to the platform.

When things quieted down, in a hushed silence, punctuated by a [14] few ecstatic "Amens," all the new young lambs were blessed in the name of God. Then joyous singing filled the room.

That night, for the last time in my life but one—for I was a big [15] boy twelve years old—I cried. I cried, in bed alone, and couldn't stop. I buried my head under the quilts, but my aunt heard me. She woke up and told my uncle I was crying because the Holy Ghost had come into my life, and because I had seen Jesus. But I was really crying because I couldn't bear to tell her that I had lied, that I had deceived everybody in the church, that I hadn't seen Jesus, and that now I didn't believe there was a Jesus any more, since he didn't come to help me.

## QUESTIONS FOR DISCUSSION

1  This brief narrative is grounded in situational irony (that is, when the opposite of what is expected happens). Briefly explain the irony. Can you also explain what misunderstanding caused the ironic situation to occur?

2  How would the account be different without the mention of young Westley in paragraph 6? What does his role contribute to the effectiveness of the narrative? Is it important that Westley's father is a "rounder"—a person given to drinking and general dissipation?

3  Hughes chooses in paragraphs 6, 8, 9, and 10 to give us the exact words of Westley, of the minister, and of Auntie Reed instead of summarizing what they said as he does in the final paragraph when letting us know what Auntie Reed has said to his uncle. What does he achieve by reproducing the exact conversation?

**4** Why does Hughes set off two short sentences as single paragraphs (paragraphs 5 and 12)?

**5** In paragraph 15 Hughes reinforces the already obvious irony of the story. Would the piece be more effective without that final paragraph? Why or why not?

**6** Writers of narratives often deliberately avoid stating a clear thesis; instead they convey their meaning indirectly and count on their readers to be sensitive enough to deduce their meaning. What does Hughes want us to learn from this brief account? Can you state his implied thesis in a single sentence?

# My Mother's Dream for Me

Gordon Parks

[1] The full meaning of my mother's death had settled over me before they lowered her into the grave. They buried her at two-thirty in the afternoon; now, at nightfall, our big family was starting to break up. Once there had been fifteen of us and, at sixteen, I was the youngest. There was never much money, so now my older brothers and sisters were scraping up enough for my coach ticket north. I would live in St. Paul, Minnesota, with my sister Maggie Lee, as my mother had requested a few minutes before she died.

[2] Poppa, a good quiet man, spent the last hours before our parting moving aimlessly about the yard, keeping to himself and avoiding me. A sigh now and then belied his outer calm. Several times I wanted to say that I was sorry to be going, and that I would miss him very much. But the silence that had always lain between us prevented this. Now I realized that probably he hadn't spoken more than a few thousand words to me during my entire childhood. It was always: "Mornin', boy"; "Git your chores done, boy"; "Goodnight, boy." If I asked for a dime or nickel, he would look beyond me for a moment, grunt, then dig through the nuts and bolts in his blue jeans and hand me the money. I loved him in spite of his silence.

[3] For his own reasons Poppa didn't go to the depot, but as my sister and I were leaving he came up, a cob pipe jutting from his mouth, and stood sideways, looking over the misty Kansas countryside. I stood awkwardly waiting for him to say something. He just grunted—three

short grunts. "Well," Maggie Lee said nervously, "won't you be kissin' your poppa goodbye?" I picked up my cardboard suitcase, turned and kissed his stubbly cheek and started climbing into the taxicab. I was halfway in when his hand touched my shoulder. "Boy, remember your momma's teachin'. You'll be all right. Just you remember her teachin'." I promised, then sat back in the Model T taxi. As we rounded the corner, Poppa was already headed for the hog pens. It was feeding time.

Our parents had filled us with love and a staunch Methodist [4] religion. We were poor, though I did not know it at the time; the rich soil surrounding our clapboard house had yielded the food for the family. And the love of this family had eased the burden of being black. But there were segregated schools and warnings to avoid white neighborhoods after dark. I always had to sit in the peanut gallery (the Negro section) at the movies. We weren't allowed to drink a soda in the drugstore in town. I was stoned and beaten and called "nigger," "black boy," "darky," "shine." These indignities came so often I began to accept them as normal. Yet I always fought back. Now I considered myself lucky to be alive; three of my close friends had already died of senseless brutality, and I was lucky that I hadn't killed someone myself. Until the very day that I left Fort Scott on that train for the North, there had been a fair chance of being shot or perhaps beaten to death. I could easily have been the victim of mistaken identity, of a sudden act of terror by hate-filled white men, or, for that matter, I could have been murdered by some violent member of my own race. There had been a lot of killing in the border states of Kansas, Oklahoma and Missouri, more than I cared to remember.

I was nine years old when the Tulsa riots took place in 1921. [5] Whites had invaded the Negro neighborhood, which turned out to be an armed camp. Many white Tulsans were killed, and rumors had it that the fight would spread into Kansas and beyond. About this time, a grown cousin of mine decided to go south to work in a mill. My mother, knowing his hot temper, pleaded with him not to go, but he caught a freight going south. Months passed and we had no word of him. Then one day his name flashed across the nation as one of the most-wanted men in the country. He had killed a white millhand who spat in his face and called him "nigger." He killed another man while fleeing the scene and shot another on the viaduct between Kansas City, Missouri, and Kansas City, Kansas.

[6]     I asked Momma questions she couldn't possibly answer. Would they catch him? Would he be lynched? Where did she think he was hiding? How long did she think he could hold out? She knew what all the rest of us knew, that he would come back to our house if it was possible.

[7]     He came one night. It was storming, and I lay in the dark of my room, listening to the rain pound the roof. Suddenly, the window next to my bed slid up, and my cousin, wet and cautious, scrambled through the opening. I started to yell as he landed on my bed, but he quickly covered my mouth with his hand, whispered his name, and cautioned me into silence. I got out of bed and followed him. He went straight to Momma's room, kneeled down and shook her awake. "Momma Parks," he whispered, "it's me, it's me. Wake up." And she awoke easily and put her hand on his head. "My Lord, son," she said, "you're in such bad trouble." Then she sat up on the side of the bed and began to pray over him. After she had finished, she tried to persuade him to give himself up. "They'll kill you, son. You can't run forever." But he refused. Then, going to our old icebox, he filled a sack with food and went back out my window into the cornfield.

[8]     None of us ever saw or heard of him again. And I would lie awake nights wondering if the whites had killed my cousin, praying that they hadn't. I remember the huge sacks of peanut brittle he used to bring me and the rides he gave me on the back of his battered motorcycle. And my days were full of fantasies in which I helped him escape imaginary white mobs.

[9]     When I was eleven, I became possessed of an exaggerated fear of death. It started one quiet summer afternoon with an explosion in the alley behind our house. I jumped up from under a shade tree and tailed Poppa toward the scene. Black smoke billowed skyward, a large hole gaped in the wall of our barn and several maimed chickens and a headless turkey flopped about on the ground. Then Poppa stopped and muttered, "Good Lord." I clutched his overalls and looked. A man, or what was left of him, was strewn about in three parts. A gas main he had been repairing had somehow ignited and blown everything around it to bits.

[10]    Then once, with two friends, I had swum along the bottom of the muddy Marmaton River, trying to locate the body of a Negro man. We had been promised fifty cents apiece by the same white policeman

who had shot him while he was in the water trying to escape arrest. The dead man had been in a crap game with several others who had managed to get away. My buddy, Johnny Young, was swimming beside me; we swam with ice hooks which we were to use for grappling. The two of us touched the corpse at the same instant. Fear streaked through me and the memory of his bloated body haunted my dreams for nights.

One night at the Empress Theater, I sat alone in the peanut gallery [11] watching a motion picture, *The Phantom of the Opera*. When the curious heroine, against Lon Chaney's warning, snatched away his mask, and the skull of death filled the screen, I screamed out loud and ran out of the theater. I didn't stop until I reached home, crying to Momma, "I'm going to die! I'm going to die."

Momma, after several months of cajoling, had all but destroyed [12] this fear when another cruel thing happened. A Negro gambler called Captain Tuck was mysteriously killed on the Frisco tracks. Elmer Kinard, a buddy, and I had gone to the Cheney Mortuary out of youthful, and perhaps morbid, curiosity. Two white men, standing at the back door where bodies were received, smiled mischievously and beckoned to us. Elmer was wise and ran, but they caught me. "Come on in, boy. You want to see Captain Tuck, don't you?"

"No, no," I pleaded. "No, no, let me go."                                [13]

The two men lifted me through the door and shoved me into a [14] dark room. "Cap'n Tuck's in here, boy. You can say hello to him." The stench of embalming fluid mixed with fright. I started vomiting, screaming and pounding the door. Then a smeared light bulb flicked on and, there before me, his broken body covering the slab, was Captain Tuck. My body froze and I collapsed beside the door.

After they revived me and put me on the street, I ran home with [15] the old fear again running the distance beside me. My brother Clem evened the score with his fists the next day, but from then on Poppa proclaimed that no Parks would ever be caught dead in Cheney's. "The Koonantz boys will do all our burying from now on," he told Orlando Cheney.

Another time, I saw a woman cut another woman to death. There [16] were men around, but they didn't stop it. They all stood there as if they were watching a horror movie. Months later, I would shudder at the sight of Johnny Young, one of my closest buddies, lying, shot to death, at the feet of his father and the girl he loved. His murderer had been in love with the same girl. And not long after, Emphry Hawkins, who had helped us bear Johnny's coffin, was also shot to death.

[17]     As the train whistled through the evening, I realized that only hours before, during what seemed like a bottomless night, I had left my bed to sleep on the floor beside my mother's coffin. It was, I knew now, a final attempt to destroy this fear of death.

[18]     But in spite of the memories I would miss this Kansas land that I was leaving. The great prairies filled with green and cornstalks; the flowering apple trees, the tall elms and oaks bordering the streams that gurgled and the rivers that rolled quiet. The summers of long, sleepy days for fishing, swimming and snatching crawdads from beneath the rocks. The endless tufts of high clouds billowing across the heavens. The butterflies to chase through grass high as the chin. The swallow-tails, bobolinks and robins. Nights filled with soft laughter, with fireflies and restless stars, and the winding sound of the cricket rubbing dampness from its wing. The silver of September rain, the orange-red-brown Octobers and Novembers, and the white Decembers with the hungry smells of hams and pork butts curing in the smokehouses. Yet, as the train sped along, the telegraph poles whizzing toward and past us, I had a feeling that I was escaping a doom which had already trapped the relatives and friends I was leaving behind. For, although I was departing from this beautiful land, it would be impossible ever to forget the fear, hatred and violence that Negroes had suffered upon it.

[19]     It was all behind me now. By the next day, there would be what my mother had called "another kind of world, one with more hope and promising things." She had said, "Make a man of yourself up there. Put something into it, and you'll get something out of it." It was her dream for me. When I stepped onto the chilly streets of St. Paul, Minnesota, two days later, I was determined to fulfill that dream.

## QUESTIONS FOR DISCUSSION

1   Although this essay is a narrative, Parks does not relate the events in chronological order, as Langston Hughes did in telling his story. Can you figure out how this account is arranged? Do you find this organization effective? Why or why not?
2   Can you describe the tone of paragraph 4 in which Parks begins to recount his first experiences with racial prejudice?
3   Parks exhibits an extraordinary gift for choosing details. Reread paragraphs

7, 9, 10, and 14. Can you explain how those details convey the fear and horror that the boy experienced?

4  In paragraph 18, which begins with the transitional word *but*, the mood of the essay changes. How do the details here differ from the ones you examined in the previous paragraphs?

5  Reread the introduction and the conclusion. What elements do they share? Can you decide what makes the conclusion effective?

6  Can you find a thesis statement in this piece, or do you think the thesis is implied? What is the main point that Parks wants to convey to his readers?


# Selling the *Post*

Russell Baker

I began working in journalism when I was eight years old. It was [1] my mother's idea. She wanted me to "make something" of myself and, after a levelheaded appraisal of my strengths, decided I had better start young if I was to have any chance of keeping up with the competition.

The flaw in my character which she had already spotted was lack [2] of "gumption." My idea of a perfect afternoon was lying in front of the radio rereading my favorite Big Little Book, *Dick Tracy Meets Stooge Viller*. My mother despised inactivity. Seeing me having a good time in repose, she was powerless to hide her disgust. "You've got no more gumption than a bump on a log," she said. "Get out in the kitchen and help Doris do those dirty dishes."

My sister Doris, though two years younger than I, had enough [3] gumption for a dozen people. She positively enjoyed washing dishes, making beds, and cleaning the house. When she was only seven she could carry a piece of short-weighted cheese back to the A&P, threaten the manager with legal action, and come back triumphantly with the full quarter-pound we'd paid for and a few ounces extra thrown in for forgiveness. Doris could have made something of herself if she hadn't been a girl. Because of this defect, however, the best she could hope for was a career as a nurse or schoolteacher, the only work that capable females were considered up to in those days.

This must have saddened my mother, this twist of fate that had [4] allocated all the gumption to the daughter and left her with a son who was content with Dick Tracy and Stooge Viller. If disappointed, though, she wasted no energy on self-pity. She would make me make something of myself whether I wanted to or not. ''The Lord helps those who help themselves,'' she said. That was the way her mind worked.

[5]    She was realistic about the difficulty. Having sized up the material the Lord had given her to mold, she didn't overestimate what she could do with it. She didn't insist that I grow up to be President of the United States.

[6]    Fifty years ago parents still asked boys if they wanted to grow up to be President, and asked it not jokingly but seriously. Many parents who were hardly more than paupers still believed their sons could do it. Abraham Lincoln had done it. We were only sixty-five years from Lincoln. Many a grandfather who walked among us could remember Lincoln's time. Men of grandfatherly age were the worst for asking if you wanted to grow up to be President. A surprising number of little boys said yes and meant it.

[7]    I was asked many times myself. No, I would say, I didn't want to grow up to be President. My mother was present during one of these interrogations. An elderly uncle, having posed the usual question and exposed my lack of interest in the Presidency, asked, ''Well, what *do* you want to be when you grow up?''

[8]    I loved to pick through trash piles and collect empty bottles, tin cans with pretty labels, and discarded magazines. The most desirable job on earth sprang instantly to mind. ''I want to be a garbage man,'' I said.

[9]    My uncle smiled, but my mother had seen the first distressing evidence of a bump budding on a log. ''Have a little gumption, Russell,'' she said. Her calling me Russell was a signal of unhappiness. When she approved of me I was always ''Buddy.''

[10]    When I turned eight years old she decided that the job of starting me on the road toward making something of myself could no longer be safely delayed. ''Buddy,'' she said one day, ''I want you to come home right after school this afternoon. Somebody's coming and I want you to meet him.''

[11]    When I burst in that afternoon she was in conference in the parlor with an executive of the Curtis Publishing Company. She introduced me. He bent low from the waist and shook my hand. Was it true as my mother had told him, he asked, that I longed for the opportunity to conquer the world of business?

My mother replied that I was blessed with a rare determination to [12] make something of myself.

"That's right," I whispered.

"But have you got the grit, the character, the never-say-quit spirit [13] it takes to succeed in business?"

My mother said I certainly did. [14]

"That's right," I said.

He eyed me silently for a long pause, as though weighing whether [15] I could be trusted to keep his confidence, then spoke man-to-man. Before taking a crucial step, he said, he wanted to advise me that working for the Curtis Publishing Company placed enormous responsibility on a young man. It was one of the great companies of America. Perhaps the greatest publishing house in the world. I had heard, no doubt, of the *Saturday Evening Post?*

Heard of it? My mother said that everyone in our house had heard [16] of the *Saturday Post* and that I, in fact, read it with religious devotion.

Then doubtless, he said, we were also familiar with those two [17] monthly pillars of the magazine world, the *Ladies Home Journal* and the *Country Gentleman.*

Indeed we were familiar with them, said my mother. [18]

Representing the *Saturday Evening Post* was one of the weightiest [19] honors that could be bestowed in the world of business, he said. He was personally proud of being a part of that great corporation.

My mother said he had every right to be. [20]

Again he studied me as though debating whether I was worthy of [21] a knighthood. Finally: "Are you trustworthy?"

My mother said I was the soul of honesty. [22]

"That's right," I said. [23]

The caller smiled for the first time. He told me I was a lucky [24] young man. He admired my spunk. Too many young men thought life was all play. Those young men would not go far in this world. Only a young man willing to work and save and keep his face washed and his hair neatly combed could hope to come out on top in a world such as ours. Did I truly and sincerely believe that I was such a young man?

"He certainly does," said my mother. [25]

"That's right," I said. [26]

He said he had been so impressed by what he had seen of me that [27] he was going to make me a representative of the Curtis Publishing Company. On the following Tuesday, he said, thirty freshly printed copies of the *Saturday Evening Post* would be delivered at our door. I would place these magazines, still damp with the ink of the presses, in a handsome canvas bag, sling it over my shoulder, and set forth through the streets to bring the best in journalism, fiction, and cartoons to the American public.

[28]   He had brought the canvas bag with him. He presented it with reverence fit for a chasuble. He showed me how to drape the sling over my left shoulder and across the chest so that the pouch lay easily accessible to my right hand, allowing the best in journalism, fiction, and cartoons to be swiftly extracted and sold to a citizenry whose happiness and security depended upon us soldiers of the free press.

[29]   The following Tuesday I raced home from school, put the canvas bag over my shoulder, dumped the magazines in, and, tilting to the left to balance their weight on my right hip, embarked on the highway of journalism.

[30]   We lived in Belleville, New Jersey, a commuter town at the northern fringe of Newark. It was 1932, the bleakest year of the Depression. My father had died two years before, leaving us with a few pieces of Sears, Roebuck furniture and not much else, and my mother had taken Doris and me to live with one of her younger brothers. This was my Uncle Allen. Uncle Allen had made something of himself by 1932. As salesman for a soft-drink bottler in Newark, he had an income of $30 a week; wore pearl-gray spats, detachable collars, and a three-piece suit; was happily married; and took in threadbare relatives.

[31]   With my load of magazines I headed toward Belleville Avenue. That's where the people were. There were two filling stations at the intersection with Union Avenue, as well as an A&P, a fruit stand, a bakery, a barber shop, Zuccarelli's drugstore, and a diner shaped like a railroad car. For several hours I made myself highly visible, shifting position now and then from corner to corner, from shop window to shop window, to make sure everyone could see the heavy black lettering on the canvas bag that said THE SATURDAY EVENING POST. When the angle of the light indicated it was suppertime, I walked back to the house.

[32]   "How many did you sell, Buddy?" my mother asked.

[33]   "None."

[34]   "Where did you go?"

"The corner of Belleville and Union Avenues." [35]

"What did you do?" [36]

"Stood on the corner waiting for somebody to buy a *Saturday* [37] *Evening Post*."

"You just stood there?" [38]

"Didn't sell a single one." [39]

"For God's sake, Russell!" [40]

Uncle Allen intervened. "I've been thinking about it for some [41] time," he said, "and I've about decided to take the *Post* regularly. Put me down as a regular customer." I handed him a magazine and he paid me a nickel. It was the first nickel I earned.

Afterwards my mother instructed me in salesmanship. I would [42] have to ring doorbells, address adults with charming self-confidence, and break down resistance with a sales talk pointing out that no one, no matter how poor, could afford to be without the *Saturday Evening Post* in the home.

I told my mother I'd changed my mind about wanting to succeed [43] in the magazine business.

"If you think I'm going to raise a good-for-nothing," she replied, [44] "you've got another think coming." She told me to hit the streets with the canvas bag and start ringing doorbells the instant school was out next day. When I objected that I didn't feel any aptitude for salesmanship, she asked how I'd like to lend her my leather belt so she could whack some sense into me. I bowed to superior will and entered journalism with a heavy heart.

My mother and I had fought this battle almost as long as I could [45] remember. It probably started even before memory began, when I was a country child in northern Virginia and my mother, dissatisfied with my father's plain workman's life, determined that I would not grow up like him and his people, with calluses on their hands, overalls on their backs, and fourth-grade educations in their heads. She had fancier ideas of life's possibilities. Introducing me to the *Saturday Evening Post*, she was trying to wean me as early as possible from my father's world where men left with their lunch pails at sunup, worked with their hands until the grime ate into the pores, and died with a few sticks of mail-order furniture as their legacy. In my mother's vision of the better life there were desks and white collars, well-pressed suits, evenings of reading and lively talk, and perhaps—if a man were very, very lucky and hit the jackpot, really made something important of himself—perhaps there might be a fantastic salary of $5,000 a year to support a big house and a Buick with a rumble seat and a vacation in Atlantic City.

[46]     And so I set forth with my sack of magazines. I was afraid of the dogs that snarled behind the doors of potential buyers. I was timid about ringing the doorbells of strangers, relieved when no one came to the door, and scared when someone did. Despite my mother's instructions, I could not deliver an engaging sales pitch. When a door opened I simply asked, "Want to buy a *Saturday Evening Post*?" In Belleville few persons did. It was a town of 30,000 people, and most weeks I rang a fair majority of its doorbells. But I rarely sold my thirty copies. Some weeks I canvassed the entire town for six days and still had four or five unsold magazines on Monday evening; then I dreaded the coming of Tuesday morning, when a batch of thirty fresh *Saturday Evening Post*s was due at the front door.

[47]     "Better get out there and sell the rest of those magazines tonight," my mother would say.

[48]     I usually posted myself then at a busy intersection where a traffic light controlled commuter flow from Newark. When the light turned red I stood on the curb and shouted my sales pitch at the motorists.

[49]     "Want to buy a *Saturday Evening Post*?"

[50]     One rainy night when car windows were sealed against me I came back soaked and with not a single sale to report. My mother beckoned to Doris.

[51]     "Go back down there with Buddy and show him how to sell these magazines," she said.

[52]     Brimming with zest, Doris, who was then seven years old, returned with me to the corner. She took a magazine from the bag, and when the light turned red she strode to the nearest car and banged her small fist against the closed window. The driver, probably startled at what he took to be a midget assaulting his car, lowered the window to stare, and Doris thrust a *Saturday Evening Post* at him.

[53]     "You need this magazine," she piped, "and it only costs a nickel."

[54]     Her salesmanship was irresistible. Before the light changed half a dozen times she disposed of the entire batch. I didn't feel humiliated. To the contrary. I was so happy I decided to give her a treat. Leading

her to the vegetable store on Belleville Avenue, I bought three apples, which cost a nickel, and gave her one.

"You shouldn't waste money," she said.                                    [55]

"Eat your apple." I bit into mine.                                        [56]

"You shouldn't eat before supper," she said. "It'll spoil your [57] appetite."

Back at the house that evening, she dutifully reported me for [58] wasting a nickel. Instead of a scolding, I was rewarded with a pat on the back for having the good sense to buy fruit instead of candy. My mother reached into her bottomless supply of maxims and told Doris, "An apple a day keeps the doctor away."

By the time I was ten I had learned all my mother's maxims by [59] heart. Asking to stay up past normal bedtime, I knew that a refusal would be explained with, "Early to bed and early to rise, makes a man healthy, wealthy, and wise." If I whimpered about having to get up early in the morning, I could depend on her to say, "The early bird gets the worm."

The one I most despised was, "If at first you don't succeed, try, [60] try again." This was the battle cry with which she constantly sent me back into the hopeless struggle whenever I moaned that I had rung every doorbell in town and knew there wasn't a single potential buyer left in Belleville that week. After listening to my explanation, she handed me the canvas bag and said, "If at first, you don't succeed . . ."

Three years in that job, which I would gladly have quit after the [61] first day except for her insistence, produced at least one valuable result. My mother finally concluded that I would never make something of myself by pursuing a life in business and started considering careers that demanded less competitive zeal.

One evening when I was eleven I brought home a short "compo- [62] sition" on my summer vacation which the teacher had graded with an A. Reading it with her own schoolteacher's eye, my mother agreed that it was top-drawer seventh grade prose and complimented me. Nothing more was said about it immediately, but a new idea had taken life in her mind. Halfway through supper she suddenly interrupted the conversation.

"Buddy," she said, "maybe you could be a writer."                        [63]

I clasped the idea to my heart. I had never met a writer, had shown [64] no previous urge to write, and hadn't a notion how to become a writer, but I loved stories and thought that making up stories must surely be almost as much fun as reading them. Best of all, though, and what really gladdened my heart, was the ease of the writer's life. Writers did not have to trudge through the town peddling from canvas bags, defending themselves against angry dogs, being rejected by surly strangers. Writers did not have to ring doorbells. So far as I could make out, what writers did couldn't even be classified as work.

[65]     I was enchanted. Writers didn't have to have any gumption at all. I did not dare tell anybody for fear of being laughed at in the school-yard, but secretly I decided that what I'd like to be when I grew up was a writer.

## QUESTIONS FOR DISCUSSION

1   What does Baker's description of himself as lacking in "gumption" contribute to the effectiveness of this piece?
2   Why is the time at which these events took place important?
3   Baker discusses four other people besides himself in this narrative: his mother, his sister Doris, his uncle, and the man from the Curtis Publishing Company. How does the author feel about each of them? Can you explain what he achieves by including these characters in his narrative?
4   Why is it sad for the boy's mother that Doris is a girl (see paragraphs 3 and 4)? Do you think it might have been sad for Doris also?
5   In paragraph 27, Baker reports that the man from the *Saturday Evening Post* "said he had been so impressed by what he had seen of me that he was going to make me a representative of the Curtis Publishing Company." Has the boy said or done anything impressive? Why, in reality, is the man going to give the lad the job?
6   The thesis of this narrative essay is not stated but implied. What is the point that Baker conveys?

## SUGGESTIONS FOR WRITING

1 Almost everyone sooner or later succumbs to social pressure such as Langston Hughes describes in "Salvation." Try to remember a time in which you went against your conscience or your better judgment for the sake of conformity. Then write an account of that experience, trying to capture the immediacy of the event through the use of concrete details and quoted conversations the way Hughes does. Try also to convey some insight into human behavior, as Hughes does, but refrain from telling your readers the point directly. Allow them to infer your meaning from the narrative. Write your essay for possible publication in *Newsweek on Campus*.

2 The essay by Gordon Parks conveys strongly the horrors that result from racial prejudice and the bone-deep fear that these events instilled in him as he was growing up. If you have ever encountered racial prejudice, either as the victim, as the perpetrator, or as an observer, write an account of the incident. Try to choose precisely the right details to convey the emotion you felt and to make your readers feel the dreadful wrongness of the prejudice. Write this essay for possible publication in *The Reader's Digest* feature entitled "My Most Unforgettable Experience."

3 If you have ever been coerced into doing some task you had no desire to do and little aptitude for, write an account of the experience. Try using people as characters and creating scenes in which you record conversation, as Russell Baker does. You might adopt a humorous tone, if you have a flair for writing humorously; otherwise, try to make your readers feel what you felt at the time: your qualms, your distaste, your dread, or your embarrassment. Choose your details carefully, and try to give your narrative a point (but don't come right out and state it). Write this piece for possible publication in *The Reader's Digest* feature, "My Most Unforgettable Experience."

# Chapter 12

# Considering Discrimination

## I Have a Dream

Martin Luther King

[1] I am happy to join with you today in what will go down in history as the greatest demonstration for freedom in the history of our nation.

[2] Five score years ago, a great American, in whose symbolic shadow we stand today, signed the Emancipation Proclamation. This momentous decree came as a great beacon light of hope to millions of Negro slaves who had been seared in the flames of withering injustice. It came as a joyous daybreak to end the long night of their captivity. But one hundred years later, the Negro still is not free. One hundred years later, the life of the Negro is still sadly crippled by the manacles of segregation and the chains of discrimination. One hundred years later, the Negro lives on a lonely island of poverty in the midst of a vast ocean of material prosperity. One hundred years later, the Negro

is still anguished in the corners of American society and finds himself in exile in his own land. And so we have come here today to dramatize a shameful condition.

In a sense we have come to our nation's capital to cash a check. [3] When the architects of our republic wrote the magnificent words of the Constitution and the Declaration of Independence, they were signing a promissory note to which every American was to fall heir. This note was the promise that all men—yes, Black men as well as white men— would be guaranteed the inalienable rights of life, liberty, and the pursuit of happiness.

It is obvious today that America has defaulted on this promissory [4] note insofar as her citizens of color are concerned. Instead of honoring this sacred obligation, America has given the Negro people a bad check, a check which has come back marked "insufficient funds." But we refuse to believe that the bank of justice is bankrupt. We refuse to believe that there are insufficient funds in the great vaults of opportunity of this nation; and so we have come to cash this check, a check that will give us upon demand the riches of freedom and the security of justice.

We have also come to this hallowed spot to remind America of [5] the fierce urgency of *now*. This is no time to engage in the luxury of cooling off or to take the tranquilizing drug of gradualism. *Now* is the time to make real the promises of democracy. *Now* is the time to rise from the dark and desolate valley of segregation to the sunlit path of racial justice. *Now* is the time to lift our nation from the quicksands of racial injustice to the solid rock of brotherhood. *Now* is the time to make justice a reality for all of God's children.

It would be fatal for the nation to overlook the urgency of the [6] moment. This sweltering summer of the Negro's legitimate discontent will not pass until there is an invigorating autumn of freedom and equality. Nineteen Sixty-three is not an end, but a beginning. And those who hope that the Negro needed to blow off steam and will now be content will have a rude awakening if the nation returns to business as usual. There will be neither rest nor tranquility in America until the Negro is granted his citizenship rights. The whirlwinds of revolt will continue to shake the foundations of our nation until the bright day of justice emerges.

But there is something that I must say to my people who stand on [7] the warm threshold which leads into the palace of justice. In the process of gaining our rightful place, we must not be guilty of wrongful deeds. Let us not seek to satisfy our thirst for freedom by drinking from the cup of bitterness and hatred. We must forever conduct our struggle on the high plane of dignity and discipline. We must not allow our creative protest to degenerate into physical violence. Again and again we must rise to the majestic heights of meeting physical force with soul force. And the marvelous new militancy which has engulfed the Negro community must not lead us to a distrust of all white people; for many of our white brothers, as evidenced by their presence here today, have come to realize that their destiny is tied up with our destiny, and they have come to realize that their freedom is inextricably bound to our freedom.

[8]        We cannot walk alone. And as we walk we must make the pledge that we shall always march ahead. We cannot turn back. There are those who are asking the devotees of civil rights, "When will you be satisfied?" We can never be satisfied as long as the Negro is the victim of the unspeakable horrors of police brutality. We can never be satisfied as long as our bodies, heavy with the fatigue of travel, cannot gain lodging in the motels of the highways and the hotels of the cities. We cannot be satisfied as long as the Negro's basic mobility is from a smaller ghetto to a larger one. We can never be satisfied as long as our children are stripped of their selfhood and robbed of their dignity by signs stating "For Whites Only." We cannot be satisfied as long as the Negro in Mississippi cannot vote and a Negro in New York believes he has nothing for which to vote. No, no, we are not satisfied, and we will not be satisfied until justice rolls down like waters and righteousness like a mighty stream.

[9]        I am not unmindful that some of you have come here out of great trials and tribulations. Some of you have come fresh from narrow jail cells. Some of you have come from areas where your quest for freedom left you battered by the storms of persecution and staggered by the winds of police brutality. You have been the veterans of creative suffering. Continue to work with the faith that unearned suffering is redemptive.

[10]       Go back to Mississippi, and go back to Alabama. Go back to South Carolina. Go back to Georgia. Go back to Louisiana. Go back to the slums and ghettos of our Northern cities, knowing that somehow

this situation can and will be changed. Let us not wallow in the valley of despair.

I say to you today, my friends, even though we face the difficulties [11] of today and tomorrow, I still have a dream. It is a dream deeply rooted in the American dream. I have a dream that one day this nation will rise up and live out the true meaning of its creed: ''We hold these truths to be self-evident, that all men are created equal.'' I have a dream that one day, on the red hills of Georgia, sons of former slaves and the sons of former slave owners will be able to sit down together at the table of brotherhood. I have a dream that one day even the state of Mississippi, a state sweltering with the heat of injustice, sweltering with the heat of oppression, will be transformed into an oasis of freedom and justice. I have a dream that my four children will one day live in a nation where they will not be judged by the color of their skin, but by the content of their character.

I have a dream today. I have a dream that one day down in [12] Alabama—with its vicious racists, with its governor's lips dripping with the words of interposition and nullification—one day right there in Alabama, little Black boys and Black girls will be able to join hands with little white boys and white girls as sisters and brothers.

I have a dream today. I have a dream that one day every valley [13] shall be exalted and every hill and mountain shall be made low, the rough places will be made plain and the crooked places will be made straight, and the glory of the Lord shall be revealed, and all flesh shall see it together.

This is our hope. This is the faith that I go back to the South with. [14] And with this faith we will be able to hew out of the mountain of despair a stone of hope. With this faith we will be able to transform the jangling discords of our nation into a beautiful symphony of brotherhood. With this faith we will be able to work together, to play together, to struggle together, to go to jail together, to stand up for freedom together, knowing that we will be free one day.

And this will be the day—this will be the day when all of God's [15] children will be able to sing with new meaning:

> My country, 'tis of thee,
> Sweet land of liberty,
> Of thee I sing;

> Land where my fathers died,
> Land of the Pilgrims' pride,
> From every mountainside
> Let freedom ring.

And if America is to be a great nation, this must become true.

[16]    And so let freedom ring from the prodigious hilltops of New Hampshire. Let freedom ring from the mighty mountains of New York. Let freedom ring from the heightening Alleghenies of Pennsylvania. Let freedom ring from the snow-capped Rockies of Colorado. Let freedom ring from the curvaceous slopes of California.

[17]    But not only that. Let freedom ring from Stone Mountain of Georgia. Let freedom ring from Lookout Mountain of Tennessee. Let freedom ring from every hill and molehill of Mississippi. ''From every mountainside let freedom ring.''

[18]    And when this happens—when we allow freedom to ring, when we let it ring from every village and every hamlet, from every state and every city—we will be able to speed up that day when all of God's children, Black men and white men, Jews and Gentiles, Protestants and Catholics, will be able to join hands and sing in the words of the old Negro spiritual: ''Free at last! Free at last! Thank God Almighty. We are free at last!''

## QUESTIONS FOR DISCUSSION

1   Dr. King delivered this speech before a crowd of 250,000 people during the March on Washington, a civil rights demonstration in 1963. What is the ''dream'' referred to in the title?

2   In paragraph 2, with the phrase ''one hundred years later,'' Dr. King begins his masterful use of deliberate repetition which reverberates throughout the speech. (The rhetorical term for this repetition at the beginning of sentences or of lines in poetry is *anaphora*.) Read the paragraph aloud. Can you describe the effect he achieves with this technique? Can you point out other examples of deliberate repetition that you find effective?

3   Another device that Dr. King employs frequently is metaphor. You remember that a metaphor is an imaginative figure of speech in which two unlike things are compared by means of some quality they have in common. For example, in the second paragraph he speaks of the Emancipation Proclamation as a ''great beacon light of hope.'' He continues this metaphor associating hope with the promise of dawn as he goes on to say that the

proclamation "came as a joyous daybreak to end the long night of [the Negro slaves'] captivity." Other metaphors in the same paragraph are "the flames of withering injustice," "the manacles of segregation and the chains of discrimination," and "a lonely island of poverty in the midst of a vast ocean of material prosperity." Can you find similar examples of metaphor in other paragraphs? Comment on their effectiveness.

4   In paragraphs 3 and 4, Dr. King uses an extended analogy (which is a kind of metaphor) to describe the condition of black people in America. Can you describe this comparison? Do you find it effective? Why or why not?

5   The transitional term "But," which begins paragraph 7, signals a change in Dr. King's thinking. What has he been arguing for in the first six paragraphs? What qualification does he add in paragraph 7?

6   Read the final paragraph aloud with as much genuine feeling as you can muster. What elements make this conclusion effective?

# The Rabbits Who Caused All the Trouble

James Thurber

Within the memory of the youngest child there was a family of rabbits [1] who lived near a pack of wolves. The wolves announced that they did not like the way the rabbits were living. (The wolves were crazy about the way they themselves were living, because it was the only way to live.) One night several wolves were killed in an earthquake and this was blamed on the rabbits, for it is well known that rabbits pound on the ground with their hind legs and cause earthquakes. On another night one of the wolves was killed by a bolt of lightning and this was also blamed on the rabbits, for it is well known that lettuce-eaters cause lightning. The wolves threatened to civilize the rabbits if they didn't behave, and the rabbits decided to run away to a desert island. But the other animals, who lived at a great distance, shamed them, saying, "You must stay where you are and be brave. This is no world for escapists. If the wolves attack you, we will come to your aid, in all probability." So the rabbits continued to live near the wolves and one day there was a terrible flood which drowned a great many wolves. This was blamed on the rabbits, for it is well known that carrot-nibblers with long ears cause floods. The wolves descended on the rabbits, for their own good, and imprisoned them in a dark cave, for their own protection.

[2]     When nothing was heard about the rabbits for some weeks, the other animals demanded to know what had happened to them. The wolves replied that the rabbits had been eaten and since they had been eaten the affair was a purely internal matter. But the other animals warned that they might possibly unite against the wolves unless some reason was given for the destruction of the rabbits. So the wolves gave them one. "They were trying to escape," said the wolves, "and, as you know, this is no world for escapists."

*Moral: Run, don't walk, to the nearest desert island.*

## QUESTIONS FOR DISCUSSION

1   Thurber's piece is taken from a volume entitled *Fables for Our Time* (1939). Do you think a fable is an effective way to get a point across? Why or why not?

2   When Thurber published this piece in 1939, he probably intended the rabbits to represent the Jews then being herded into concentration camps by Hitler's storm troopers, the wolves in the tale. Can you think of any people the rabbits could represent today? Who, then, would be the wolves?

3   Why does Thurber refrain from telling us what the rabbits were doing that annoyed the wolves?

4   Who do "the other animals" represent? Thurber mentions that they "lived at a great distance." Does he mean this literally? If not, what does the statement mean?

5   The fable is, of course, humorous, but what more accurate term can you think of to describe the tone?

6   Thurber's moral at the end is fitting, but besides conveying this humorous point, the fable has a broader meaning. Can you state the theme in a single sentence?

# Darkness at Noon

Harold Krents

[1]  Blind from birth, I have never had the opportunity to see myself and have been completely dependent on the image I create in the eye of the observer. To date it has not been narcissistic.

[2]     There are those who assume that since I can't see, I obviously also cannot hear. Very often people will converse with me at the top

of their lungs, enunciating each word very carefully. Conversely, people will also often whisper, assuming that since my eyes don't work, my ears don't either.

For example, when I go to the airport and ask the ticket agent for [3] assistance to the plane, he or she will invariably pick up the phone, call a ground hostess and whisper: "Hi, Jane, we've got a 76 here." I have concluded that the word "blind" is not used for one of two reasons: Either they fear that if the dread word is spoken, the ticket agent's retina will immediately detach, or they are reluctant to inform me of my condition of which I may not have been previously aware.

On the other hand, others know that of course I can hear, but [4] believe that I can't talk. Often, therefore, when my wife and I go out to dinner, a waiter or waitress will ask Kit if "*he* would like a drink" to which I respond that "indeed *he* would."

This point was graphically driven home to me while we were in [5] England. I had been given a year's leave of absence from my Washington law firm to study for a diploma in law degree at Oxford University. During the year I became ill and was hospitalized. Immediately after admission, I was wheeled down to the X-ray room. Just at the door sat an elderly woman—elderly I would judge from the sound of her voice. "What is his name?" the woman asked the orderly who had been wheeling me.

"What's your name?" the orderly repeated to me.                    [6]

"Harold Krents," I replied.                                        [7]

"Harold Krents," he repeated.                                      [8]

"When was he born?"                                                [9]

"When were you born?"                                              [10]

"November 5, 1944," I responded.                                   [11]

"November 5, 1944," the orderly intoned.                           [12]

This procedure continued for approximately five minutes at which [13] point even my saint-like disposition deserted me. "Look," I finally blurted out, "this is absolutely ridiculous. Okay, granted I can't see, but it's got to have become pretty clear to both of you that I don't need an interpreter."

"He says he doesn't need an interpreter," the orderly reported to [14] the woman.

The toughest misconception of all is the view that because I can't [15] see, I can't work. I was turned down by over forty law firms because of my blindness, even though my qualifications included a cum laude degree from Harvard College and a good ranking in my Harvard Law School class.

[16]    The attempt to find employment, the continuous frustration of being told that it was impossible for a blind person to practice law, the rejection letters, not based on my lack of ability but rather on my disability, will always remain one of the most disillusioning experiences of my life.

[17]    Fortunately, this view of limitation and exclusion is beginning to change. On April 16, the Department of Labor issued regulations that mandate equal-employment opportunities for the handicapped. By and large, the business community's response to offering employment to the disabled has been enthusiastic.

[18]    I therefore look forward to the day, with the expectation that it is certain to come, when employers will view their handicapped workers as a little child did me years ago when my family still lived in Scarsdale.

[19]    I was playing basketball with my father in our backyard according to procedures we had developed. My father would stand beneath the hoop, shout, and I would shoot over his head at the basket attached to our garage. Our next-door neighbor, aged five, wandered over into our yard with a playmate. "He's blind," our neighbor whispered to her friend in a voice that could be heard distinctly by Dad and me. Dad shot and missed; I did the same. Dad hit the rim: I missed entirely: Dad shot and missed the garage entirely. "Which one is blind?" whispered back the little friend.

[20]    I would hope that in the near future when a plant manager is touring the factory with the foreman and comes upon a handicapped and nonhandicapped-person working together, his comment after watching them work will be, "Which one is disabled?"

## QUESTIONS FOR DISCUSSION

1   Although this essay is conveyed largely through the use of narrative, the organization is not chronological. Can you explain how the material is organized?

2   Krents employs a lot of direct quotations. What does he gain by repeating the actual remarks instead of summarizing what people said?

3 Krents begins by telling us that he has been blind from birth. Throughout the piece he mentions other personal details about his job and his education. Why are these details an important part of his strategy?

4 Can you describe the tone of the last sentence of paragraph 3? What are your verbal clues?

5 Although Krents does not state his thesis, you can tell that he is trying to make a point. Can you express his thesis in a single sentence?

## SUGGESTIONS FOR WRITING

1  You have always heard about the American dream. Think about what the phrase means to you. Consider whether all people have an equal chance of achieving that dream of success. Think about the essays by Gordon Parks and Russell Baker in the previous chapter; both deal indirectly with the dream.

   Write an essay addressed to a group of Chicano (or Asian or Haitian) immigrants to this country who are about to be granted citizenship. Explain to them—using plenty of specific details—what the American dream entails. Then, warn them of the difficulties you think they may encounter. If possible, conclude by offering advice for overcoming these obstacles.

2  Imitating Dr. King's splendid rhetorical techniques, write your own ''I Have a Dream'' speech in which you envision an America free from toxic wastes or rape or hunger—or whatever your dream entails for improving our society. Your audience will be a joint session of your state legislature.

3  Write a brief fable for junior high school students in which your purpose is to convince them not to use alcohol or to warn them of the danger of AIDS.

4  If you are physically handicapped, write an editorial for your school newspaper explaining to the unhandicapped how to feel more comfortable around you. Pattern your essay on the one by Harold Krents. Think of three or four ways in which thoughtless people annoy you or hurt your feelings and suggest ways to avoid this behavior. Tone is important here. Don't be accusatory; be genial—if possible, humorous.

Chapter 13

# Considering Ethical Issues

## A Teenager's Tragedy:
## Birth and Death in a Florida Town

Charlene Mitchell
Thomas Burdick

The 16-year-old girl hesitates at the doorway. There's a hush as [1] everyone turns. Her features, untouched by makeup, are soft and youthful. She has large eyes that seem to be looking off in the distance. The light hits her face, evoking a luminescent glow. She is obviously weak. She has just been released that day from the hospital, still recovering from the physical and emotional trauma of giving birth alone in her family's home.

A chorus of gasps breaks the silence as onlookers see the iron [2] shackles binding the girl's wrists and ankles. As she shuffles into the courtroom for the preliminary hearing, the girl sees her mother and tears fall down her cheeks. As she sits beside her lawyer at the huge mahogany table, staring at her bound wrists, the spectators scrutinize her face. She looks so much like an ethereal child-martyr, they cannot imagine what drove her to allegedly commit murder.

[3]     When you go as far as you can on the habitable area of southwestern Florida, you reach the pristine resort of Naples. The community is divided into two types of people. The monied reside in estates on the Gulf beaches. The service people live inland in suburbs like Golden Gate, where the homes are well tended and the residents conservative.

[4]     On the morning of January 14, 1987, Michelle Clark broke her routine. Typically, she would accompany her mother, Gail Conyer, from Golden Gate to an island off the coast where Gail managed a delicatessen and Michelle attended a Baptist high school.

[5]     But this morning, Michelle was sick. She said she was having an especially bad period. Since it was nothing serious, her mother and her stepfather, a heavy-machine operator, went to work. As the day passed, Michelle's pain became searing. Finally, half-delirious, she collapsed on the floor as a baby pushed from her body. She hacked at the umbilical cord with a pair of scissors.

[6]     When Gail Conyer returned home that evening, she found blood throughout the house. Insisting that her daughter open her locked bedroom door, Gail saw towels, bed sheets, and clothes soaked with blood. Michelle, who was only semiconscious by then, said, ''I think my liver passed through my body.'' Seeing blood seeping from a bag in the closet, Gail discovered a newborn infant. Gail rushed them both to the hospital. Michelle survived after four blood transfusions. Her son was dead.

[7]     In the hospital, the doctor told Gail the shocking end to Michelle's ordeal. The full-term infant had been born healthy. Then it was stabbed, beaten, and strangled. Michelle was placed under psychiatric care at the hospital. After six weeks, her doctor recommended she return home and undergo outpatient treatment. Instead, she was arrested and held without bail at a youth detention facility pending a first-degree murder charge.

[8]     Over the next several months, the community would reverberate with the repercussions of the incident. No one even tangentially

involved would remain untouched; at least one official would lose his job outright. But more than politics, it was religion that kept cropping up. Not a few people were reminded of the fact-based movie *Agnes of God*, for Michelle was a "good" girl raised in a "religious" home and educated at a "Christian" school. She was steeped in a strict moral code that forbade premarital sex and abortion. Yet despite this—or perhaps because of it—Michelle Clark had allegedly committed murder.

It is perhaps all too easy to see in this story just another sensa- [9] tional tale of blood and hysteria, to forget how pervasive the attitudes are that created the tragedy of Michelle Clark and her baby. This is not just an isolated incident of a teenager trapped by the extremist views of a fundamentalist church. It is a story that could happen in any family where ideology clashes with reality. The outmoded but still prevalent notion that teenagers don't engage in sex and therefore don't need birth control information means that many young women find themselves carrying an unwanted child.

Michelle's story is also a tale of denial. Her family ignored her [10] problems and her needs; her religion also denied Michelle's emotional and sexual needs. It is a pattern mirrored in American society: young women are denied reasonable sex education, affordable abortions, and effective counseling. Many women in America, like Michelle, are struggling to cope with an environment that denies them any "real" choice.

Gail Conyer is nervous. It's two months since Michelle's arrest. [11] For most of our conversation her hands twist constantly in her lap. She speaks softly as if her words will sound better whispered. She is in her mid-thirties, pale by Floridian standards. Adhering to the Scriptures, she wears no makeup, her outfit is modest, and her hair very long. Gail is recalling a dispute she had with her daughter in 1985 that became a turning point in their relationship.

Michelle was 14 then and she wanted her hair cut in the medium- [12] length style popular in her public high school. Mrs. Conyer forbade it because "the Bible says Mary [Magdalene] had long hair and she wiped Jesus' feet with it. That gave a symbol a woman's hair should be long." Michelle didn't care what the Bible said, she wanted to be like the other girls.

According to Rosa Hernandez, then a youth relations officer [13] covering Michelle's high school, "Michelle had problems dealing with her mother being so strict, so religious." Soon after the arguments about her hairstyle, Michelle and a friend scratched their wrists in what Hernandez considered a symbolic suicide attempt. It was the first sign that Gail's intense beliefs were beginning to affect the otherwise normal child. Gail finally relented and Michelle was allowed to cut her hair.

[14]     Gail Conyer embraces her religion unquestioningly. She is a Pentecostal Apostolic—"we believe what the apostles believed." Religion is the one strong foundation in her troubled life. Her first husband, Michelle's father, reportedly beat her. Eight years ago he disappeared and is presumed dead. (There are rumors that something went wrong in a drug-smuggling deal.) Gail's second husband is emotionally distanced from the family.

[15]     As her worldly problems increased, Conyer wrapped herself more tightly in her faith. Mother and daughter were caught in a vicious cycle—the more Gail pushed Michelle toward religion, the more troubles arose between them. Toward the end of Michelle's ninth-grade year, Gail transferred her daughter from a public school to a private fundamentalist school. At the school, she and the other students were lectured ceaselessly about the evils of abortion and premarital sex. Her only close friend there, Cara Scarpa, said, "It seems like they tell us every day."

[16]     Michelle was not even allowed to date, according to psychiatrist José Lombillo, who has treated her. He adds: "But she was allowed to go out with her cousin. He had a twenty-year-old friend." The friend suggested they go to a motel—Michelle apparently thought they were going to watch movies. But the young man wanted sex—and Michelle agreed. "There was only one thing on her mind," Lombillo asserts. "She was thinking of what her mother would say." According to Lombillo, it was the first time Michelle had sex, and she became pregnant.

[17]     "If you're teaching teenagers the right approach to God, then they won't go out and be committing sin," says Gail's pastor, Larry Sims. "So you don't have to worry about birth control." The Reverend is hoarse from his "fire and brimstone" sermons—he calls them "fervent."

[18]     The fundamentalist minister supports Gail's stance with Michelle. "The Scriptures say hair is given to you for a covering." He says the

Bible is a literal guide for contemporary life. "We believe you don't walk around half-naked as they do today. I don't believe in makeup. This is my standpoint and my wife's."

Since everything is grounded in the Bible, members do not accept [19] recent changes in society concerning women. "The man is subjected to the Lord, the woman is subjected to the man," asserts Sims. "As far as going out and dancing in a bar, I don't see how anything could be Christian in that. Especially if you're dancing with the opposite sex. The Bible teaches us to flee the mere appearance of evil and there's more than the appearance there on a dance floor."

Premarital sex is a "sin in the eyes of God," says Reverend Sims. [20] "I tell them the consequences down the road. Pregnancies. Diseases. Not just that this is a sin and you're going to hell."

What if a teenager should get pregnant? The church advocates that [21] the teenager have the child rather than an abortion. "Then I would want them to go on and live their normal life," Sims says.

Assistant State Attorney Jerry Brock is assigned to prosecute [22] Michelle Clark. He is southwest Florida's own shrewd country lawyer—a deceptively mild-looking attorney with the tenacity of a hound dog and an impressive track record. Lately he's been receiving mixed signals about how to handle Clark's case.

"There was a lot of high-level political pressure in this baby- [23] killing," says Harold Young, the sheriff department's chief homicide investigator on the case. He notes that at first a number of officials— he includes himself—pushed for the filing of first-degree murder charges, which carry the death penalty as the maximum punishment. But as the prosecution machinery began to grind, Michelle made her appearance in court forlorn and shackled. A color photo of her ran on the front page of the local paper and galvanized public opinion. "There were lots of letters to the editors in favor of the young girl," recalls Young. Overnight the case turned from "star-maker" to "political hot potato."

The state, in its initial eagerness to prosecute, had backed itself [24] into a corner with strong public pronouncements about the "brutal" murder. Now, they began looking for a face-saving way out, and settled on the sheriff's department. Young says his office became the scapegoat—officials suddenly began to claim that Young's homicide unit had messed up the crime scene, providing them with a much needed excuse for dropping the case.

[25]     Young began taping his conversations with Jerry Brock, to show that it was actually the D.A.'s office doing the backpedaling. In Florida it is illegal in most cases to tape your own phone calls if the other party is not told, so when someone leaked the story to the press, Young, a well-liked officer, was forced to step down after 17 years on the force.

[26]     According to Young, a grand jury was "on the verge of indicting her for first-degree murder," when Brock went back and asked them to wait, saying there would be more evidence in the future. "It was a clever way to throw the case," says Young. "They didn't get an indictment because they didn't ask for one." Michelle was eventually charged with a more politically "acceptable" crime, second-degree murder, which doesn't carry the death penalty. As of press time, the case had yet to go to trial.

[27]     All but forgotten in the scramble was Michelle. First she was in the psychiatric ward, then she was in the county jail for a few hours. Conyer says, "The psychiatrists said they [the officials] had destroyed in those five hours what it had taken them over two months to do." Next, she was placed in a youth holding facility; after the second-degree murder charge was brought in, bail was finally set. Michelle was incarcerated for three months.

[28]     Gail recalls that for the first few weeks in the youth holding facility "Michelle cried day and night. So they put her on a heavier drug." But the guards didn't want Michelle, drugged or not. "They were getting aggravated," recalls Conyer, "and yelled a lot. When you yell at her, she just cries. Then they'd get more aggravated with her."

[29]     Originally Conyer expected more sympathy from officials. When the police came that January night, "they said they were my friends. So I'm comforted. I didn't realize we needed an attorney. I thought they were going to help. Then down the road they're really against us. They treated Michelle not like a person with a problem, but like a mass murderer."

[30]     Young agrees that the investigators were initially understanding and the female officer in charge of the questioning was quite sympathetic. "She said Michelle was a cute, freckle-faced, little girl," recalls

Young. "I took her to the autopsy and said look at the baby. Her attitude immediately became different." Young, a grandfather, can't forget the baby. "[It] was perfect in every way," he says. "A very pretty baby."

"She never had a baby in her mind. It was like a monster, a [31] creature," says her psychiatrist, Dr. José Lombillo, who testified in court about Michelle and is noted for his professional involvement in a number of celebrated murder cases. During those last months before the birth, he says Michelle became obsessed with horror movies of the kind where creatures erupt from human bodies and women give birth to demonic babies.

"This is the most fascinating case of denial I've ever encoun- [32] tered," says Lombillo. "The intensity is just tremendous. So much drama. Pressure. You have the denial not only through the whole pregnancy but even while she is having the baby."

According to Lombillo, the extreme circumstances of the birth [33] had a profound effect on Michelle. "You're losing blood, losing control of yourself. You're alone. I have women delivering a baby and they have all the support of their family and doctors and they're in the hospital. It's still a traumatic experience. But when you are alone, and you're passing in and out of consciousness, that is very different." Lombillo says Michelle nearly died because she lost almost half of her blood.

Michelle had no recollection of anything right after the birth. "If [34] you can block your pregnancy you can block all that too," explains Lombillo. "Denial was very important in the family. Michelle didn't have any trouble convincing people she wasn't pregnant because she didn't believe she was. . . ." Her mother approaches everything "in terms of black and white," adds Lombillo. "You forget anything that is black. It is complete, total denial." As for Michelle's stepfather, "Gail's husband is like a wall hanging," says Lombillo. "He has nothing to say in the family."

Harold Young would probably agree with that assessment. [35] According to him, Conyer was not the first to arrive home on January 14. Her husband and stepson were there already watching the television—which had a puddle of blood in front of it. Both have denied seeing the blood.

[36]       Michelle is still at home. Gail has also been keeping her stepson
out of school because classmates were taunting him. Despite the fact
that Michelle is slated for trial, with prison as a possible outcome,
Conyer is making plans. "When this is all over we have an area picked
out. They have the same type of school." Conyer insists everything is
back to normal. "Michelle sees a psychiatrist once a week. At home
it's just like she's back into it: she laughs and pokes and tickles. She's
doing good. When she came back home we let her have our bedroom.
And she's having a ball. She has her own bathroom and telephone. I
know she probably thinks about everything. But they helped her quite
a bit at the hospital—you know, and life goes on."

*Editor's note:* Following her trial, Michelle was granted probation which included
extensive psychiatric counseling.

## QUESTIONS FOR DISCUSSION

1   What descriptive details in the introduction immediately engage your attention and make you want to continue reading?

2   Why do the authors mention the young woman's age and lack of makeup
in the first paragraph but wait until the fourth paragraph to give her name?

3   What is your response to the phrase "iron shackles" in the first sentence
of paragraph 2? Would the effect have been the same if the authors had
written "metal chains"? Can you explain why? In paragraph 23, the
sheriff's investigator refers to "this baby-killing." Can you think of a more
neutral term he could have used if he felt sympathy for Michelle?

4   This essay involves a controversy—the question of Michelle's criminal guilt
in the death of her baby. Locate details within the first ten paragraphs that
clearly indicate which side the authors support.

5   Why do the authors focus on Michelle's mother in paragraphs 11 through
16? On her pastor in paragraphs 17 through 21? Why do they save the
observations of her psychiatrist until last in paragraphs 31 through 35?

6   Why do the authors include these details: Michelle's step-father "is
emotionally distanced from the family" (paragraph 14); her minister "is
hoarse from his 'fire and brimstone' sermons . . ." (paragraph 17)?

7   Like many narratives, this article does not begin with a clearly stated thesis,
but the authors are definitely trying to make a point. Can you state their
purpose in writing? What do they want their readers to learn from this
piece? In which paragraph do the authors come closest to stating their thesis?

# A Priest's Painful Choice

Charles R. Burns

"How odd," I thought, "that he should come to see me." The young [1] man was obviously distressed and experiencing great difficulty trying to verbalize his pain. He was 25 years old, darkly handsome and dying of AIDS. His parents knew neither that he had AIDS nor that he was an active homosexual. And he had come to me, a Roman Catholic priest, for help.

It was yet another of those times when I knew all the right things [2] to say but knew, too, that the right things were wrong. Bobby resurrected ghosts in my psyche and for a moment I knew the terror of an Orestes pursued by the Furies. In all my religious training I had been given rules that embodied good intentions. But upon application in particular cases, they revealed an inflexibility that could drive you crazy. Bobby had asked me a very simple thing: would I stand with him as he tried to talk to his parents?

Church law forbids homosexual acts, however, and according to [3] the rules, I should have condemned him. But I stood with Bobby and helped his parents accept him as I was also learning to do. He was a man of faith who happened to be a homosexual. And I was struck by his obvious sincerity. We talked many hours after that, and I managed to pry open, with his help, a steamer trunk of past regrets—of relationships I had run away from because my training taught me that any relationship could become sexual. It also taught me to fear homosexual men, and so I dealt with them as nonpersons; I did the same with women.

When I entered the seminary 30 years ago, everything was set and [4] sure. You knew what the rules were. Anything not within their purview belonged to that hazy limbo labeled "a mystery." Seminary living is just slightly less natural than foot-binding. We were 70-odd men gathered together in our late teens and herded into a totally male environment. We slept in the same huge dormitory and studied in the same huge hall. We had individual desks, but nothing about them was allowed any trace of individual expression. The world we lived in was impersonal, a long black line of marching heads bent at the same angle. Is it any wonder some of us became depersonalized?

[5]     We were trained and taught to have the right answers. A few years later when each of us had his own room, we were forbidden to visit anyone else's room without the door being ajar. Aside from the sniggering and unspoken fear of homosexuality, such arrangements also precluded intimacy. The preclusion was worse than the fear; how does one grow as a person without intimacy? We were also warned about the danger of having a "particular friendship." Particular friendships became the altar upon which intimacy was sacrificed.

[6]     I always suspected that drawing close to a man or a woman would automatically lead to sexual involvement. One learned to avoid involvement. One learned to follow the directives and to "fit in" with all the others. One learned never to be particularly noteworthy—either by doing something well or by doing it badly. Getting along with others was prized. I learned how to banter and to make clever remarks; this smoothed relationships. It was a life devoted to getting others to accept me rather than of accepting myself.

[7]     Bobby once asked me why I always kidded him. He told me that he knew that I loved him and cared deeply about him, but he wondered why I always tried to have something funny to say. I had no answer. Instead we began talking about my past, and his, and how I developed the essentially defensive bantering device. In his pajamas, with tubes running into his body, Bobby became a healer for me. Gradually, I learned how to lean over his bed and kiss him goodbye without any trace of fear or suspicion of lust. Each time I left him I began to realize it might be a final leave-taking, and so I wanted him to know at the last that I loved him very much.

[8]     My earlier training had been how to get along in an institution, how to be a person whose intellect always controlled his emotions. Bobby helped me to realize that I was starving even as he lost more weight than he could possibly afford. I began to understand that old verity: if you deal with the dying, they will give you life.


## ACCEPTANCE AND FORGIVENESS

[9]  Two months after Bobby died, Kevin's family called and I was all set to perform another good deed. Again I would appear at an AIDS victim's side, help him receive the sacraments, and I would be properly recognized. There was even an added thrill because, at the time, visits

to AIDS patients were still suspect and filled with the fear of contamination. But Kevin's situation did not work out according to my scenario. He refused my sacramental ministrations.

During the 17 years of my priesthood, I had grown accustomed [10] to people bringing me their love and their hate. But it was surprising to me that I respected Kevin for refusing. It was consistent with the faith with which he had grown comfortable: a faith that says we cannot limit acceptance and forgiveness. The wasted body was not about to give in to superstition, nor was he about to feign being accepted into the arms of a church that had spent the greater part of his life rejecting him. I became awed by the power of the man and almost asked his blessing. Now, I wish I had.

In the 23rd chapter of Matthew's Gospel, Jesus admonished his [11] disciples: "Call no one on earth your father. . . ." It is a favored text among the more vigorous fundamentalists who are angry at my church. Bobby and Kevin taught me that I am not their father: that I had enough trouble just trying to be their friend. I try to be a good person, as did they. I try to help, and so did they. I bumble and strive at love, and so did they.

My seminary training would have led me to be distant from those [12] whom, I have learned, I would rather love. There are those in power in my church who would make themselves distant from me in the same way. Yet, I now make the conscious choice to love and to befriend. I do it for Kevin and for Bobby. I do it for all who are like them. And there are moments when I stand before the altar and I hear them calling out to me, "Way to go, Charlie. Don't let anyone call you father. Don't keep anyone away."

## QUESTIONS FOR DISCUSSION

1 What techniques does Burns employ in his introduction to engage your attention?
2 Why does Burns devote two paragraphs (4 and 5) to describing his seminary training?
3 Can you comment on the meaning and effectiveness of these figures of speech: "I knew the terror of an Orestes pursued by the Furies" (paragraph 2); "I managed to pry open, with his help, a steamer trunk of past regrets . . ." (paragraph 3); "Seminary living is just slightly less natural than foot-binding" (paragraph 4); and "Particular friendships became the altar upon which intimacy was sacrificed" (paragraph 5)?

4  Why does Burns put the phrase "particular friendships" in quotation marks the first time he uses it in paragraph 5? What does the phrase actually mean?

5  Can you explain the effectiveness of the last three sentences in paragraph 11?

6  What is the purpose of this essay? Does Burns ever state his thesis? What is his main point?

# A Hanging

## George Orwell

[1]  It was in Burma, a sodden morning of the rains. A sickly light, like yellow tinfoil, was slanting over the high walls into the jail yard. We were waiting outside the condemned cells, a row of sheds fronted with double bars, like small animal cages. Each cell measured about ten feet by ten and was quite bare within except for a plank bed and a pot of drinking water. In some of them brown silent men were squatting at the inner bars, with their blankets draped round them. These were the condemned men, due to be hanged within the next week or two.

[2]      One prisoner had been brought out of his cell. He was a Hindu, a puny wisp of a man, with a shaven head and vague liquid eyes. He had a thick, sprouting moustache, absurdly too big for his body, rather like the moustache of a comic man on the films. Six tall Indian warders were guarding him and getting him ready for the gallows. Two of them stood by with rifles with fixed bayonets, while the others handcuffed him, passed a chain through his handcuffs and fixed it to their belts, and lashed his arms tight to his sides. They crowded very close about him, with their hands always on him in a careful, caressing grip, as though all the while feeling him to make sure he was there. It was like men handling a fish which is still alive and may jump back into the water. But he stood quite unresisting, yielding his arms limply to the ropes, as though he hardly noticed what was happening.

[3]      Eight o'clock struck and a bugle call, desolately thin in the wet air, floated from the distant barracks. The superintendent of the jail, who was standing apart from the rest of us, moodily prodding the gravel with his stick, raised his head at the sound. He was an army doctor, with a grey toothbrush moustache and a gruff voice. "For God's sake

hurry up, Francis,'' he said irritably. ''The man ought to have been dead by this time. Aren't you ready yet?''

Francis, the head jailer, a fat Dravidian in a white drill suit and [4] gold spectacles, waved his black hand. ''Yes sir, yes sir,'' he bubbled. All iss satisfactorily prepared. The hangman iss waiting. We shall proceed.''

''Well, quick march, then. The prisoners can't get their breakfast [5] till this job's over.''

We set out for the gallows. Two warders marched on either side [6] of the prisoner, with their rifles at the slope; two others marched close against him, gripping him by arm and shoulder, as though at once pushing and supporting him. The rest of us, magistrates and the like, followed behind. Suddenly, when we had gone ten yards, the procession stopped short without any order or warning. A dreadful thing had happened—a dog, come goodness knows whence, had appeared in the yard. It came bounding among us with a loud volley of barks, and leapt round us wagging its whole body, wild with glee at finding so many human beings together. It was a large woolly dog, half Airedale, half pariah. For a moment it pranced round us, and then, before anyone could stop it, it had made a dash for the prisoner, and jumping up tried to lick his face. Everyone stood aghast, too taken aback even to grab at the dog.

''Who let that bloody brute in here?'' said the superintendent [7] angrily. ''Catch it, someone!''

A warder, detached from the escort, charged clumsily after the [8] dog, but it danced and gambolled just out of his reach, taking everything as part of the game. A young Eurasian jailer picked up a handful of gravel and tried to stone the dog away, but it dodged the stones and came after us again. Its yaps echoed from the jail walls. The prisoner, in the grasp of the two warders, looked on incuriously, as though this was another formality of the hanging. It was several minutes before someone managed to catch the dog. Then we put my handkerchief through its collar and moved off once more, with the dog still straining and whimpering.

It was about forty yards to the gallows. I watched the bare brown [9] back of the prisoner marching in front of me. He walked clumsily with his bound arms, but quite steadily, with that bobbing gait of the Indian who never straightens his knees. At each step his muscles slid neatly into place, the lock of hair on his scalp danced up and down, his feet printed themselves on the wet gravel. And once, in spite of the men who gripped him by each shoulder, he stepped slightly aside to avoid a puddle on the path.

[10]     It is curious, but till that moment I had never realised what it means to destroy a healthy, conscious man. When I saw the prisoner step aside to avoid the puddle, I saw the mystery, the unspeakable wrongness, of cutting a life short when it is in full tide. This man was not dying, he was alive just as we were alive. All the organs of his body were working—bowels digesting food, skin renewing itself, nails growing, tissues forming—all toiling away in solemn foolery. His nails would still be growing when he stood on the drop, when he was falling through the air with a tenth of a second to live. His eyes saw the yellow gravel and the grey walls, and his brain still remembered, foresaw, reasoned—reasoned even about puddles. He and we were a party of men walking together, seeing, hearing, feeling, understanding the same world; and in two minutes, with a sudden snap, one of us would be gone—one mind less, one world less.

[11]     The gallows stood in a small yard, separate from the main grounds of the prison, and overgrown with tall prickly weeds. It was a brick erection like three sides of a shed, with planking on top, and above that two beams and a crossbar with the rope dangling. The hangman, a greyhaired convict in the white uniform of the prison, was waiting beside his machine. He greeted us with a servile crouch as we entered. At a word from Francis the two warders, gripping the prisoner more closely than ever, half led, half pushed him to the gallows and helped him clumsily up the ladder. Then the hangman climbed up and fixed the rope round the prisoner's neck.

[12]     We stood waiting, five yards away. The warders had formed in a rough circle round the gallows. And then, when the noose was fixed, the prisoner began crying out on his god. It was a high, reiterated cry of ''Ram! Ram! Ram! Ram!'', not urgent and fearful like a prayer or a cry for help, but steady, rhythmical, almost like the tolling of a bell. The dog answered the sound with a whine. The hangman, still standing on the gallows, produced a small cotton bag like a flour bag and drew it down over the prisoner's face. But the sound, muffled by the cloth, still persisted, over and over again: ''Ram! Ram! Ram! Ram! Ram!''

[13]     The hangman climbed down and stood ready, holding the lever.

Minutes seemed to pass. The steady, muffled crying from the prisoner went on and on. "Ram! Ram! Ram!" never faltering for an instant. The superintendent, his head on his chest, was slowly poking the ground with his stick; perhaps he was counting the cries, allowing the prisoner a fixed number—fifty, perhaps, or a hundred. Everyone had changed colour. The Indians had gone grey like a bad coffee, and one or two of the bayonets were wavering. We looked at the lashed, hooded man on the drop, and listened to his cries—each cry another second of life; the same thought was in all our minds: oh, kill him quickly, get it over, stop that abominable noise!

Suddenly the superintendent made up his mind. Throwing up his [14] head he made a swift motion with his stick. "Chalo!" he shouted almost fiercely.

There was a clanking noise, and then dead silence. The prisoner [15] had vanished, and the rope was twisting on itself. I let go of the dog, and it galloped immediately to the back of the gallows; but when it got there it stopped short, barked, and then retreated into a corner of the yard, where it stood among the weeds, looking timorously out at us. We went round the gallows to inspect the prisoner's body. He was dangling with his toes straight downwards, very slowly revolving, as dead as a stone.

The superintendent reached out with his stick and poked the bare [16] body; it oscillated, slightly. "*He's* all right," said the superintendent. He backed out from under the gallows, and blew out a deep breath. The moody look had gone out of his face quite suddenly. He glanced at his wristwatch. "Eight minutes past eight. Well, that's all for this morning, thank God."

The warders unfixed bayonets and marched away. The dog, [17] sobered and conscious of having misbehaved itself, slipped after them. We walked out of the gallows yard, past the condemned cells with their waiting prisoners, into the big central yard of the prison. The convicts, under the command of warders armed with lathis, were already receiving their breakfast. They squatted in long rows, each man holding a tin pannikin, while two warders with buckets marched round ladling out rice; it seemed quite a homely, jolly scene, after the hanging. An enormous relief had come upon us now that the job was done. One felt an impulse to sing, to break into a run, to snigger. All at once everyone began chattering gaily.

[18]     The Eurasian boy walking beside me nodded towards the way we had come, with a knowing smile: "Do you know, sir, our friend (he meant the dead man), when he heard his appeal had been dismissed, he pissed on the floor of his cell. From fright.—Kindly take one of my cigarettes, sir. Do you not admire my new silver case, sir? From the boxwallah, two rupees eight annas. Classy European style."

[19]     Several people laughed—at what, nobody seemed certain.

[20]     Francis was walking by the superintendent, talking garrulously: "Well, sir, all hass passed off with the utmost satisfactoriness. It wass all finished—flick! like that. It iss not always so—oah, no! I have known cases where the doctor wass obliged to go beneath the gallows and pull the prisoner's legs to ensure decease. Most disagreeable!"

[21]     "Wriggling about, eh? That's bad," said the superintendent.

[22]     "Ach, sir, it iss worse when they become refractory! One man, I recall, clung to the bars of hiss cage when we went to take him out. You will scarcely credit, sir, that it took six warders to dislodge him, three pulling at each leg. We reasoned with him. 'My dear fellow,' we said, 'think of all the pain and trouble you are causing to us!' But no, he would not listen! Ach, he wass very troublesome!"

[23]     I found that I was laughing quite loudly. Everyone was laughing. Even the superintendent grinned in a tolerant way. "You'd better all come out and have a drink," he said quite genially. "I've got a bottle of whisky in the car. We could do with it."

[24]     We went through the big double gates of the prison, into the road. "Pulling at his legs!" exclaimed a Burmese magistrate suddenly, and burst into a loud chuckling. We all began laughing again. At that moment Francis's anecdote seemed extraordinarily funny. We all had a drink together, native and European alike, quite amicably. The dead man was a hundred years away.

## QUESTIONS FOR DISCUSSION

1   How does Orwell engage your attention in his introduction?

2   Why is the appearance of the dog in paragraph 6 described as "a terrible thing"? The dog is mentioned again in paragraphs 12 and 15. Can you tell why?

3   Why does the superintendent seem so irritable before the hanging? Why are all the officials in such a good humor following the hanging?

4   Can you explain what makes the conclusion effective?

5 In this narrative, Orwell comes right out and states the point he wants to make in paragraph 10. Do you consider this thesis statement effective, or would the essay have been better without that paragraph? Why do you think Orwell included it?

# The Penalty of Death

H. L. Mencken

Of the arguments against capital punishment that issue from uplifters, [1] two are commonly heard most often, to wit:

1 That hanging a man (or frying him or gassing him) is a dreadful business, degrading to those who have to do it and revolting to those who have to witness it.

2 That it is useless, for it does not deter others from the same crime.

The first of these arguments, it seems to me, is plainly too weak [2] to need serious refutation. All it says, in brief, is that the work of the hangman is unpleasant. Granted. But suppose it is? It may be quite necessary to society for all that. There are, indeed, many other jobs that are unpleasant, and yet no one thinks of abolishing them—that of the plumber, that of the soldier, that of the garbage-man, that of the priest hearing confessions, that of the sand-hog, and so on. Moreover, what evidence is there that any actual hangman complains of his work? I have heard none. On the contrary, I have known many who delighted in their ancient art, and practiced it proudly.

In the second argument of the abolitionists there is rather more [3] force, but even here, I believe, the ground under them is shaky. Their fundamental error consists in assuming that the whole aim of punishing criminals is to deter other (potential) criminals—that we hang or electrocute A simply in order to so alarm B that he will not kill C. This, I believe, is an assumption which confuses a part with the whole. Deterrence, obviously, is *one* of the aims of punishment, but it is surely not the only one. On the contrary, there are at least a half dozen, and some are probably quite as important. At least one of them, practically considered, is *more* important. Commonly, it is described as revenge, but revenge is really not the word for it. I borrow a better term from the late Aristotle: *katharsis*. *Katharsis*, so used, means a salubrious discharge of emotions, a healthy letting off of steam. A school-boy, disliking his teacher, deposits a tack upon the pedagogical chair; the teacher jumps and the boy laughs. This is *katharsis*. What I contend is that one of the prime objects of all judicial punishments is to afford the same grateful relief (*a*) to the immediate victims of the criminal punished, and (*b*) to the general body of moral and timorous men.

[4]     These persons, and particularly the first group, are concerned only indirectly with deterring other criminals. The thing they crave primarily is the satisfaction of seeing the criminal actually before them suffer as he made them suffer. What they want is the peace of mind that goes with the feeling that accounts are squared. Until they get that satisfaction they are in a state of emotional tension, and hence unhappy. The instant they get it they are comfortable. I do not argue that this yearning is noble; I simply argue that it is almost universal among human beings. In the face of injuries that are unimportant and can be borne without damage it may yield to higher impulses; that is to say, it may yield to what is called Christian charity. But when the injury is serious Christianity is adjourned, and even saints reach for their sidearms. It is plainly asking too much of human nature to expect it to conquer so natural an impulse. A keeps a store and has a bookkeeper, B. B steals $700, employs it in playing at dice or bingo, and is cleaned out. What is A to do? Let B go? If he does so he will be unable to sleep at night. The sense of injury, of injustice, of frustration will haunt him like pruritus. So he turns B over to the police, and they hustle B to prison. Therefore A can sleep. More, he has pleasant dreams. He pictures B chained to the wall of a dungeon a hundred feet underground, devoured by rats and scorpions. It is so agreeable that it makes him forget his $700. He has got his *katharsis*.

[5]     The same thing precisely takes place on a larger scale when there is a crime which destroys a whole community's sense of security. Every law-abiding citizen feels menaced and frustrated until the criminals have been struck down—until the communal capacity to get even with them, and more than even, has been dramatically demonstrated. Here, manifestly, the business of deterring others is no more than an afterthought. The main thing is to destroy the concrete scoundrels whose act has alarmed everyone, and thus made everyone unhappy. Until they are brought to book that unhappiness continues; when the law has been

executed upon them there is a sigh of relief. In other words, there is *katharsis*.

I know of no public demand for the death penalty for ordinary [6] crimes, even for ordinary homicides. Its infliction would shock all men of normal decency of feeling. But for crimes involving the deliberate and inexcusable taking of human life, by men openly defiant of all civilized order—for such crimes it seems, to nine men out of ten, a just and proper punishment. Any lesser penalty leaves them feeling that the criminal has got the better of society—that he is free to add insult to injury by laughing. That feeling can be dissipated only by a recourse to *katharsis*, the invention of the aforesaid Aristotle. It is more effectively and economically achieved, as human nature now is, by wafting the criminal to realms of bliss.

The real objection to capital punishment doesn't lie against the [7] actual extermination of the condemned, but against our brutal American habit of putting it off so long. After all, every one of us must die soon or late, and a murderer, it must be assumed, is one who makes that sad fact the cornerstone of his metaphysic. But it is one thing to die, and quite another thing to lie for long months and even years under the shadow of death. No sane man would choose such a finish. All of us, despite the Prayer Book, long for a swift and unexpected end. Unhappily, a murderer, under the irrational American system, is tortured for what, to him, must seem a whole series of eternities. For months on end he sits in prison while his lawyers carry on their idiotic buffoonery with writs, injunctions, mandamuses, and appeals. In order to get his money (or that of his friends) they have to feed him with hope. Now and then, by the imbecility of a judge or some trick of juridic science, they actually justify it. But let us say that, his money all gone, they finally throw up their hands. Their client is now ready for the rope or the chair. But he must still wait for months before it fetches him.

That wait, I believe, is horribly cruel. I have seen more than one [8] man sitting in the death-house, and I don't want to see any more. Worse, it is wholly useless. Why should he wait at all? Why not hang him the day after the last court dissipates his last hope? Why torture him as not even cannibals would torture their victims? The common answer is that he must have time to make his peace with God. But how long does that take? It may be accomplished, I believe, in two hours quite as comfortably as in two years. There are, indeed, no temporal limitations upon God. He could forgive a whole herd of murderers in a millionth of a second. More, it has been done.

## QUESTIONS FOR DISCUSSION

1 Do you consider Mencken's introduction effective? Explain why or why not.
2 Mencken uses a couple of rhetorical questions in paragraph 2. What function do they serve? He employs several more questions near the beginning of his final paragraph. How do the questions in the conclusion differ from those in the second paragraph?
3 Why do you think Mencken argues in paragraph 3 that "revenge is really not the right word" and suggests instead the term *katharsis*? Can you explain the distinction that he's trying to make?
4 In paragraph 4 Mencken observes that unimportant injuries "may yield to what is called Christian charity. But when the injury is serious Christianity is adjourned, and even saints reach for their sidearms." Do you think this appraisal of human nature is accurate? Why or why not?
5 Despite the seriousness of his argument, Mencken's essay is often humorous. Can you explain a couple of his techniques for achieving humor?

## SUGGESTIONS FOR WRITING

1 Can you think of any way to prevent teenage pregnancies—any way other than instilling fear, that is? Michelle Clark's mother and minister tried that method and it failed. Do you think sex education in the schools helps—or is the need of teenaged girls to be "loved" by someone of the opposite sex too strong to be resisted? Consider what social pressures may contribute to that need. Do you think that females are enculturated to want to please males? Why are very young girls so eager to wear makeup, shave their legs, and wear jewelry? Does having a boyfriend make a teenaged girl feel more important, more popular, more successful than having a girlfriend? Why should that be so? What influences in society contribute to these values? What influences try to counteract them—with little success? What role should young males play in preventing pregnancy? Can you think of any way to persuade young men to behave with equal responsibility when young women are the ones who bear the consequences? And what about AIDS? Will the fear of an early death be strong enough to counteract social and biological pressures?

After thinking about these difficult questions and perhaps doing some reading in the library about teenage pregnancy, write an essay directed toward the students of the junior high school you once attended. Suggest in as convincing a tone as possible some reasonable ways in which they could alter their behavior and alleviate the problem. Remember that your main challenge will be to convince these readers of the need to change their ways.

2 Charles Burns went against the teachings of his church in order to follow the dictates of his conscience in providing spiritual comfort to dying AIDS victims. He justifies his actions on grounds of compassion.

Think of a time when you did something that you knew in your heart to be right but something that others might consider wrong—perhaps helping a friend get an abortion (or refusing to do so), resisting the draft registration, rejecting your parents' religion, testifying against a friend on trial for drunk driving, reporting (or not reporting) a friend for shoplifting, or turning in your neighbors for child abuse.

Describe your ethical dilemma and explain how you worked it out. Your purpose will be to show that one must always make the right choice, not the easy choice. You could address your remarks to your classmates, but should you wish to address a wider audience, you could write for publication in *Newsweek*'s "My Turn" column which prints personal opinion pieces from readers, including Charles Burns's "A Priest's Painful Choice."

**3**  George Orwell and H. L. Mencken take opposite sides in the death penalty
argument. Which writer offers the more convincing case? Try to be objective about your analysis of the two essays. Discuss the effectiveness of the
rhetorical strategies of each writer; consider how skillfully they present
their viewpoints. Since Orwell makes no attempt to review the reasons for
opposing the death penalty, you should not focus simply on the strength of
their arguments. Instead, focus on how well each essay convinces. You
may conclude by stating your views on the matter and admitting that your
preconceptions may have influenced your response. Your audience for this
piece should be your instructor in this course. You could include your
classmates in your audience, if all have read both essays.

Chapter 14

# Considering Gender Roles

## Shakespeare's Sister

Virginia Woolf

It would have been impossible, completely and entirely, for any woman [1] to have written the plays of Shakespeare in the age of Shakespeare. Let me imagine, since facts are so hard to come by, what would have happened had Shakespeare had a wonderfully gifted sister, called Judith, let us say. Shakespeare himself went, very probably—his mother was an heiress—to the grammar school, where he may have learnt Latin—Ovid, Virgil and Horace—and the elements of grammar and logic. He was, it is well known, a wild boy who poached rabbits, perhaps shot a deer, and had, rather sooner than he should have done, to marry a woman in the neighbourhood, who bore him a child rather quicker than was right. That escapade sent him to seek his fortune in London. He had, it seemed, a taste for the theatre; he began by holding horses at the stage door. Very soon he got work in the theatre, became a successful actor, and lived at the hub of the universe, meeting everybody, knowing everybody, practising his art on the boards, exercising his wits in the streets, and even getting access to the palace of the queen. Meanwhile his extraordinarily gifted sister, let us suppose, remained at home. She was as adventurous, as imaginative, as agog to see the world as he was. But she was not sent to school. She had no chance of learning grammar and logic, let alone of reading Horace and Virgil. She picked up a book now and then, one of her brother's perhaps, and read a few pages. But then her parents came in and told her to mend the stockings or mind the stew and not moon about with books and papers. They would have spoken sharply but kindly, for they were substantial people who knew the conditions of life for a woman and loved their daughter—indeed, more likely than not she was the apple of her father's eye. Perhaps she scribbled some pages up in an apple loft on the sly, but was careful to hide them or set fire to them. Soon, however, before she was out of her teens, she was to be betrothed to the son of a neighbouring wool-stapler. She cried out that marriage was hateful to her, and for that she was severely beaten by her father. Then he ceased to scold her. He begged her instead not to hurt him, not to shame him in this matter of her marriage. He would give her a chain of beads or a fine petticoat, he said; and there were tears in his eyes. How could she disobey him? How could she break his heart? The force of her own gift alone drove her to it. She made up a small parcel of her belongings, let herself down by a rope one summer's night and took the road to London. She was not seventeen. The birds that sang in the hedge were not more musical than she was. She had the quickest fancy, a gift like her brother's, for the tune of words. Like him, she had a taste for the theatre. She stood at the stage door; she wanted to act, she said. Men laughed in her face. The manager—a fat, loose-lipped man—guffawed. He bellowed something about poodles dancing and women acting—no woman, he said, could possibly be an actress. He hinted—you can imagine what. She could get no training in her craft. Could she even seek her dinner in a tavern or roam the streets at midnight? Yet her genius was for fiction and lusted to feed abundantly upon the lives of men and women and the study of their ways. At last—for she was very young, oddly like Shakespeare the poet in her face, with the same grey eyes and rounded brows—at last Nick Greene the actor-manager took pity on her; she found herself with child by that gentleman and so—who shall measure the heat and violence of the poet's heart when caught and tangled in a woman's body?—killed herself one winter's night and lies buried at some cross-roads where the omnibuses now stop outside the Elephant and Castle.

That, more or less, is how the story would run, I think, if a woman [2] in Shakespeare's day had had Shakespeare's genius.

## QUESTIONS FOR DISCUSSION

1  Do you know why Woolf suggests that Shakespeare's imaginary sister might have been named Judith? Look up the name in an encyclopedia and see if you can tell.
2  Why does Woolf give us a brief sketch of Shakespeare's early life when her focus is on the sister?
3  The theater manager in London "hinted—you can imagine what" about Judith. What do you imagine? Why doesn't Woolf say? (This selection was taken from *A Room of One's Own*, published in 1919.)
4  Near the end of the first long paragraph, we are told, "at last Nick Greene the actor-manager took pity" on Judith. Would you call what he did to the young girl "taking pity"? Why does Woolf choose those terms?
5  Woolf has created this narrative about an imaginary sister in order to make a point. What is her thesis?

# Women Divided: Family or Career?

Ellen Goodman

Every few months, there is another public announcement of retirement [1] from the ranks of superwoman. The notice may be posted in a newspaper or in a magazine, the woman may be a disillusioned lawyer or a disillusioned MBA, but she is sure to be a high-powered professional who decided to go home.

The articles invariably contain a paragraph or two explaining how [2] "the feminists" convinced her that she should do it all: work, wife, mother. Anything less was, well, less. But there came a moment, or a second child, when she felt something had to give and so she gave up the office. Family came first.

The responses to these announcements are almost as familiar by [3] now as the notices. In letters to the editor, one woman will surely (and perhaps angrily) remind the author that not every mother has an economic choice. Another will resent the fact that the author blames feminism for the stress. A third will bristle at the implication that the children of employed mothers suffer.

[4]     And then, in a little while, the argument that has no final answer, that remains as emotional as any in our public private life, fades out of print only to recycle over and over again.

[5]     This time it has been written large onto the cover of a new book, *A Mother's Work*. The author flags the dilemma this way: "Like many women I was educated to feel that my career and my family should both come first. One day I had to make a choice."

[6]     The "I" is Deborah Fallows, a woman who wrote an early retirement notice that ran some years ago in the capital city of work obsession, Washington, D.C. It got notice and notoriety. Now in a more subtle mood, Fallows struggles to defend her decision to go home, without attacking mothers who are employed. Her desire to be fair, to employed mothers and even to day care, is palpable. But in an odd way, the very delicacy, the very carefulness of the book, reminded me of how difficult it is for one woman to make claims on the turf of motherhood without raising the defenses of other women.

[7]     The qualified bottom line for Fallows is this: "Whenever possible, parents should care for children themselves. . . . Other conditions being equal, children are more likely to thrive when they spend most of their day with a parent. . . ."

[8]     There is nothing intrinsically hostile about such statements. Yet it is as hard for an employed mother to read those declarations neutrally as it is for a mother at home to react impersonally when an employed friend exclaims: "All things considered, the woman who stays at home has less impact on the world. . . . On the whole, the woman in the work place feels much better about her life."

[9]     The reality is that women take these statements personally because they are personal. The social argument that has filled two decades is not about the behavior of rats in mazes, but about how women should live their lives and treat the people they love.

[10]     We are in a particularly uneasy state of balance now. There are almost equal numbers of mothers of young children in and out of the work force. It is one thing for these women in "mixed company" to join hands and mouth support for each other's right to choose. It is

quite another to believe it. Mothers may feel judged, challenged, by nothing more than another's decision.

Every time a woman in an office leaves for home, every time a [11] woman in a neighborhood leaves for work, there is a ripple effect. The waves of ambivalence can swamp self-confidence and even friend-ships. In such an atmosphere, employed mothers share their anxieties most easily with each other; mothers at home circle their own wagons. Each group may still, more than occasionally, feel the other attacking.

This social argument goes on and on because, in fact, there is no [12] certainty, no right way to live. Even Fallows' bottom line that children do best when they are in the day care of their own parents is a belief, not a fact. In the business of creating our own lives, or caring for our children, we are all experts and amateurs, opinionated and uncertain, wildly subjective.

We have only one sample of children and a limited number of [13] years and no guaranteed rewards for our behavior. Parents—mostly mothers—who have choices must make them. Not in a vacuum but in a space inundated with worries about our psyches and pocketbooks, our children and selves, the present and future. We do make these choices but our confidence may be fragile and our skin thin. The shifting winds of the social argument, blowing pros and cons at us, all too easily raise the hackles of our own anxieties.

## QUESTIONS FOR DISCUSSION

1  Goodman's article, which appeared in newspapers across the country, has short paragraphs because it was printed in narrow columns of type to make it easier to read. If you had written this piece as an essay, where would you have indented for paragraphs? Be prepared to explain your choices.

2  What does the phrase ''mixed company'' mean in paragraph 10? Why does Goodman put quotation marks around it?

3  In the final paragraph, Goodman uses a sentence fragment (beginning ''Not in a vacuum . . .''). Why do you think she chose this construction instead of using a complete sentence?

4  In paragraph 11, she employs a metaphor: ''. . . mothers at home circle their own wagons.'' Read the entire sentence in which this figure of speech appears and then explain what it means. Do you find it effective? Why or why not?

5  Goodman is examining a controversy which, as she says, ''has no final

answer.'' Does she attempt to present both sides of the issue? If not, why not?

**6** Can you tell which side of the argument Goodman is on? Is she trying to convince her readers to take one side or the other? If not, then what is her purpose? Can you state her thesis?

# Why I Want a Wife

Judy Syfers

[1] I belong to that classification of people known as wives. I am A Wife. And, not altogether incidentally, I am a mother.

[2] Not too long ago a male friend of mine appeared on the scene fresh from a recent divorce. He had one child, who is, of course, with his ex-wife. He is looking for another wife. As I thought about him while I was ironing one evening, it suddenly occurred to me that I, too, would like to have a wife. Why do I want a wife?

[3] I would like to go back to school so that I can become economically independent, support myself, and, if need be, support those dependent upon me. I want a wife who will work and send me to school. And while I am going to school I want a wife to take care of my children. I want a wife to keep track of the children's doctor and dentist appointments. And to keep track of mine, too. I want a wife to make sure my children eat properly and are kept clean. I want a wife who will wash the children's clothes and keep them mended. I want a wife who is a good nurturing attendant to my children, who arranges for their schooling, makes sure that they have an adequate social life with their peers, takes them to the park, the zoo, etc. I want a wife who takes care of the children when they are sick, a wife who arranges to be around when the children need special care, because, of course, I cannot miss classes at school. My wife must arrange to lose time at work and not lose the job. It may mean a small cut in my wife's income from time to time, but I guess I can tolerate that. Needless to say, my wife will arrange and pay for the care of the children while my wife is working.

[4] I want a wife who will take care of *my* physical needs. I want a wife who will keep my house clean. A wife who will pick up after my children, a wife who will pick up after me. I want a wife who will keep my clothes clean, ironed, mended, replaced when need be, and

who will see to it that my personal things are kept in their proper place so that I can find what I need the minute I need it. I want a wife who cooks the meals, a wife who is a *good* cook. I want a wife who will plan the menus, do the necessary grocery shopping, prepare the meals, serve them pleasantly, and then do the cleaning up while I do my studying. I want a wife who will care for me when I am sick and sympathize with my pain and loss of time from school. I want a wife to go along when our family takes a vacation so that someone can continue to care for me and my children when I need a rest and change of scene.

I want a wife who will not bother me with rambling complaints [5] about a wife's duties. But I want a wife who will listen to me when I feel the need to explain a rather difficult point I have come across in my course of studies. And I want a wife who will type my papers for me when I have written them.

I want a wife who will take care of the details of my social life. [6] When my wife and I are invited out by my friends, I want a wife who will take care of the babysitting arrangements. When I meet people at school that I like and want to entertain, I want a wife who will have the house clean, will prepare a special meal, serve it to me and my friends, and not interrupt when I talk about things that interest me and my friends. I want a wife who will have arranged that the children are fed and ready for bed before my guests arrive so that the children do not bother us. I want a wife who takes care of the needs of my guests so that they feel comfortable, who makes sure that they have an ashtray, that they are passed the hors d'oeuvres, that they are offered a second helping of the food, that their wine glasses are replenished when necessary, that their coffee is served to them as they like it. And I want a wife who knows that sometimes I need a night out by myself.

I want a wife who is sensitive to my sexual needs, a wife who [7] makes love passionately and eagerly when I feel like it, a wife who makes sure that I am satisfied. And, of course, I want a wife who will not demand sexual attention when I am not in the mood for it. I want a wife who assumes the complete responsibility for birth control, because I do not want more children. I want a wife who will remain sexually faithful to me so that I do not have to clutter up my intellectual life with jealousies. And I want a wife who understands that *my* sexual needs may entail more than strict adherence to monogamy. I must, after all, be able to relate to people as fully as possible.

[8]     If, by chance, I find another person more suitable as a wife than the wife I already have, I want the liberty to replace my present wife with another one. Naturally, I will expect a fresh, new life; my wife will take the children and be solely responsible for them so that I am left free.

[9]     When I am through with school and have a job, I want my wife to quit working and remain at home so that my wife can more fully and completely take care of a wife's duties.

[10]     My God, who *wouldn't* want a wife?

## QUESTIONS FOR DISCUSSION

1   Can you explain who Syfers's audience is?

2   In paragraph 2 Syfers explains how she came to discover that she wants a wife. What transition does she use then to move into the main body of the essay?

3   What does Syfers achieve through the deliberate repetition of the phrase "I want a wife . . ."?

4   Can you describe the tone of this essay?

5   Syfers's description of a wife's duties indicates that she is writing about a wife and mother who also holds a job outside of the home. Is the role of the husband she presents equally demanding? What does he appear to do? Why do you think she fails to mention any rewards of being a wife and mother?

6   Syfers punctuates her last sentence as a paragraph. What does she achieve by doing this? Do you consider this conclusion effective? Why or why not?

7   What point is Syfers trying to get across in this essay?

# The Androgynous Man

Noel Perrin

The summer I was 16, I took a train from New York to Steamboat [1]
Springs, Colo., where I was going to be assistant horse wrangler at a
camp. The trip took three days, and since I was much too shy to talk
to strangers, I had quite a lot of time for reading. I read all of "Gone
With the Wind." I read all the interesting articles in a couple of
magazines I had, and then I went back and read all the dull stuff. I also
took all the quizzes, a thing of which magazines were even fuller then
than now.

The one that held my undivided attention was called "How [2]
Masculine/Feminine Are You?" It consisted of a large number of
inkblots. The reader was supposed to decide which of four objects each
blot most resembled. The choices might be a cloud, a steam engine, a
caterpillar and a sofa.

When I finished the test, I was shocked to find that I was barely [3]
masculine at all. On a scale of 1 to 10, I was about 1.2. Me, the horse
wrangler? (And not just wrangler, either. That summer, I had to skin
a couple of horses that died—the camp owner wanted the hides.)

The results of that test were so terrifying to me that for the first [4]
time in my life I did a piece of original analysis. Having unlimited
time on the train, I looked at the "masculine" answers over and over,
trying to find what it was that distinguished real men from people like
me—and eventually I discovered two very simple patterns. It was
"masculine" to think the blots looked like man-made objects, and
"feminine" to think they looked like natural objects. It was masculine
to think they looked like things capable of causing harm, and feminine
to think of innocent things.

Even at 16, I had the sense to see that the compilers of the test [5]
were using rather limited criteria—maleness and femaleness are both
more complicated than *that*—and I breathed a huge sigh of relief. I
wasn't necessarily a wimp, after all.

That the test did reveal something other than the superficiality of [6]
its makers I realized only many years later. What it revealed was that
there is a large class of men and women both, to which I belong, who

are essentially androgynous. That doesn't mean we're gay, or low in the appropriate hormones, or uncomfortable performing the jobs traditionally assigned our sexes. (A few years after that summer, I was leading troops in combat and, unfashionable as it now is to admit this, having a very good time. War is exciting. What a pity the 20th century went and spoiled it with high-tech weapons.)

[7]     What it does mean to be spiritually androgynous is a kind of freedom. Men who are all-male, or he-man, or 100 percent red-blooded Americans, have a little biological set that causes them to be attracted to physical power, and probably also to dominance. Maybe even to watching football. I don't say this to criticize them. Completely masculine men are quite often wonderful people: good husbands, good (though sometimes overwhelming) fathers, good members of society. Furthermore, they are often so unself-consciously at ease in the world that other men seek to imitate them. They just aren't as free as us androgynes. They pretty nearly have to be what they are; we have a range of choices open.

[8]     The sad part is that many of us never discover that. Men who are not 100 percent red-blooded Americans—say, those who are only 75 percent red-blooded—often fail to notice their freedom. They are too busy trying to copy the he-men ever to realize that men, like women, come in a wide variety of acceptable types. Why this frantic imitation? My answer is mere speculation, but not casual. I have speculated on this for a long time.

[9]     Partly they're just envious of the he-man's unconscious ease. Mostly they're terrified of finding that there may be something wrong with them deep down, some weakness at the heart. To avoid discovering that, they spend their lives acting out the role that the he-man naturally lives. Sad.

[10]    One thing that men owe to the women's movement is that this kind of failure is less common than it used to be. In releasing themselves from the single ideal of the dependent woman, women have more or less incidentally released a lot of men from the single ideal of the dominant male. The one mistake the feminists have made, I think, is in supposing that *all* men need this release, or that the world would be a better place if all men achieved it. It would just be duller.

[11]    So far I have been pretty vague about just what the freedom of the androgynous man is. Obviously it varies with the case. In the case

I know best, my own, I can be quite specific. It has freed me most as a parent. I am, among other things, a fairly good natural mother. I like the nurturing role. It makes me feel good to see a child eat—and it turns me to mush to see a 4-year-old holding a glass with both small hands, in order to drink. I even enjoyed sewing patches on the knees of my daughter Amy's Dr. Dentons when she was at the crawling stage. All that pleasure I would have lost if I had made myself stick to the notion of the paternal role that I started with.

Or take a smaller and rather ridiculous example. I feel free to kiss [12] cats. Until recently it never occurred to me that I would want to, though my daughters have been doing it all their lives. But my elder daughter is now 22, and in London. Of course, I get to look after her cat while she is gone. He's a big, handsome farm cat named Petrushka, very unsentimental, though used from kittenhood to being kissed on the top of the head by Elizabeth. I've gotten very fond of him (he's the adventurous kind of cat who likes to climb hills with you), and one night I simply felt like kissing him on the top of the head, and did. Why did no one tell me sooner how silky cat fur is?

Then there's my relation to cars. I am completely unembarrassed [13] by my inability to diagnose even minor problems in whatever object I happen to be driving, and don't have to make some insider's remark to mechanics to try to establish that I, too, am a "Man With His Machine."

The same ease extends to household maintenance. I do it, of [14] course. Service people are expensive. But for the last decade my house has functioned better than it used to because I've had the aid of a volume called "Home Repairs Any Woman Can Do," which is pitched just right for people at my technical level. As a youth, I'd as soon have touched such a book as I would have become a transvestite. Even though common sense says there is really nothing sexual whatsoever about fixing sinks.

Or take public emotion. All my life I have easily been moved by [15] certain kinds of voices. The actress Siobhan McKenna's, to take a notable case. Give her an emotional scene in a play, and within 10 words my eyes are full of tears. In boyhood, my great dread was that someone might notice. I struggled manfully, you might say, to suppress this weakness. Now, of course, I don't see it as a weakness at all, but as a kind of fulfillment. I even suspect that the true he-men feel the same way, or one kind of them does, at least, and it's only the poor imitators who have to struggle to repress themselves.

[16]     Let me come back to the inkblots, with their assumption that masculine equates with machinery and science, and feminine with art and nature. I have no idea whether the right pronoun for God is He, She or It. But this I'm pretty sure of. If God could somehow be induced to take that test, God would not come out macho, and not feminismo, either, but right in the middle. Fellow androgynes, it's a nice thought.

## QUESTIONS FOR DISCUSSION

1   Why does Perrin make a point of telling us in the first paragraph that he was employed as a horse wrangler and in the sixth paragraph that he led troops in combat?

2   What does the word *androgynous* mean to you? Does it have any positive or negative connotations? How do you think most people would respond to the idea of being an androgynous person? If you think they would respond negatively, what implications might that attitude have on Perrin's choice of writing strategies?

3   In paragraph 5 Perrin uses the slang word ''wimp.'' Why is it a better choice than the standard English term *sissy*?

4   Perrin tells us that being ''spiritually androgynous'' has given him ''a kind of freedom'' (paragraph 7). What sort of freedom does he mean?

5   Why does Perrin include the little story about learning to kiss the cat in paragraph 12? Do you find the example effective? Why or why not?

6   What point is Perrin trying to get across? Can you state the thesis of his essay in a single sentence?

## SUGGESTIONS FOR WRITING

1  Imagine that you are Shakespeare's mother (or father). Write a letter to
   your daughter Judith trying to convince her that she will be better off
   marrying the wool-stapler's son instead of going to London to become an
   actress and playwright.
2  Ellen Goodman, in considering the controversy about whether mothers
   should work outside the home, focuses on the effects of this argument upon
   women—not on the controversy itself. If you have strong feelings about
   the matter, respond by writing a letter to the editor of the Chicago *Tribune*
   (or any other newspaper in which the article appeared). In your letter you
   could either agree with or question this assertion which Goodman quotes:
   "Whenever possible, parents should care for children themselves. . . .
   Other conditions being equal, children are more likely to thrive when they
   spend most of their day with a parent. . . ." Be sure to supply plenty of
   specific evidence. And remember that while personal experience can prove
   effective in this kind of persuasive writing, you must be careful not to draw
   conclusions from your experience that are too sweeping.
3  Interview at least twenty women to discover how they feel about this issue
   of mothers' holding a job outside the home. Try to get a fairly representative sampling of women—older women and younger, married and single,
   with children and childless—all from various economic levels, if possible.
   Plan your questions carefully in advance. You'll want to inquire about such
   matters as the mother's motivation for working outside the home or for
   staying at home, about her degree of job satisfaction whether in or out of
   the home; and about any guilt feelings about working at a job or staying
   at home. Analyze your findings and report your conclusions in a letter to
   Ellen Goodman, c/o The Washington Post Writer's Group, 1150 15th Street
   NW, Washington, DC   20071.
4  Making use of some of the ideas in Syfers's "Why I Want a Wife," write
   an essay contrasting the roles of the working man and the working woman.
   Think about the complete lives of each—at work and at leisure. Compose
   this piece for an audience of female high school seniors who plan to combine
   marriage, motherhood, and a career.
5  With the help of several classmates or friends, make a list of personality
   traits that people tend to accept as typically masculine. Then list traits that
   are typically considered feminine. Does either list describe what you think
   of as a well-rounded individual? Would people in our society be better off
   if we were encouraged to develop traits from both lists? Write an article
   for *Parents* magazine in which you encourage the readers to allow their
   children to grow up as androgynous human beings instead of inculcating

sex roles by giving guns to boys, dolls to girls, doctor kits to boys, nurse kits to girls, allowing boys to be boisterous but encouraging girls to be quiet, etc. Or, if you prefer, reassure the readers that since our present gender roles are important in preserving a smoothly functioning society, male children should continue to be brought up with typically masculine traits, females with typically feminine traits.

6  Consider the relationships between men and women as they are presented on soap operas or situation comedies. Do these programs offer a realistic portrayal of gender roles? If not, do you consider the influence of these presentations to be damaging to either sex—or perhaps to both sexes? Write an article for *Newsweek on Campus* in which you focus on the presentation of sex roles in one of these types of programs.

# Chapter 15

# Considering Television

## Life According to TV

Harry F. Waters

*You people sit there, night after night. You're beginning to believe this illusion we're spinning here. You're beginning to think the tube is reality and your own lives are unreal. This is mass madness!*

—Anchorman Howard Beale
in the film "Network"

*If you can write a nation's stories, you needn't worry about who makes its laws. Today television tells most of the stories to most of the people most of the time.*

—George Gerbner, Ph.D.

The late Paddy Chayefsky, who created Howard Beale, would have [1] loved George Gerbner. In "Network," Chayefsky marshaled a scathing, fictional assault on the values and methods of the people who control the world's most potent communications instrument. In real life, Gerbner, perhaps the nation's foremost authority on the social impact of television, is quietly using the disciplines of behavioral research to construct an equally devastating indictment of the medium's images and messages. More than any spokesman for a pressure group, Gerbner has become the man that television watches. From his cramped, book-lined office at the University of Pennsylvania springs a steady flow of studies that are raising executive blood pressures at the networks' sleek Manhattan command posts.

[2]     George Gerbner's work is uniquely important because it transports the scientific examination of television far beyond familiar children-and-violence arguments. Rather than simply studying the link between violence on the tube and crime in the streets, Gerbner is exploring wider and deeper terrain. He has turned his lens on TV's hidden victims—women, the elderly, blacks, blue-collar workers and other groups—to document the ways in which video-entertainment portrayals subliminally condition how we preceive ourselves and how we view those around us. Gerbner's subjects are not merely the impressionable young; they include all the rest of us. And it is his ominous conclusion that heavy watchers of the prime-time mirror are receiving a grossly distorted picture of the real world that they tend to accept more readily than reality itself.

[3]     The 63-year-old Gerbner, who is dean of Penn's Annenberg School of Communications, employs a methodology that meshes scholarly observation with mundane legwork. Over the past 15 years, he and a tireless trio of assistants (Larry Gross, Nancy Signorielli and Michael Morgan) videotaped and exhaustively analyzed 1,600 prime-time programs involving more than 15,000 characters. They then drew up multiple-choice questionnaires that offered correct answers about the world at large along with answers that reflected what Gerbner perceived to be the misrepresentations and biases of the world according to TV. Finally, these questions were posed to large samples of citizens from all socioeconomic strata. In every survey, the Annenberg team discovered that heavy viewers of television (those watching more than four hours a day), who account for more than 30 percent of the population, almost invariably chose the TV-influenced answers, while light viewers (less than two hours a day), selected the answers corre-

sponding more closely to actual life. Some of the dimensions of television's reality warp:

## SEX

Male prime-time characters out-number females by 3 to 1 and, with a [4] few star-turn exceptions, women are portrayed as weak, passive satellites to powerful, effective men. TV's male population also plays a vast variety of roles, while females generally get typecast as either lovers or mothers. Less than 20 percent of TV's married women with children work outside the home—as compared with more than 50 percent in real life. The tube's distorted depictions of women, concludes Gerbner, reinforce stereotypical attitudes and increase sexism. In one Annenberg survey, heavy viewers were far more likely than light ones to agree with the proposition: ''Women should take care of running their homes and leave running the country to men.''

## AGE

People over 65, too, are grossly underrepresented on television. Corre- [5] spondingly, heavy-viewing Annenberg respondents believe that the elderly are a vanishing breed, that they make up a smaller proportion of the population today than they did 20 years ago. In fact, they form the nation's most rapidly expanding age group. Heavy viewers also believe that old people are less healthy today than they were two decades ago, when quite the opposite is true. As with women, the portrayals of old people transmit negative impressions. In general, they are cast as silly, stubborn, sexually inactive and eccentric. ''They're often shown as feeble grandparents bearing cookies,'' says Gerbner. ''You never see the power that real old people often have. The best and possibly only time to learn about growing old with decency and grace is in youth. And young people are the most susceptible to TV's messages.''

## RACE

The problem with the medium's treatment of blacks is more one of [6] image than of visibility. Though a tiny percentage of black characters come across as "unrealistically romanticized," reports Gerbner, the overwhelming majority of them are employed in subservient, supporting roles—such as the white hero's comic sidekick. "When a black child looks at prime time," he says, "most of the people he sees doing interesting and important things are white." That imbalance, he goes on, tends to teach young blacks to accept minority status as naturally inevitable and even deserved. To assess the impact of such portrayals on the general audience, the Annenberg survey forms included questions like "Should white people have the right to keep blacks out of their neighborhoods?" and "Should there be laws against marriages between blacks and whites?" The more that viewers watched, the more they answered "Yes" to each question.

## WORK

[7] Heavy viewers greatly overestimated the proportion of Americans employed as physicians, lawyers, athletes and entertainers, all of whom inhabit prime-time in hordes. A mere 6 to 10 percent of television characters hold blue-collar or service jobs vs. about 60 percent in the real work force. Gerbner sees two dangers in TV's skewed division of labor. On the one hand, the tube so overrepresents and glamorizes the elite occupations that it sets up unrealistic expectations among those who must deal with them in actuality. At the same time, TV largely neglects portraying the occupations that most youngsters will have to enter. "You almost never see the farmer, the factory worker or the small businessman," he notes. "Thus not only do lawyers and other professionals find they cannot measure up to the image TV projects of them, but children's occupational aspirations are channeled in unrealistic directions." The Gerbner team feels this emphasis on high-powered jobs poses problems for adolescent girls, who are also presented with views of women as homebodies. The two conflicting views, Gerbner says, add to the frustration over choices they have to make as adults.

## HEALTH

[8] Although video characters exist almost entirely on junk food and quaff alcohol 15 times more often than water, they manage to remain slim,

healthy and beautiful. Frequent TV watchers, the Annenberg investigators found, eat more, drink more, exercise less and possess an almost mystical faith in the curative powers of medical science. Concludes Gerbner: "Television may well be the single most pervasive source of health information. And its overidealized images of medical people, coupled with its complacency about unhealthy life-styles, leaves both patients and doctors vulnerable to disappointment, frustration and even litigation."

## CRIME

On the small screen, crime rages about 10 times more often than in [9] real life. But while other researchers concentrate on the propensity of TV mayhem to incite aggression, the Annenberg team has studied the hidden side of its imprint: fear of victimization. On television, 55 percent of prime-time characters are involved in violent confrontations once a week; in reality, the figure is less than 1 percent. In all demographic groups in every class of neighborhood, heavy viewers overestimated the statistical chance of violence in their own lives and harbored an exaggerated mistrust of strangers—creating what Gerbner calls a "mean-world syndrome." Forty-six percent of heavy viewers who live in cities rated their fear of crime "very serious" as opposed to 26 percent for light viewers. Such paranoia is especially acute among TV entertainment's most common victims: women, the elderly, nonwhites, foreigners and lower-class citizens.

Video violence, proposes Gerbner, is primarily responsible for [10] imparting lessons in social power: it demonstrates who can do what to whom and get away with it. "Television is saying that those at the bottom of the power scale cannot get away with the same things that a white, middle-class American male can," he says. "It potentially conditions people to think of themselves as victims."

At a quick glance, Gerbner's findings seem to contain a cause- [11] and-effect, chicken-or-the-egg question. Does television make heavy viewers view the world the way they do or do heavy viewers come from the poorer, less experienced segment of the populace that regards the world that way to begin with? In other words, does the tube create or simply confirm the unenlightened attitudes of its most loyal audience? Gerbner, however, was savvy enough to construct a methodology largely immune to such criticism. His samples of heavy viewers cut across all ages, incomes, education levels and ethnic backgrounds—and every category displayed the same tube-induced misconceptions of the world outside.

[12]     Needless to say, the networks accept all this as enthusiastically as they would a list of news-coverage complaints from the Ayatollah Khomeini. Even so, their responses tend to be tinged with a singular respect for Gerbner's personal and professional credentials. The man is no ivory-tower recluse. During World War II, the Budapest-born Gerbner parachuted into the mountains of Yugoslavia to join the partisans fighting the Germans. After the war, he hunted down and personally arrested scores of high Nazi officials. Nor is Gerbner some videophobic vigilante. A Ph.D. in communications, he readily acknowledges TV's beneficial effects, noting that it has abolished parochialism, reduced isolation and loneliness and provided the poorest members of society with cheap, plug-in exposure to experiences they otherwise would not have. Funding for his research is supplied by such prestigious bodies as the National Institute of Mental Health, the surgeon general's office and the American Medical Association, and he is called to testify before congressional committees nearly as often as David Stockman.

## MASS ENTERTAINMENT

[13]  When challenging Gerbner, network officials focus less on his findings and methods than on what they regard as his own misconceptions of their industry's function. "He's looking at television from the perspective of a social scientist rather than considering what is mass entertainment," says Alfred Schneider, vice president of standards and practices at ABC. "We strive to balance TV's social effects with what will capture an audience's interests. If you showed strong men being victimized as much as women or the elderly, what would comprise the dramatic conflict? If you did a show truly representative of society's total reality, and nobody watched because it wasn't interesting, what have you achieved?"

[14]     CBS senior vice president Gene Mater also believes that Gerbner is implicitly asking for the theoretically impossible. "TV is unique in its problems," says Mater. "Everyone wants a piece of the action.

Everyone feels that their racial or ethnic group is underrepresented or should be portrayed as they would like the world to perceive them. No popular entertainment form, including this one, can or should be an accurate reflection of society.''

On that point, at least, Gerbner is first to agree; he hardly expects [15] television entertainment to serve as a mirror image of absolute truth. But what fascinates him about this communications medium is its marked difference from all others. In other media, customers carefully choose what they want to hear or read: a movie, a magazine, a best seller. In television, notes Gerbner, viewers rarely tune in for a particular program. Instead, most just habitually turn on the set—and watch by the clock rather than for a specific show. ''Television viewing fulfills the criteria of a ritual,'' he says. ''It is the only medium that can bring to people things they otherwise would not select.'' With such unique power, believes Gerbner, comes unique responsibility: ''No other medium reaches into every home or has a comparable, cradle-to-grave influence over what a society learns about itself.''

## MATCH

In Gerbner's view, virtually all of TV's distortions of reality can be [16] attributed to its obsession with demographics. The viewers that prime-time sponsors most want to reach are white, middle-class, female and between 18 and 49—in short, the audience that purchases most of the consumer products advertised on the tube. Accordingly, notes Gerbner, the demographic portrait of TV's fictional characters largely matches that of its prime commercial targets and largely ignores everyone else. ''Television,'' he concludes, ''reproduces a world for its own best customers.''

Among TV's more candid executives, that theory draws consid- [17] erable support. Yet by pointing a finger at the power of demographics, Gerbner appears to contradict one of his major findings. If female viewers are so dear to the hearts of sponsors, why are female characters cast in such unflattering light? ''In a basically male-oriented power structure,'' replies Gerbner, ''you can't alienate the male viewer. But you can get away with offending women because most women are pretty well brainwashed to accept it.'' The Annenberg dean has an equally tidy explanation for another curious fact. Since the corporate world provides network television with all of its financial support, one would expect businessmen on TV to be portrayed primarily as good guys. Quite the contrary. As any fan of "Dallas," "Dynasty" or "Falcon Crest" well knows, the image of the company man is usually that of a mendacious, dirty-dealing rapscallion. Why would TV snap at the hand that feeds it? "Credibility is the way to ratings," proposes Gerbner. "This country has a populist tradition of bias against anything big, including big business. So to retain credibility, TV entertainment shows businessmen in relatively derogatory ways."

[18]     In the medium's Hollywood-based creative community, the gospel of Gerbner finds some passionate adherents. Rarely have TV's best and brightest talents viewed their industry with so much frustration and anger. The most sweeping indictment emanates from David Rintels, a two-time Emmy-winning writer and former president of the Writers Guild of America, West. "Gerbner is absolutely correct and it is the people who run the networks who are to blame," says Rintels. "The networks get bombarded with thoughtful, reality-oriented scripts. They simply won't do them. They slam the door on them. They believe that the only way to get ratings is to feed viewers what conforms to their biases or what has limited resemblance to reality. From 8 to 11 o'clock each night, television is one long lie."

[19]     Innovative thinkers such as Norman Lear, whose work has been practically driven off the tube, don't fault the networks so much as the climate in which they operate. Says Lear: "All of this country's institutions have become totally fixated on short-term bottom-line thinking. Everyone grabs for what might succeed today and the hell with tomorrow. Television just catches more of the heat because it's more visible." Perhaps the most perceptive assessment of Gerbner's conclusions is offered by one who has worked both sides of the industry street. Deanne Barkley, a former NBC vice president who now helps run an independent production house, reports that the negative depictions of women on TV have made it "nerve-racking" to function as a woman within TV. "No one takes responsibility for the social impact of their shows," says Barkley. "But then how do you decide where it all begins? Do the networks give viewers what they want? Or are the networks conditioning them to think that way?"

[20]     Gerbner himself has no simple answer to that conundrum. Neither a McLuhanesque shaman nor a Naderesque crusader, he hesitates to suggest solutions until pressed. Then out pops a pair of provocative

notions. Commercial television will never democratize its treatments of daily life, he believes, until it finds a way to broaden its financial base. Coincidentally, Federal Communications Commission chairman Mark Fowler seems to have arrived at much the same conclusion. In exchange for lifting such government restrictions on TV as the fairness doctrine and the equal-time rule, Fowler would impose a modest levy on station owners called a spectrum-use fee. Funds from the fees would be set aside to finance programs aimed at specialized tastes rather than the mass appetite. Gerbner enthusiastically endorses that proposal: "Let the ratings system dominate most of prime time but not every hour of every day. Let some programs carry advisories that warn: 'This is not for all of you. This is for nonwhites, or for religious people or for the aged and the handicapped. Turn it off unless you'd like to eavesdrop.' That would be a very refreshing thing."


## ROLE

In addition, Gerbner would like to see viewers given an active role in [21] steering the overall direction of television instead of being obliged to passively accept whatever the networks offer. In Britain, he points out, political candidates debate the problems of TV as routinely as the issue of crime. In this country, proposes Gerbner, "every political campaign should put television on the public agenda. Candidates talk about schools, they talk about jobs, they talk about social welfare. They're going to have to start discussing this all-pervasive force."

There are no outright villains in this docudrama. Even Gerbner [22] recognizes that network potentates don't set out to proselytize a point of view; they are simply businessmen selling a mass-market product. At the same time, their 90 million nightly customers deserve to know the side effects of the ingredients. By the time the typical American child reaches the age of reason, calculates Gerbner, he or she will have absorbed more than 30,000 electronic "stories." These stories, he suggests, have replaced the socializing role of the preindustrial church: they create a "cultural mythology" that establishes the norms of approved behavior and belief. And all Gerbner's research indicates that this new mythological world, with its warped picture of a sizable portion of society, may soon become the one most of us think we live in.

[23]     Who else is telling us that? Howard Beale and his eloquent alarms have faded into off-network reruns. At the very least, it is comforting to know that a real-life Beale is very much with us . . . and *really* watching.

## QUESTIONS FOR DISCUSSION

1  Those italicized quotations at the beginning of the article are called *epigraphs*. Why do you think Waters included them?

2  Study the opening and closing paragraphs. Can you describe the strategy Waters is using?

3  In what paragraph does the author state his thesis?

4  Why does the author include the information in paragraph 12?

5  Do you find Waters's reporting of Gerbner's findings completely objective? If he seems to favor one side in this controversy, whose side is he on? How can you tell? Can you point out any words with negative connotations that serve as clues?

# Sin, Suffer, and Repent
## Donna Woolfolk Cross

*Soap operas reverse Tolstoy's famous assertion in* Anna Karenina *that "Happy families are all alike; every unhappy family is unhappy in its own way." On soaps, every family is unhappy, and each is unhappy in more or less the same way.*

—Marjorie Perloff

*It is the hope of every advertiser to habituate the housewife to an engrossing narrative whose optimum length is forever and at the same time to saturate all levels of her consciousness with the miracle of a given product, so she will be aware of it all the days of her life and mutter its name in her sleep.*

—James Thurber

[1]     In July 1969, when the entire nation was glued to television sets watching the first man walk on the moon, an irate woman called a Wausau, Wisconsin, TV station to complain that her favorite soap opera

was not being shown that day and why was that. The station manager replied, "This is probably the most important news story of the century, something you may never again see the equal of." Unimpressed, the lady replied, "Well, I hope they crash."

One can hardly blame her. For weeks, she had been worrying that [2] Audrey might be going blind, that Alice would marry that scoundrel Michael, and that Dr. Hardy might not discover his patient Peter to be his long-lost natural son before the boy died of a brain tumor. Suddenly, in the heat of all these crises, she was cut off from all information about these people and forced to watch the comings and goings of men in rubber suits whom she had never met. It was enough to unhinge anybody.

Dedicated watchers of soap operas often confuse fact with fiction.[1] [3] Sometimes this can be endearing, sometimes ludicrous. During the Senate Watergate hearings (which were broadcast on daytime television), viewers whose favorite soap operas were preempted simply adopted the hearings as substitute soaps. Daniel Shorr reports that the listeners began "telephoning the networks to criticize slow-moving sequences, suggesting script changes and asking for the return of favorite witnesses, like 'that nice John Dean.'"

Stars of soap operas tell hair-raising stories of their encounters [4] with fans suffering from this affliction. Susan Lucci, who plays the promiscuous Erica Kane on "All My Children," tells of a time she was riding in a parade: "We were in a crowd of about 250,000, traveling in an antique open car moving ver-r-ry slowly. At that time in the series I was involved with a character named Nick. Some man broke through, came right up to the car and said to me, 'Why don't you give *me* a little bit of what you've been giving Nick?'" The man hung onto the car, menacingly, until she was rescued by the police. Another time, when she was in church, the reverent silence was broken by a woman's astonished remark, "Oh my god, Erica prays!" Margaret Mason, who plays the villainous Linda Anderson in "Days of Our

---

[1]Contrary to popular belief, soap operas are not the harmless pastime of lonely housewives only. Recent surveys show that many high school and college students, as well as many working and professional people, are addicted to soaps. A sizable chunk of the audience is men. Such well-known people as Sammy Davis, Jr., Van Cliburn, John Connally, and Supreme Court Justice Thurgood Marshall admit to being fans of one or more soap operas.

Lives,'' was accosted by a woman who poured a carton of milk all over her in the supermarket. And once a woman actually tried to force her car off the Ventura Freeway.

[5]     Just as viewers come to confuse the actors with their roles, so too they see the soap image of life in America as real. The National Institute of Mental Health reported that a majority of Americans actually adopt what they see in soap operas to handle their own life problems. The images are not only ''true to life''; they are a guide for living.

[6]     What, then, is the image of life on soap operas? For one thing, marriage is touted as the *ne plus ultra* of a woman's existence. Living together is not a respectable condition and is tolerated only as long as one of the partners (usually the woman) is bucking for eventual marriage. Casual sex is out; only the most despicable villains engage in it: ''Diane has no respect for marriage or any of the values we were brought up with. She's a vicious, immoral woman.'' Occasionally, a woman will speak out against marriage, but it's clear that in her heart of hearts she really wants it. Women who are genuinely not interested in marriage do not appear on soap operas except as occasional caricatures, misguided and immature in their thinking. Reporter Martha McGee appeared on ''Ryan's Hope'' just long enough to titillate the leading man with remarks like, ''I don't know if you're my heart's desire, but you're sexy as hell.'' Punished for this kind of heretical remark, she was last seen sobbing brokenly in a telephone booth.

[7]     No, love and marriage still go together like a horse and carriage in soap operas, though many marriages don't last long enough for the couple to put away all the wedding gifts. As Cornell professor Rose Goldsen says, this is a world of ''fly-apart marriages, throwaway husbands, throwaway wives.'' There is rarely any clear logic behind the dissolution of these relationships; indeed, the TV formula seems to be: the happier the marriage, the more perilous the couple's future. A blissful marriage is the kiss of death: ''I just can't believe it about Alice and Steve. I mean, they were the *perfect* couple, the absolute *perfect* couple!''

[8]     Most marriages are not pulled apart by internal flaws but by external tampering—often by a jealous rival: ''C'mon, Peter. Stay for just one more drink. Jan won't mind. And anyway, the night's still young. Isn't it nice to be together all nice and cozy like this?''

[9]     Often the wife has willfully brought this state of affairs on herself by committing that most heinous of all offenses: neglecting her man.

"NHM" almost always occurs when the woman becomes too wrapped up in her career. Every time Rachel Corey went to New York City for a weekend to further her career as a sculptress, her marriage tottered. At this writing, Ellen Dalton's marriage to Mark appears to be headed for big trouble as a result of her business trip to Chicago:

*Erica:* I warned you, Ellen, not to let your job interfere with your marriage.

*Ellen:* I have tried to do my best for my marriage *and* my job . . . Mark had no right to stomp out of here just now.

*Erica:* Don't you understand? He just couldn't take any more.

*Ellen:* What do you mean?

*Erica:* It's not just the trip to Chicago that Mark resents. It's your putting your job before having a family.

*Ellen:* I demand the right to be treated as an equal. I don't have to apologize because I don't agree to have a child the minute my husband snaps his fingers. I'm going to Chicago like a big girl and I'm going to do the job I was hired to do. (stalks out the door)

*Erica:* (musing to herself) Well, I may be old-fashioned, but that's no way to hold onto your man.

Career women do appear frequently on soap operas, but the ones [10] who are romantically successful treat their careers as a kind of sideline. Female cardiologists devote fifteen years of their lives to advanced medical training, then spend most of their time in the hospital coffee shop. One man remarked to a career woman who was about to leave her job, "Oh Kate, you'll miss working. Those long lunches, those intimate cocktail hours!" Women residents apparently schedule all their medical emergencies before dinnertime, because if they should have to stay late at the hospital, it's the beginning of the end for their marriages. It's interesting to speculate how they might work this out:

*Nurse:* Oh my God, Dr. Peterson, the patient's hemorrhaging!

*Dr. Peterson:* Sorry, nurse, it'll have to wait. If I don't get my meat loaf in by a quarter to six, it'll never be ready before my husband gets home.

Husbands, weak-minded souls, cannot be expected to hold out [11] against the advances of any attractive woman, even one for whom they have contempt, if their wives aren't around. Meatloafless, they are very easily seduced. The clear suggestion is that they could hardly have been expected to do otherwise:

> "Well, after all, Karen, you weren't around very much during that time. It's not surprising that Michael turned to Pat for a little comfort and understanding."

[12] If, in the brief span of time allotted to them, a couple manage to have intercourse, the woman is certain to become pregnant. Contraception on soap operas is such a sometime thing that even the Pope could scarcely object to it. The birthrate on soaps is eight times as high as the United States birthrate; indeed it's higher than the birthrate of any underdeveloped nation in the world. This rabbitlike reproduction is fraught with peril. One recent study revealed that out of nineteen soap opera pregnancies, eight resulted in miscarriages and three in death for the mother. Rose Goldsen has estimated that the odds are 7 to 10 against any fetus making it to full term, worse if you include getting through the birth canal. Women on soap operas miscarry at the drop of a pin. And of course, miscarriages are rarely caused by any defect with mother or baby: again, external forces are to blame. Often, miscarriage is brought on by an unappreciative or unfaithful mate. For example, on "Another World," Alice, the heroine, suffered a miscarriage when her husband visited his ex-wife Rachel. One woman lost her baby because her husband came home drunk. This plot twist is no doubt particularly appealing to women viewers because of the instant revenge visited upon the transgressing mate. They can fantasize about similar punishment for husbandly malfeasance in their own lives—and about his inevitable guilt and repentance:

> *Husband:* (stonily) Jennifer, these potatoes are too gluey. I can't eat this!
>
> *Wife:* (clutches her belly) Oh no!
>
> *Husband:* What? What is it?
>
> *Wife:* It's the baby! Something's wrong—call the doctor!
>
> *Husband:* Oh my God, what have I done?
>
> *Later, at the hospital:*
>
> *Doctor:* I'm sorry, Mr. Henson, but your wife has lost the baby.
>
> *Husband:* (brokenly) I didn't know, I didn't know. How could I have attacked her potatoes so viciously with her in such a delicate condition.
>
> *Doctor:* Now, now. You mustn't blame yourself. We still don't know exactly what causes miscarriages except that they happen for a complicated set of physical and emotional reasons.

*Husband:* Oh, thank you, Doctor.

*Doctor:* Of course, carping about the potatoes couldn't have *helped.*

Miscarriage is effective as a punishment because it is one of the [13] very worst things that can happen to a woman on a soap opera. In the world of soaps, the one thing every good and worthwhile woman wants is a baby. Soap operas never depict childless women as admirable. These "real people" do not include women like Katharine Hepburn, who once announced that she never wanted to have children because "the first time the kid said no to me, I'd kill it!" Childless women are either to be pitied, if there are physical reasons that prevent them from getting pregnant, or condemned, if they are childless by choice.

Second only to neglecting her man in her hierarchy of female crime [14] is having an abortion. No admirable character *ever* gets an abortion on a soap opera. Occasionally, however, a virtuous woman will consider it, usually for one of two reasons: she doesn't want the man she loves to feel "trapped" into marrying her; or she has been "violated" by her husband's best friend, a member of the underworld, or her delivery boy, who may also be her long-lost half brother. But she always "comes around" in the end, her love for "the new life growing inside me" conquering her misgivings. If the baby should happen to survive the perilous journey through the birth canal (illegitimate babies get miscarried at a far higher rate than legitimate ones), she never has any regrets. Why should she? Babies on soap operas never drool, spit up, or throw scrambled eggs in their mothers' faces. Babyhood (and its inevitable counterpart, motherhood) is "sold" to American women as slickly as soap. Kimberly, of "Ryan's Hope," is so distressed when she finds out she is pregnant that she runs away from home. She has the baby, prematurely, while alone and unattended on a deserted houseboat. It is a difficult and dangerous birth. But once the baby is born, Kimberly is all maternal affection. "Where is she?" she shouts. "Why won't they let me see my little girl?" By the end of the day, she announces, "If anything happens to this baby, I don't know what I'll do!"

Mothers are never tired, sleepless, or discouraged. Radiant, they [15] boast about the baby's virtues:

Well, he's just the smartest, best little baby in the whole wide world!

He looks just like his daddy—those big blue eyes, that enchanting smile!

Look at her little hands and feet. Have you ever seen anything more adorable! And she's good as gold—really, no trouble at all. She's Mommy's precious little princess, aren't you, darling?

[16]    One producer of a (now defunct) soap opera actually wanted, as a promotion gimmick for one of the plotlines, to give away one baby a week as a prize! The idea was abandoned only because of the lack of cooperation from adoption agencies.

[17]    After the age of about ten months, children are of no interest in soap operas unless they are hit by a car or contract a fever of unknown origin, in which case they occasion a lot of hand-wringing and pious sentiments from all the adults. If the producers cannot arrange any such misfortune, the rule is that children are not to be seen or heard. Having a young child around would interrupt the endless raveling of the sleeve of romance. It won't do to have little Bobby need to go on the potty or have his nose blown in the middle of the adults' complicated lives, which have, as one critic says, "all the immediacy of a toothache and the urgency of a telegram."

[18]    You may hear a good deal of pious talk about a young child's need for stability and love, but usually only when a couple's marriage is on the rocks. Children on soap operas still go to sleep at night having no idea whether one or both of their parents will be around in the morning—a situation which brings to mind Lady Bracknell's remark in *The Importance of Being Earnest:* "Losing one parent might be regarded as a misfortune; losing two seems like carelessness."

[19]    Children on soap operas are secondary. Because they serve largely as foils for the adult characters, their development does not follow the slow, steady pattern of the rest of the action.[2] Their growth is marked

---

[2] The pace of many soap operas has picked up considerably in the last few years, as audience surveys have revealed a strong viewer interest in action-and-adventure stories. Before 1980, however, plot movement on the soaps was glacierlike, and on the earliest soaps, almost imperceptible. James Thurber claimed that it took one male character in a soap three days to get an answer to the simple question, "Where have you been?" He wrote, "If . . . you missed an automobile accident that occurred on a Monday broadcast, you could pick it up the following Thursday and find the leading woman character still unconscious and her husband still moaning over her beside the wrecked car. In one program . . . [a character] said, 'It doesn't seem possible to me that Ralph Wilde arrived here only yesterday.' It should not have seemed possible to anyone else, either, since Ralph Wilde had arrived, as mortal time goes, thirteen days before."

by a series of sudden and unsettling metamorphoses as new and older juvenile actors assume the role. On Tuesday, little Terence is cooing in his cradle. On Monday next, he is the terror of the Little League. By Thursday, his voice begins to change. Friday night is his first date. He wakes up on Monday a drug-crazed teenager, ready to be put to use creating heartbreak and grief for his devoted mother and her new husband. He stays fifteen years old for about two to five years (more if he managed to get into lots of scrapes), and then one day he again emerges from the off-camera cocoon transformed into a full-fledged adult, with all the rights, privileges, pain, and perfidy of that elite corps. And so the cycle continues.

Under the surface of romantic complications, soap operas sell a [20] vision of morality and American family life, of a society where marriage is the highest good, sex the greatest evil, where babies are worshipped and abortion condemned, where motherhood is exalted and children ignored. It is a vision of a world devoid of social conflict. There are hardly any short-order cooks, bus drivers, mechanics, construction workers, or farmers on soap operas. Blue-collar problems do not enter these immaculate homes. No one suffers from flat feet or derrière spread from long hours spent at an unrewarding or frustrating job. The upwardly mobile professionals who populate soap operas love their work, probably because they are hardly ever at it—one lawyer clocked in at his office exactly once in three months. Their problems are those of people with time on their hands to covet the neighbor's wife, track down villains, betray friends, and enjoy what one observer has called "the perils of Country Club Place."

## QUESTIONS FOR DISCUSSION

1  Cross precedes her introductory paragraph with two epigraphs. Can you explain how these quotations function?

2  What strategy does Cross employ in her introduction?

3  What is her most common method of paragraph development?

4  In the last paragraph, Cross delineates the "vision of morality and American family life" conveyed by soap operas. Do you consider that presentation to be positive or negative if accepted as reality by people watching the programs?

5  In what ways does the evidence offered by Cross corroborate the findings of Gerbner's study reported in "Life According to TV"?

6   Why do you think certain audiences find soap operas so appealing?
7   To what audience do you think this piece is addressed—soap opera fans or people who never watch soaps? How can you tell?

# How TV Violence Damages Your Children

Victor B. Cline

[1]   ITEM: Shortly after a Boston TV station showed a movie depicting a group of youths dousing a derelict with gasoline and setting him afire for "kicks," a woman was burned to death in that city—turned into a human torch under almost identical circumstances.

[2]   ITEM: Several months ago, NBC-TV presented in early-evening, prime viewing time a made-for-TV film, *Born Innocent*, which showed in explicit fashion the sexual violation of a young girl with a broom handle wielded by female inmates in a juvenile detention home. Later a California mother sued NBC and San Francisco TV station KRON for $11,000,000, charging that this show had inspired three girls, ages 10 to 15, to commit a similar attack on her 9-year-old daughter and an 8-year-old friend three days after the film was aired.

[3]   ITEM: A 14-year-old boy, after watching rock star Alice Cooper engage in a mock hanging on TV, attempted to reproduce the stunt and killed himself in the process.

[4]   ITEM: Another boy laced the family dinner with ground glass after seeing it done on a television crime show.

[5]   ITEM: A British youngster died while imitating his TV hero, Batman. The boy was hanged while leaping from a cabinet in a garden shed. His neck became caught in a nylon loop hanging from the roof. His father blamed the TV show for his death—and for encouraging children to attempt the impossible.

[6]   These are just a sampling of many well-documented instances of how TV violence can cause antisocial behavior—instances that are proving that TV violence is hazardous to your child's health.

[7]   TV broadcasters can no longer plead that they are unaware of the potential adverse effects of such programs as *Born Innocent*. During the last decade, two national violence commissions and an overwhelming number of scientific studies have continually come to one conclusion: televised and filmed violence can powerfully teach,

suggest—even legitimatize—extreme antisocial behavior, and can in some viewers trigger specific aggressive or violent behavior. The research of many behavioral scientists has shown that a definite cause-effect relationship exists between violence on TV and violent behavior in real life.

When U.S. Surgeon General Jesse Steinfeld appeared before the [8] U.S. Senate subcommittee reviewing two years of scientific research on the issue, he bluntly concluded, "The overwhelming consensus and the unanimous Scientific Advisory Committee's report indicate that televised violence, indeed, does have an adverse effect on certain members of our society. . . . It is clear to me that the causal relationship between televised violence and antisocial behavior is sufficient to warrant appropriate and immediate remedial action. . . . There comes a time when the data are sufficient to justify action. That time has come.''

The Federal Communications Commission was ordered by [9] Congress to come up with a report by December 31, 1974, on how children can be protected from televised violence (and sex). Hopefully, some concrete proposals will develop.

The television moguls have repeatedly paraded before various [10] Congressional subcommittees over the last ten years, solemnly promising to reduce the overall amount of violence programmed, especially in time slots that had large numbers of child viewers. However, if we look at the data compiled throughout the 1960's and early 1970's, we find very little change in the average number of violent episodes per program broadcast by all three networks. In one study, the staff of U.S. Congressman John M. Murphy of New York found NBC leading the pack with violent sequences in 71 percent of its prime-time shows, followed by ABC with 67 percent and CBS with 57 percent.

With more and more mega-violent films coming to TV from the [11] commercial theater market, as well as the increasing violence injected into made-for-TV movies, we find that the promise of television has been shamelessly ignored. In too many TV films, we see a glorification of violence that makes heroes of killers. The primary motivation for all of this is money and the fierce scramble for ratings. Thus the television industry's "repentance" for past wrongs, occurring after major national tragedies such as the assassination of the Kennedy brothers and Martin Luther King, Jr., with the transient public outrage and demand for change, has been all ritual with little substance.

[12]     We are a great free society with the power to shape our destiny and create almost any social-cultural environment we wish, but as the late President John F. Kennedy put it, "We have the power to make this the best generation in the history of mankind, or the last." If one looks at crime statistics, we find that we are by far the most violent of all the great Western nations. Our homicide rate is about ten times greater than, say, the Scandinavian countries', or four times greater than Scotland's or Australia's. There are more murders per year on the island of Manhattan or in the city of Philadelphia than in the entire United Kingdom, with its nearly 60,000,000 people. Violent crime has been increasing at six to ten times the rate of population growth in this country. And interestingly, if one analyzes the content of TV programs in England, we find that their rate of televised violence is half that of ours; in the Scandinavian countries it is much less even than that.

[13]     Thus one of the major social-cultural differences between the United States with its high homicide and violence rates and those countries with low violence rates is the amount of violence screened on public television.


## "MONKEY SEE, MONKEY DO"

[14]  Much of the research that has led to the conclusion that TV and movie violence could cause aggressive behavior in some children has stemmed from work in the area of imitative learning or modeling which, reduced to its simplest expression, might be termed "monkey see, monkey do." Research by Stanford psychologist Albert Bandura has shown that even brief exposure to novel aggressive behavior *on a one-time basis* can be repeated in free play by as high as 88 percent of the young children seeing it on TV. Dr. Bandura also demonstrated that even a single viewing of a novel aggressive act could be recalled and produced by children six months later, without any intervening exposure. Earlier studies have estimated that the average child between the ages of 5 and 15 will witness, during this 10-year period, the violent destruction of more than 13,400 fellow humans. This means that through several hours of TV-watching, a child may see more violence than the average adult experiences in a lifetime. Killing is as common as taking a walk,

a gun more natural than an umbrella. Children are thus taught to take pride in force and violence and to feel ashamed of ordinary sympathy.

According to the Nielsen Television Index, preschoolers watch [15] television an average of 54 hours a week. During one year, children of school age spend more time in front of a TV set than they do in front of a teacher; in fact, they spend more time watching TV than any other type of waking activity in their lives.

So we might legitimately ask, What are the major lessons, values [16] and attitudes that television teaches our children? Content analyses of large numbers of programs broadcast during children's viewing hours suggest that the major message taught in TV entertainment is that violence is the way to get what you want.

## WHO ARE THE "GOOD GUYS"?

Another major theme that many TV studies have shown to occur [17] repeatedly is that violence is acceptable if the victim "deserved" it. This, of course, is a very dangerous and insidious philosophy. It suggests that aggression, while reprehensible in criminals, is acceptable for the "good guys" who have right on their side. But, of course, nearly every person feels that he or she is "right." And often the "good guys" are criminals whom the film happens to depict sympathetically, as in *The Godfather*. Who is "good" and who is "bad" merely depends on whose side you're on.

Studies by McLeod and Associates of boys and girls in junior and [18] senior high school found that the more the youngster watched violent television fare, the more aggressive he or she was likely to be. Other studies revealed that the amount of television violence watched by children (especially boys) at age 9 influenced the degree to which they were aggressive 10 years later, at age 19.

The problem becomes increasingly serious because, even if your [19] child is not exposed to a lot of media violence, the youngster still could become the *victim or target* of aggression by a child who is stimulated by the violence that he or she sees on TV.

And criminals are too frequently shown on TV as daring heroes. [20] In the eyes of many young viewers, these criminals possess all that's worth having in life—fast cars, beautiful, admiring women, super-potent guns, modish clothes, etc. In the end they die like heroes—

almost as martyrs—but then only to appease the "old folks" who insist on "crime-does-not-pay" endings.

[21]     The argument that you can't get high ratings for your show unless it is hyped up with violence is, of course, not true—as 20 years of *I Love Lucy* and, more recently, *All in the Family*, *Sanford and Son*, *The Waltons* and scores of other shows have demonstrated. Action shows featuring themes of human conflict frequently have appeal, yet even they needn't pander to the antisocial side of man's nature or legitimatize evil.

[22]     The hard scientific evidence clearly demonstrates that watching television violence, sometimes for only a few hours, and in some studies even for a few minutes, can and often does instigate aggressive behavior that would not otherwise occur. If only 1 percent of the possibly 40,000,000 people who saw *The Godfather* on TV were stimulated to commit an aggressive act, this would involve 400,000 people. Or if it were only one in 10,000, it would involve 4,000 people—plus their victims.

[23]     Some parents believe that if their children are suitably loved, properly brought up and emotionally well-balanced, they will not be affected by TV violence. However, psychiatrist Frederic Wertham responds to this by noting that all children are impressionable and therefore susceptible. We flatter ourselves if we think that our social conditions, our family life, our education and our entertainment are so far above reproach that only emotionally sick children can get into trouble. As Dr. Wertham points out, if we believe that harm can come only to the predisposed child, this leads to a contradictory and irresponsible attitude on the part of adults. Constructive TV programs are praised for giving children constructive ideas, but we deny that destructive scenes give children destructive ideas.

[24]     It should also be noted that the "catharsis theory" in vogue a few years ago, which suggested that seeing violence is good for children because it allows them vicariously to discharge their hostile feelings, has been convincingly discarded. Just the opposite has been found to be true. Seeing violence stimulates children aggressively; it also shows them how to commit aggressive acts.

[25]     The author of this article has conducted research studying the "desensitization" of children to TV violence and its potential effects.

[26]     In our University of Utah laboratories, we set up two six-channel

physiographs which had the capacity to measure emotional responsiveness in children while they watched violent TV shows. When most
of our subjects saw violent films, those instruments measuring heart
action, respiration, perspiration, etc., all hooked up to the autonomic
nervous system, did indeed record strong emotional arousal. We studied
120 boys between the ages of 5 and 14. Half had seen little or no TV
in the previous two years (hence had seen little media violence), and
the other half had seen an average of 42 hours of TV a week for the
past two years (hence a lot of violence). As our violent film, we chose
an eight-minute sequence from the Kirk Douglas prizefighting film,
*The Champion,* which had been shown many times on TV reruns but
which none of the boys tested had ever seen. We considered other,
more violent films, but they were too brutal, we felt, to be shown to
children—even for experimental purposes. The boxing match seemed
like a good compromise. Nobody was killed or seriously injured.
Nothing illegal occurred. Yet the fight did depict very graphically
human aggression that was emotionally arousing.

These two groups of boys watched our film while we recorded [27]
their emotional responses on the physiograph. The results showed that
the boys with a history of heavy violence watching were significantly
less aroused emotionally by what they saw—they had become habit-
uated or "desensitized" to violence. To put it another way, our findings
suggested that the heavy TV watchers appeared to be somewhat desensitized or "turned off" to violence, suggesting the possibility of an
emotional blunting or less "conscience and concern" in the presence
of witnessed violence. This means that they had developed a tolerance
fo it, and possibly an indifference toward human life and suffering.
They were no longer shocked or horrified by it. It suggested to us the
many instances of "bystander apathy," in which citizens in large urban
areas have witnessed others being assaulted, yet did not come to their
rescue or try to secure aid or help. Or incidents such as the My Lai
massacre, in which American soldiers killed Vietnamese civilians. This
suggests an unfeeling, indifferent, noncaring, dehumanized response
to suffering or distress.

In any event, our research has presented the first empirical [28]
evidence that children who are exposed to a lot of TV violence do to
some extent become blunted emotionally or desensitized to it.

Since our children are an important national resource, these [29]

findings suggest that we should teach them wisely. The kinds of fantasies to which we expose them may make a great deal of difference as
to what kind of adults they become, and whether we will survive as a
society.

[30]     The author, who is a psychotherapist and who treats many
damaged children and families, was then faced with the problem of
what to do about his own TV set and his own children, who regularly
watched TV and had their favorite programs. The evidence had been
stacking up in my laboratory—so what should I do about it at home?
The thing that finally turned me from being the permissive, tolerant,
"good-guy" dad to the concerned parent was the realization that
whenever my children looked at TV for any lengthy period, especially
violent action shows, they became frequently touchy, cross and irritable. Instead of playing outside, even on beautiful days, discharging
tensions in healthy interaction with others, they sat passive for hours,
too often hypnotized by whatever appeared on the tube. Frequently,
homework didn't get done, chores were neglected, etc. One Saturday
morning I was shocked to find my bright, 15-year-old son watching
cartoons for four straight hours, having let all chores and other responsibilities go. It was then that we finally decided to turn off the TV set
on a relatively permanent basis.

## "NO TV" IS A TURN-ON

[31]     When we announced this decision, we found ourselves faced with a
family revolt. There was much wailing and gnashing of teeth. It was
as if the alcoholic had been deprived of his bottle, or as if we had
suddenly announced that no more food would be served at our table.

[32]     However, the "storm" lasted only one week. Interestingly, during
that week, the children went outside and played with each other and
the neighbors much more, a lot more good books got read, homework
was done on time, chores got finished, and the children got along with
each other better. And very interestingly, the complaints about "no
TV" suddenly stopped at the end of that week. Now, several years
later, we do occasionally look at TV—some sports specials, a good
movie, something required for school, even a mystery. But it's almost
never on school nights—and it is no longer an issue in our home.
Nobody feels deprived. It's now just not a major part of our lifestyle.

[33]     It should be stated, in all fairness, that television has the potential

for great good—to teach children pro-social values and behavior, such as sharing with others, controlling one's impulses, solving problems through reason and discussion, being kind and thoughtful. Such programs as *The Waltons* suggest to me that such content can have wide popular appeal and be commercially marketable—if done with talent, care and commitment. In other words, television could be used for far more constructive programming than we have seen in the past. For the time being, parents should, in my judgment, be very cautious about what they expose their children to on television (as well as in movies). If something particularly objectionable is broadcast during children's prime-time hours, there are three things that can be done: (1) turn the television set off; (2) phone your local station expressing your concern; (3) write to the program's sponsor, indicating your objections (the firm's address will be found on the label of his merchandise).

The evidence is clear: a child's mind can be polluted and corrupted [34] just as easily as his body can be poisoned by contaminants in the environment. Children are essentially powerless to deal with such problems. This means that the responsibility for effecting change rests with every adult citizen. Meaning you. Meaning me. Meaning us.

## QUESTIONS FOR DISCUSSION

1  What strategy does Cline use to engage your attention at the beginning of the essay?
2  Paragraph 12 is developed primarily with statistics. Do you find this evidence convincing? Does the inference conveyed by the last sentence bear any causal relationship to the statistics preceding it?
3  In paragraph 25 and again in paragraph 30, the writer refers to himself in the third person ("The author of this article has conducted research . . ." and "The author, who is a psychotherapist . . ."). Why do you suppose he doesn't just say, "I"? Do you think his writing would be more effective if he did? Why or why not?
4  Do you think Cline overstates his case in paragraph 29? Or is the matter truly that crucial?
5  How do you respond to the headings used throughout this article? Why do you suppose they are there? Have you ever used headings in your own writing? If so, what kind of writing were you doing?
6  Do you find Cline's "No TV is a turn-on" believable? Do you think the results would be the same if you instituted the rule in your family? Why or why not?

## SUGGESTIONS FOR WRITING

1  The Gerbner study discussed by Harry Waters was published in 1982. Have TV shows changed since then? Consider the categories analyzed in the research: sex, age, race, work, and crime. Write an update reporting what you observe to be happening in those areas in today's programs. Be as specific as possible in describing the attitudes you see portrayed. Your audience for this report could be Professor Gerbner.

2  Choose a TV series that you think significantly distorts reality and analyze the images that are presented there. Or choose a category of people (like mothers, fathers, children, police officers, private detectives) and analyze the way their roles are depicted on several shows. Write this piece for publication in your school newspaper or in *Newsweek*'s ''My Turn'' column.

3  In ''Sin, Suffer, and Repent,'' Donna Woolfolk Cross analyzes soap operas in terms of their presentation of marriage, career women, infidelity, pregnancy, miscarriage, abortion, motherhood, and children. Considering some or all of these factors, write a similar analysis of true confession stories or Harlequin romances. You might conclude, as Cross does, by explaining what ''vision of morality and American family life'' is being sold in these fictions. Write your essay for publication in the national *PTA Newsletter* with your purpose being to let parents know what values are conveyed to teenagers who read these works.

4  Throughout his article ''How TV Violence Damages Your Children,'' Victor Cline uses ''he'' to refer to children of both sexes. If you were offended by this eclipsing of the female, write a letter to Cline explaining how sexist language damages your children. Before beginning, you might want to read Robin Lakoff's article, ''You Are What You Say,'' in Chapter 17.

5  Cline's article appeared in 1975. Has the amount of violence on television decreased—or have people just quit worrying about it? For a week, study TV programming during prime time, including the movies shown, and write a report to Cline delivering the good news if you find that violence has diminished since he published his article, the bad news if you find that violence remains about the same, or the crushing blow if you find that violence has actually increased. Be sure to cite plenty of specific evidence.

Chapter 16

# Considering Violence

## Kill 'Em! Crush 'Em! Eat 'Em Raw!

John McMurtry

A few months ago my neck got a hard crick in it. I couldn't turn my [1]
head; to look left or right I'd have to turn my whole body. But I'd had
cricks in my neck since I started playing grade-school football and
hockey, so I just ignored it. Then I began to notice that when I reached
for any sort of large book (which I do pretty often as a philosophy
teacher at the University of Guelph) I had trouble lifting it with one
hand. I was losing the strength in my left arm, and I had such a steady
pain in my back I often had to stretch out on the floor of the room I
was in to relieve the pressure.

A few weeks later I mentioned to my brother, an orthopedic [2]
surgeon, that I'd lost the power in my arm since my neck began to
hurt. Twenty-four hours later I was in a Toronto hospital not sure

whether I might end up with a wasted upper limb. Apparently the steady pounding I had received playing college and professional football in the late Fifties and early Sixties had driven my head into my backbone so that the discs had crumpled together at the neck—"acute herniation"—and had cut the nerves to my left arm like a pinched telephone wire (without nerve stimulation, of course, the muscles atrophy, leaving the arm crippled). So I spent my Christmas holidays in the hospital in heavy traction and much of the next three months with my neck in a brace. Today most of the pain has gone, and I've recovered most of the strength in my arm. But from time to time I still have to don the brace, and surgery remains a possibility.

[3]     Not much of this will surprise anyone who knows football. It is a sport in which body wreckage is one of the leading conventions. A few days after I went into the hospital for that crick in my neck, another brother, an outstanding football player in college, was undergoing spinal surgery in the same hospital two floors above me. In his case it was a lower, more massive herniation, which every now and again buckled him so that he was unable to lift himself off his back for days at a time. By the time he entered the hospital for surgery he had already spent several months in bed. The operation was successful, but, as in all such cases, it will take him a year to recover fully.

[4]     These aren't isolated experiences. Just about anybody who has ever played football for any length of time, in high school, college or one of the professional leagues, has suffered for it later physically.

[5]     Indeed, it is arguable that body shattering is the very *point* of football, as killing and maiming are of war. (In the United States, for example, the game results in 15 to 20 deaths a year and about 50,000 major operations on knees alone.) To grasp some of the more conspicuous similarities between football and war, it is instructive to listen to the imperatives most frequently issued to the players by their coaches, teammates and fans. "Hurt 'em!" "Level 'em!" "Kill 'em!" "Take 'em apart!" Or watch for the plays that are most enthusiastically applauded by the fans. Where someone is "smeared," "knocked silly," "creamed," "nailed," "broken in two," or even "crucified." (One of my coaches when I played corner linebacker with the Calgary Stampeders in 1961 elaborated, often very inventively, on this language of destruction: admonishing us to "unjoin" the opponent, "make 'im remember you" and "stomp 'im like a bug.") Just as in hockey, where

a fight will bring fans to their feet more often than a skillful play, so in football the mouth waters most of all for the really crippling block or tackle. For the kill. Thus the good teams are ''hungry,'' the best players are ''mean,'' and ''casualties'' are as much a part of the game as they are of a war.

The family resemblance between football and war is, indeed, [6] striking. Their languages are similar: ''field general,'' ''long bomb,'' ''blitz,'' ''take a shot,'' ''front line,'' ''pursuit,'' ''good hit,'' ''the draft'' and so on. Their principles and practices are alike: mass hysteria, the art of intimidation, absolute command and total obedience, territorial aggression, censorship, inflated insignia and propaganda, blackboard manoeuvres and strategies, drills, uniforms, formations, marching bands and training camps. And the virtues they celebrate are almost identical: hyper-aggressiveness, coolness under fire and suicidal bravery. All this has been implicitly recognized by such jock-loving Americans as media stars General Patton and President Nixon, who have talked about war as a football game. Patton wanted to make his Second World War tank men look like football players. And Nixon, as we know, was fond of comparing attacks on Vietnam to football plays and drawing coachly diagrams on a blackboard for TV war fans.

One difference between war and football, though, is that there is [7] little or no protest against football. Perhaps the most extraordinary thing about the game is that the systematic infliction of injuries excites in people not concern, as would be the case if they were sustained at, say, a rock festival, but a collective rejoicing and euphoria. Players and fans alike revel in the spectacle of a combatant felled into semiconsciousness, ''blindsided,'' ''clotheslined'' or ''decapitated.'' I can remember, in fact, being chided by a coach in pro ball for not ''getting my hat'' injuriously into a player who was already lying helpless on the ground. (On another occasion, after the Stampeders had traded the celebrated Joe Kapp to BC, we were playing the Lions in Vancouver and Kapp was forced on one play to run with the ball. He was coming ''down the chute,'' his bad knee wobbling uncertainly, so I simply dropped on him like a blanket. After I returned to the bench I was reproved for not exploiting the opportunity to unhinge his bad knee.)

After every game, of course, the papers are full of reports on the [8] day's injuries, a sort of post-battle ''body count,'' and the respective teams go to work with doctors and trainers, tape, whirlpool baths, cortisone and morphine to patch and deaden the wounds before the next game. Then the whole drama is reenacted—injured athletes held together by adhesive, braces and drugs—and the days following it are filled with even more feverish activity to put on the show yet again at the end of the next week. (I remember being so taped up in college that I earned the nickname "mummy.") The team that survives this merry-go-round spectacle of skilled masochism with the fewest incapacitating injuries usually wins. It is a sort of victory by ordeal: "We hurt them more than they hurt us."

[9]      My own initiation into this brutal circus was typical. I loved the game from the moment I could run with a ball. Played shoeless on a green open field with no one keeping score and in a spirit of reckless abandon and laughter, it's a very different sport. Almost no one gets hurt and it's rugged, open and exciting (it still is for me). But then, like everything else, it starts to be regulated and institutionalized by adult authorities. And the fun is over.

[10]     So it was as I began the long march through organized football. Now there was a coach and elders to make it clear by their behavior that beating other people was the only thing to celebrate and that trying to shake someone up every play was the only thing to be really proud of. Now there were severe rule enforcers, audiences, formally recorded victors and losers, and heavy equipment to permit crippling bodily moves and collisions (according to one American survey, more than 80% of all football injuries occur to fully equipped players). And now there was the official "given" that the only way to keep playing was to wear suffocating armor, to play to defeat, to follow orders silently and to renounce spontaneity for joyless drill. The game had been, in short, ruined. But because I loved to play and play skillfully, I stayed. And progressively and inexorably, as I moved through high school, college and pro leagues, my body was dismantled. Piece by piece.

[11]     I started off with torn ligaments in my knee at 13. Then, as the organization and the competition increased, the injuries came faster and harder. Broken nose (three times), broken jaw (fractured in the first half and dismissed as a "bad wisdom tooth," so I played with it for the rest of the game), ripped knee ligaments again. Torn ligaments in one ankle and a fracture in the other (which I remember feeling relieved about because it meant I could honorably stop drill-blocking

a 270-pound defensive end). Repeated rib fractures and cartilage tears (usually carried, again, through the remainder of the game). More dislocations of the left shoulder than I can remember (the last one I played with because, as the Calgary Stampeder doctor said, it "couldn't be damaged any more"). Occasional broken or dislocated fingers and toes. Chronically hurt lower back (I still can't lift with it or change a tire without worrying about folding). Separated right shoulder (as with many other injuries, like badly bruised hips and legs, needled with morphine for the games). And so on. The last pro game I played— against Winnipeg Blue Bombers in the Western finals in 1961—I had a recently dislocated left shoulder, a more recently wrenched right shoulder and a chronic pain centre in one leg. I was so tied up with soreness I couldn't drive my car to the airport. But it never occurred to me or anyone else that I miss a play as a corner linebacker.

By the end of my football career, I had learned that physical [12] injury—giving it and taking it—is the real currency of the sport. And that in the final analysis the "winner" is the man who can hit to kill even if only half his limbs are working. In brief, a warrior game with a warrior ethos into which (like almost everyone else I played with) my original boyish enthusiasm had been relentlessly taunted and conditioned.

In thinking back on how all this happened, though, I can pick out [13] no villains. As with the social system as a whole, the game has a life of its own. Everyone grows up inside it, accepts it and fulfills its dictates as obediently as helots. Far from ever questioning the principles of the activity, people simply concentrate on executing these principles more aggressively than anybody around them. The result is a group of people who, as the leagues become of a higher and higher class, are progressively insensitive to the possibility that things could be otherwise. Thus, in football, anyone who might question the wisdom or enjoyment of putting on heavy equipment on a hot day and running full speed at someone else with the intention of knocking him senseless would be regarded simply as not really a devoted athlete and probably "chicken." The choice is made straightforward. Either you, too, do your very utmost to efficiently smash and be smashed, or you admit incompetence or cowardice and quit. Since neither of these admissions is very pleasant, people generally keep any doubts they have to themselves and carry on.

[14]       Of course, it would be a mistake to suppose that there is more blind acceptance of brutal practices in organized football than elsewhere. On the contrary, a recent Harvard study has approvingly argued that football's characteristics of "impersonal acceptance of inflicted injury," an overriding "organization goal," the "ability to turn oneself on and off" and being, above all, "out to win" are of "inestimable value" to big corporations. Clearly, our sort of football is no sicker than the rest of our society. Even its organized destruction of physical well-being is not anomalous. A very large part of our wealth, work and time is, after all, spent in systematically destroying and harming human life. Manufacturing, selling and using weapons that tear opponents to pieces. Making ever bigger and faster predator-named cars with which to kill and injure one another by the million every year. And devoting our very lives to outgunning one another for power in an ever more destructive rat race. Yet all these practices are accepted without question by most people, even zealously defended and honored. Competitive, organized injuring is integral to our way of life, and football is simply one of the more intelligible mirrors of the whole process: a sort of colorful morality play showing us how exciting and rewarding it is to Smash Thy Neighbor.

[15]       Now it is fashionable to rationalize our collaboration in all this by arguing that, well, man *likes* to fight and injure his fellows and such games as football should be encouraged to discharge this original-sin urge into less harmful channels than, say, war. Public-show football, this line goes, plays the same sort of cathartic role as Aristotle said stage tragedy does: without real blood (or not much), it releases players and audience from unhealthy feelings stored up inside them.

[16]       As an ex-player in this seasonal coast-to-coast drama, I see little to recommend such a view. What organized football did to me was make me *suppress* my natural urges and re-express them in an alienating, vicious form. Spontaneous desires for free bodily exuberance and fraternization with competitors were shamed and forced under ("If it ain't hurtin' it ain't helpin'") and in their place were demanded armored mechanical moves and cool hatred of all opposition. Endless authoritarian drill and dressing-room harangues (ever wonder why competing teams can't prepare for a game in the same dressing room?) were the kinds of mechanisms employed to reconstruct joyful energies into mean and alien shapes. I am quite certain that everyone else around

me was being similarly forced into this heavily equipped military precision and angry antagonism, because there was always a mutinous attitude about full-dress practices, and everybody (the pros included) had to concentrate incredibly hard for days to whip themselves into just one hour's hostility a week against another club. The players never speak of these things, of course, because everyone is so anxious to appear tough.

The claim that men like seriously to battle one another to some [17] sort of finish is a myth. It only endures because it wears one of the oldest and most propagandized of masks—the romantic combatant. I sometimes wonder whether the violence all around us doesn't depend for its survival on the existence and preservation of this tough-guy disguise.

As for the effect of organized football on the spectator, the fan is [18] not released from supposed feelings of violent aggression by watching his athletic heroes perform it so much as encouraged in the view that people-smashing is an admirable mode of self-expression. The most savage attackers, after all, are, by general agreement, the most efficient and worthy players of all (the biggest applause I ever received as a football player occurred when I ran over people or slammed them so hard they couldn't get up). Such circumstances can hardly be said to lessen the spectators' martial tendencies. Indeed it seems likely that the whole show just further develops and titillates the North American addiction for violent self-assertion. . . . Perhaps, as well, it helps explain why the greater the zeal of U.S. political leaders as football fans (Johnson, Nixon, Agnew), the more enthusiastic the commitment to hard-line politics. At any rate there seems to be a strong correlation between people who relish tough football and people who relish intimidating and beating the hell out of commies, hippies, protest marchers and other opposition groups.

Watching well-advertised strong men knock other people around, [19] make them hurt, is in the end like other tastes. It does not weaken with feeding and variation in form. It grows.

I got out of football in 1962. I had asked to be traded after Calgary [20] had offered me a $25-a-week-plus-commissions off-season job as a clothing-store salesman. ("Dear Mr. Finks:" I wrote. [Jim Finks was then the Stampeders' general manager.] "Somehow I do not think the dialectical subtleties of Hegel, Marx and Plato would be suitably oriented amidst the environmental stimuli of jockey shorts and herring-bone suits. I hope you make a profitable sale or trade of my contract to the East.'') So the Stampeders traded me to Montreal. In a preseason intersquad game with the Alouettes I ripped the cartilages in my ribs on the hardest block I'd ever thrown. I had trouble breathing and I had to shuffle-walk with my torso on a tilt. The doctor in the local hospital said three weeks rest, the coach said scrimmage in two days. Three days later I was back home reading philosophy.

## QUESTIONS FOR DISCUSSION

1 How does McMurtry engage your interest in his introduction?
2 Can you find a thesis statement in the first few paragraphs of the essay? If so, where? Why do you think he placed it where he did?
3 In paragraph 3 he asserts that football ''is a sport in which body wreckage is one of the leading conventions,'' and presents persuasive evidence from his immediate family. Can you explain then why boys (and men) continue to risk (and suffer) injury in order to play?
4 McMurtry develops a substantial portion of his essay with an analogy—a comparison of football and war. Have you encountered this analogy before? Do you find it convincing? Why or why not?
5 In paragraph 14 McMurtry extends his indictment of violence in football to include the violence in society in general. Do you agree that ''competitive, organized injuring is integral to our way of life . . .''? Can you add any examples to the ones he cites in the paragraph?
6 What is McMurtry's purpose in writing this essay? Does he just want to warn his readers about the dangers that football players face? Or is he making a broader point than that?

# Fifty Million Handguns

Adam Smith

[1] ''You people,'' said my Texas host, ''do not understand guns or gun people.'' By ''you people'' he meant not just me, whom he happened to be addressing, but anyone from a large eastern or midwestern city. My Texas host is a very successful businessman, an intelligent man. ''There are two cultures,'' he said, ''and the nongun culture looks down on the gun culture.''

My Texas host had assumed—correctly—that I do not spend a lot [2] of time with guns. The last one I knew intimately was a semiautomatic M-14, and, as any veteran knows, the Army bids you call it a weapon, not a gun. I once had to take that weapon apart and reassemble it blind-folded, and I liked it better than the heavy old M-1. We were also given a passing introduction to the Russian Kalashnikov and the AK-47, the Chinese copy of that automatic weapon, presumably so we could use these products of our Russian and Chinese enemies if the need arose. I remember that you could drop a Kalashnikov in the mud and pick it up and it would still fire. I also remember blowing up a section of railroad track using only an alarm clock, a primer cord, and a plastic called C-4. The day our little class blew up the track at Fort Bragg was rather fun. These experiences give me some credibility with friends from the ''gun culture.'' (Otherwise, they have no lasting social utility whatsoever.) And I do not share the fear of guns—at least of ''long guns,'' rifles and shotguns—that some of my college-educated city-dweller friends have, perhaps because of my onetime intimacy with that Army rifle, whose serial number I still know.

In the gun culture, said my Texas host, a boy is given a .22 rifle [3] around the age of twelve, a shotgun at fourteen, and a .30-caliber rifle at sixteen. The young man is taught to use and respect these instru-ments. My Texas host showed me a paragraph in a book by Herman Kahn in which Kahn describes the presentation of the .22 as a rite of passage, like a confirmation or a bar mitzvah. ''Young persons who are given guns,'' he wrote, ''go through an immediate maturing experience because they are thereby given a genuine and significant responsibility.'' Any adult from the gun culture, whether or not he is a relative, can admonish any young person who appears to be careless with his weapon. Thus, says Kahn, the gun-culture children take on ''enlarging and maturing responsibilities'' that their coddled upper-middle-class counterparts from the nongun culture do not share. The children of my Texas host said ''sir'' to their father and ''ma'am'' to their mother.

I do not mean to argue with the rite-of-passage theory. I am quite [4] willing to grant it. I bring it up because the subjects of guns and gun control are very emotional ones, and if we are to solve the problems associated with them, we need to arrive at a consensus within and between gun and nongun cultures in our country.

[5]     Please note that the rite-of-passage gifts are shotguns and rifles. Long guns have sporting uses. Nobody gives a child a handgun, and nobody shoots a flying duck with a .38 revolver. Handguns have only one purpose.

[6]     Some months ago, a college friend of mine surprised a burglar in his home in Washington, D.C. Michael Halberstam was a cardiologist, a writer, and a contributor to this magazine.* The burglar shot Halberstam, but Halberstam ran him down with his car on the street outside before he died, and the case received widespread press. I began to work on this column, in high anger, right after his death. A few days later, John Lennon was killed in New York. These two dreadful murders produced an outpouring of grief, followed immediately by intense anger and the demand that something be done, that Congress pass a gun-control law. The National Rifle Association was quick to point out that a gun-control law would not have prevented either death; Halberstam's killer had already violated a whole slew of existing laws, and Lennon's was clearly sufficiently deranged or determined to kill him under any gun law. The National Rifle Association claims a million members, and it is a highly organized lobby. Its Political Victory Fund "works for the defeat of antigun candidates and for the support and election of progun office seekers." Let us grant the National Rifle Association position that the accused killers in these two recent spectacular shootings might not have been deterred even by severe gun restrictions.

[7]     In the course of researching this column, I talked to representatives of both the progun and the antigun lobbies. Anomalies abound. Sam Fields, a spokesman for the National Coalition to Ban Handguns, is an expert rifleman who was given a gun at age thirteen by his father, a New York City policeman. The progun banner is frequently carried by Don Kates Jr., who describes himself as a liberal, a former civil rights worker, and a professor of constitutional law. Fields and Kates have debated each other frequently. Given their backgrounds, one might expect their positions to be reversed.

[8]     Some of the progun arguments run as follows:

[9]     Guns don't kill people, people kill people. Gun laws do not deter criminals. (A 1976 University of Wisconsin study of gun laws

*This article appeared in *Esquire* magazine in 1981.

concluded that "gun-control laws have no individual or collective effect in reducing the rate of violent crime.") A mandatory sentence for carrying an unlicensed gun, says Kates, would punish the "ordinary decent citizens in high-crime areas who carry guns illegally because police protection is inadequate and they don't have the special influence necessary to get a 'carry' permit." There are fifty million handguns out there in the United States already; unless you were to use a giant magnet, there is no way to retrieve them. The majority of people do not want guns banned. A ban on handguns would be like Prohibition—widely disregarded, unenforceable, and corrosive to the nation's sense of moral order. Federal registration is the beginning of federal tyranny; we might someday need to use those guns against the government.

Some of the antigun arguments go as follows: [10]

People kill people, but handguns make it easier. When other [11] weapons (knives, for instance) are used, the consequences are not so often deadly. Strangling or stabbing someone takes a different degree of energy and intent than pulling a trigger. Registration will not interfere with hunting and other rifle sports but will simply exercise control over who can carry handguns. Ordinary people do not carry handguns. If a burglar has a gun in his hand, it is quite insane for you to shoot it out with him, as if you were in a quick-draw contest in the Wild West. Half of all the guns used in crimes are stolen; 70 percent of the stolen guns are handguns. In other words, the supply of handguns used by criminals already comes to a great extent from the households these guns were supposed to protect.

"I'll tell you one thing," said a lieutenant on the local police [12] force in my town. "You should never put that decal in your window, the one that says THIS HOUSE IS PROTECTED BY AN ARMED CITIZEN. The gun owners love them, but that sign is just an invitation that says 'Come and rob my guns.' Television sets and stereos are fenced at a discount; guns can actually be fenced at a premium. The burglar doesn't want to meet you. I have had a burglar tell me, 'If I wanted to meet people, I would have been a mugger.'"

After a recent wave of burglaries, the weekly newspaper in my [13] town published a front-page story. "Do not buy a gun—you're more likely to shoot yourself than a burglar," it said. At first the police agreed with that sentiment. Later, they took a slightly different line. "There is more danger from people having accidents or their kids getting hold of those guns than any service in defending their houses; but there was a flap when the paper printed that, so now we don't say anything,'' said my local police lieutenant. "If you want to own a gun legally, okay. Just be careful and know the laws.''

[14]        What police departments tell inquiring citizens seems to depend not only on the local laws but also on whether or not that particular police department belongs to the gun culture.

[15]        Some of the crime statistics underlying the gun arguments are surprising. Is crime-ridden New York City the toughest place in the country? No: your chances of being murdered are higher in Columbus, Georgia, in Pine Bluff, Arkansas, and in Houston, Texas, among others. Some of the statistics are merely appalling: we had roughly ten thousand handgun deaths last year. The British had forty. In 1978, there were 18,714 Americans murdered. Sixty-four percent were killed with handguns. In that same year, *we had more killings with handguns by children ten years old and younger than the British had by killers of all ages.* The Canadians had 579 homicides last year; we had more than twenty thousand.

[16]        H. Rap Brown, the Sixties activist, once said, "Violence is as American as apple pie.'' I guess it is. We think fondly of Butch Cassidy and the Sundance Kid; we do not remember the names of the trainmen and the bank clerks they shot. Four of our Presidents have died violently; the British have never had a prime minister assassinated. *Life* magazine paid $8,000 to Halberstam's accused killer for photos of his boyhood. Now he will be famous, like Son of Sam. The list could go on and on.

[17]        I am willing to grant to the gunners a shotgun in every closet. Shotguns are not used much in armed robberies, or even by citizens in arguments with each other. A shotgun is a better home-defense item anyway, say my police friends, if only because you have to be very accurate with a handgun to knock a man down with one. But the arguments over which kinds of guns are best only demonstrate how dangerously bankrupt our whole society is in ideas on personal safety.

[18]        Our First Lady has a handgun.

[19]        Would registry of handguns stop the criminal from carrying the unregistered gun? No, and it might afflict the householder with some extra red tape. However, there is a valid argument for registry. Such

a law might have no immediate effect, but we have to begin somewhere. We license automobiles and drivers. That does not stop automobile deaths, but surely the highways would be even more dangerous if populated with unlicensed drivers and uninspected cars. The fifty million handguns outstanding have not caused the crime rate to go down. Another two million handguns will be sold this year, and I will bet that the crime rate still does not go down.

Our national behavior is considered close to insane by some of [20] the other advanced industrial nations. We have gotten so accustomed to crime and violence that we have begun to take them for granted; thus we are surprised to learn that the taxi drivers in Tokyo carry far more than five dollars in cash, that you can walk safely around the streets of Japan's largest cities, and that Japan's crime rate is going *down*. I know there are cultural differences; I am told that in Japan the criminal is expected to turn himself in so as not to shame his parents. Can we imagine that as a solution to crime here?

In a way, the tragic killings of Michael Halberstam and John [21] Lennon have distracted us from a larger and more complex problem. There is a wave of grief, a wave of anger—and then things go right on as they did before. We become inured to the violence and dulled to the outrage. Perhaps, indeed, no legislation could stop murders like these, and perhaps national gun legislation would not produce overnight change. The hard work is not just to get the gunners to join in; the hard work is to do something about our ragged system of criminal justice, to shore up our declining faith in the institutions that are supposed to protect us, and to promote the notion that people should take responsibility for their own actions.

What makes us so different from the Japanese and the British and [22] the Canadians? They are not armed, as we are, yet their streets and houses are far safer. Should we not be asking ourselves some sober questions about whether we are living the way we want to?

## QUESTIONS FOR DISCUSSION

1  Do you find Smith's opening strategy effective? What does he achieve with the quoted conversation?
2  Why do you think he includes the recollection of his war experiences in paragraph 2?
3  Do you agree with author Herman Kahn (quoted by Smith in paragraph 3):

''Young persons who are given guns . . . go through an immediate maturing experience because they are thereby given a genuine and significant responsibility''? Would the same hold true, for instance, if these young persons were given cars?

4  At the end of paragraph 6, Smith concedes that the murderers of Michael Halberstam and John Lennon ''might not have been deterred even by severe gun restrictions.'' Why, then, did he bother to mention these notorious murders?

5  In paragraphs 8 through 11, Smith presents the standard arguments for and against gun control. Does either side strike you as having noticeably better arguments?

6  Why does Smith set off a single sentence as paragraph 18?

7  How persuasive do you find Smith's arguments that other societies are far safer than ours because their citizens are not armed with handguns?

8  Do you think we have any chance of accomplishing the ''hard work'' that Smith suggests as a possible solution to the problem in the last sentence of paragraph 21? If so, how? If not, why not?

# Sexual Abuse on Campus: Where Is the True Gentleman Today?

T. A. Stoll

*The situation is typical. The brothers have been socialized the way most young men are; they have learned to suppress their feelings, and they would* **never** *back down from a fight—that would be a sign of weakness, and therefore not ''masculine.'' These brothers have formed a ''bond''; they view their fraternity with the attitude of ''we're in this together, we're brothers, we're fighting 'the others,' we're unstoppable together . . .''*

*A group of guys in the house have been checking out a new ''fraternity row'' calendar featuring scantily clad women, accompanied by sexist remarks such as ''wouldn't you like her for a little sister?'' or ''who can get a date with this babe?'' etc.*

*While looking at the calendar, they are unaware that they have started objectifying women they know by discussing which ones are ''loose.'' ''Groupthink'' has taken over with these guys; each man's individual consciousness has been lowered; their senses of right and wrong have been numbed.*

*The house has a party. Sally Jones, one of the coeds they consider ''loose,'' arrives. She, like almost everyone there, drinks some alcohol. She is attracted to brother Joe Smith.*[1] *Sally goes with Joe to his room and they start kissing. The other guys think Sally is open prey, fair game. They filter into Joe's room and start to tease her, to cajole her, "Come on, Sally, kiss me, too. Aren't we friends, Sally?"*

*Initially, Sally goes along with the teasing. These are her friends, guys she has respected. Then the young men start to exert pressure . . .*

*Sally leaves feeling frightened, degraded and confused about the fraternity guys. She has been coerced by the group to do something against her will. She has been abused.*

*The brothers have a feeling of conquest. They all keep up the facade that this is an O.K. thing to do. After all, Sally went along with it. If one guy starts to say, "I think we did something wrong to Sally . . . ," the groupthink will pressure him to feel he's being a weak man.*

*All these young men know they have not acted in a just way, and they will eventually pay a price. They realize things got out of hand; that they acted far beyond ungentlemanly; that what they have done is morally unacceptable.*

Some of us may recall similar incidences on our own campuses, or [1] even in the chapter house. We thought the friendly "gang bang" was O.K. After all, the woman went along with it.

Wrong, brothers. Not only is the "gang bang" itself wrong by [2] legal standards—it's rape, no matter how you rationalize it—but it's an act of violence based on a perverted myth of masculinity and sexuality.

The problem of sexual abuse on campus is not a new one, although [3] the issue has received greater attention in the media and on campuses due to growing awareness of changing social codes and mores, and the redefined roles of men and women.

Brother Tom Goodale, a dean who has worked on college [4] campuses for 25 years, said sexually abusive behavior has been occurring all along.

"Now the problem is out of the closet, thank goodness," he said. [5] "Society isn't going to tolerate sexual abuse as appropriate behavior any more. The whole consciousness has changed. Everyone views their body as private."

The need for ΣAE to address the sexual abuse problem on campus [6] is clear: Recently, a chapter of Sigma Alpha Epsilon was closed

---

[1]These names refer to fictional characters. Any similarity to or resemblance to real-life college students is purely coincidental.

following an incident of gang rape at the chapter house. In addition, current statistics on "acquaintance rape" cry out for a solution to this growing problem:

- A study sponsored by the Association of American Colleges found evidence that 50 gang rapes occurred in fraternity houses across the country in a recent two- to three-year period.
- FBI statistics show that about one of four women will be raped in her lifetime. One out of eight women will be raped during her educational stay.
- *Newsweek on Campus* reported results of a study that revealed 15 percent of the women surveyed at 33 colleges had been raped by strict legal standards, and that in 84 percent of the assaults, the women knew their attackers. Hence the term "acquaintance rape."
- A study of 200 college women reported that 15 percent had been forced to have sex against their will; 50 percent had clothing unfastened against their will; 35 percent had the genital area touched against their will; and only 43 percent had not been forced to do anything against their will.
- In a study conducted at a college in the southern United States, it was learned that 61 percent of the men surveyed had touched a woman sexually against her will.

[7]     The National Interfraternity Conference (NIC) House of Delegates unanimously passed a resolution last fall recognizing "inappropriate behavior in human interaction" being practiced by some collegians, including fraternity members, and urging each fraternity to intensify efforts to educate its members in fraternal principles and ideals regarding expected gentlemanly conduct and "positive human interaction."

[8]     "I think we have been shocked into taking some very immediate action," commented Ed King, chairman of the newly formed NIC Values and Ethics Committee.

[9]     "Not long ago, we felt one of the safest places for a woman to be was in a fraternity house. In a very short period of time," King continued, "we were finding out there were some horrendous things happening right under our own roofs."

[10]    King's Values and Ethics Committee finds its purpose in a comment from a recent NIC survey of fraternity executives, campus

Greek advisors and others. It reads, "fraternity ideals, values and brotherhood are not sufficiently understood and practiced by the undergraduates. Herein lies our greatest weakness; and at the same time, our opportunity for greatness."

The Greek community is conducting a nationwide crusade against [11] sexual abuse on campus, but many are quick to point out that fraternities are not the sole perpetrators of sexual abuse.

"This problem is not localized to fraternities," said Mary Barbee, [12] an assistant dean of students at the University of New Mexico and a past chairman of the National Panhellenic Conference.

"Residence halls are just as convenient an environment for the [13] abuse to occur," she contends. "Sexual abuse can be prevalent in any place where people are living together."

Barbee explained that universities often are in a better position [14] than fraternity chapters to keep quiet incidences that occur in student housing. An institution can conduct an internal investigation and shun any negative publicity.

"They can tell guilty students 'clean up your act or get out of [15] school'," she said.

Often a fraternity's national officers have an opportunity to inves- [16] tigate a chapter incident only after a local authority has reported it to them—as well as reporting it to the local media.

"Fraternities and sororities are just more publicly scrutinized [17] because they are visible organized groups," Barbee said.

Clinical psychologist Mark Stevens asserts that our society, courts [18] and media are more open to hearing about sexual abuse incidences today.

"It used to be that a woman had to be 'raped' again in court by a [19] skeptical public. She had to prove *her* innocence, instead of the accused man's guilt," Stevens said.

Prosecutors, juries, judges and lawmakers are increasingly aware [20] that rape cannot and should not be blamed on the victim. Civil lawsuits, in which rape victims sue rapists for damages, have increased in recent years. Additionally, there is the possibility that victims will bring third-party liability suits against fraternities and/or institutions.

A brochure provided to students at the University of Miami stipu- [21] lates that sexual harassment can constitute grounds for dismissal from the university. Sexual harassment, it states,

includes, but is not limited to, physical or verbal abuse of a sexual nature
including: graphic commentaries about an individual's body; sexually
degrading remarks used to describe an individual; or unwelcome propo-
sitions and physical advances of a sexual nature. . . .

[22]    Note the use of the word "unwelcome." How are we supposed
to determine what is "unwelcome"? We are often confused about
sexual roles; about the "rules" of the "game." Our confusion stems
from outdated, traditional assumptions that are no longer valid.

[23]    "Many men think that a woman is going to jump up and slap him
and walk out of the room in a huff" if he's acting against her will,
explains Dave Westol, an assistant prosecuting attorney.

[24]    "The mistake that most guys make is the assumption that if the
woman doesn't react that strongly, then she's giving in," he explained.

[25]    "Often the problem is that a woman, particularly a young college
woman, becomes so frightened or intimidated—often compounded by
alcohol consumption or drugs—that she is not certain what is
happening.

[26]    "But she does know one thing: That she did not give her consent
for sexual intercourse or contact," Westol said.

[27]    Although consent is defined in various ways by state laws,
"sobriety is an ingredient necessary to give consent," explains attorney
Ron Doleac.

[28]    "Consent from a drunk person doesn't count," Doleac said,
"because her judgment is impaired by the alcohol. Consent requires
an *informed* decision about one's conduct."

[29]    We have all heard arguments such as "no means yes," that a
woman who dresses promiscuously is "asking for it," that a woman
who has had sex with one man loses her right to say no to others, or,
even worse, that a woman *enjoys* being overpowered. Many of us
understand that these myths are wrong, but others never stop to question
them.

[30]    "If a girl has had sex before—that automatically means she has
to sleep with you?" asks Andrew Merton, a University of New
Hampshire professor.

[31]    "*You* have had sex before—does that mean that you have to sleep
with every woman who finds you attractive?"

[32]    Merton queries college men "to remember when you were small

boys—maybe five, six, or seven years old. Think of a time, when someone larger than you—an abusive adult, or an older boy—bullied you. Began punching you, kicking you, restraining you. And you yelled, 'No! Let go!' over and over again. And the person didn't stop.''

"That's the kind of terror that a woman experiences when you're [33] forcing yourself on her,'' Merton contends.

"There is no enjoyment in it at all. And it is called rape.'' [34]

The authors of the study on campus gang rape sponsored by the [35] Association of American Colleges wrote,

> No person asks to be hurt and degraded, just as no one asks to be robbed because they are carrying money in their pocket. No woman—whatever her behavior—"deserves" to be raped by one or seven or eleven men. Rape is the responsibility of the rapist(s), not the victim.

A group of college men in a rape awareness program defined rape [36] as "an act of forcing physical or mental aggression on another person *with or without having sexual intercourse.*''

In an article circulated last year by Alpha Tau Omega Fraternity, [37] High Council Secretary John Lawlor asserted that "sexually touching a woman against her will is a form of assault, and even done without coercion is still appallingly rude and insensitive.

"A man who brings a date back to the fraternity house and takes [38] sexual liberties—even if it's only unwanted touching—is hurting a human being he presumably likes and respects,'' Lawlor wrote.

"Forced sex itself isn't sex at all, but an act of violence,'' writes [39] Lawlor of Alpha Tau Omega.

Dave Westol explained that college students tend to think there [40] are two sets of laws—one for everybody else and one for undergraduates.

"When we're in school, we think, 'college students don't commit [41] crimes. A *criminal* is not a church-going college sophomore with good grades, from a good family','' Westol said.

"The fact that someone's a nice person is not a defense. Your [42] character does not come into play in a criminal sexual conduct case.''

In Michigan, where Westol is a criminal prosecutor, a jury can [43] be instructed that the victim need not resist.

[44]     "The word 'no' is sufficient," he said.

[45]     Additionally, physical violence (bruises or signs of a struggle) is not necessary to substantiate a criminal sexual conduct charge.

[46]     "The testimony of the victim is sufficient to get the case to the jury," Westol explained.

[47]     There are varying degrees of criminal sexual conduct laws. These include contact with certain, specified parts of the body—*even if clothing covers those parts of the body.* Sexual assault does not always include penetration.

[48]     In gang rape situations, the laws can be harsh. In Michigan, if two or more perpetrators are involved in a forcible act of sexual penetration, the crime can be punishable by life imprisonment or any term of years.

[49]     "If someone aids or assists anyone else in committing the crime, they are considered equally responsible," Westol said. "Some guys think, 'well, I never had sex with her . . .' but if you help hold her down, or threaten her verbally to comply, you're aiding in the crime."

[50]     Gang rape is the most extreme example of sexual abuse. But even in more "innocent" situations, we can face criminal charges.

[51]     Westol cautions us that voluntary intoxication is not a defense in a sexual assault case. He said that a young man might say "I was drunk, I didn't know what I was doing."

[52]     "That isn't going to let him off the hook," he said.

[53]     "We rely too much on traditional assumptions," Westol asserts. "Say a woman comes to your room at two a.m. with a bottle of wine. You make the assumption without talking with her, that 'this is the night; this is the big score.'

[54]     "It's easier to make that assumption than to talk with the woman, than to discuss it. That assumption is what gets a lot of people in trouble.

[55]     "Common sense and communication on the part of both people will dispel any misunderstandings," he added.

[56]     To prevent acquaintance rape is to understand the differing expectations between individuals; between the sexes. Societal changes have created confusion among college students, who are typically away from homes, families and parental guidance for the first time in their lives.

[57]     We were traditionally socialized to believe that women are

responsible for the outcome of sexual encounters, that if a woman is sexually victimized, it is her own fault. This was a prevalent attitude in the 1950s. There were "good girls" and there were "bad girls."

Although there is a return to the conservatism of the 1950s and a [58] resurgence in the popularity of fraternities, we are in a different era today. In the 1980s, "women claim the same right as men to sexual activity when and with whom they choose, provided both parties consent" wrote Andrew Merton in a *Ms.* magazine article.

People have also traditionally believed that men are expected to [59] sow their wild oats, to be aggressive. College presents a big challenge to a man's identity; nobody knows him, so he has to prove himself to his new peers. Historically he did so by being "tough." This attitude often fuses sexuality and aggression, which can be reinforced by single-sex groups, such as occur in dorms, fraternities, locker rooms. These environments can foster "backroom" humor—an extention of the kind of talk adolescent boys learn when they start reading pornography and talking "dirty."

Callous, sexually abusive humor takes many forms. Among them: [60]

• Rush posters or brochures with scantily clad women as the main feature, rush promises of "all the beautiful women and beer any man could want," rush slide shows featuring the little sisters in bathing suits (What do these say about brotherhood, mutual respect, scholarship, leadership?)
• A graph compiled by a fraternity tallying the number of beers needed to seduce each little sister
• Party themes such as "Minerva's Period" and "Pimp & Hooker"
• Slang used which is typically "dirty"—descriptive of body parts and body functions (Women are referred to as tails, pelts, cracks, slits, pieces and worse.)
• Watching a brother and a woman in bed together, through a window, closet door, etc.
• Performing lewd, obscene and otherwise sexually abusive skits and/or songs at Greek or all-campus competitions

"The fact is that when a young man joins a fraternity, he does [61] not do so for the purpose of abusing alcohol, or women, or the underclassmen who will follow him in years to come," says Merton. "You want to be able to say, honestly, that the active brothers are model citizens—gentlemen, scholars, leaders.''

[62]     Merton asserts that despite good intentions, some fraternity brothers wind up committing exactly those transgressions. They are "a minority, to be sure, but a sizable enough minority to affect the whole system.''

[63]     "When you join a fraternity, you vow to function within a value set that is progressive and human, and you are responsible for behaving within that set of values,'' said Mary Barbee.

[64]     "There are some things that are right and some things that are wrong. You are responsible for behaving right. There is never an excuse for the wrong behavior,'' she added.

[65]     "In most gang rape situations,'' people are not behaving responsibly, due to the group synergy and often due to alcohol and/or drugs. The group thinking feeds on itself and builds to a crescendo.

[66]     "But your responsibility way back before the group synergy started was to behave responsibly,'' Barbee contends.

[67]     Dr. Stevens explains that by nature men are not evil, "but peer pressure to follow the group prevails, because we want to be accepted.''

[68]     "Often adolescent males mistake this group 'bonding' as a way to gain intimacy or friendship with each other,'' Stevens said. "They think things like, 'we're in this together, we'll feel closer to each other because we're real men when we team up this way.' Then the group develops an *illusory* sense of masculinity and power; individual feelings of responsibility for the violence are minimized.''

[69]     The recently released feature film "Platoon" included a scene where groupthink had superseded the soldiers' individual consciences. Several of the men were starting to rape a Vietnamese girl. The protagonist, Chris Taylor, screamed at them to stop, and managed to rescue her from his fellow soldiers. He said, "You just don't get it, do you? She's a ----ing human being, man!''

[70]     As young boys, we are usually encouraged by our peers to think of women as objects of gratification, rather than as human beings. After a date, an adolescent male is typically asked to describe his date in terms of "conquest.'' Rarely do we ask each other after dates about the girls' aspirations, interests, feelings, etc. Instead, we talk about sexual activity. "There is a tremendous pressure from peers, parents,

society and even religion to be heterosexual,'' Stevens explained, ''and to be *active* as a heterosexual.''

Media and pornography have a tremendous influence on us, and [71] they can teach us to associate sexuality with physical aggression. Young boys' early idols are cartoon superheroes, and later people like Don Johnson, Sylvester Stallone, Walter Payton and Michael Jordan; ''quiet guys who let their bodies do the talking. Guys who play hurt and don't complain. 'Macho' guys,'' says Merton.

Rock videos, song lyrics, advertising and prime time television [72] enhance the image of men as physical beings, conquering the world and often its female inhabitants as well. Young adolescents reading ''skin'' magazines can learn to associate their physical arousal with women's body parts, and with women featured in vulnerable positions. Exposure to these media makes it easy to view women as objects.[2]

''The myth of male sexuality teaches us that 'conquests make me [73] feel better about myself and make me look better to my peers','' Stevens said.

While boys are usually socialized to objectify women, girls are [74] socialized to seek intimate relationships, Dr. Stevens contends. ''Men equate sexual intercourse with intimacy and women equate the relationship with intimacy.''

When a man and a woman go into a date with these different [75] understandings, their expectations will differ as well.

''The guy is thinking, 'we'll get really close because we're going [76] to go all the way tonight','' Stevens said. ''The girl thinks, 'I want to get close to him, get to know him, feel something for him, so maybe we'll make love sometime'.''

If the young man becomes physically aggressive with the young [77] woman, he may recognize subconsciously that she is uncomfortable. ''But if we don't recognize our own feelings, we aren't going to recognize the feelings of another human being,'' he explained.

Often the woman is caught in a trap; she wants to tell the man to [78] stop doing something that makes her feel uncomfortable, but she's

---

[2]Dr. Stevens points out that parents can help their children to develop healthy attitudes toward the opposite sex. ''The key is to be open with them and really discuss things like relationships with them, even when they're young. If you find your son reading *Playboy*, don't make him feel guilty, talk to him about the importance of emotional intimacy in a relationship with a woman,'' Stevens said.

afraid saying so will make him dislike her, or discontinue dating her. She is confused and does not know what to do.

[79]     Acquaintance rape victims are most often younger college women, who are less experienced in dealing with people and therefore less assertive than upperclass women. This points to the need to build assertiveness among women entering college.

[80]     Assertiveness is often a problem among fraternity brothers as well. John Lawlor wrote that he has "memories of which I am not so proud . . . *of knowing about wrongs being committed, and of keeping silent for the sake of brotherhood.*"

[81]     Brother Ron Doleac said there are times when we feel a brother is acting inappropriately, perhaps because he's had too much to drink. We are afraid to speak up, to confront him.

[82]     "It's okay to go talk to him, and say, 'hey, let's settle down; this isn't an appropriate way to act'," Doleac said. "You may not want to speak up initially because you're afraid of rejection by your peers, or of dissention in the chapter, but in the end, after it's been discussed, the brothers will come around to your side and respect you for speaking up."

[83]     It was to address these issues that the delegates to the Sigma Alpha Epsilon National Convention passed the fraternity's position statement on sexual abuse in 1985. In addition, the Supreme Council last fall adopted a mandated policy on sexual abuse.

[84]     Sigma Alpha Epsilon is not alone. Alpha Tau Omega passed a resolution on "Human Dignity in an undignified World." Pi Kappa Phi Fraternity has adopted a similar position statement. Others have followed suit, and are publishing in their journals articles on sexism and sexual abuse.

[85]     Pi Kappa Phi has also produced a widely circulated poster on the sexual abuse issue. The poster features the art print, "The Rape of the Sabine Women" above the words, "Today's Greeks Call It Date Rape. Just a reminder from Pi Kappa Phi. Against her will is against the law."

*   *   *   *   *   *   *   *

[86]     "All persons, regardless of age, economic status, educational level or social standing want to be treated with dignity by others. When we ignore that need, when we begin to treat each other as less than individ-

uals of value, we enhance the atmosphere in which despicable acts can occur,'' wrote Margaret Hess Watkins, executive director of Delta Gamma Fraternity in a recent issue of *The Anchora.*

Treating people with dignity, *as fellow human beings*, is the [87] essence of The True Gentleman, the model every Sigma Alpha Epsilon strives to emulate.

''One of these days, we will realize that we can feel intimate with [88] a woman without having sex with her, that it's okay to go out on a date without 'scoring,' and to share our feelings and fears with others,'' contends Dr. Stevens. ''And we will see that these behaviors and attitudes are valued by society.''

John O. Moseley once wrote, ''Every fraternity chapter is [89] endowed with the awesome responsibility of a tremendous power of coercive group pressure. The direction of that pressure unerringly indicates if the chapter is to 'weaken' or to 'greaten'.''

## QUESTIONS FOR DISCUSSION

1   Why does the author begin with the imaginary narrative about Sally Jones and the fraternity brothers?
2   Can you tell who the audience is for this piece?
3   In light of that audience, can you determine why the author includes the material in paragraphs 12 through 17?
4   What is the purpose of Stoll's article? Do you find it persuasive? Why or why not?
5   In paragraph 44, Stoll quotes a prosecution lawyer as saying, ''The word 'no' is sufficient.'' Why do you think men of college age would need to be told such a seemingly obvious fact?
6   Do you find Stoll's concluding paragraph effective? Why or why not?

## SUGGESTIONS FOR WRITING

1 The movie *North Dallas Forty* focuses on violence in professional football. Rent the videotape and watch it a couple of times. (If you don't have access to a VCR, you can probably arrange to view the tape at your school's audiovisual center.) Once you have studied the movie, write an essay similar to McMurtry's in which you argue the case against pro football using evidence drawn from the film. If you welcome a challenge, your audience for this piece could be the booster club for the pro football team in your region. Remember—that group will be a hostile audience. Good luck!

2 Adam Smith suggests that the prevalence of handguns in our society contributes to violent death. Write an essay in which you speculate on the source of America's tolerance for gun ownership. Besides the obvious lobbying of the National Rifle Association, consider the influence of movies and television. Remember to mention specific examples. You might also want to draw on some of the ideas presented by Cline in "How TV Violence Damages Your Children." Address your remarks to the membership of the National Coalition to Ban Handguns.

3 Consider the sexual attitudes of men toward women as you see them displayed in several macho rock videos or in a sexist movie like Prince's *Purple Rain*. Then write an essay addressed to your classmates to raise their awareness of the influence that such presentations exert in perpetuating the misunderstandings between the sexes discussed by Stoll in "Sexual Abuse on Campus." Or, if you prefer, argue that these sexist presentations serve to increase the already intolerably high level of violence against women in our society.

4 With the help of a classmate, draw up a questionnaire requesting "agree" or "disagree" responses to queries about sexual relationships between men and women (e.g., "A woman has an obligation to repay a man who takes her out on an expensive date"; "A woman often says 'no' when she means 'yes'"; "A man will think less of a woman if she has sex with him on the first date"). Ask friends and friendly faculty members to suggest questions and perhaps to critique your list.

Type your completed list on a ditto or a stencil so that you can reproduce 75 or 100 copies. Take these questionnaires to the campus cafeteria or coffee shop and gather responses from equal numbers of males and females.

Then, get together with your coresearcher, examine and analyze the results, and present your findings in a written report to your composition class. If time permits, you might hold a class discussion on your findings.

# Chapter 17

# Considering Language

## You Are What You Say

Robin Lakoff

"Women's language" is that pleasant (dainty?), euphemistic, never- [1]
aggressive way of talking we learned as little girls. Cultural bias was
built into the language we were allowed to speak, the subjects we were
allowed to speak about, and the ways we were spoken of. Having
learned our linguistic lesson well, we go out in the world, only to
discover that we are communicative cripples—damned if we do, and
damned if we don't.

If we refuse to talk "like a lady," we are ridiculed and criticized [2]
for being unfeminine. ("She thinks like a man" is, at best, a left-
handed compliment.) If we do learn all the fuzzy-headed, unassertive
language of our sex, we are ridiculed for being unable to think clearly,
unable to take part in a serious discussion, and therefore unfit to hold
a position of power.

[3]     It doesn't take much of this for a woman to begin feeling she deserves such treatment because of inadequacies in her own intelligence and education.

[4]     "Women's language" shows up in all levels of English. For example, women are encouraged and allowed to make far more precise discriminations in naming colors than men do. Words like *mauve, beige, ecru, aquamarine, lavender*, and so on, are unremarkable in a woman's active vocabulary, but largely absent from that of most men. I know of no evidence suggesting that women actually *see* a wider range of colors than men do. It is simply that fine discriminations of this sort are relevant to women's vocabularies, but not to men's; to men, who control most of the interesting affairs of the world, such distinctions are trivial—irrelevant.

[5]     In the area of syntax, we find similar gender-related peculiarities of speech. There is one construction, in particular, that women use conversationally far more than men: the tag question. A tag is midway between an outright statement and a yes-no question; it is less assertive than the former, but more confident than the latter.

[6]     A *flat statement* indicates confidence in the speaker's knowledge and is fairly certain to be believed; a *question* indicates a lack of knowledge on some point and implies that the gap in the speaker's knowledge can and will be remedied by an answer. For example, if, at a Little League game, I have had my glasses off, I can legitimately ask someone else: "Was the player out at third?" A *tag question*, being intermediate between statement and question, is used when the speaker is stating a claim, but lacks full confidence in the truth of that claim. So if I say, "Is Joan here?" I will probably not be surprised if my respondent answers "no"; but if I say, "Joan is here, isn't she?" instead, chances are I am already biased in favor of a positive answer, wanting only confirmation. I still want a response, but I have enough knowledge (or think I have) to predict that response. A tag question, then, might be thought of as a statement that doesn't demand to be believed by anyone but the speaker, a way of giving leeway, of not forcing the addressee to go along with the views of the speaker.

[7]     Another common use of the tag question is in small talk when the speaker is trying to elicit conversation: "Sure is hot here, isn't it?"

[8]     But in discussing personal feelings or opinions, only the speaker normally has any way of knowing the correct answer. Sentences such

as "I have a headache, don't I?" are clearly ridiculous. But there are other examples where it is the speaker's opinions, rather than perceptions, for which corroboration is sought, as in "The situation in Southeast Asia is terrible, isn't it?"

While there are, of course, other possible interpretations of a [9] sentence like this, one possibility is that the speaker has a particular answer in mind—"yes" or "no"—but is reluctant to state it baldly. This sort of tag question is much more apt to be used by women than by men in conversation. Why is this the case?

The tag question allows a speaker to avoid commitment, and [10] thereby avoid conflict with the addressee. The problem is that, by so doing, speakers may also give the impression of not really being sure of themselves, or looking to the addressee for confirmation of their views. This uncertainty is reinforced in more subliminal ways, too. There is a peculiar sentence intonation-pattern, used almost exclusively by women, as far as I know, which changes a declarative answer into a question. The effect of using the rising inflection typical of a yes-no question is to imply that the speaker is seeking confirmation, even though the speaker is clearly the only one who has the requisite information, which is why the question was put to her in the first place:

(Q) When will dinner be ready?
(A) Oh . . . around six o'clock . . . ?

It is as though the second speaker were saying, "Six o'clock—if that's okay with you, if you agree." The person being addressed is put in the position of having to provide confirmation. One likely consequence of this sort of speech-pattern in a woman is that, often unbeknownst to herself, the speaker builds a reputation of tentativeness, and others will refrain from taking her seriously or trusting her with any responsibilities, since she "can't make up her mind," and "isn't sure of herself."

Such idiosyncrasies may explain why women's language sounds [11] much more "polite" than men's. It is polite to leave a decision open, not impose your mind, or views, or claims, on anyone else. So a tag question is a kind of polite statement, in that it does not force agreement or belief on the addressee. In the same way a request is a polite command, in that it does not force obedience on the addressee, but rather suggests something be done as a favor to the speaker. A clearly stated order implies a threat of certain consequences if it is not followed, and—even more impolite—implies that the speaker is in a superior position and able to enforce the order. By couching wishes in the form of a request, on the other hand, a speaker implies that if the request is not carried out, only the speaker will suffer; noncompliance cannot harm the addressee. So the decision is really left up to addressee. The distinction becomes clear in these examples:

> Close the door.
> Please close the door.
> Will you close the door?
> Will you please close the door?
> Won't you close the door?

[12]     In the same ways as words and speech patterns used *by* women undermine her image, those used to *describe* women make matters even worse. Often a word may be used of both men and women (and perhaps of things as well); but when it is applied to women, it assumes a special meaning that, by implication rather than outright assertion, is derogatory to women as a group.

[13]     The use of euphemisms has this effect. A euphemism is a substitute for a word that has acquired a bad connotation by association with something unpleasant or embarrassing. But almost as soon as the new word comes into common usage, it takes on the same old bad connotations, since feelings about the things or people referred to are not altered by a change of name; thus new euphemisms must be constantly found.

[14]     There is one euphemism for *women* still very much alive. The word, of course, is *lady*. *Lady* has a masculine counterpart, namely *gentleman*, occasionally shortened to *gent*. But for some reason *lady* is very much commoner than *gent(leman)*.

[15]     The decision to use *lady* rather than *woman*, or vice versa, may considerably alter the sense of a sentence, as the following examples show:

(a)     A woman (lady) I know is a dean at Berkeley.
(b)     A woman (lady) I know makes amazing things out of shoelaces and old boxes.

The use of *lady* in (a) imparts a frivolous, or nonserious, tone to [16] the sentence: the matter under discussion is not one of great moment. Similarly, in (b), using *lady* here would suggest that the speaker considered the ''amazing things'' not to be serious art, but merely a hobby or an aberration. If *woman* is used, she might be a serious sculptor. To say *lady doctor* is very condescending, since no one ever says *gentleman* doctor or even *man doctor*. For example, mention in the *San Francisco Chronicle* of January 31, 1972, of Madalyn Murray O'Hair as the *lady atheist* reduces her position to that of scatterbrained eccentric. Even *woman atheist* is scarcely defensible: sex is irrelevant to her philosophical position.

Many women argue that, on the other hand, *lady* carries with it [17] overtones recalling the age of chivalry: conferring exalted stature on the person so referred to. This makes the term seem polite at first, but we must also remember that these implications are perilous: they suggest that a ''lady'' is helpless, and cannot do things by herself.

*Lady* can also be used to infer frivolousness, as in titles of organi- [18] zations. Those that have a serious purpose (not merely that of enabling ''the ladies'' to spend time with one another) cannot use the word *lady* in their titles, but less serious ones may. Compare the *Ladies' Auxiliary* of a men's group, or the *Thursday Evening Ladies' Browning and Garden Society* with *Ladies' Liberation* or *Ladies' Strike for Peace*.

What is curious about this split is that *lady* is in origin a euphe- [19] mism—a substitute that puts a better face on something people find uncomfortable—for *women*. What kind of euphemism is it that subtly denigrates the people to whom it refers? Perhaps *lady* functions as a euphemism for *women* because it does not contain the sexual impli- cations present in *woman*: it is not ''embarrassing'' in that way. If this is so, we may expect that, in the future, *lady* will replace woman as the primary word for the human female, since *woman* will have become too blatantly sexual. That this distinction is already made in some contexts at least is shown in the following examples, where you can try replacing *woman* with *lady:*

(a)    She's only twelve, but she's already a woman.
(b)    After ten years in jail, Harry wanted to find a woman.
(c)    She's my woman, see, so don't mess around with her.

Another common substitute for *woman* is *girl*. One seldom hears [20] a man past the age of adolescence referred to as a boy, save in expressions like "going out with the boys," which are meant to suggest an air of adolescent frivolity and irresponsibility. But women of all ages are "girls": one can have a man—not a boy—Friday, but only a girl—never a woman or even a lady—Friday; women have girlfriends, but men do not—in a nonsexual sense—have boyfriends. It may be that this use of *girl* is euphemistic in the same way the use of *lady* is: in stressing the idea of immaturity, it removes the sexual connotations lurking in *woman*. *Girl* brings to mind irresponsibility: you don't send a girl to do a woman's errand (or even, for that matter, a boy's errand). She is a person who is both too immature and too far from real life to be entrusted with responsibilities or with decisions of any serious or important nature.

[21]     Now let's take a pair of words which, in terms of the possible relationships in an earlier society, were simple male-female equivalents, analogous to *bull : cow*. Suppose we find that, for independent reasons, society has changed in such a way that the original meanings now are irrelevant. Yet the words have not been discarded, but have acquired new meanings, metaphorically related to their original senses. But suppose these new metaphorical uses are no longer parallel to each other. By seeing where the parallelism breaks down, we discover something about the different roles played by men and women in this culture. One good example of such a divergence through time is found in the pair, *master : mistress*. Once used with reference to one's power over servants, these words have become unusable today in their original master-servant sense as the relationship has become less prevalent in our society. But the words are still common.

[22]     Unless used with reference to animals, *master* now generally refers to a man who has acquired consummate ability in some field, normally nonsexual. But its feminine counterpart cannot be used this way. It is practically restricted to its sexual sense of "paramour." We start out with two terms, both roughly paraphrasable as "one who has power over another." But the masculine form, once one person is no longer able to have absolute power over another, becomes usable metaphorically in the sense of "having power over *something*." *Master* requires as its object only the name of some activity, something inanimate and abstract. But *mistress* requires a masculine noun in the possessive to precede it. One cannot say: "Rhonda is a mistress." One must be

*someone's* mistress. A man is defined by what he does, a woman by her sexuality, that is, in terms of one particular aspect of her relationship to men. It is one thing to be an *old master* like Hans Holbein, and another to be an *old mistress*.

The same is true of the words *spinster* and *bachelor*—gender words [23] for "one who is not married." The resemblance ends with the definition. While *bachelor* is a neutral term, often used as a compliment, *spinster* normally is used pejoratively, with connotations of prissiness, fussiness, and so on. To be a bachelor implies that one has the choice of marrying or not, and this is what makes the idea of a bachelor existence attractive, in the popular literature. He has been pursued and has successfully eluded his pursuers. But a spinster is one who has not been pursued, or at least not seriously. She is old, unwanted goods. The metaphorical connotations of *bachelor* generally suggest sexual freedom; of *spinster*, puritanism or celibacy.

These examples could be multiplied. It is generally considered a [24] *faux pas*, in society, to congratulate a woman on her engagement, while it is correct to congratulate her fiancé. Why is this? The reason seems to be that it is impolite to remind people of things that may be uncomfortable to them. To congratulate a woman on her engagement is really to say, "Thank goodness! You had a close call!" For the man, on the other hand, there was no such danger. His choosing to marry is viewed as a good thing, but not something essential.

The linguistic double standard holds throughout the life of the [25] relationship. After marriage, bachelor and spinster become man and wife, not man and woman. The woman whose husband dies remains "John's widow"; John, however, is never "Mary's widower."

Finally, why is it that salesclerks and others are so quick to call [26] women customers "dear," "honey," and other terms of endearment they really have no business using? A male customer would never put up with it. But women, like children, are supposed to enjoy these endearments, rather than being offended by them.

In more ways than one, it's time to speak up. [27]

## QUESTIONS FOR DISCUSSION

1 What audience is addressed in this essay? How can you tell? If Lakoff had written this piece for *Esquire* magazine (instead of for *Ms.*), what changes do you think she would need to make in the first three paragraphs?

2  Can you explain in your own words what a "tag question" is? Do you think Lakoff is correct in suggesting that women use this syntactic construction far more frequently than men?

3  The question that ends paragraph 9 is not a tag question. What kind of question is it, and why does she use it?

4  Can you think of other terms like *master* and *mistress* that have different connotations, perhaps even different meanings? Consider *governor* and *governess*, *major* and *majorette*, *poet* and *poetess*.

5  Lakoff's conclusion is quite abrupt—a single sentence. Do you find it effective? Why or why not?

6  Can you state Lakoff's main point in a single sentence?

# Weasel Words: God's Little Helpers

## Paul Stevens

[1]  First of all, you know what a weasel is, right? It's a small, slimy animal that eats small birds and other animals, and is especially fond of devouring vermin. Now, consider for a moment the kind of winning personality he must have. I mean, what kind of a guy would get his jollies eating rats and mice? Would you invite him to a party? Take him home to meet your mother? This is one of the slyest and most cunning of all creatures; sneaky, slippery, and thoroughly obnoxious. And so it is with great and warm personal regard for these attributes that we humbly award this King of All Devious the honor of bestowing his name upon our golden sword: the weasel word.

[2]  A weasel word is "a word used in order to evade or retreat from a direct or forthright statement or position" (Webster). In other words, if we can't say it, we'll weasel it. And, in fact, a weasel word has become more than just an evasion or retreat. We've trained our weasels. They can do anything. They can make you hear things that aren't being said, accept as truths things that have only been implied, and believe things that have only been suggested. Come to think of it, not only do we have our weasels trained, but they, in turn, have got you trained. When *you* hear a weasel word, you automatically hear the implication. Not the real meaning, but the meaning *it* wants *you* to hear. So if you're ready for a little re-education, let's take a good look under a strong light at the two kinds of weasel words.

## WORDS THAT MEAN THINGS THEY REALLY DON'T MEAN

### Help

That's it. "Help." It means "aid" or "assist." Nothing more. Yet, [3] "help" is the one single word which, in all the annals of advertising, has done the most to say something that couldn't be said. Because "help" is the great qualifier; once you say it, you can say almost anything after it. In short, "help" has helped help us the most.

*Helps keep you young*
*Helps prevent cavities*
*Helps keep your house germ-free*

"Help" qualifies everything. You've never heard anyone say, [4] "This product will keep you young," or "This toothpaste will positively prevent cavities for all time." Obviously, we can't say anything like that, because there aren't any products like that made. But by adding that one little word, "help," in front, we can use the strongest language possible afterward. And the most fascinating part of it is, you are immune to the word. You literally don't hear the word "help." You only hear what comes after it. And why not? That's strong language, and likely to be much more important to you than the silly little word at the front end.

I would guess that 75 percent of all advertising uses the word [5] "help." Think, for a minute, about how many times each day you hear these phrases:

*Helps stop . . .*
*Helps prevent . . .*
*Helps fight . . .*
*Helps overcome . . .*
*Helps you feel . . .*
*Helps you look . . .*

I could go on and on, but so could you. Just as a simple exercise, call it homework if you wish, tonight when you plop down in front of the boob tube for your customary three and a half hours of violence and/ or situation comedies, take a pad and pencil, and keep score. See if you can count how many times the word "help" comes up during the commercials. Instead of going to the bathroom during the pause before Marcus Welby operates, or raiding the refrigerator prior to witnessing the Mod Squad wipe out a nest of dope pushers, stick with it. Count the "helps," and discover just how dirty a four-letter word can be.

Like

[6] Coming in second, but only losing by a nose, is the word "like," used in comparison. Watch:

> *It's like getting one bar free*
> *Cleans like a white tornado*
> *It's like taking a trip to Portugal*

[7]     Okay. "Like" is a qualifier, and is used in much the same way as "help." But "like" is also a comparative element, with a very specific purpose; we use "like" to get you to stop thinking about the product per se, and to get you thinking about something that is bigger or better or different from the product we're selling. In other words, we can make you believe that the product is more than it is by likening it to something else.

[8]     Take a look at that first phrase, straight out of recent Ivory Soap advertising. On the surface of it, they tell you that four bars of Ivory cost about the same as three bars of most other soaps. So, if you're going to spend a certain amount of money on soap, you can buy four bars instead of three. Therefore, it's like getting one bar free. Now, the question you have to ask yourself is, "Why the weasel? Why do they say 'like'? Why don't they just come out and say, 'You get one bar free'?" The answer is, of course, that for one reason or another, you really don't. Here are two possible reasons. One: sure, you get four bars, but in terms of the actual amount of soap that you get, it may very well be the same as in three bars of another brand. Remember, Ivory has a lot of air in it—that's what makes it float. And air takes up room. Room that could otherwise be occupied by more soap. So, in terms of pure product, the amount of actual soap in four bars of Ivory may be only as much as the actual amount of soap in three bars of most others. That's why we can't—or won't—come out with a straightforward declaration such as, "You get 25 percent more soap," or "Buy three bars, and get the fourth one free."

Reason number two: the actual cost and value of the product. Did [9]
it ever occur to you that Ivory may simply be a cheaper soap to make
and, therefore, a cheaper soap to sell? After all, it doesn't have any
perfume or hexachlorophene, or other additives that can raise the cost
of manufacturing. It's plain, simple, cheap soap, and so it can be sold
for less money while still maintaining a profit margin as great as more
expensive soaps. By way of illustrating this, suppose you were trying
to decide whether to buy a Mercedes-Benz or a Ford. Let's say the
Mercedes cost $7,000, and the Ford $3,500. Now the Ford salesman
comes up to you with this deal: as long as you're considering spending
$7,000 on a car, buy my Ford for $7,000 and I'll give you a second
Ford, free! Well, the same principle can apply to Ivory: as long as
you're considering spending 35 cents on soap, buy my cheaper soap,
and I'll give you more of it.

I'm sure there are other reasons why Ivory uses the weasel "like." [10]
Perhaps you've thought of one or two yourself. That's good. You're
starting to think.

Now, what about that wonderful white tornado? Ajax pulled that [11]
one out of the hat some eight years ago, and you're still buying it. It's
a classic example of the use of the word "like" in which we can force
you to think, not about the product itself, but about something bigger,
more exciting, certainly more powerful than a bottle of fancy ammonia.
The word "like" is used here as a transfer word, which gets you away
from the obvious—the odious job of getting down on your hands and
knees and scrubbing your kitchen floor—and into the world of fantasy,
where we can imply that this little bottle of miracles will supply all the
elbow grease you need. Isn't that the name of the game? The whirlwind
activity of the tornado replacing the whirlwind motion of your arm?
Think about the swirling of the tornado, and all the work it will save
you. Think about the power of that devastating windstorm; able to lift
houses, overturn cars, and now, pick the dirt up off your floor. And
we get the license to do it simply by using the word "like."

It's a copywriter's dream, because we don't have to substantiate [12]
anything. When we compare our product to "another leading brand,"
we'd better be able to prove what we say. But how can you compare
ammonia to a windstorm? It's ludicrous. It can't be done. The whole
statement is so ridiculous it couldn't be challenged by the government
or the networks. So it went on the air, and it worked. Because the little

word "like" let us take you out of the world of reality, and into your own fantasies.

[13]     Speaking of fantasies, how about that trip to Portugal? Mateus Rosé is actually trying to tell you that you will be transported clear across the Atlantic Ocean merely by sipping their wine. "Oh, come on," you say. "You don't expect me to believe that." Actually, we don't expect you to believe it. But we do expect you to get our meaning. This is called "romancing the product," and it is made possible by the dear little "like." In this case, we deliberately bring attention to the word, and we ask you to join us in setting reality aside for a moment. We take your hand and gently lead you down the path of moonlit nights, graceful dancers, and mysterious women. Are we saying that these things are all contained inside our wine? Of course not. But what we mean is, our wine is part of all this, and with a little help from "like," we'll get you to feel that way, too. So don't think of us as a bunch of peasants squashing a bunch of grapes. As a matter of fact, don't think of us at all. Feel with us.

[14]     "Like" is a virus that kills. You'd better get immune to it.

## Other Weasels

[15] "Help" and "like" are the two weasels so powerful that they can stand on their own. There are countless other words, not quite so potent, but equally effective when used in conjunction with our two basic weasels, or with each other. Let me show you a few.

[16]     **Virtual _or_ Virtually**  How many times have you responded to an ad that said:

> *Virtually trouble-free . . .*
> *Virtually foolproof . . .*
> *Virtually never needs service . . .*

Ever remember what "virtual" means? It means "in essence or effect, but not in fact." Important—"but not in fact." Yet today the word "virtually" is interpreted by you as meaning "almost or just about the same as. . . ." Well, gang, it just isn't true. "Not," in fact, means not, in fact. I was scanning, rather longingly I must confess, through the brochure Chevrolet publishes for its Corvette, and I came to this phrase: "The seats in the 1972 Corvette are virtually handmade." They had me, for a minute. I almost took the bait of that lovely little weasel. I almost decided that those seats were just about completely handmade. And then I remembered. Those seats were not, *in fact,* handmade. Remember, "virtually" means "not, in fact," or you will, in fact, get sold down the river.

**Acts *or* Works**   These two action words are rarely used alone, [17] and are generally accompanied by "like." They need help to work, mostly because they are verbs, but their implied meaning is deadly, nonetheless. Here are the key phrases:

*Acts like . . .*
*Acts against . . .*
*Works like . . .*
*Works against . . .*
*Works to prevent (or help prevent) . . .*

You see what happens? "Acts" or "works" brings an action to the product that might not otherwise be there. When we say that a certain cough syrup "acts on the cough control center," the implication is that the syrup goes to this mysterious organ and immediately makes it better. But the implication here far exceeds what the truthful promise should be. An act is simply a deed. So the claim "acts on" simply means it performs a deed on. What that deed is, we may never know.

The rule of thumb is this: if we can't say "cures" or "fixes" or [18] use any other positive word, we'll nail you with "acts like" or "works against," and get you thinking about something else. Don't.

## Miscellaneous Weasels

**Can Be**   This is for comparison, and what we do is to find an [19] announcer who can really make it sound positive. But keep your ears open. "Crest can be of significant value when used in . . . ," etc., is indicative of an ideal situation, and most of us don't live in ideal situations.

**Up To**   Here's another way of expressing an ideal situation. [20] Remember the cigarette that said it was aged, or "cured for up to eight long, lazy weeks''? Well, that could, and should, be interpreted as meaning that the tobaccos used were cured anywhere from one hour to eight weeks. We like to glamorize the ideal situation; it's up to you to bring it back to reality.

[21]     **As Much As**   More of the same. "As much as 20 percent greater mileage" with our gasoline again promises the ideal, but qualifies it.

[22]     **Refreshes, Comforts, Tackles, Fights, Comes On**   Just a handful of the same action weasels, in the same category as "acts" and "works," though not as frequently used. The way to complete the thought here is to ask the simple question, "How?" Usually, you won't get an answer. That's because, usually, the weasel will run and hide.

[23]     **Feel *or* the Feel Of**   This is the first of our subjective weasels. When we deal with a subjective word, it is simply a matter of opinion. In our opinion, Naugehyde has the feel of real leather. So we can say it. And, indeed, if you were to touch leather, and then touch Nauge-hyde, you may very well agree with us. But that doesn't mean it is real leather, only that it feels the same. The best way to handle subjective weasels is to complete the thought yourself, by simply saying, "But it isn't." At least that way you can remain grounded in reality.

[24]     **The Look of *or* Looks Like**   "Look" is the same as "feel," our subjective opinion. Did you ever walk into a Woolworth's and see those $29.95 masterpieces hanging in their "Art Gallery"? "The look of a real oil painting," it will say. "But it isn't," you will now reply. And probably be $29.95 richer for it.

## WORDS THAT HAVE NO SPECIFIC MEANING

[25]   If you have kids, then you have all kinds of breakfast cereals in the house. When I was a kid, it was Rice Krispies, the breakfast cereal that went snap, crackle, and pop. (One hell of a claim for a product that is supposed to offer nutritional benefits.) Or Wheaties, the break-fast of champions, whatever that means. Nowadays, we're forced to a confrontation with Quisp, Quake, Lucky Stars, Cocoa-Puffs, Clunkers, Blooies, Snarkles and Razzmatazz. And they all have one thing in

common: they're all "fortified." Some are simply "fortified with vitamins," while others are specifically "fortified with vitamin D," or some other letter. But what does it all mean?

"Fortified" means "added on to." But "fortified," like so many [26] other weasel words of indefinite meaning, simply doesn't tell us enough. If, for instance, a cereal were to contain one unit of vitamin D, and the manufacturers added some chemical which would produce two units of vitamin D, they could then claim that the cereal was "fortified with twice as much vitamin D." So what? It would still be about as nutritional as sawdust.

The point is, weasel words with no specific meaning don't tell us [27] enough, but we have come to accept them as factual statements closely associated with something good that has been done to the product. Here's another example.

### Enriched

We use this one when we have a product that starts out with nothing. [28] You mostly find it in bread, where the bleaching process combined with the chemicals used as preservatives renders the loaves totally void of anything but filler. So the manufacturer puts a couple of drops of vitamins into the batter, and presto! It's enriched. Sounds great when you say it. Looks great when you read it. But what you have to determine is, is it really great? Figure out what information is missing, and then try to supply that information. The odds are, you won't. Even the breakfast cereals that are playing it straight, like Kellogg's Special K, leave something to be desired. They tell you what vitamins you get, and how much of each in one serving. The catch is, what constitutes a serving? They say, one ounce. So now you have to whip out your baby scale and weigh one serving. Do you have any idea how much that is? Maybe you do. Maybe you don't care. Okay, so you polish off this mound of dried stuff, and now what? You have ostensibly received the minimum, repeat, minimum dosage of certain vitamins for the day. One day. And you still have to go find the vitamins you didn't get. Try looking it up on a box of frozen peas. Bet you won't find it. But do be alert to "fortified" and "enriched." Asking the right questions will prove beneficial.

Did you buy that last sentence? Too bad, because I weaseled you, [29] with the word "beneficial." Think about it.

### Flavor and Taste

[30] These are two totally subjective words that allow us to claim marvelous things about products that are edible. Every cigarette in the world has claimed the best taste. Every supermarket has advertised the most flavorful meat. And let's not forget "aroma," a subdivision of this category. Wouldn't you like to have a nickel for every time a room freshener (a weasel in itself) told you it would make your home "smell fresh as all outdoors"? Well, they can say it, because smell, like taste and flavor, is a subjective thing. And, incidentally, there are no less than three weasels in that phrase. "Smell" is the first. Then, there's "as" (a substitute for the ever-popular "like"), and finally, "fresh," which, in context, is a subjective comparison, rather than the primary definition of "new."

[31]     Now we can use an unlimited number of combinations of these weasels for added impact. "Fresher-smelling clothes." "Fresher-tasting tobacco." "Tastes like grandma used to make." Unfortunately, there's no sure way of bringing these weasels down to size, simply because you can't define them accurately. Trying to ascertain the meaning of "taste" in any context is like trying to push a rope up a hill. All you can do is be aware that these words are subjective, and represent only one opinion—usually that of the manufacturer.

### Style and Good Looks

[32] Anyone for buying a new car? Okay, which is the one with the good looks? The smart new styling? What's that you say? All of them? Well, you're right. Because this is another group of subjective opinions. And it is the subjective and collective opinion of both Detroit and Madison Avenue that the following cars have "bold new styling": Buick Riviera, Plymouth Satellite, Dodge Monaco, Mercury Brougham, and you can fill in the spaces for the rest. Subjectively, you have to decide on which bold new styling is, indeed, bold new styling. Then, you might spend a minute or two trying to determine what's going on under that styling. The rest I leave to Ralph Nader.

### Different, Special, and Exclusive

[33] To be different, you have to be not the same as. Here, you must rely on your own good judgment and common sense. Exclusive formulas and special combinations of ingredients are coming at you every day, in every way. You must constantly assure yourself that, basically, all

products in any given category are the same. So when you hear "special," "exclusive," or "different," you have to establish two things: on what basis are they different, and is that difference an important one? Let me give you a hypothetical example.

All so-called "permanent" antifreeze is basically the same. It is [34] made from a liquid known as ethylene glycol, which has two amazing properties: It has a lower freezing point than water, and a higher boiling point than water. It does not break down (lose its properties), nor will it boil away. And every permanent antifreeze starts with it as a base. Also, just about every antifreeze has now got antileak ingredients, as well as antirust and anticorrosion ingredients. Now, let's suppose that, in formulating the product, one of the companies comes up with a solution that is pink in color, as opposed to all the others, which are blue. Presto—an exclusivity claim. "Nothing else looks like it, nothing else performs like it." Or how about, "Look at ours, and look at anyone else's. You can see the difference our exclusive formula makes." Granted, I'm exaggerating. But did I prove a point?

## QUESTIONS FOR DISCUSSION

1  Is Stevens being fair to weasels in his opening paragraph? Why does he deliberately malign the weasel?
2  What is the level of usage of this essay? Cite specific examples to indicate how you made your decision.
3  What audience does Stevens address?
4  Stevens writes in first-person plural. Who, besides himself, is included in the *we* and *us*?
5  How does Stevens organize his exposé of slippery advertising practices?
6  Why do you think he uses headings throughout the essay?
7  Can you describe Stevens's tone? Do you find it effective? Why or why not?

# Nukespeak and the War Strategists

Stephen Hilgartner
Richard C. Bell
Rory O'Connor

The world of nuclear warfare is a world of doublethink, a hall of [1] mirrors, where *peace* is preserved through the constant threat of war, *security* is obtained through mutual insecurity, and nuclear war planners ''think about the *unthinkable*,'' holding millions of civilians hostage to the most powerful death machines in history.

[2]     Nuclear war strategists have developed an esoteric, highly specialized vocabulary. In their ultrarational world, they talk in cool, clinical language about *megatons* and *megadeaths*. Cities are *bargaining chips*; they are not destroyed, they are *taken out* with *clean*, *surgical strikes*—as if they were tumors.

[3]     Since there is no way to defend cities and industry against nuclear attack, *global stability* is now preserved through a system called the *balance of terror*. The balance of terror is based upon the principle of *deterrence*. Nuclear deterrence is, in effect, a mutual suicide pact: if you attack me, it may kill me, but I will kill you before I die. The civilian population of each superpower is held hostage by the opposite power. The same is true of the allies covered by the *nuclear umbrellas* of the superpowers. If either side attacks, all the hostages will be destroyed.

[4]     The U.S. Department of *Defense* (known as the War Department until 1948) is incapable of defending the United States against a nuclear attack by the USSR. But it is capable of killing many millions of Russian citizens at the push of a button, and the Russians are incapable of doing anything to prevent the carnage. If the Russians were to attack the U.S. or its allies with nuclear weapons, the U.S. would retaliate by attacking the USSR. Since the Russians know this, the reasoning goes, they will be deterred from striking first. A mirror-image argument describes how Russia deters the U.S. from striking its people.

[5]     Military analysts classify nuclear attacks as either *counterforce* or *countervalue* attacks. A counterforce attack is one that is directed primarily against the other side's military forces; countervalue attacks are directed against cities and industry.

[6]     That a counterforce attack is directed primarily against military forces does not mean that there would be few civilian casualties. On the contrary, counterforce attacks could leave millions of civilians dead from the fallout produced by attacks on missile silos. A large airport might be construed as a military target because it could serve as a base for military planes. A naval base situated in a metropolitan area is another example of a target that could be interpreted as either counter-force or countervalue. The difference between a counterforce and a

countervalue attack is not whether civilians die, but whether this is the main goal or a side effect. The deaths of civilians and the destruction of nonmilitary property in a counterforce attack is called *collateral damage*.

Nuclear war planners have always been afraid that the other side [7] might try to launch a *preemptive first strike* (also known as a *splendid first strike*), that is, a counterforce attack designed to cripple the enemy's ability to retaliate. The reasoning behind a preemptive first-strike strategy goes as follows: If country X can destroy a large enough number of country Y's missiles in a first-strike attack, then X can also threaten to destroy Y's remaining cities in a second *nuclear salvo* if Y retaliates with any remaining missiles. It is assumed that Y will be *rational* and surrender to X rather than ensure its total destruction by launching an attack for revenge. X can then impose its will on Y, thus *winning* the nuclear war.

In its public statements, the USSR has renounced the first use of [8] nuclear weapons; the United States has not. Nevertheless, military planners in both countries prepare for *worst-case* situations and tend not to believe verbal declarations. In war, the argument goes, *capabilities* count more than *intentions*, since intentions change without warning.

As a result of this perception of the possibility of an enemy [9] attempting a splendid first strike, the two superpowers have engaged in a massive *arms race*, reaching higher and higher levels of destructive power. Some years ago, each superpower attained *overkill*, the ability to kill every citizen on the other side more than once. Nevertheless, the arms race continues, and each side continues to expand and *modernize* its nuclear arsenal.

The driving force behind the arms race is a treacherous double- [10] bind known as the *security dilemma*. Since X is afraid of Y's weapons, X adds to its arsenal. X's arms buildup, which is conceived of as *defensive* by X, is perceived as *offensive* by Y, prompting Y to build more weapons to deter an attack by X. X looks at this and concludes that Y must be planning to attack; otherwise Y would not have expanded its arsenal. X therefore decides to build still more weapons, and the cycle continues.

The security dilemma has led to the creation of huge military [11] establishments in both the U.S. and the USSR. The superpowers' *hawks* watch each other closely, passing what they see through the gloomy filter of worst-case *scenarios*. The hawks of one nation contribute to the prestige and power of the hawks of the other, and arms budgets climb.

[12]     The arms race has produced a wide array of nuclear weapons and delivery systems for getting them to their targets. The weapons are designed for use in different situations and vary considerably in explosive power. Nuclear warriors generally divide these weapons into three categories: strategic, tactical, and theater.

[13]     *Strategic nuclear weapons* have high-yield warheads; each warhead may be hundreds of times as powerful as the bomb that destroyed Hiroshima. The Hiroshima bomb had a *yield* of 13,000 tons of TNT, or 13 *kilotons;* strategic weapons often have a yield measured in *megatons*—millions of tons of TNT. Strategic weapons are capable of striking targets many thousands of miles away. Both superpowers have deployed their strategic weapons in bombers, in land-based missiles, and in submarines. In the U.S., this three-legged war machine is called the *strategic TRIAD*. Bombers armed with nuclear weapons wait for the *go code*. Land-based *Intercontinental Ballistic Missiles* (*ICBMs*) are ready to strike at the push of a button. Submarines bearing nuclear-armed missiles are *on-station*, waiting for a transmission that would order them to launch their cargo. Radar systems scan the sky for incoming missiles or bombers. At least one of the *Strategic Air Command's* flying command posts, officially called the *Looking Glass Planes* and unofficially known as the *Doomsday Planes*, is in the air at all times. And overhead, a network of satellites circles the earth, watching Soviet ICBM fields and maintaining *command, control and communications*, or $C^3$ (C cubed)—the capability to transmit and receive information and orders.

[14]     *Tactical nuclear weapons* are designed for use on the *nuclear battlefield*. They have much smaller yields than strategic weapons; their yields usually range from as low as one kiloton to several times the yield of the Hiroshima bomb. Tactical nuclear weapons are designed for use in conjunction with *conventional military forces*. In a land war, tactical nuclear weapons might be used to *take out* enemy tank columns. On the sea, they could be used to sink enemy warships. They can be shot from artillery, dropped from planes, shot in short-range missiles, used in depth charges or torpedoes, or placed in land mines.

*Theater nuclear weapons* have powerful warheads like those of [15] strategic weapons. They do not have intercontinental range, however, and are designed for use in a *limited theater of operations*—like Europe, for example. These weapons include bombers and missiles with medium to long ranges. They are *deployed* on land and on aircraft carriers.

The U.S. government has also developed a new kind of nuclear [16] weapon called the *neutron bomb* or *enhanced radiation warhead*. Neutron bombs produce less explosive blast than other nuclear weapons, releasing a greater fraction of their energy in a deadly burst of neutron radiation. Neutron bombs purportedly make it possible to kill enemy troops while reducing blast damage to the surrounding countryside. In its war games, the Defense Department envisions using neutron bombs to stop Soviet tank attacks in western Europe.

Equipped with this array of armaments, nuclear warriors are ready [17] to play the game of *escalation*, using threats and counterthreats to deter, influence, coerce, and block their opponents.

The theory of *limited war*—war which the combatant nations limit [18] in scope or intensity by tacit or explicit agreement—is important to escalation strategy. This theory holds that war can be limited by restricting the geographic region in which it is conducted, by limiting the kinds of weapons used, or by limiting the kinds of targets attacked.

Nuclear war strategist Herman Kahn outlined a theory of escala- [19] tion and limited war in a 1965 book called *On Escalation: Metaphors and Scenarios*. Kahn developed an *escalation ladder* with forty-four rungs, or levels of conflict. The rungs Kahn described range from "Political, Economic and Diplomatic *Gestures*" through "*Nuclear 'Ultimatums'*" and limited evacuation of cities, before crossing the "*No Nuclear Use Threshold*." From "*Local Nuclear War*," the ladder rises to "*Exemplary Attacks*" on property and population, before reaching "*Slow-Motion Countercity War*." As the intensity of the conflict climbs, the level of "*Countervalue Salvo*" is reached, and finally, the orgasmic release of "*Spasm or Insensate War*," as everyone lets loose with everything they have got.

Escalation strategy is a complex game of *nuclear chicken*. [20] Opposing strategists, like two drivers headed on a collision course, try to force each other to back down by threatening terrible consequences for both unless somebody backs down. A disagreement might escalate into a crisis, a crisis into a conventional war. The use of tactical nuclear weapons would escalate conventional war into *limited nuclear war*. If this happens, no one knows whether the use of nuclear force could be neatly contained. Some analysts fear that crossing the *no-nuclear-use threshold* would ultimately lead to a *spasm war*.

[21] Escalation strategy, also known as *brinksmanship*, is ripe with paradox. Survival depends on everyone being *rational*, yet it is hard to tell what the word rational means. Sometimes it seems rational to pretend to be irrational, even to act irrationally, making the illusion more credible by making it more real. In a game of chicken, the driver who throws his steering wheel out the window has won control of the road. Similarly, the nuclear warrior can seize the advantage by throwing away options, or by convincing the opponent he is willing to plunge over the brink. President Nixon, for example, developed a strategy he called the "*Madman Theory*" to try to force the North Vietnamese to negotiate. According to Nixon operative H. R. Haldeman, convicted in the Watergate coverup, Nixon said:

> I want the North Vietnamese to believe I've reached the point where I might do *anything* [original emphasis] to stop the war. We'll just slip the word to them that "for God's sake, you know Nixon is obsessed about Communism. We can't restrain him when he's angry—and he has his hand on the *nuclear button*"—and Ho Chi Minh himself will be in Paris in two days begging for peace.

[22] Over the years, the U.S. government has developed a number of theories about how to maintain deterrence; these are known as *strategic doctrines*. The best known is the strategy of *mutually assured destruction (MAD)*, developed by Robert McNamara, Secretary of Defense during the Kennedy and Johnson administrations. Under this strategy, nuclear war is deterred by the threat that any attack would promptly lead to a *nuclear exchange* that would destroy both superpowers.

[23] For the balance of terror to remain *stable*, nuclear war strategists must keep escalation under control. Each side must believe that everyone's nuclear forces have *survivability*, the ability to survive a counterforce attack and still deliver a crippling retaliatory blow. Both sides must believe that the *costs of striking* would be greater than the *costs of not striking*.

[24] If the survivability of either side's forces is in question, the whole

situation becomes a hall of mirrors. What if X thinks Y thinks X could take out Y's weapons in a preemptive first strike? Should X strike? If X doesn't, Y might strike first, because X thinks Y might think it has nothing to lose. And what might Y think about all this? A terrifying web of perceptions and misperceptions is possible. *Spiraling tensions* could start a thermonuclear war even if no one wanted it.

During the late 1960s and the early 1970s, the survivability of [25] each superpower's nuclear forces was not in question. In the past decade, however, improvements in weapons technology have made the survivability of land-based missiles less certain. This erosion of survivability is the result of what is known as *technological creep*, improvements in weapons technology that seem to have a momentum of their own.

One of the most *destabilizing* technological developments of the [26] 1970s was the deployment of *MIRVs, multiple independently targetable reentry vehicles*. MIRVs make it possible for a single missile to carry a number of nuclear warheads, each of which can be aimed at a separate target. The U.S. began deploying MIRVs in 1970, and the Soviet Union began in 1975.

MIRVs tend to give the advantage to the side which strikes first [27] in a nuclear exchange. A quick look at the following example will illustrate why this is so. Imagine a situation in which each side has 1,000 missiles with 10 MIRVed warheads on each missile. By striking first with 100 missiles—MIRVed with 1,000 warheads—the attacker could eliminate all of the other side's missiles. This would leave the attacker 900 missiles to use as a deterrent against retaliation. While this example is hypothetical, the message is clear; MIRVs are destabilizing.

A second case of technological creep has occurred in the area of [28] missile accuracy. Extreme accuracy is not important for *city-busting*, since the target is large and *soft*—unprotected and easily destroyed. Accuracy is important for counterforce attacks, however. Underground missile silos, with their heavy shieldings, are very *hard* targets, and to destroy them, it is necessary to make a *direct hit*. Over the past decade, each superpower has greatly improved the accuracy of its missiles, so much so that they can now land within a few hundred feet of their targets. Weapons specialists refer to this increase in accuracy as a decrease in the *CEP*, or the *circular error probable*, which is the radius of the circle in which a missile has a 50 percent chance of landing if aimed at its center. As a result of the increase in accuracy, land-based missiles in both the U.S. and the USSR are vulnerable to counterforce attack.

[29]     No one has developed *antisubmarine warfare* (*ASW*) technology capable of threatening the survivability of either U.S. or USSR submarines, and the subs remain a *credible* deterrent. Work to *improve* antisubmarine warfare is under way in both countries, however.

[30]     The $C^3$ systems both superpowers depend on to coordinate their nuclear forces might be vulnerable to nuclear attack. This could provide a *strong incentive* to strike first. As the newsletter of the Federation of American Scientists (FAS) noted in October 1980,

> A nation that strikes first with strategic forces does so with its command structure, control mechanisms, and communications devices wholly intact, alerted, and ready. Each and every telephone line, satellite, and antenna is functioning and every relevant person is alive and well. By contrast, the nation which seeks to launch a retaliatory attack may find its chain of command highly disrupted, its telephone lines dead, its satellites inoperative, its radio signals interfered with, and its communications officers out of action.

[31]     The FAS called attacks on $C^3$ "a kind of supercounterforce and correspondingly destabilizing." The Federation predicted: "Should either side carry out deliberate efforts to attack the $C^3$ of the other, it appears almost certain that a spasm war would result in which the attacked nation gave its military commanders either by prior agreement or by last desperate message, the authority to *fire at will*. As its ability to communicate gave out, it could and would do no less than use its last communications channel for *the final order*.

[32]     Another threat to the stability of deterrence is the possibility that a system failure in either superpower's nuclear-war-fighting computers could trigger an accidental nuclear war. Three recent *alerts* caused by computer errors show that this threat may not be as insignificant as the Department of Defense claims:

> In November of 1979, data from a computer *war game* accidentally flowed into a live warning and command network, triggering a low-level alert. The computer's mistake was not detected for six minutes. In the meantime, B-52 pilots were told to man their planes, and the launch

officers in ICBM silos unlocked a special strong box, removed the *attack verification codes*, and inserted the *keys* into their slots. When two keys ten feet apart are turned within two seconds of each other, the missiles blast off.

In June, 1980, on two separate occasions, a computer error caused by a faulty circuit chip worth 46¢ sent out false signals that the USSR had launched missiles headed for the U.S. In both cases, some of the B-52 fleet started its engines before the error was detected.

The Pentagon maintains that there is *"no chance that any* [33] *irretrievable actions* would be taken on the basis of *ambiguous computer information,"* noting that the computers do not make decisions alone and that *human intervention* has always detected the errors.

Nevertheless, there is little time for the people involved to read [34] the signals properly and make decisions. Land-based missiles can reach the U.S. in about thirty minutes, while submarine-launched missiles might take only half that time. Moreover, the threat exists that an erroneous alert could generate a nuclear attack as if by a trick of mirrors. If in response to a computer error the B-52s were suddenly to take off from their air bases, the Russians would immediately detect the maneuver. Soviet officers would have even less time to reach a judgment about how to respond, since their *early warning systems* are not as sophisticated as those of the U.S. If the Soviets dispatched their bombers, the U.S. warning system would in turn detect the planes, and the computer's message, though originally erroneous, would be *confirmed.*

The Pentagon claims that such a *chain reaction is a "highly* [35] *unlikely scenario."* A full public discussion of the issues involved is impossible because most of the relevant information is classified.

## QUESTIONS FOR DISCUSSION

1  Can you describe the audience for this essay?
2  For what reason do you think our government changed the name of the *War Department* to the *Department of Defense* following World War II?
3  What do you think of the practice of considering the deaths of civilians as *collateral damage* (paragraph 6) and calling the neutron bomb an *enhanced radiation warhead* (paragraph 16)? The neutron bomb, you will remember,

is designed to kill people while "reducing blast damage" to their surround-ings. Look up the words *collateral* and *enhanced*, if you are unsure of their meanings.

4   Do you remember the name for the figure of speech employed by the authors at the beginning of paragraph 20? Do you consider the technique appro-priate? Why or why not?

5   The essay has an extremely brief conclusion. Do you think it needs to be longer?

6   Can you state the authors' purpose in writing this piece?

## SUGGESTIONS FOR WRITING

1   With the help of your friends, list as many names as possible of animals
    and foods that are applied to women, like *chick, dish, dog, cupcake, bird*,
    etc. At the same time, think of similar names that are typically applied to
    men, like *hoss, buck, stud, old goat*. Analyze your results. Consider, for
    instance, what is the difference between the kinds of animals whose names
    are associated with females and those associated with males? What is the
    significance of that difference? Why are so many edibles associated with
    women, so few with men? Do any terms that can be applied to both sexes
    have different connotations when applied to females—like *cat*, for instance?
    Can you draw any conclusions from your study? If you come up with inter-
    esting observations, write a report of your findings to present at the next
    meeting of the local chapter of the National Organization for Women.

2   Look up the words *manly* and *womanly* and *manlike* and *womanlike* in a
    large dictionary in your college library. Copy the definitions and analyze
    the differences. Write an essay for *Newsweek on Campus* in which you
    explain how these definitions reveal society's attitudes toward women. You
    might want to remind your readers that dictionaries don't make up the
    meanings of words; they only record the ways in which words are used by
    people.

3   Write a one-page advertisement aimed at convincing other students at your
    school to sign up for your favorite class. Use as many of Stevens's weasel
    words as possible. Next, rewrite the same advertisement without using any
    weasel words. Then, analyze the effect of the changes you made. In a final
    paragraph, explain how those changes affected your tone, your level of
    usage, your sincerity, and your effectiveness in persuading fellow students
    to take the course.

4   Examine the ads in several issues of a woman's (or man's) magazine to
    see if you can detect visual "weaseling" techniques—ways in which the
    ads manipulate the viewer to purchase the products. You could include
    verbal weaseling also if space permits. Write a report of your findings for
    the readership of the magazine in which the ads appeared.

5   Can you think of other areas in our society in which deceptive language is
    used to make some questionable activity acceptable to the public? Consider
    the language employed by executives of companies operating nuclear power
    plants, for instance, in discussing the possibility of accidents. Write a letter
    to the president of your nearest nuclear power plant complaining that the
    deliberate use of deceptive language is both inaccurate and immoral.

# Chapter 18

# Considering Nuclear Destruction

## Atomic Bombing of Nagasaki Told by Flight Member

William L. Laurence

[1] *With the atomic-bomb mission to Japan, August 9 (Delayed)*—We are on our way to bomb the mainland of Japan. Our flying contingent consists of three specially designed B-29 Superforts, and two of these carry no bombs. But our lead plane is on its way with another atomic bomb, the second in three days, concentrating in its active substance an explosive energy equivalent to twenty thousand and, under favorable conditions, forty thousands tons of TNT.

[2]     We have several chosen targets. One of these is the great industrial and shipping center of Nagasaki, on the western shore of Kyushu, one of the main islands of the Japanese homeland.

[3]     I watched the assembly of this man-made meteor during the past

two days and was among the small group of scientists and Army and Navy representatives privileged to be present at the ritual of its loading in the Superfort last night, against a background of threatening black skies torn open at intervals by great lightning flashes.

It is a thing of beauty to behold, this "gadget." Into its design [4] went millions of man-hours of what is without doubt the most concentrated intellectual effort in history. Never before had so much brain power been focused on a single problem.

This atomic bomb is different from the bomb used three days ago [5] with such devastating results on Hiroshima.

I saw the atomic substance before it was placed inside the bomb. [6] By itself it is not at all dangerous to handle. It is only under certain conditions, produced in the bomb assembly, that it can be made to yield up its energy, and even then it gives only a small fraction of its total contents—a fraction, however, large enough to produce the greatest explosion on earth.

The briefing at midnight revealed the extreme care and the [7] tremendous amount of preparation that had been made to take care of every detail of the mission, to make certain that the atomic bomb fully served the purpose for which it was intended. Each target in turn was shown in detailed maps and in aerial photographs. Every detail of the course was rehearsed—navigation, altitude, weather, where to land in emergencies. It came out that the Navy had rescue craft, known as Dumbos and Superdumbos, stationed at various strategic points in the vicinity of the targets, ready to rescue the fliers in case they were forced to bail out.

The briefing period ended with a moving prayer by the chaplain. [8] We then proceeded to the mess hall for the traditional early-morning breakfast before departure on a bombing mission.

A convoy of trucks took us to the supply building for the special [9] equipment carried on combat missions. This included the Mae West [a life jacket], a parachute, a lifeboat, an oxygen mask, a flak suit, and a survival vest. We still had a few hours before take-off time, but we all went to the flying field and stood around in little groups or sat in jeeps talking rather casually about our mission to the Empire, as the Japanese home islands are known hereabouts.

In command of our mission is Major Charles W. Sweeney, twenty- [10] five, of 124 Hamilton Avenue, North Quincy, Massachusetts. His flagship, carrying the atomic bomb, is named *The Great Artiste*, but the name does not appear on the body of the great silver ship, with its unusually long, four-bladed, orange-tipped propellers. Instead, it carries the number 77, and someone remarks that it was ''Red'' Grange's winning number on the gridiron.

[11] We took off at 3:50 this morning and headed northwest on a straight line for the Empire. The night was cloudy and threatening, with only a few stars here and there breaking through the overcast. The weather report had predicted storms ahead part of the way but clear sailing for the final and climactic stages of our odyssey.

[12] We were about an hour away from our base when the storm broke. Our great ship took some heavy dips through the abysmal darkness around us, but it took these dips much more gracefully than a large commercial air liner, producing a sensation more in the nature of a glide than a ''bump,'' like a great ocean liner riding the waves except that in this case the air waves were much higher and the rhythmic tempo of the glide was much faster.

[13] I noticed a strange eerie light coming through the window high above the navigator's cabin, and as I peered through the dark all around us I saw a startling phenomenon. The whirling giant propellers had somehow become great luminous disks of blue flame. The same luminous blue flame appeared on the plexiglas windows in the nose of the ship, and on the tips of the giant wings. It looked as though we were riding the whirlwind through space on a chariot of blue fire.

[14] It was, I surmised, a surcharge of static electricity that had accumulated on the tips of the propellers and on the di-electric material of the plastic windows. One's thoughts dwelt anxiously on the precious cargo in the invisible ship ahead of us. Was there any likelihood of danger that this heavy electric tension in the atmosphere all about us might set it off?

[15] I expressed my fears to Captain Bock, who seems nonchalant and unperturbed at the controls. He quickly reassured me.

[16] ''It is a familiar phenomenon seen often on ships. I have seen it many times on bombing missions. It is known as St. Elmo's fire.''

[17] On we went through the night. We soon rode out the storm and our ship was once again sailing on a smooth course straight ahead, on a direct line to the Empire.

[18] Our altimeter showed that we were traveling through space at a height of seventeen thousand feet. The thermometer registered an

outside temperature of thirty-three degrees below zero Centigrade, about thirty below Fahrenheit. Inside our pressurized cabin the temperature was that of a comfortable air-conditioned room and a pressure corresponding to an altitude of eight thousand feet. Captain Bock cautioned me, however, to keep my oxygen mask handy in case of emergency. This, he explained, might mean either something going wrong with the pressure equipment inside the ship or a hole through the cabin by flak.

The first signs of dawn came shortly after five o'clock. Sergeant [19] Curry, of Hoopeston, Illinois, who had been listening steadily on his earphones for radio reports, while maintaining a strict radio silence himself, greeted it by rising to his feet and gazing out the window.

"It's good to see the day," he told me. "I get a feeling of claus- [20] trophobia hemmed in this cabin at night."

He is a typical American youth, looking even younger than his [21] twenty years. It takes no mind reader to read his thoughts.

"It's a long way from Hoopeston," I find myself remarking. [22]

"Yep," he replies, as he busies himself decoding a message from [23] outer space.

"Think this atomic bomb will end the war?" he asks hopefully. [24]

"There is a very good chance that this one may do the trick," I [25] assured him, "but if not, then the next one or two surely will. Its power is such that no nation can stand up against it very long." This was not my own view. I had heard it expressed all around a few hours earlier, before we took off. To anyone who had seen this manmade fireball in action, as I had less than a month ago in the desert of New Mexico, this view did not sound overoptimistic.

By 5:50 it was really light outside. We had lost our lead ship, but [26] Lieutenant Godfrey, our navigator, informs me that we had arranged for that contingency. We have an assembly point in the sky above the little island of Yakushima, southeast of Kyushu, at 9:10. We are to circle there and wait for the rest of our formation.

Our genial bombardier, Lieutenant Levy, comes over to invite me [27] to take his front-row seat in the transparent nose of the ship, and I accept eagerly. From that vantage point in space, seventeen thousand feet above the Pacific, one gets a view of hundreds of miles on all sides, horizontally and vertically. At that height the vast ocean below and the sky above seem to merge into one great sphere.

I was on the inside of that firmament, riding above the giant [28] mountains of white cumulus clouds, letting myself be suspended in infinite space. One hears the whirl of the motors behind one, but it soon becomes insignificant against the immensity all around and is before long swallowed by it. There comes a point where space also swallows time and one lives through eternal moments filled with an oppressive loneliness, as though all life had suddenly vanished from the earth and you are the only one left, a lone survivor traveling endlessly through interplanetary space.

[29]     My mind soon returns to the mission I am on. Somewhere beyond these vast mountains of white clouds ahead of me there lies Japan, the land of our enemy. In about four hours from now one of its cities, making weapons of war for use against us, will be wiped off the map by the greatest weapon ever made by man: In one tenth of a millionth of a second, a fraction of time immeasurable by any clock, a whirlwind from the skies will pulverize thousands of its buildings and tens of thousands of its inhabitants.

[30]     But at this moment no one yet knows which one of the several cities chosen as targets is to be annihilated. The final choice lies with destiny. The winds over Japan will make the decision. If they carry heavy clouds over our primary target, that city will be saved, at least for the time being. None of its inhabitants will ever know that the wind of a benevolent destiny had passed over their heads. But that same wind will doom another city.

[31]     Our weather planes ahead of us are on their way to find out where the wind blows. Half an hour before target time we will know what the winds have decided.

[32]     Does one feel any pity or compassion for the poor devils about to die? Not when one thinks of Pearl Harbor and of the Death March on Bataan.

[33]     Captain Bock informs me that we are about to start our climb to bombing altitude.

[34]     He manipulates a few knobs on his control panel to the right of him, and I alternately watch the white clouds and ocean below me and the altimeter on the bombardier's panel. We reached our altitude at nine o'clock. We were then over Japanese waters, close to their mainland. Lieutenant Godfrey motioned to me to look through his radar scope. Before me was the outline of our assembly point. We shall soon meet our lead ship and proceed to the final stage of our journey.

We reached Yakushima at 9:12 and there, about four thousand [35] feet ahead of us, was *The Great Artiste* with its precious load. I saw Lieutenant Godfrey and Sergeant Curry strap on their parachutes and I decided to do likewise.

We started circling. We saw little towns on the coastline, heedless [36] of our presence. We kept on circling, waiting for the third ship in our formation.

It was 9:56 when we began heading for the coastline. Our weather [37] scouts had sent us code messages, deciphered by Sergeant Curry, informing us that both the primary target as well as the secondary were clearly visible.

The winds of destiny seemed to favor certain Japanese cities that [38] must remain nameless. We circled about them again and again and found no opening in the thick umbrella of clouds that covered them. Destiny chose Nagasaki as the ultimate target.

We had been circling for some time when we noticed black puffs [39] of smoke coming through the white clouds directly at us. There were fifteen bursts of flak in rapid succession, all too low. Captain Bock changed his course. There soon followed eight more bursts of flak, right up to our altitude, but by this time were too far to the left.

We flew southward down the channel and at 11:33 crossed the [40] coastline and headed straight for Nagasaki, about one hundred miles to the west. Here again we circled until we found an opening in the clouds. It was 12:01 and the goal of our mission had arrived.

We heard the prearranged signal on our radio, put on our arc [41] welder's glasses, and watched tensely the maneuverings of the strike ship about half a mile in front of us.

"There she goes!" someone said. [42]

Out of the belly of *The Great Artiste* what looked like a black [43] object went downward.

Captain Bock swung to get out of range; but even though we were [44] turning away in the opposite direction, and despite the fact that it was broad daylight in our cabin, all of us became aware of a giant flash that broke through the dark barrier of our arc welder's lenses and flooded our cabin with intense light.

We removed our glasses after the first flash, but the light still [45] lingered on, a bluish-green light that illuminated the entire sky all around. A tremendous blast wave struck our ship and made it tremble from nose to tail. This was followed by four more blasts in rapid succession, each resounding like the boom of cannon fire hitting our plane from all directions.

[46] Observers in the tail of our ship saw a giant ball of fire rise as though from the bowels of the earth, belching forth enormous white smoke rings. Next they saw a giant pillar of purple fire, ten thousand feet high, shooting skyward with enormous speed.

[47] By the time our ship had made another turn in the direction of the atomic explosion the pillar of purple fire had reached the level of our altitude. Only about forty-five seconds had passed. Awe-struck, we watched it shoot upward like a meteor coming from the earth instead of from outer space, becoming ever more alive as it climbed skyward through the white clouds. It was no longer smoke, or dust, or even a cloud of fire. It was a living thing, a new species of being, born right before our incredulous eyes.

[48] At one stage of its evolution, covering millions of years in terms of seconds, the entity assumed the form of a giant square totem pole, with its base about three miles long, tapering off to about a mile at the top. Its bottom was brown, its center was amber, its top white. But it was a living totem pole, carved with many grotesque masks grimacing at the earth.

[49] Then, just when it appeared as though the thing had settled down into a state of permanence, there came shooting out of the top a giant mushroom that increased the height of the pillar to a total of forty-five thousand feet. The mushroom top was even more alive than the pillar, seething and boiling in a white fury of creamy foam, sizzling upward and then descending earthward, a thousand Old Faithful geysers rolled into one.

[50] It kept struggling in an elemental fury, like a creature in the act of breaking the bonds that held it down. In a few seconds it had freed itself from its gigantic stem and floated upward with tremendous speed, its momentum carrying it into the stratosphere to a height of about sixty thousand feet.

[51] But no sooner did this happen when another mushroom, smaller in size than the first one, began emerging out of the pillar. It was as though the decapitated monster was growing a new head.

[52] As the first mushroom floated off into the blue it changed its shape into a flowerlike form, its giant petals curving downward, creamy white

outside, rose-colored inside. It still retained that shape when we last gazed at it from a distance of about two hundred miles. The boiling pillar of many colors could also be seen at that distance, a giant mountain of jumbled rainbows, in travail. Much living substance had gone into those rainbows. The quivering top of the pillar was protruding to a great height through the white clouds, giving the appearance of a monstrous prehistoric creature with a ruff around its neck, a fleecy ruff extending in all directions, as far as the eye could see.

## QUESTIONS FOR DISCUSSION

1   How does Laurence engage your interest in his introduction? Does the term "favorable" strike you as a strange word choice in the last sentence of paragraph 1? Can you explain why he uses it?
2   Underline all the words and phrases that the writer chooses to describe the bomb. What is his attitude toward it? Why does he put "gadget" in quotation marks in paragraph 4?
3   Does it strike you as paradoxical that the men are sent off on their mission of death "with a moving prayer by the chaplain" (paragraph 8)? Why or why not?
4   Why is the description of the St. Elmo's fire a particularly apt detail? Consider especially the last sentence of paragraph 13. Can you explain the allusion to "riding the whirlwind"?
5   Why does Laurence include so many details about the crew—even mentioning their hometowns?
6   Why do you think he refers in paragraph 32 to the prospective victims as "poor devils" instead of "people" or "human beings"? What happened at Pearl Harbor? What do you know about the Bataan Death March?
7   Laurence twice mentions that "destiny" chose Nagasaki as the target (paragraphs 30 and 38). Is that observation in any way misleading?
8   Analyze the description of the mushroom cloud in the final paragraph. Are the images positive or negative? What is the meaning of this sentence: "Much living substance had gone into those rainbows"?

# "I Thought My Last Hour Had Come . . ."
## Robert Guillain

"It was in Hiroshima, that morning of August 6. I had joined a team [1] of women who, like me, worked as volunteers in cutting firepaths against incendiary raids by demolishing whole rows of houses. My husband, because of a raid alert the previous night, had stayed at the *Chunichi (Central Japan Journal)*, where he worked.

[2]      "Our group had passed the Tsurumi bridge, Indian-file, when there was an alert; an enemy plane appeared all alone, very high over our heads. Its silver wings shone brightly in the sun. A woman exclaimed, 'Oh, look—a parachute!' I turned toward where she was pointing, and just at that moment a shattering flash filled the whole sky.

[3]      "Was it the flash that came first, or the sound of the explosion, tearing up my insides? I don't remember. I was thrown to the ground, pinned to the earth, and immediately the world began to collapse around me, on my head, my shoulders. I couldn't see anything. It was completely dark. I thought my last hour had come. I thought of my three children, who had been evacuated to the country to be safe from the raids. I couldn't move; debris kept falling, beams and tiles piled up on top of me.

[4]      "Finally I did manage to crawl free. There was a terrible smell in the air. Thinking the bomb that hit us might have been a yellow phosphorus incendiary like those that had fallen on so many other cities, I rubbed my nose and mouth hard with a *tenugui* (a kind of towel) I had at my waist. To my horror, I found that the skin of my face had come off in the towel. Oh! The skin on my hands, on my arms, came off too. From elbow to fingertips, all the skin on my right arm had come loose and was hanging grotesquely. The skin of my left hand fell off too, the five fingers, like a glove.

[5]      "I found myself sitting on the ground, prostrate. Gradually I registered that all my companions had disappeared. What had happened to them? A frantic panic gripped me, I wanted to run, but where? Around me was just debris, wooden framing, beams and roofing tiles; there wasn't a single landmark left.

[6]      "And what had happened to the sky, so blue a moment ago? Now it was as black as night. Everything seemed vague and fuzzy. It was as though a cloud covered my eyes and I wondered if I had lost my senses. I finally saw the Tsurumi bridge and I ran headlong toward it, jumping over the piles of rubble. What I saw under the bridge then horrified me.

[7]      "People by the hundreds were flailing in the river. I couldn't tell

if they were men or women; they were all in the same state: their faces were puffy and ashen, their hair tangled, they held their hands raised and, groaning with pain, threw themselves into the water. I had a violent impulse to do so myself, because of the pain burning through my whole body. But I can't swim and I held back.

"Past the bridge, I looked back to see that the whole Hachobori [8] district had suddenly caught fire, to my surprise, because I thought only the district I was in had been bombed. As I ran, I shouted my children's names. Where was I going? I have no idea, but I can still see the scenes of horror I glimpsed here and there on my way.

"A mother, her face and shoulders covered with blood, tried [9] frantically to run into a burning house. A man held her back and she screamed, 'Let me go! Let me go! My son is burning in there!' She was like a mad demon. Under the Kojin bridge, which had half collapsed and had lost its heavy, reinforced-concrete parapets, I saw a lot of bodies floating in the water like dead dogs, almost naked, with their clothes in shreds. At the river's edge, near the bank, a woman lay on her back with her breasts ripped off, bathed in blood. How could such a frightful thing have happened? I thought of the scenes of the Buddhist hell my grandmother had described to me when I was little.

"I must have wandered for at least two hours before finding myself [10] on the Eastern military parade ground. My burns were hurting me, but the pain was different from an ordinary burn. It was a dull pain that seemed somehow to come from outside my body. A kind of yellow pus oozed from my hands, and I thought that my face must also be horrible to see.

"Around me on the parade ground were a number of grade-school [11] and secondary-school children, boys and girls, writhing in spasms of agony. Like me, they were members of the anti-air raid volunteer corps. I heard them crying 'Mama! Mama!' as though they'd gone crazy. They were so burned and bloody that looking at them was insupportable. I forced myself to do so just the same, and I cried out in rage. 'Why? Why these children?' But there was no one to rage at and I could do nothing but watch them die, one after the other, vainly calling for their mothers.

"After lying almost unconscious for a long time on the parade [12] ground, I started walking again. As far as I could see with my failing sight, everything was in flames, as far as the Hiroshima station and the

Atago district. It seemed to me that my face was hardening little by little. I cautiously touched my hands to my cheeks. My face felt as though it had doubled in size. I could see less and less clearly. Was I going blind, then? After so much hardship, was I going to die? I kept on walking anyway and I reached a suburban area.

[13]    "In that district, farther removed from the center, I found my elder sister alive, with only slight injuries to the head and feet. She didn't recognize me at first, then she burst into tears. In a handcart, she wheeled me nearly three miles to the first-aid center at Yaga. It was night when we arrived. I later learned there was a pile of corpses and countless injured there. I spent two nights there, unconscious; my sister told me that in my delirium I kept repeating, 'My children! Take me to my children!'

[14]    "On August 8, I was carried on a stretcher to a train and transported to the home of relatives in the village of Kasumi. The village doctor said my case was hopeless. My children, recalled from their evacuation refuge, rushed to my side. I could no longer see them; I could recognize them only by smelling their good odor. On August 11, my husband joined us. The children wept with joy as they embraced him.

[15]    "Our happiness soon ended. My husband, who bore no trace of injury, died suddenly three days later, vomiting blood. We had been married sixteen years and now, because I was at the brink of death myself, I couldn't even rest his head as I should have on the pillow of the dead.

[16]    "I said to myself, 'My poor children, because of you I don't have the right to die!' And finally, by a miracle, I survived after I had again and again been given up for lost.

[17]    "My sight returned fairly quickly, and after twenty days I could dimly see my children's features. The burns on my face and hands did not heal so rapidly, and the wounds remained pulpy, like rotten tomatoes. It wasn't until December that I could walk again. When my bandages were removed in January, I knew that my face and hands would always be deformed. My left ear was half its original size. A streak of cheloma, a dark brown swelling as wide as my hand, runs from the side of my head across my mouth to my throat. My right hand is striped with a cheloma two inches wide from the wrist to the little finger. The five fingers on my left hand are now fused at the base. . . ."

## QUESTIONS FOR DISCUSSION

1  Guillain, a French journalist, recorded Mrs. Futaba Kitayama's description of her ordeal as a first-person account. The narrative is full of specific details which enable the readers to see and all but feel the horror of her experience. Choose three paragraphs and explain what makes the details in each particularly effective.
2  Why is the mention of the parachute significant in paragraph 2?
3  The narrator employs a number of rhetorical questions; reread the ones posed in paragraphs 5, 8, 9, 11, and 12. What effect, in general, does the narrator achieve with these questions?
4  What do you think killed Mrs. Kitayama's husband, who "bore no trace of injury" but "died suddenly three days later, vomiting blood" (paragraph 15)?
5  Clearly, the unstated purpose of this narrative is to oppose the use of atomic weapons. Do you feel any differently about William Laurence's account of his experience of watching the bomb drop after reading about the devastation of all below?

# This Beautiful Planet

Helen Caldicott

This beautiful planet of ours is terminally ill. Unless we face it and do [1] something about it, almost certainly it will die along with us and the whales. It is important to examine this terminally ill planet, which presently is infected with lethal "macrobes," the nuclear weapons, which are metastasizing rapidly.

The nuclear age began in the late 1930s and early 1940s when [2] Einstein wrote to President Roosevelt telling him that he thought Hitler was developing nuclear weapons and that America should be doing the same thing. This led to the Manhattan Project, which was funded by huge amounts of government money and through which many scientists became involved in the challenge of their lifetime.

A film shown on PBS, "The Day After Trinity," described the [3] history of the experiment. It took the scientists about three years to develop enough enriched uranium and plutonium to make three bombs. Even after it became apparent that Hitler, in fact, was not going to make nuclear weapons, and even after VE day, when Germany surrendered, they kept going. Some of the scientists had a meeting to discuss whether they should proceed, but because they were absolutely fascinated by what they were doing, they decided it would be better to make the bombs and use them to show mankind how dreadful they were, and then they would never be made again.

[4] The first bomb was named Trinity and it was called a "gadget." The "gadget" was hoisted to the top of a tower in Alamagordo Desert in July 1945. On a stormy night with lightning everywhere, the "gadget" exploded. One scientist described how he felt when it blew up. He said, "The noise went on, and on, and on, like thunder, never stopping. The desert suddenly became small."

[5] They were not sure before they blew up the bomb that the whole atmosphere would not go critical. They were worried about this probability, so they redid their calculations and the probability remained the same. It was not extremely small. One technician was upset to hear Enrico Fermi taking side bets as the "gadget" was hoisted to the tower, that New Mexico would be incinerated.

[6] After the explosion, the radioactive cloud hovered overhead for some time, worrying the scientists, because if it did not blow away in the direction they had prescribed, it could have killed them or injured them severely. However, it did eventually blow away. That night the scientists had a party.

[7] The next bomb was blown up or tested over a human population on August 6, 1945, at 8:15 in the morning. In fact, the air force had been told to spare two cities in Japan so that we could see the effects of these weapons on human populations. The bomb was dropped from a plane called the *Enola Gay*, which flew over Hiroshima. Men looking up saw one parachute opening and they were pleased because they thought the plane had been shot down. Another parachute opened adjacent to the first. Then there was a blinding flash and tens of thousands of people were vaporized. People, in fact, when they disappeared, left their shadows on concrete sidewalks behind them. Children were seen running along streets shedding skin from their bodies like veils; a man was standing in a state of acute clinical shock holding his eyeball in the palm of his hand; and a woman lay dying in a gutter with her back totally burned with her baby suckling at her breast as she lay dying.

[8] Some people who escaped Hiroshima migrated then to the only Christian center in Japan, Nagasaki, thinking that it would never be

bombed by the Americans. They arrived three days later, just in time to receive the second bomb. Many Japanese will say, if you visit there, "We can sort of understand the first bomb, but why the second?" One of the physicists who celebrated at the party the night after Trinity recounted in "The Day After Trinity" how he felt after the bomb in Hiroshima was used. He said, "I was so nauseated that night I had to go to bed, and I was profoundly depressed. We are scientists. We never thought of human beings as matter."

After the war, Robert Oppenheimer thought that if the nuclear [9] secret were shared with Russia, neither country would develop the weapons. But it was decided that the secret should remain. This, he said, was the beginning of the Cold War. However, several years later Russia developed the secret and the arms race began. Oppenheimer was interviewed 20 years later in the PBS documentary. The then gaunt man was asked, "What do you think?"

In a very didactic, scientific way, puffing on his pipe, he said, "It [10] is too late."

"What should have happened?" the filmmakers asked. [11]

He said, "It should have been stopped the day after Trinity." [12]

This was in the sixties. Today we have tens of thousands of [13] hydrogen bombs on this planet, with more being built every day.

During the sixties, Robert McNamara, who was Secretary of [14] Defense, determined that if America had 400 one megaton bombs, this would be an adequate deterrent. A one megaton bomb is equivalent to one million tons of TNT. The bomb used on Hiroshima was equivalent to approximately 13,000 tons of TNT. The maximum payload any plane could carry during the Second World War was four tons of bombs. The four hundred bombs would be sufficient to kill one third of the Russian population and destroy two thirds of their industry. I thought about that statement the other day from an ethical, moral and medical perspective and I realized that the last person who spoke like that in my lifetime wrote a book called *Mein Kampf*. To kill one third of the Russian people is to kill nearly one hundred million human beings. We have been anesthetized and we practice psychic numbing. We listen to the Pentagon jargon which is, I think, meant to confuse. It is rather like the medical jargon which we use to confuse the patients, so they do not understand what is actually wrong with them.

That is the history of this terminally ill planet. At the time 400 [15] bombs were determined to be an adequate deterrent force, the air force had control of all the nuclear weapons, but traditionally the army and navy have rivalries, and they were jealous. It was then decided to develop a triad of nuclear weapons, so everybody could have them. The arms race really began in earnest. Also, at that time it was decided to nuclearize all forms of conventional weapons. So now there are atomic bombs in torpedoes and in land mines, and men who go into battle with 18-inch howitzers on their shoulders, carry with them atomic bombs.

[16]     What is the physical condition of our planet today? America now has some 30 to 35 thousand hydrogen bombs. The Pentagon says, however, there are only five thousand worthwhile targets in the Soviet Union. According to the Pentagon's estimates, there are enough weapons in this country to overkill (a Pentagon word) every Russian human being 40 times. There are, in fact, enough weapons on one Trident submarine to destroy every major city in the Northern Hemisphere, and America is building 11 Trident submarines.

[17]     The Soviet Union has some 20,000 hydrogen bombs, which are bigger than the American bombs because they are less accurate. The Soviets have enough weapons to overkill every American human being some 20 times. Collectively, the superpowers can overkill every human being on earth 12 times.

[18]     I have heard statements recently that America is behind Russia. I do not understand that statement. How can one be behind or ahead when both countries can kill each other many times over? I have heard talk of Russian expansionism, and I investigated that thoroughly. I found that, according to the Pentagon, America has 200 major bases in 45 nations in the world and 20 major ports; the Soviet Union has none.

[19]     The world spends over $600 billion a year on the arms race. That is over a million dollars a minute. Incidentally, the cost of one third of one Trident submarine would eradicate malaria in the world. Two thirds of the world's children are malnourished and starving. Over half the scientists in this country work for the military-industrial complex.

[20]     What, therefore, is the prognosis of our terminally ill planet? It is gloomy. In 1975, the Joint Chiefs of Staff testified before a Senate Committee and predicted a 50-50 chance of a nuclear war occurring before 1985. A Harvard-MIT study done later verified that prediction.

*The Bulletin of the Atomic Scientists*, which commenced publication during Einstein's era, has a doomsday clock on its cover. Its hands have been moved only ten times since 1945. During the years of détente when there was some relaxation and a little bit of confidence and hope about the future, the clock was at nine minutes to midnight. After Afghanistan, it was moved to seven. In January 1981, the hands moved to four minutes to midnight.

Dr. George Kistiakowsky, Professor Emeritus of Chemistry at [21] Harvard University, who was Eisenhower's science advisor and who devised the implosion, or triggering, mechanism for the first atomic bomb, has serious doubts that we will survive to the year 1990. Presidential advisors, some of them coming from Harvard, at the moment are making statements that we must psychologically prepare ourselves for a nuclear war. As a physician who knows something about psychiatry, I am not sure how one does that. Other advisors are writing articles in *Foreign Affairs* saying it is possible to fight and win a nuclear war. Let me describe the terminal or agonal event of this planet if such a war should occur.

A nuclear war between the superpowers, using only strategic [22] weapons, would take about half an hour to complete. In fact, the weapons on the submarines off the coast of this country and the Soviet Union need only ten minutes to a quarter of an hour to reach their targets. The reason for this is that once the weapons are launched, they go out into space, reenter the earth's atmosphere at 20 times the speed of sound and land accurately on target. Meanwhile, the other country's satellites, radar, and other instruments detect the attack and the button is pressed on the other side. The weapons cross in mid-space, practically. And they land within about half an hour.

According to the Arms Control and Disarmament Agency, there [23] are enough weapons to target every town and city with a population of ten thousand people or more. Apparently the nuclear reactors are also targeted. Inside each thousand-megawatt nuclear reactor is as much long-lived radiation as that released by 1,000 Hiroshima-sized bombs. Apparently the major airports, the major oil refineries, and industry are also targeted.

Let me describe now a 20-megaton bomb dropping on Boston, [24] using a series of articles published in *The New England Journal of Medicine* in 1962. A 20-megaton bomb is equal to 20 million tons of

TNT. That is four times the collective size of all the bombs dropped during the Second World War. It is a small sun. It explodes with the heat of the sun. It will do this to Boston: It will carve out a crater about half a mile to a mile wide and 300 feet deep. Everything in that volume will be converted to radioactive fallout. Every human being within a radius of six miles from the hypo-center will be vaporized, as will most buildings. Concrete and steel will burn. Out to a radius of 20 miles, most people will be dead, or lethally injured, with tens of thousands of severe burn victims, when there are only facilities for 2000 acute burn victims in the whole of the United States of America. There will be injuries such as compound fractures, ruptured lungs from the overpressure, ruptured internal organs and massive hemorrhage. What is left of the buildings will be lying in what is left of the streets. Most hospitals will be destroyed, most medical personnel dead or injured. If one doctor works for two weeks, eighteen hours a day, he or she will only be able to see each patient once for a ten-minute period during that time, meaning every patient would die. If you happen just to glance at the blast from 35 to 40 miles away, the flash would instantly burn the retina and blind you. It will create a fire storm of 15,000 to 30,000 square miles, in which everything will spontaneously ignite, creating a holocaust fanned by hurricane-force winds, so if you were in a fallout shelter, you would be pressure-cooked and asphyxiated as the fire used all the oxygen. The explosion will create an electromagnetic pulse damaging all electronic equipment and all communications equipment.

[25]     As most towns and cities in this country are so targeted, what happens if you are in a rural area that is not targeted? Now you must not be asleep. You must be listening to the radio or television to hear the emergency signal. You sometimes hear it tested, don't you? "Oooooooooh, we are testing the emergency signal." This time I guess they will tell you you have 15 minutes to run to the nearest shelter. Medically, you will not be able to emerge for 2 to 6 weeks because the short-lived isotopes in the fallout will be so intensely radioactive that you will die within days of acute radiation sickness if you are exposed to it.

[26]     When you reemerge, the world will be different. This building will be gone; Harvard will be gone. All the magnificent architecture we have inherited from our ancestors will be destroyed. The Bach, the

Handel, the Beethoven will be gone from the planet. The art, the literature, the poetry, everything will be gone. There will be no one to come and help as there was in Hiroshima because most people will be dead. There will be nobody to bring medical help, because doctors will be dead or injured. There will be no drugs for the dying patients. Just last year the Boston *Globe* reported that President Carter was stockpiling huge quantities of opium just in case there was to be a nuclear war. Of course, that would be used for euthanasia, if anyone knew where it was.

The National Academy of Science did a study in 1975 that stated [27] if the superpowers used only 10 percent of their nuclear arsenals, that could destroy 50 to 80 percent of the ozone layer in the Northern Hemisphere and 30 to 40 percent in the Southern Hemisphere because of the nitrous oxide released in the explosions. Some scientists predict that if only 30 percent of the ozone layer (which protects the earth from the ultraviolet radiation of the sun) is destroyed, it could blind every organism on earth, including the insects and bees, which literally means the death of the ecosphere as we know it. If people stay in the sun for half an hour, they will get third-degree sunburn, which is lethal, and be blinded. Survivors will die of a synergistic combination of acute radiation sickness, sunburn, blindness, starvation and epidemics of disease (as bacteria mutate and multiply in the millions of dead bodies, to become more virulent while our immune mechanism is depleted by background radiation) and people die of grief.

In the symposia that Physicians for Social Responsibility hold on [28] the medical consequences of nuclear war, addressed by some of the most famous physicians in this country, it is predicted that within 30 days after an all-out nuclear exchange, 90 percent of American human beings will be dead. And not just in America, you know, but in Canada, Mexico, all of Europe, all of England, all of Russia, and much of China.

What is the etiology or cause of the present situation, our termi- [29] nally ill planet? It is psychiatric. We are causing the illness. We are very intelligent, but we are motivated by our emotions. How did we let it happen? One of the reasons we have let it happen, according to Robert Lifton, is that we practice psychic numbing. We block it out. We push it back into our subconscious because we do not like to think about it. Because if, in fact, we take this on emotionally, it is as if I have told you just now that you have a terminal illness. You, the planet, us. If you have a cancer, you might die in a year. If you understand this fact emotionally, you enter the stages of grief which are, first, shock and disbelief. "She must be mad. Anyway, one of her facts is wrong, so I will discount the lot." The next stage is profound depression. You would prefer to feel the pain of a fractured arm than the pain of the depression, followed by profound anger, followed perhaps eventually, by adjustment. The human being would do anything to avoid those feelings, so we practice psychic numbing and avoid the feelings.

[30]         During the early sixties, the days of atmospheric testing and the Cuban missile crisis, we were not psychically numbed, but then we developed the partial test ban treaty, and the bombs were tested underground. Out of sight is out of mind. The Vietnam war was unthinkable, Watergate was a little bit of fun, if not very serious, and we forgot that the weapons were being made, and that this country makes or recycles three to 10 new hydrogen bombs per day.

[31]         We also practice adaptation. When animals are in the jungle and are threatened with some stimulus they perceive to be life-threatening, they will immediately be alert. But if the stimulus persists and nothing bad happens, they adapt and move on to receive new stimuli which may be threatening. Adaptation is what we have done with the threat of nuclear war.

[32]         Another thing we do is project the fear of the nuclear age. The fear is profound. I am sure we have all had nuclear nightmares. I am sure some of you in the 1950s and 1960s used to practice hiding under your desk in schools in case a bomb exploded, or put bits of paper on your head so that you would be protected from the flash. The fear is so profound that we normally tend to project it onto other people. At a recent meeting of physicians from 11 countries, we worked out that we are projecting that fear onto the Russians. The fear is so profound in the nuclear age that in our fear, the Russians, or whoever, become inanimate objects. If they are inanimate objects, we can talk about killing tens or hundreds of millions of them and it does not feel bad at all. In so doing, we have lost our own humanity.

[33]         The other thing we tend to do is use what I call the "but what about the Russians" syndrome. When I talk on television about the medical effects of nuclear war, the first question that comes back to

me is "But what about the Russians?" It is as if the people have streamlined all the information so it goes over their heads, and the fear is still projected onto the Russians. Therefore, I say I am not worried about the Russians, I am worried about you and your children being incinerated. It is rather like telling a patient, you have a bad disease and if the patient does not comply medically with what you prescribe, you are psychologically a little more brutal at the next appointment.

What about the adolescents? The Harvard psychiatrists' recent [34] study of 1,000 adolescents in Boston shows that one of the main reasons they think the children are taking drugs and drinking alcohol is that most of these children expressed a profound fear of the future and a feeling that they probably won't grow up and will probably never survive to have children.

It is interesting treating children, which is what I do. Children can [35] face death more openly and readily than adults. I think they are less conditioned. They are less like Pavlovian dogs than we are.

What about the scientists, the leaders of the countries of the world, [36] and the industrialists who make the weapons? Partly these people are stuck in old thinking. They see nuclear weapons as they saw bows and arrows or conventional weapons. The more one has, the safer one is, because you can destroy your enemy and rebuild from the rubble. There are very few leaders in the world who have seen a hydrogen bomb explode and seen battleships become like splinters in the water or felt the heat or the blast. In their imaginations, can they possibly foresee what that is like? So they think of more hydrogen bombs as providing more security, when in fact this thinking is leading us to total insecurity. Einstein put it best. He said, "The splitting of the atom changed everything save man's mode of thinking, thus we drift toward unparalleled catastrophe."

America's leaders also practice psychic numbing. During the [37] SALT hearings, they talked about how many bombs the Russians have and how many more we need to counter them. They sound like nine-year-old boys, a little like my younger son.

I called the Senate Foreign Relations Committee and asked, "Why [38] hasn't anybody testified about the medical consequences of thermonuclear war?"

They said, "The senators don't like to hear that sort of thing, it [39] makes them feel uncomfortable."

[40]     I think many politicians are practicing power games or projecting their dark sides onto other people, which we all tend to do. It takes much more courage for men and women to face their own anger, fear and hostility and understand where it comes from and grow emotionally than it does to project one's fear and anger onto other people and blame them.

[41]     I also think there is another mechanism that is operating. We all have a profound fear of our own death, which we don't think about. Some people cope with that by using a counter-phobic mechanism by dealing in death or playing with it. Perhaps that is what the scientists and engineers are doing as they make these weapons for mass genocide without contemplating the end result of what they are actually doing.

[42]     What would be the pathogenesis of the terminal event, or of nuclear war? If you look back through history, you see that wars are often started for totally illogical reasons, inane reasons. Often wars are started by sane men. Adolf Eichmann, when psychoanalyzed after the war, was found to be, psychiatrically, totally sane. Moreover, a third-world leader could initiate a nuclear war. Libya's Colonel Qaddafi is financing a Pakistani bomb program and so he will soon have his own nuclear weapon. I don't know what will happen then in the Middle East.

[43]     Nuclear war could be initiated by pathology within leaders of the world. In medicine, we see pathology a lot. I have seen sane people develop an acute psychosis suddenly, under severe stress. Or the president of either country or the chairman of the Soviet Union could develop a cerebral tumor and, before getting a CAT scan, could do something which is totally insane.

[44]     A nuclear war could be started by accident. Over the last 18 months, computers within the Pentagon and elsewhere have made 151 errors that predicted that nuclear weapons were coming from the Soviet Union. One such error was started by a man who plugged a war-game tape into the fail-safe computer at the Pentagon in November 1979. The computer detected weapons coming from Russia. The whole world went on nuclear alert for six minutes. Some planes took off with nuclear weapons heading toward the Soviet Union. At the seventh minute, the President was to be officially notified, but he could not be found. If the error had not been determined at that time, in 14 minutes we would have been annihilated.

[45]     What is the therapy for this planet, and for us? First, as physi-

cians, we must shatter people's psychic numbing. It is inappropriate for any person on this planet to be psychologically comfortable in this day and age. As the psychic numbing is shattered, people will enter the phases of the grieving reaction. This then motivates individuals to become active in doing something about the problem. The anger can be very profound. It is therapeutic to do something, it feels better. We must also deal with our own dark side and stop projecting it like children onto other people and stop blaming other people for things we ourselves can fix and for which we are responsible.

We must also have a total commitment to save this planet. Now, [46] a marriage or a relationship with two people will never work unless each partner is totally committed to that marriage. If there is so much as one toe out the door, saying if you don't do this I will leave, the marriage will eventually disintegrate, because neither partner will go through the pain and humiliation of personal growth to reach the stage where the relationship matures. Similarly, both superpowers must be totally committed to saving this planet. For nothing else really matters. War is no longer appropriate. Even conventional war is no longer appropriate because of nuclear reactors and huge nuclear radioactive waste dumps everywhere that would produce, to a degree, genetic suicide. These weapons are biologically inapplicable and cannot be used. The only weapon we have at our disposal in this day and age is the larynx.

Kübler-Ross studies people who are terminally ill. Many people [47] who are terminally ill find it very hard to die: The people who find it hardest to die and are clinging on to life are those who have never really loved and given and who have been selfish and greedy. Often the people who die with grace and dignity and at peace are those people who have given to other people and loved. In other words, the way to true happiness is through helping other people on this planet, not to make yourself happy. Therefore, our challenge today is to help each other and to help the planet survive. It does not really matter if you get a good job; it does not really matter if you have children and make sure they clean their teeth and eat good, nutritious food, if we don't survive. In fact, if we continue practicing psychic numbing, we are passively suicidal. If a patient comes into my office who is suicidal, I hospitalize him immediately because this is an acute clinical emergency.

This is the ultimate in preventive medicine, because nuclear war [48] will create the final medical epidemic for which there will be no cure. We as physicians are extremely concerned about this. The American Medical Association has passed a resolution against nuclear war. We are also negotiating with Soviet physicians now. Dr. Chazov, Soviet President Brezhnev's personal cardiologist, said recently, "You know, the politicians are our patients."

[49]     Governments were instituted partly because of our medical knowledge. Our knowledge has produced hygienic sewage systems, clean water supplies and immunization programs, but the vectors of disease today are not flies, rats, mosquitoes and poor sanitation. They are us. They are the scientists who make the weapons, the industry who build them, and the politicians who use them for power. We must confront these vectors of disease.

[50]     This is the greatest challenge the human race has ever had since we stood on our hind legs and developed the opposing thumb to use weapons. Unless we mature and stop behaving like children, we will not survive.

[51]     I saw a bumper sticker the other day that said, "God Bless America," but every person on earth is the son or daughter of God, including the Russian people. We are together on a small, fragile planet. We will either live together or we will die together.

[52]     What is our responsibility toward evolution? To continue this beautiful life process. If you take this on, life becomes very precious. Even the things you dislike most about your life become precious. Go outside and look at a rose and smell it, or look at a baby to know what I mean.

[53]     We are curators of all life on this planet. We hold it in our hands. It is a beautiful planet, maybe the only life in the whole universe, and I refuse to believe we are silly enough to destroy it.


## QUESTIONS FOR DISCUSSION

1   Can you explain the metaphor that Caldicott, a physician, employs in her introduction and repeats throughout the essay? What does the term "metastasizing" mean?

2   Why does Dr. Caldicott devote paragraphs 2 through 15 to recounting the history of the atom bomb? How does this information support her antinuclear arguments? Be as specific as possible in your response.

3  Dr. Caldicott reports, "Over the last 18 months, computers within the Pentagon and elsewhere have made 151 errors that predicted that nuclear weapons were coming from the Soviet Union" (paragraph 44). How can that statement be true when everyone knows that computers don't make mistakes?

4  Who wrote the book called *Mein Kampf* (paragraph 14)?

5  What is the purpose of the opening questions in paragraphs 16, 20, 29, 36, 42, 45, and 52? Can you tell from these questions how the author has organized her material? Look also at the opening sentence of paragraph 15.

6  Dr. Caldicott delivered this piece in 1981 as a lecture at Harvard University in Boston. Can you state her thesis?

## SUGGESTIONS FOR WRITING

1  Laurence's narrative is told from the point of view of the men who dropped
   the bomb; Guillain's transcription presents the point of view of those on
   the ground. Compare these two accounts using evidence from both readings.
   For instance, Laurence speculates, "Does one feel any pity or compassion
   for the poor devils about to die? Not when one thinks of Pearl Harbor and
   of the Death March on Bataan" (paragraph 32). Poor Mrs. Kitayama cries
   out in rage, " 'Why? Why these children?' But there was no one to rage at
   and I could do nothing but watch them die, one after the other, vainly
   calling for their mothers" (paragraph 11). Consider also such differences
   as the coolly scientific tone of Laurence's account contrasted with the
   anguished tone of the woman's story; the images of beauty, spaciousness,
   and control employed by Laurence contrasted with the images of devastation, decay, and helplessness recounted by the woman; the warm camara-
   derie of the men in the plane contrasted with the lonely wandering of the
   injured woman searching for her family.

   Write this essay for the members of your composition class who have
   also studied both essays. Be sure to make a point about how these differences affected your response to the readings or perhaps about how the
   readings affected your opinion concerning the morality of dropping the
   bomb.

2  Using the *Short Story Index* in your library, find and read Walter Van
   Tilburg Clark's "The Portable Phonograph." Discuss the compelling way
   in which the story illustrates Helen Caldicott's contention, "All the magnificent architecture we have inherited from our ancestors will be destroyed.
   The Bach, the Handel, the Beethoven will be gone from the planet. The
   art, the literature, the poetry, everything will be gone" (paragraph 26).
   Write this essay for your instructor.

3  Dr. Caldicott devotes several paragraphs to explaining how she thinks we
   manage to put the nuclear threat out of our minds: through "psychic
   numbing" (paragraph 29), through adaptation (paragraph 31), through
   "projecting that fear onto the Russians" (paragraph 32), and through
   "taking drugs and drinking alcohol" (paragraph 34). If you have ever
   suffered nuclear nightmares, think about the ways in which you consciously
   or unconsciously dealt with the anxiety. Did you resort to any or all of the
   methods that Caldicott mentions? Write an essay for your classmates who
   may have experienced similar psychic trauma describing your fear,
   explaining how you learned to live with the threat, and suggesting a more
   positive way to dispel the fear in the future.

4  In paragraph 36, Dr. Caldicott argues that the "scientists, the leaders of
   the countries of the world, and the industrialists who make the weapons"

are "stuck in the old thinking. They see nuclear weapons as they saw bows and arrows or conventional weapons. The more one has, the safer one is, because you can destroy your enemy and rebuild from the rubble." Review the essay entitled "Nukespeak and the War Strategists" (in the preceding chapter). Then, write an essay in which you attempt to convince the members of a Reserve Officers Training Corps (ROTC) unit that this "old thinking" underlies the Pentagon's nuclear strategies. Since your audience will probably be hostile to your ideas, you will need to be extremely careful about your tone.

5 Write instructions detailing what to do in case of a nuclear attack. If you believe the chance of survival is minimal, adopt a humorous, heavily ironic tone and select details to illustrate the futility of the entire attempt. Address your advice to the students at your university; tell them what to do from the time of the alert, explaining procedures for evacuating a classroom, a dormitory, or an off-campus apartment. Your purpose, of course, will not be to help people survive the holocaust; your purpose will be to illustrate the madness of tolerating such a suicidal governmental policy as the arms race. Submit your completed article for publication in your campus newspaper.

# ACKNOWLEDGMENTS

CHAPTER 11   CONSIDERING TIMES PAST

Langston Hughes, "Salvation." From *The Big Sea* by Langston Hughes. Copyright ©
1940 by Langston Hughes; renewed 1968 by Arna Bontemps and George Houston Bass.
Reprinted by permission of Hill and Wang, a division of Farrar, Straus and Giroux, Inc.

Gordon Parks, "My Mother's Dream for Me." From *A Choice of Weapons* by Gordon
Parks. Copyright © 1965, 1966 by Gordon Parks. Reprinted by permission of Harper
and Row, Publishers, Inc.

Russell Baker, "Selling the Post." From *Growing Up* by Russell Baker. Copyright ©
1982 by Russell Baker. Reprinted by permission of Congdon & Weed, Inc.

CHAPTER 12   CONSIDERING DISCRIMINATION

Martin Luther King Jr., "I Have a Dream." Copyright © 1963 by Martin Luther King,
Jr. Reprinted by permission of Joan Daves.

James Thurber, "The Rabbits Who Caused All the Trouble." From *Fables For Our
Time* published by Harper & Row. Copyright © 1940 by James Thurber; renewed 1968
by Helen Thurber.

Harold Krents, "Darkness at Noon." From *The New York Times*, May 26, 1976.
Copyright © 1976 by The New York Times Company. Reprinted by permission.

CHAPTER 13   CONSIDERING ETHICAL ISSUES

Charlene Mitchell and Thomas Burdick, "A Teenager's Tragedy: Birth and Death in a
Florida Town." From *Ms.* magazine, December, 1987. Copyright by Charlene Mitchell
and Thomas Burdick. Reprinted by permission.

Charles R. Burns, "A Priest's Painful Choice." From *Newsweek*, February 2, 1987.
Copyright © 1987 by Newsweek, Inc. All rights reserved. Reprinted by permission.

George Orwell, "A Hanging." From *Shooting an Elephant and Other Essays* by George
Orwell. Copyright © 1950 by Sonia Brownell Orwell; renewed 1978 by Sonia Pitt-
Rivers. Reprinted by permission of Harcourt Brace Jovanovich, Inc.

H. L. Mencken, "The Penalty of Death." From *A Mencken Chrestomathy* by H. L.
Mencken. Copyright © 1926 by Alfred A. Knopf, Inc.; renewed 1954 by H. L.
Mencken. Reprinted by permission of Alfred A. Knopf., Inc.

CHAPTER 14   CONSIDERING GENDER ROLES

Virginia Woolf, "Shakespeare's Sister." From *A Room of One's Own* by Virginia Woolf.
Copyright © 1929 by Harcourt Brace Jovanovich, Inc.; renewed 1957 by Leonard Woolf.
Reprinted by permission of Harcourt Brace Jovanovich, Inc.

Ellen Goodman, "Women Divided: Family or Career?" First appeared in *The Boston
Globe*. Copyright © 1988 by The Boston Globe Newspaper Company/Washington Post
Writers Group. Reprinted by permission.

Judy Syfers, "Why I Want a Wife." From *Ms.* magazine, December, 1971. Copyright
by Judy Syfers. Reprinted by permission.

Noel Perrin, "The Androgynous Man." From *The New York Times*, February 5, 1984. Copyright © 1984 by The New York Times Company. Reprinted by permission.

## CHAPTER 15   CONSIDERING TELEVISION

Harry F. Waters, "Life According to TV." From *Newsweek*, December 6, 1982. Copyright © 1982 by Newsweek, Inc. All rights reserved. Reprinted by permission.

Donna Woolfolk Cross, "Sin, Suffer, and Repent." From *Mediaspeak: How Television Makes Your Mind Up* by Donna Woolfolk Cross. Copyright © 1985 by Donna Woolfolk Cross. Reprinted by permission of The Putnam Publishing Group.

Victor B. Cline, "How TV Violence Damages Your Children." From *Ladies' Home Journal* magazine, February, 1975. Copyright © 1975 by the Meredith Corporation. All rights reserved. Reprinted by permission.

## CHAPTER 16   CONSIDERING VIOLENCE

John McMurtry, "Kill 'Em! Crush 'Em! Eat 'Em Raw!" From *Maclean's* magazine, October, 1971. Copyright by John McMurty. Reprinted by permission.

Adam Smith, "Fifty Million Handguns." From *Esquire* magazine, April, 1981. Copyright © 1981 by Esquire Associates. Reprinted by permission.

T. A. Stoll, "Sexual Abuse on Campus: Where Is the True Gentleman Today?" From *The Record*, Spring, 1987. Copyright © 1987 by Sigma Alpha Epsilon. Reprinted by permission.

## CHAPTER 17   CONSIDERING LANGUAGE

Robin Lakoff, "You Are What You Say." From *Ms.* magazine. Copyright by Robion Lakoff. Reprinted by permission.

Stephen Hilgartner, Richard C. Bell, and Rory O'Connor, "War Strategists and Nukespeak." From *Nukespeak* by Hilgartner, Bell, & O'Connor. Copyright © 1982 by Stephen Hilgartner, Richard C. Bell, & Rory O'Connor. Reprinted by permission of Sierra Club Books.

## CHAPTER 18   CONSIDERING NUCLEAR DESTRUCTION

William L. Laurence, "Atomic Bombing of Nagasaki Told by Flight Member." From *The New York Times*, September 9, 1945. Copyright © 1945 by The New York Times Company. Reprinted by permission.

Robert Guillain, "I Thought My Last Hour Had Come . . ." From *I Saw Tokyo Burning* by Robert Guillain. Translated by William R. Bryan. Copyright © 1980, 1981 by Doubleday, a division of Bantam, Doubleday, Dell Publishing Group, Inc. Reprinted by permission of the publisher.

Helen Caldicott, "This Beautiful Planet." From *Speak Out Against the New Right* by Herbert Vetter. Copyright © by Dr. Helen Caldicott. Reprinted by generous permission of Dr. Caldicott.

# Index

# Theme-Grading Guide